WEBSTER'S
CONCISE WORLD ATLAS

WEBSTER'S
CONCISE WORLD ATLAS

THIS EDITION PRINTED IN 1995

Published by Blitz Editions, an imprint of Bookmart Limited
Registered Number 2372865
Trading as Bookmart Limited
Desford Road
Enderby
Leicester LE9 5AD

Published by arrangement with De Agostini Editions Limited,
Griffin House, 161 Hammersmith Road, London W6 8SD

ISBN 1856052818

© Istituto Geografico De Agostini 1995

Printed in the EU, Officine Grafiche De Agostini - Novara 1995

CONTENTS

Plate Page Title
number

     5 Contents
   6-7 Key to World Maps
     8 Key to European Maps

**A GEOGRAPHICAL
DICTIONARY OF
COUNTRIES, CONTINENT
BY CONTINENT**

Europe 10, Asia 18, Africa 24,
Australia and Oceania 32,
North America 34,
South America 38

 10-15 Europe
 16-17 The Commonwealth of
         Independent States (CIS)
 18-23 Asia
 24-31 Africa
 32-33 Australia and Oceania
 34-37 North and Central America
 38-39 South America

WORLD MAPS

1 42-43 The World: Physical
          Map Symbols
2 44-45 The World: Political

Europe

3 46-47 Europe: Political
4 48-49 Scandinavia and the
          Baltic States
5 50-51 Central Europe
6 52-53 Central and Eastern Europe
7 54-55 British Isles
8 56-57 France
9 58-59 Spain and Portugal
10 60-61 Italy
11 62-63 The Balkan States
12 64-65 Baltic States and
          Western CIS
13 66-67 CIS: West
14 68-69 CIS: East

Asia

15 70-71 Asia: Political
16 72-73 Eastern Asia
17 74-75 Japan

18 76-77 South-East Asia
19 78-79 Mainland South-East Asia
20 80-81 Southern Asia
21 82-83 South-West Asia
22 84-85 Turkey and the Near East

Africa

23 86-87 Africa: Political
24 88-89 Northwestern Africa
25 90-91 Northeastern Africa
26 92-93 Central and Southern
          Africa

Oceania

27 94-95 Australia and New
          Zealand
28 96-97 Pacific Islands
29 98-99 Australia

**North and Central
America**

30 100-101 North America: Political
31 102-103 Canada
32 104-105 Central and Eastern
          United States
33 106-107 Central and Western
          United States
34 108-109 Mexico
35 110-111 Central America
          and West Indies

South America

36 112-113 South America: Political
37 114-115 South America:
          North-West
38 116-117 South America:
          North-East
39 118-119 South America: Central
40 120-121 South America: South

Polar Regions

41 122 Arctic Ocean
42 123 Antarctica

INDEX

   124-192 Index

WORLD: Key to map pages

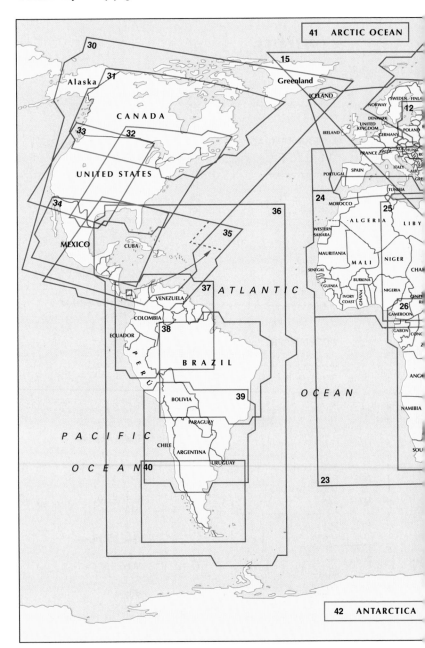

41 ARCTIC OCEAN

30

15

31 Alaska

Greenland

ICELAND

SWEDEN FINLA

NORWAY

12

CANADA

DENMARK

UNITED KINGDOM

IRELAND

GERMANY

POLAND

33

32

FRANCE SWITZ AUSTR HUNG

RO

UNITED STATES

PORTUGAL SPAIN

ITALY

ALB

GRE

34

TUNISIA

24

MOROCCO

25

36

ALGERIA

LIBY

WESTERN SAHARA

35

MEXICO

CUBA

MAURITANIA

MALI

NIGER

CHA

SENEGAL

BURKINA

GUINEA

NIGERIA

37

ATLANTIC

VENEZUELA

IVORY COAST

GHANA

CENT RI

COLOMBIA

26

CAMEROON

38

GABON

CONG

ECUADOR

P E R U

BRAZIL

ANG

OCEAN

39

BOLIVIA

NAMIBIA

PARAGUAY

P A C I F I C

CHILE

ARGENTINA

SOU

O C E A N 40

URUGUAY

23

42 ANTARCTICA

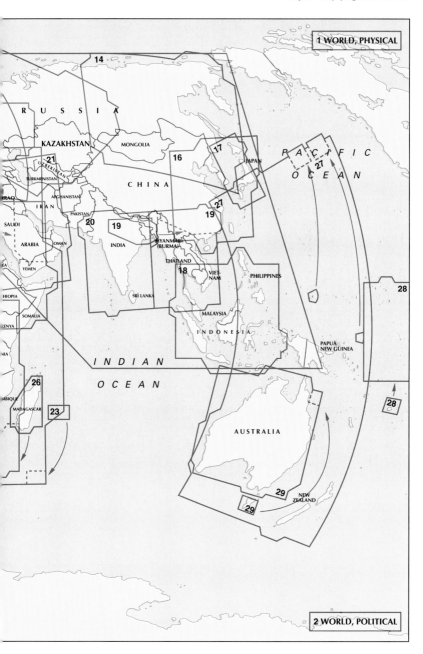

1 WORLD, PHYSICAL

14

RUSSIA

KAZAKHSTAN

MONGOLIA

21

UZBEKISTAN

TURKMENISTAN

AFGHANISTAN

IRAQ

IRAN

PAKISTAN

SAUDI

ARABIA

OMAN

YEMEN

CHINA

16

17

JAPAN

27

19

20

19

INDIA

MYANMAR
(BURMA)

THAILAND

18

VIET-
NAM

PHILIPPINES

SRI LANKA

MALAYSIA

INDONESIA

PAPUA
NEW GUINEA

HIOPIA

SOMALIA

KENYA

NIA

26

ABIQUE

MADAGASCAR

23

INDIAN

OCEAN

PACIFIC

OCEAN

27

27

28

28

AUSTRALIA

29

NEW
ZEALAND

29

2 WORLD, POLITICAL

7

EUROPE: Key to map pages

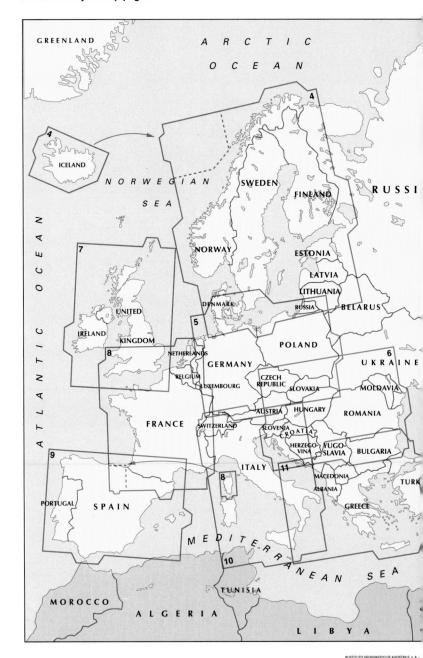

© ISTITUTO GEOGRAFICO DE AGOSTINI S. p.A. -

A GEOGRAPHICAL DICTIONARY OF COUNTRIES, CONTINENT BY CONTINENT

Europe	10
Asia	18
Africa	24
Australia and Oceania	32
North America	34
South America	38

STATE (official name/ English translation)	CAPITAL ① inhabitants	AREA (sq km)	POPULATION	DENSITY (inhab/sq km)	LIF EXPE AN (in ye M
ALBANIA (Republika e Shqipërisë/ Republic of Albania)	Tirana (Tiranë) 243 000	28 748	3 256 000	113	69.6
ANDORRA (Principat d'Andorra/ Principauté d'Andorre/ Principality of Andorra)	Andorra la Vella (Andorre-la-Vieille) 15 600	453	52 000	115	74.0
AUSTRIA (Republik Österreich/ Republic of Austria)	Vienna (Wien) 1 533 000	83 859	7 712 000	92	72.1
BELGIUM (Koninkrijk België/ Royaume de Belgique/ Kingdom of Belgium)	Brussels (Brussel/Bruxelles) 960 000	30 518	9 950 000	326	70.0
BOSNIA-HERZEGOVINA (Republika Bosnia i Hercegovina)	Sarajevo 526 000	51 129	4 350 000	85	68.0
BULGARIA (Republika Bulgarija/ Republic of Bulgaria)	Sofia (Sofiya) 1 221 000	110 994	8 990 000	81	68.3
CROATIA (Republika Hrvatska/ Republic of Croatia)	Zagreb 763 000	56 538	4 750 000	84	67.0
CZECH REPUBLIC (Ceská Republika)	Prague (Praha) 1 212 000	78 864	10 365 000	131	68.1
DENMARK (Kongeriget Danmark/ Kingdom of Denmark)	Copenhagen (København) 467 000	43 093	5 140 000	119	71.9
ESTONIA (Eesti Vabariik/ Republic of Estonia)	Tallinn 484 000	45 100	1 578 000	35	65.8
FINLAND (Suomen Tasavalta/ Republiken Finland/ Republic of Finland)	Helsinki (Helsingfors) 491 000	338 145	4 986 000	15	70.7
FRANCE (République Française/ French Republic)	Paris 2 152 000	543 965	56 600 000	104	72.7
GERMANY (Bundesrepublik Deutschland/Federal Republic of Germany)	Berlin 3 410 000	356 957	79 479 000	223	72.2

SS NAL UCT)	LANGUAGES	RELIGIONS	ECONOMY
740	Albanian (Gheg and Tosc [off.])	Muslim 70%; Orthodox 20%	**Economy** Mainly agriculture (cereals, potatoes, sugar beet, olives, fruit), animal farming and industry (food processing, textile and tobacco production, building materials). **Mineral resources** Substantial reserves of chromite and petroleum.
500	Catalan (off.); Spanish; French	Catholic	**Economy** As a free-trade (duty-free) zone, considerable income is generated by tourism, trade and banking. **Agriculture** Another main economic activity. Cattle and pigs are the chief livestock, cereals, potatoes and tobacco the principal crops.
360	German	Catholic 84%; Protestant 6%	**Industry** Dominates the economy (mechanical, chemical, wood, paper, textile and food production). Tourism is thriving. **Mineral resources** Iron, magnesite, petroleum, lignite, lead. **Agriculture** Almost self-sufficient (cereals, sugar beet).
390	Flemish; French	Catholic	**Economy** Relies mainly on manufacturing. Brussels profits from being the HQ of the EC. **Agriculture** Main crops: cereals, potatoes, beet. Dairy farming is thriving. **Industry** Coal mining and the production of machinery, textiles, chemicals, food, diamonds.
741	Serbo-Croat	Muslim; Christian	**Economy** Based on agriculture (cereals, tobacco, fruit) and animal farming. **Mineral resources** Copper, lead, zinc, gold and iron. **Industry** Mechanical, electronics, chemical, textile and food industries.
320	Bulgarian	Orthodox 80%; Muslim 13%	**Economy** Essentially agricultural (cereals, potatoes, beet, vines, tobacco). Roses are traditionally grown too. **Mineral resources** Coal, iron, copper, lead and zinc. **Industry** The food, mechanical and electronic sectors are well established.
226	Croat	Catholic 76%; Orthodox 11%	**Agriculture** Principal crops: cereals, potatoes, beet, vines, olives. Animal farming is productive. **Principal resources** Timber from the large forests, coal, bauxite, hydrocarbons. **Industry** Mechanical, chemical, food, textiles and wood.
200	Czech	Catholic	**Economy** Dominated by heavy industry, although the country has profited from its considerable timber and coal reserves. **Agriculture** Cereals, hops and beet are cultivated widely. **Industry** Food, textile, mechanical and chemicals.
510	Danish	Protestant	**Agriculture** Animal farming (dairy products, meat) is important to domestic and export markets. Also fishing and arable farming (cereals, potatoes, sugar beet). **Industry** Primarily food, mechanical, chemical and ceramic production.
349	Estonian	Lutheran	**Economy** Dominated by agriculture (cereals, potatoes, animal fodder crops), animal farming (pigs, cattle), forestry and mineral resources (bituminous shale, phosphorites, peat). **Industry** Food processing, wood- and metalworking.
060	Finnish; Swedish	Protestant	**Economy** Dense forestation provides great quantities of timber, much for export, the rest for wood and paper factories. **Agriculture** Dairy farming and fishing are significant. **Industry** Metalworking, shipbuilding and food processing.
830	French	Catholic	**Agriculture** Extensive fishing, arable (cereals, potatoes, beet, grapes for wine) and animal farming. **Principal resources** Coal, petrol, natural gas, timber. **Industry** Food, machinery, vehicles, chemicals, electronics, textiles, fashion, rubber.
750	German	Protestant 41%; Catholic 41%	**Economy** Very strong, notably industry (metals, mechanical, chemicals, electronics) and services. **Agriculture** Main crops: potatoes, cereals, beet, hops for brewing. Animal farming. **Mineral resources** Coal, lignite, potassium salts.

STATE (official name/ English translation)	CAPITAL ① inhabitants	AREA (sq km) POPULATION DENSITY (inhab/sq km)			L EXF A (in y M
GREECE (Ellinikí Dimokratía/ Hellenic Republic)	**Athens** (Athínai) 885 000	131 957	10 123 000	77	72.2
HUNGARY (Magyar Köztársaság/ Hungarian Republic)	**Budapest** 2 016 000	93 033	10 364 000	111	65.4
ICELAND (Lyðveldið Ísland/ Republic of Iceland)	**Reykjavík** 96 700	102 819	255 000	2	75.7
IRELAND (Poblacht na h'Éireann/ Republic of Ireland)	**Dublin** (Baile Átha Cliath) 503 000	70 283	3 503 000	50	71.0
ITALY (Repubblica Italiana/ Republic of Italy)	**Rome** (Roma) 2 693 000	301 302	56 800 000	187	73.2
LATVIA (Latvija)	**Riga** 916 000	64 500	2 683 000	41	64.2
LIECHTENSTEIN (Fürstentum Liechtenstein/ Principality of Liechtenstein)	**Vaduz** 4 900	160	29 000	181	66.1
LITHUANIA (Lietuva)	**Vilnius** 582 000	65 200	3 725 000	57	66.9
LUXEMBOURG (Grand-Duché de Luxembourg/Grand Duchy of Luxembourg)	**Luxembourg** 76 000	2 586	381 000	147	70.6
MACEDONIA (Republika Makedonija)	**Skopje** 406 000	25 713	2 030 000	79	68.0
MALTA (Republic of Malta/ Repubblika ta' Malta)	**Valletta** 9 200	316	354 000	1120	73.8
MONACO (Principauté de Monaco/ Principality of Monaco)	**Monaco** 1 234	1.9	30 000	15 789	—
THE NETHERLANDS (Koninkrijk der Nederlanden/Kingdom of the Netherlands)	**Amsterdam** 695 000	41 574	14 893 000	358	73.7

...SS ...NAL ...UCT ...	LANGUAGES	RELIGIONS	ECONOMY
340	Greek	Orthodox	**Agriculture** Important economically. Main crops: cereals, olives, vines, citrus fruits, cotton, tobacco. Livestock and fishing also important. **Industry** Tourism highly profitable; also food processing, petrochemicals, textiles, metals and chemicals.
560	Hungarian	Catholic 64%; Protestant 23%	**Agriculture** Among the major crops are cereals, potatoes, sugar beet and grapes. Animal farming is significant. **Mineral resources** Bauxite, petroleum and coal. **Industry** Machinery, textiles, chemicals and food.
240	Icelandic	Protestant	**Economy** Fishing (cod, herrings) is vital. **Agriculture** Small-scale: the inhospitable climate is most suitable for grazing and sheep rearing. **Industry** Mainly fish storage and processing; hydroelectricity fuels the profitable aluminium-smelting plants.
500	Irish (off.); English	Catholic 93%; Anglican 3%	**Economy** Essentially agricultural, with livestock (sheep and cattle) of primary importance. Main crops: cereals, potatoes and sugar beet. **Principal resources** Peat, zinc and natural gas. **Industry** Food processing, machinery and brewing.
150	Italian	Catholic	**Agriculture** Important to the domestic economy (cereals, olives, vines, citrus fruits, tomatoes, beet). Also animal farming (cattle, pigs) and fishing. **Industry** Cars, machinery, chemicals, food, textiles, clothing and tourism.
176	Lettish	Lutheran; Orthodox	**Economy** Heavily industrialized, specializing in metals, food, electronics, textiles, chemicals and wood. **Agriculture** Of secondary importance. Cereals, potatoes, flax, beet and fodder are the main crops. Also dairy farming and fishing.
000	German	Catholic	**Economy** Dominated by tourism and industry (particularly precision instruments, chemicals, pharmaceutics, food, textiles, ceramics). **Agriculture** Relatively modest. Main crops: cereals, potatoes, vegetables. Main livestock: cattle, pigs, sheep.
796	Lithuanian	Catholic	**Agriculture** Dominates the economy (cereals, potatoes, flax, beet, vegetables). Animal farming and forestry are also important activities. **Industry** Major industries are food, machinery, textiles, wood and chemicals.
860	Letzeburgish; French; German	Catholic	**Agriculture** The leading products are cereals, potatoes and grapes. Animal farming is widespread. **Industry** The most developed sector of the economy, particularly iron and steel, machinery, chemicals, rubber and plastics.
697	Macedonian	Orthodox	**Economy** Industry and mining (of iron, chromite, copper and lignite) predominate. **Agriculture** Main crops: cereals, tobacco, cotton, fruit. Also sheep breeding and forestry. **Industry** Chiefly food, metals, chemicals and textiles.
820	Maltese; English	Catholic	**Agriculture** Cereals, potatoes, vegetables, fruit and flowers. Animal farming and fishing are important. **Industry** Main sectors: clothing, food, electronics, shipbuilding, publishing and tobacco. Tourism is a major source of foreign revenue.
636	French; Monegasque	Catholic	**Economy** Light industry, banking, casinos and tourism are the main sources of revenue. **Industry** Textiles, clothing, electronics, chemicals, pharmaceutics and paper are among the chief manufactured goods.
010	Dutch	Catholic 36%; Protestant 26%	**Agriculture** Main crops: cereals, potatoes, fruit, beet, flowers (tulips, hyacinths). Animal farming and fishing are important. **Mineral resources** Natural gas, petrol. **Industry** Food, chemicals, electronics and rubber are manufactured.

	STATE (official name/ English translation)	CAPITAL ① inhabitants	AREA (sq km)	POPULATION	DENSITY (inhab/sq km)	L EXP AN (in y M
	NORWAY (Kongeriket Norge/ Kingdom of Norway)	Oslo 461 000	323 878	4 242 000	13	73.3
	POLAND (Polska Rzeczpospolita/ Republic of Poland)	Warsaw (Warszawa) 1 656 000	312 683	38 180 000	122	66.8
	PORTUGAL (República Portuguesa/ Portuguese Republic)	Lisbon (Lisboa) 830 000	91 191	10 251 000	112	70.6
	ROMANIA (România)	Bucharest (Bucureşti) 2 127 000	237 500	23 207 000	98	66.5
	SAN MARINO (Serenissima Repubblica di San Marino/Most Serene Republic of San Marino)	San Marino 2 300	60.6	23 000	379	73.2
	SLOVAKIA (Slovenská Republika/ Republic of Slovakia)	Bratislava 441 000	49 036	5 297 000	108	66.9
	SLOVENIA (Republika Slovenija/ Republic of Slovenia)	Ljubljana 267 000	20 251	1 950 000	96	67.0
	SPAIN (Reino de España/ Kingdom of Spain)	Madrid 3 121 000	498 507	36 950 000	74	73.6
	SWEDEN (Konungariket Sverige/ Kingdom of Sweden)	Stockholm 674 000	449 964	8 559 000	19	74.2
	SWITZERLAND (Schweizerische Eidgenossenschaft; Confédération Suisse)	Berne (Bern) 134 000	41 285	6 712 000	162	74.0
	UNITED KINGDOM (United Kingdom of Great Britain and Northern Ireland)	London 6 378 000	244 100	55 487 000	227	72.2
	VATICAN CITY (Stato della Città del Vaticano/ State of the Vatican City)		0.44	1 000	—	
	YUGOSLAVIA (Federativna Republika Jugoslavija/Federal Republic of Yugoslavia)	Belgrade (Beograd) 1 554 000	102 173	10 300 000	101	68.1

...SS ...NAL ...UCT	LANGUAGES	RELIGIONS	ECONOMY
...50	Bokmaal; Nynorsk	Protestant	**Agriculture** Main crops: cereals, potatoes. Animals are profitably reared for dairy products (sheep), meat (reindeer), fur. Fishing is a major industry. **Principal resources** Timber, petrol, natural gas. **Industry** Mechanical, chemical and wood-processing.
...60	Polish	Catholic	**Agriculture** Main crops: cereals, potatoes, beet, tobacco, flax, hops, hemp. Animal farming and fishing are practiced. **Mineral resources** Coal, lignite, copper, silver, sulphur. **Industry** Iron, steel, machinery, food and textiles are important.
...60	Portuguese	Catholic	**Agriculture** Cereals, potatoes, tomatoes and grapes (for prosperous wine industry) are the chief crops. Fishing (sardines). **Principal resources** Cork, pyrethrum and tungsten. **Industry** Textiles, clothes, chemicals and ceramics.
...40	Romanian	Orthodox	**Agriculture** Cereals, potatoes, beet, fruit and grapes are the main crops. Animal farming and forestry are important. **Mineral resources** Petroleum, natural gas, lignite, coal, iron. **Industry** Metallurgy, food and chemical production.
...90	Italian	Catholic	**Economy** Tourism and the sale of postage stamps are the backbone of the economy. **Agriculture** Principal crops: cereals, grapes and olives. **Industry** Principal products: food, textiles, leather goods, ceramics and other local crafts.
...60	Slovak	Catholic	**Agriculture** An important sector of the economy (cereals, potatoes, sugar beet, vines, tobacco). Cattle, pigs and sheep are reared. **Mineral resources** Copper, iron, lead and zinc. **Industry** Food, textile and metal industries.
07	Slovene	Catholic	**Agriculture** Dairy and arable farming (cereals, potatoes, beet, vegetables, fruit). **Principal resources** Timber, iron, lead, zinc, copper, lignite, mercury. **Industry** Iron, steel and textile production, mechanical and chemical engineering.
...50	Spanish (Castilian); Catalan; Basque; Galician	Catholic	**Agriculture** Dairy farming and fishing are widespread. Main crops: cereals, grapes, citrus fruits, olives. **Principal resources** Cork, coal. **Industry** Main products: consumer goods, chemicals, food, textiles. Tourism is also important.
...10	Swedish	Protestant	**Agriculture** Limited (cereals, potatoes, beet). Animal farming and fishing at a modest level. **Principal resources** Plentiful timber, iron, lead, zinc, copper and hydroelectricity. **Industry** Motor vehicles, machinery, food, paper and wood.
...70	German; French; Italian; Romansch	Catholic 48%; Protestant 44%	**Economy** Rich, as a result of its status as an international financial centre and its plentiful hydroelectricity. **Agriculture** Mainly dairy farming. **Industry** Main products: food, textiles, chemicals, pharmaceutics, precision instruments. Tourism.
70	English	Protestant; Catholic 9%	**Agriculture** Mainly dairy farming (sheep, cattle) and fishing. **Mineral resources** Rich reserves of petrol, natural gas, coal. **Industry** Services, banking, tourism and manufacturing (metals, chemicals, food, textiles and bricks).
	Italian and Latin (both off.)	Catholic	**Economy** The City attracts pilgrims and tourists from all over the world. Its revenue derives from charitable donations and income from investments.
...90	Serbo-Croat	Orthodox	**Economy** Agriculture-based, with cereals, tobacco, fruit and grapes among the main crops. Animal farming and forestry are profitable. **Industry** Major concerns are machinery, textiles, food and paper.

THE COMMONWEALTH OF INDEPENDENT STATES (CIS)

STATE (official name/ English translation)	CAPITAL ① inhabitants	AREA (sq km) POPULATION DENSITY (inhab/sq km)			L EXF AN (in y M
ARMENIA (Haikakan Hanrapetoutioun)	**Yerevan** 1 199 000	29 800	3 335 000	112	69.0
AZERBAIJAN (Republik Azarbaijchan)	**Baku** 1 150 000	86 600	7 134 000	82	66.6
BELARUS (BYELORUSSIA) (Respublika Belarus)	**Minsk** (Mensk) 1 589 000	207 600	10 260 000	49	66.8
GEORGIA (Sakartvelos Respublika/ Republic of Georgia)	**Tbilisi** 1 260 000	69 700	5 460 000	78	63.9
KAZAKHSTAN (Kazak Respublikasy)	**Alma-Ata** 1 128 000	2 717 300	16 740 000	6	63.9
KYRGYZSTAN (Kyrgyz Respublikasy)	**Bishkek** (Biškek) 616 000	198 500	4 394 000	22	64.3
MOLDOVA (Republika Moldovenească)	**Chişinău** 665 000	33 700	4 362 000	129	65.5
RUSSIA (Rossiya/Rossiyskaya Federativnaya Respublika)	**Moscow** (Moskva) 8 769 000	17 075 400	148 288 000	8	64.2
TAJIKISTAN (Respublika i Tojikiston)	**Dushanbe** (Dušanbe) 595 000	143 100	5 303 000	37	66.8
TURKMENISTAN (Türkmenostan)	**Ashkabad** 398 000	488 100	3 668 000	7	61.8
UKRAINE (Ukraïna)	**Kiev** (Kyiv) 2 587 000	603 700	51 889 000	86	66.1
UZBEKISTAN (Ozbekiston Respublikasy)	**Tashkent** 2 073 000	447 400	20 514 000	46	66.0
CIS (Commonwealth of Independent States)		22 100 900	281 347 000	13	
EUROPE Total ⒶA		10 396 569	709 019 000	68	

SS NAL UCT	LANGUAGES	RELIGIONS	ECONOMY
10	Armenian	Orthodox	**Agriculture** Chief crops are wheat, potatoes, vegetables, fruit, grapes, cotton and tobacco. Livestock includes cattle, sheep and goats. **Industry** Metalwork, machinery, chemicals, food and bricks.
50	Azerbaijani	Muslim (Shiite 75%; Sunni 25%)	**Economy** Depends mainly on its reserves of oil (plus natural gas) and manufacturing (machinery, chemicals, petrochemicals). **Agriculture** Arable (cereals, cotton, tobacco, tea, grapes, fruit) and animal farming are significant.
60	Belarussian	Orthodox; Catholic	**Economy** Based on agriculture (cereals, potatoes, sugar beet, vegetables, fruit, flax), animal farming (cattle, pigs) and industry (metals, electronics, chemicals, food, textiles).
10	Georgian	Orthodox	**Agriculture** Cereals, citrus fruits, grapes, tea, flowers and tobacco. Animals are kept for meat and wool. **Principal resources** Manganese ore, hydroelectricity. **Industry** Developing rapidly. Main products: metals, chemicals and bricks.
20	Kazakh	Muslim (Sunni); Orthodox	**Economy** Plentiful resources (coal, petrol, iron, natural gas, tungsten, copper, lead, zinc) aid industrial growth (metals, chemicals, textiles). **Agriculture** Animal farming; much of the population grows crops (cereals, cotton, sugar beet).
30	Kyrgyz	Muslim (Sunni); Orthodox	**Agriculture** Cereals, potatoes, sugar beet and fruit are the principal crops, with sheep, goats and cattle the main livestock. **Industry** Textiles, tanning, metallurgy, machinery, electronics, mining (coal, uranium).
30	Romanian	Orthodox	**Agriculture** Arable farming – cereals, potatoes, beet, fruit, grapes (for wine), vegetables, sunflower seeds – and animal herding are vital to the economy. **Industry** The major products are machinery, textiles, chemicals and processed food.
10	Russian	Orthodox	**Economy** Owing to abundant resources (hydrocarbons, combustibles, timber, minerals) all industrial sectors are highly developed. **Agriculture** Large-scale. Main crops: cereals, potatoes. Animal farming and fishing are also practiced.
40	Tajik	Muslim (Sunni)	**Agriculture** The main products are cotton, vegetables, fruit and seeds. Sheep, goats and cattle are raised. **Mineral resources** Uranium, gold, iron and lead. **Industry** Concentrates on food and textiles (carpets).
70	Turkmen	Muslim (Sunni)	**Agriculture** Cotton is one of the chief exports; animal breeding (especially karakul sheep) is also important. **Principal resources** Plentiful petroleum and natural gas. **Industry** Machinery, textiles (especially carpets) and petrochemicals.
00	Ukrainian	Christian	**Agriculture** Animal and arable farming (cereals, potatoes, sunflower seeds, beet) are widespread. **Economy** Rich deposits of minerals (coal, iron) have helped the development of the iron and steel, mechanical and chemical industries.
50	Uzbek	Muslim (Sunni)	**Agriculture** Cotton, cereals, vegetables and fruit are the main crops, sheep and goats the main livestock. **Mineral resources** Large reserves of natural gas, petrol, coal, lead, zinc and gold. **Industry** Machinery-building and chemicals.

udes the Azores Is (Portugal), Asian Greek Islands, European parts of Turkey and the CIS; excludes Canary Is (Spain) and Madeira (Portugal).

① The local form is given in brackets only when it differs from the English form

② Per inhabitant, in US$.

STATE (official name/ English translation)	CAPITAL ① inhabitants	AREA (sq km)	POPULATION	DENSITY (inhab/sq km)	LI EXPI AN (in y M
AFGHANISTAN (Da Afghānistān Jamhuriat Republic of Afghanistan)	**Kābul** 1 424 000	652 225	16 922 000	26	41.0
BAHRAIN (Dawlat al-Baḥrain)	**Manama** (Al Manāmah) 151 500	678	516 000	761	71.0
BANGLADESH (Gana Praja Tantri Bangladesh/People's Republic of Bangladesh)	**Dhaka** 6 105 000	143 998	105 000 000	729	56.9
BHUTAN (Druk-Yul/ Realm of the Dragon)	**Thimphu** 30 000	47 000	1 476 000	31	49.2
BRUNEI (Negara Brunei Darussalam/Sultanate of Brunei)	**Bandar Seri Begawan** 55 100	5 765	264 000	46	72.6
CAMBODIA (Roat Kâmpŭchéa/ State of Cambodia)	**Phnom Penh** 564 000	181 035	8 781 000	48	47.0
CHINA (Zhonghua Renmin Gongheguo/People's Republic of China)	**Peking** (Beijing) 5 770 000	9 536 499	1155 790 000	121	68.4
CYPRUS (Kypriakí Dimokratía/ Kibris Cumhuriyeti/ Republic of Cyprus)	**Nicosia** 187 000	9 251	710 000	77	73.9
INDIA (Bhārat Juktarashtra/ Republic of India)	**Delhi** 294 000	3 287 782	849 638 000	258	58.1
INDONESIA (Republik Indonesia/ Republic of Indonesia)	**Jakarta** 7 829 000	1 529 072	180 910 000	118	58.5
IRAN (Jomhurī-e-Islāmī-e-Irān/ Islamic Republic of Iran)	**Tehran** 6 620 000	1 648 196	56 250 000	34	64.0
IRAQ (Al Jumhūrīya al-'Irāqīya/ Republic of Iraq)	**Baghdād** 3 844 600	434 128	17 903 000	41	63.0
ISRAEL (Medinat Yisra'el/ State of Israel)	**Jerusalem** 524 000	20 700	4 975 000	240	74.5
JAPAN (Nihon or Nippon/ Land of the Rising Sun)	**Tōkyō** 8 163 000	372 819	123 921 000	332	75.9

SS NAL UCT)	LANGUAGES	RELIGIONS	ECONOMY
60	Dari; Pushto	Muslim (Sunni) 80%	**Economy** Mainly agricultural (cereal crops); cotton is widely cultivated for the textile industry. Animal farming is the basic livelihood of nomads. **Mineral resources** Rich, under-exploited reserves of natural gas and iron ore.
10	Arabic	Muslim 85%	**Economy** Relies on petroleum, refined locally for export. An important financial centre. **Industry** Booming, particularly food, cement, chemicals, aluminium. **Agriculture** Fishing (fish, pearls) and agriculture are the traditional activities.
20	Bengali (off.); English	Muslim 86.6%; Hindu 12.1%	**Economy** Agriculture-based. Rice is the main crop, fol-lowed by jute, tea, sugar-cane, cotton and tobacco. Animal farming is widespread and fishing is important. **Industry** Food processing and textile manufacturing are developing.
80	Dzongkha	Buddhist; Hindu	**Economy** Extremely poor. Agriculture (cereals, potatoes, fruit), stock-raising (mainly cattle, then pigs, sheep and goats) and lumbering (firewood) employ virtually the whole population of this rural country. Local crafts are exported.
60	Malay; English; Chinese	Muslim 63%; Buddhist 14%	**Economy** Rich reserves of petroleum and natural gas make Brunei one of the wealthiest countries in Asia. **Agriculture** Rice, bananas and citrus fruits; forestry and fishing. **Industry** Chiefly petrochemicals, food, wood and rubber.
00	Khmer (off.); French	Buddhist	**Agriculture** Dominates the economy, especially rice. Fish-ing and animal farming are traditional livelihoods. Forests are particularly rich (rubber and timber). **Industry** Primarily food processing, textiles, tobacco and mechanical industries.
70	Chinese; Uighur; Tibetan; Mongol	Confucian 19%; Budd. 14%; Mus. 5%; Christ.	**Economy** Essentially agricultural. The largest rice producer in the world. Pig farming, fishing and silk-worm breeding are important. **Principal resources** China is rich in minerals and fuel. **Industry** All sectors are developing rapidly.
40	Greek; Turkish	Christian; Cypriot 81%; Mus. 19%	**Economy** Based on agriculture (wine, olives, citrus fruits and potatoes). Sheep and goat farming are practiced on a modest scale, as is fishing. **Industry** Principally mineral extraction (of pyrite, chromite, asbestos) and tourism.
30	Hindi (off.); English; Telugu; Bengali; Marathi; Urdu	Hindu 80%; Muslim 11%	**Economy** Agriculture-based. Cereals and rice are the most profitable crops. Livestock are reared extensively, although mainly to meet subsistence needs. Some income raised through fishing and forestry. **Industry** Growing rapidly.
10	Bahasa Indonesia (off.); Javanese	Muslim 87%; Christian 9.6%	**Economy** Almost half the population is involved in agriculture (rice, tea, coffee, sugar-cane, palm-oil, coconuts, tobacco). Second largest rubber producer. **Principal resources** Rich mineral reserves (oil) contribute to developing industry.
20	Persian (Farsi)	Muslim (Shia)	**Principal resources** Profits from international sales of oil and natural gas are being used to enhance all sectors of the economy. **Industry** The mining, petrochemical, mechanical and textile (carpet) industries are flourishing.
50	Arabic; Kurdish	Muslim (Sunni, Shia)	**Economy** Petroleum is a major source of foreign revenue. **Agriculture** Employs a third of the population, thanks to fertile river basins. Cereals grown for domestic market; dates for export. **Industry** Textiles, chemicals, cement, food, paper.
30	Hebrew (off.); Arabic	Jewish; Muslim	**Economy** Structurally modern and well organized. All sectors are flourishing, especially agriculture. **Industry** Manufacturing (chemical, mechanical, textiles), mining (diamonds) and tourism are particularly lucrative.
20	Japanese	Shintoist; Buddhist	**Economy** Most industrialized in Asia, third world-wide. All manufacturing sectors well developed (mechanics, electro-nics, chemicals, textiles and paper). **Agriculture** Mainly rice; fishing is important to domestic and export markets.

STATE (official name/ English translation)	CAPITAL ① inhabitants	AREA (sq km) POPULATION		DENSITY (inhab/sq km)	L EXF A (in y M
JORDAN (Al Mamlaka al Urdunīyah al Hāshemīyah/Hashemite Kingdom of Jordan)	**Ammān** 936 000	97 740	3 285 000	34	64.2
KUWAIT (Dawlat al-Kuwait/ State of Kuwait)	**Kuwait City** 44 400	17 818	2 241 000	126	71.2
LAOS (Satharanarath Pasathipatai Pasason Lao/Lao People's Democratic Republic)	**Vientiane** (Viengchane) 377 400	236 800	4 262 000	18	47.8
LEBANON (Al-Jumhūrīya al-Lubnānīya)	**Beirut** (Bayrūt) 474 900	10 400	2 965 000	285	65.1
MALAYSIA (Persekutuan Tanah Malaysia/ Federation of Malaysia)	**Kuala Lumpur** 1 103 000	329 758	18 239 000	55	68.8
THE MALDIVES (Divehi Jumhuriya/ Republic of Maldives)	**Malé** 55 100	298	222 000	745	62.2
MONGOLIA (Mongol Uls/ Mongolian Republic)	**Ulan Bator** (Ulaanbaatar) 548 000	1 566 500	2 140 000	1	61.2
MYANMAR (BURMA) (Pyidaungsu Myanma Naingngandaw/ Union of Myanmar)	**Rangoon** (Yangon) 2 459 000	678 033	42 561 000	63	60.0
NEPAL (Nepāl Adhirājya/ Kingdom of Nepal)	**Kathmandu** 393 500	147 181	19 379 000	131	55.4
NORTH KOREA (Chosun Minchu-chui Inmin Konghwa-Guk/Democratic People's Republic of Korea)	**P'yŏngyang** 2 639 000	120 538	22 937 000	190	66.2
OMAN (Sulṭanat 'Umān/ Sultanate of Oman)	**Muscat** 50 000	212 457	1 559 000	7	62.2
PAKISTAN (Islāmi Jamhūrīya e-Pakistān/ Islamic Republic of Pakistan)	**Islāmābād** 204 400	796 095	115 520 000	145	59.3
PHILIPPINES (Republika ñg Pilipinas/ Republic of the Philippines)	**Manila** 1 599 000	300 000	62 000 000	207	62.5
QATAR (Dawlat al-Qaṭar/ State of Qatar)	**Doha** (Ad Dawhah) 217 000	11 437	455 000	39	66.9

OSS ONAL OUCT ②	LANGUAGES	RELIGIONS	ECONOMY
120	Arabic	Muslim	**Economy** Quite poor; the arid soil yields only vegetables, citrus fruits and cereals. **Principal resources** Phosphates and potash (the main export). **Industry** Food processing, chemical, cement and tobacco manufacture.
160	Arabic	Muslim	**Economy** Rich oil reserves make Kuwait one of the world's wealthiest countries. **Agriculture** Fishing is traditionally strong; irrigation is used to expand arable land. **Industry** Chemical, mechanical and cement plants supplied by natural gas.
230	Lao (off.); French	Buddhist	**Economy** The least developed in Indochina. Agriculture, forestry and fresh-water fishing are almost the only economic activities. **Agriculture** Rice is the principal crop. **Industry** Largely limited to the production of local crafts.
350	Arabic (off.); French	Christian 42%; Muslim 29%	**Agriculture** Olives, citrus fruits, grapes, fruit and vegetables are the main yields. Minimal animal farming and fishing. **Industry** The principal employers in this sector are the oil-refineries, cotton-mills, and cigarette and cement factories.
490	Malay (off.); English; Chinese	Mus. 53%; Buddhist; Taoist; Christian	**Agriculture** Mainly rice, coconuts, palm-oil, coffee, tea, pineapples and rubber (of which Malaysia is the world's largest exporter). **Mineral resources** Abundant tin, petrol, bauxite, copper. **Industry** Tourism is being promoted.
460	Dhivehi	Muslim	**Agriculture** The majority of the population is involved in fishing or cultivating coconuts (fish and coconut fibre being the principal exports). Most staple foods have to be imported. **Industry** Tourism is growing rapidly.
473	Mongolian	Buddhist	**Economy** Depends mainly on animal herding (sheep, goats, cattle, horses, camels). Some cereals are cultivated. **Industry** Centres on food processing. **Principal resources** The country has deposits of copper and coal.
200	Birmano (off.); English	Buddhist 88%	**Agriculture** Dominates. Teak and forestry products have replaced rice as the principal export. Crops for industrial use include sugar-cane, tobacco, jute and cotton. **Mineral resources** The country has considerable reserves of oil.
180	Nepali (off.); Bihari	Hindu 89%; Buddhist 5%	**Economy** Dominated by cultivation (cereals, potatoes, jute, sugar-cane, tobacco) and animal farming (yak, cattle, buffalo, goats). **Industry** Small-scale, mainly processing industries. Tourism is flourishing and brings in foreign revenue.
040	Korean	Buddhist; Confucian; Shintoist	**Economy** Dominated by mining (coal, iron, copper, lead). **Industry** Iron and steel production, mechanical and chemical engineering and textile manufacture all well established. **Agriculture** Principal crops are rice, maize and potatoes.
650	Arabic (off.); English	Muslim (Sunni)	**Economy** Depends on the export of petrol and natural gas. Of lesser importance: agriculture (vegetables, fruit, dates), animal farming (goats, sheep), and fishing. **Industry** Metal-lurgical (copper), petrochemical and cement production.
400	Urdu (nat.); English	Muslim	**Economy** Expanding. **Agriculture** Flourishing, the main crops being cereals, sugar-cane and cotton. Cotton is the principal export, and also supplies a productive textile in-dustry. **Mineral resources** Petroleum, natural gas and coal.
740	Tagalog (Filipino); English	Catholic 84%	**Agriculture** Fundamental to the economy (rice, maize, coconuts, sugar-cane, bananas). Fishing is also important. **Industry** Mining growing rapidly (gold, copper) along with food processing, electronics, chemicals and textiles.
870	Arabic	Muslim (Sunni)	**Economy** Relies on its plentiful reserves of petroleum and natural gas. **Industry** Petrochemicals and cement are the chief industrial products. **Agriculture** Fishing and nomadic animal herding are traditional livelihoods.

STATE (official name/ English translation)	CAPITAL ① inhabitants	AREA (sq km)	POPULATION	DENSITY (inhab/sq km)	LIF EXPE AN (in ye M
SAUDI ARABIA (Al Mamlaka al'Arabīya as-Sa'ūdīya/Kingdom of Saudi Arabia)	**Riyadh** (Ar Riyād) 1 308 000	2 153 168	15 267 000	7	61.7
SINGAPORE (Republik Singapura/ Republic of Singapore)	**Singapore**	639	2 763 000	4324	70.3
SOUTH KOREA (Daehan-Minkuk/ Republic of South Korea)	**Seoul** (Sŏul) 10 628 000	99 237	43 530 000	438	66.9
SRĪ LANKA (Srī Lanka Prajatantrika Samajawadi Janarajaya)	**Colombo** 615 000	65 610	17 247 000	263	69.1
SYRIA (Al Jumhūrīya al 'Arabīya as Sūrīya)	**Damascus** (Dimashq) 1 326 000	185 180	12 524 000	67	65.2
TAIWAN (REPUBLIC OF CHINA) (Chung-hua Min Kuo)	**Taipei** 2 718 000	36 202	20 489 000	566	71.3
THAILAND (Prathet Thai/ Kingdom of Thailand)	**Bangkok** 5 876 000	513 115	55 884 000	109	63.8
TURKEY (Türkiye Cumhuriyeti/ Republic of Turkey)	**Ankara** 2 553 000	755 688	51 277 000	69	68.0
UNITED ARAB EMIRATES (Al Imārāt al 'Arabīya al-Muttahida)	**Abu Dhabi** 243 000	83 600	1 945 000	23	68.6
VIETNAM (Công Hòa Xã Hôi Chu' Nghiã Viêt Nam/Socialist Republic of Vietnam)	**Hanoi** 1 089 000	329 566	67 589 000	205	63.7
YEMEN (Al-Jumhūrīya al-Yamanīyah/ Republic of Yemen)	**Sana'ā** 427 000	524 342	11 843 000	22	49.0

ASIA   27 140 550   3 121 179 000   115

ASIA   Total ⒶA   44 032 038   3 210 194 000   73

OSS ONAL DUCT ②	LANGUAGES	RELIGIONS	ECONOMY
070	Arabic	Muslim (Sunni)	**Economy** Petroleum is the most valuable resource (Saudi Arabia is the world's third biggest producer of crude oil). **Industry** Mainly petrochemical. Tourism is also flourishing (many pilgrims visit the sacred cities of Mecca and Medina).
890	Chinese; Malay; Tamil; English	Tao. 29%; Bud. 27%; Mus. 16%; Christ. 10%	**Economy** Dominated by industrial sector (electronics, ship-yards, textiles, chemicals, rubber, metallurgical and petro-chemical plants). A major international financial and com-mercial centre, the island also has a thriving fishing industry.
340	Korean (off.)	Budd.40%; Christ. 28%; Conf. 17%	**Agriculture** Mainly rice, potatoes, cotton and tobacco. Also fishing. **Mineral resources** Rich in coal, iron, gold and tungsten. **Industry** Well developed mechanical, electronic, textile and petrochemical sectors .
500	Sinhalese; Tamil (off.); English	Bud. 69%; Hindu 15%; Christ. 7%; Mus. 8%	**Economy** Essentially agricultural (rice, coconuts, tea, cinnamon, coffee). The forests yield caoutchouc. **Industry** Precious stones are mined; textiles, cement, rubber and chemicals are manufactured. Tourism is increasing.
110	Arabic	Muslim (Sunni) 75%; Christ. 10%	**Economy** Based on agriculture (wheat, cotton, grapes, olives, vegetables and fruit). Sheep farming is widespread. **Industry** Mining (petroleum, phosphates), textiles, food, leather, cement and glass industries are all developing.
810	Chinese	Confucian; Buddist	**Agriculture** Well-organized; rice, sugar-cane, tea and sweet potatoes are the main crops. Little animal farming, but fishing is profitable. **Industry** Textiles are the primary pro-duct, plus electronics, machinery, petrochemicals and toys.
580	Thai	Buddist	**Economy** Still fundamentally agricultural: rice, maize, cassava and sugar-cane are the chief products. Fishing, forestry (timber, caoutchouc) and mining (tin) are important. Tourism is now the primary foreign exchange earner.
820	Turkish (off.); Kurdish	Muslim	**Agriculture** Employs almost half the population (cereals, cotton, vine, olive, fruit, sugar beet, tobacco). Animal farming is widespread. **Industry** The food, textile, chemical and machinery sectors are expanding; tourism is flourishing.
870	Arabic (off.); English	Muslim 95%	**Economy** One of the wealthiest countries in the world due to extensive on- and off-shore reserves of petroleum and natural gas. Fishing and pearl cultivation are traditional livelihoods. **Industry** Petrochemical, metallurgical and cement.
110	Vietnamese	Buddist; Taoist	**Economy** Much of the work force is employed in cultivating rice. Cassava, sweet potatoes, coconuts, tea and tobacco are also grown. Fishing is important. **Industry** Mining (coal, petrol), metal, food and chemical sectors are well developed.
540	Arabic	Muslim	**Economy** Agriculture (cereals, dates, vegetables, fruit, cotton, coffee) and fishing employ most of the population, while sheep, goats and cattle are herded. **Industry** Oil is mined; chemical, textile and cement production is increasing.

cludes Christmas and Cocos Is, Hong Kong, Macao, Sinai
eninsula, Gaza Strip and the Asian parts of the CIS, but
cludes Irian Jaya and Socotra.

① The local form is given in brackets only when it differs from the English form

② Per inhabitant, in US$

STATE (official name/ English translation)	CAPITAL ① inhabitants	AREA (sq km)	POPULATION	DENSITY (inhab/sq km)	LIF EXPE AN• (in ye M
ALGERIA (Al Jumhūrīya al Jazā'iriya ad Dīmūqrātīya ash-Sha'bīya)	**Algiers** (Al Jazair) 1 687 600	2 381 741	25 660 000	11	65.0
ANGOLA (República de Angola/ Republic of Angola)	**Luanda** 1 136 000	1 246 700	10 303 000	8	44.9
BENIN (République du Bénin/ Republic of Benin)	**Porto-Novo** 164 000	112 622	4 889 000	43	49.0
BOTSWANA (Republic of Botswana)	**Gaborone** 134 000	600 372	1 320 000	2	52.7
BURKINA FASO (République de Burkina Faso/ Republic of Burkina Faso)	**Ouagadougou** 442 200	274 200	9 242 000	34	47.6
BURUNDI (République du Burundi/ Republika y'Uburundi/ Republic of Burundi)	**Bujumbura** 235 400	27 834	5 600 000	201	50.0
CAMEROON (République du Cameroun/ Republic of Cameroon)	**Yaoundé** 653 700	475 442	11 932 000	25	53.5
CAPE VERDE (República de Cabo Verde/ Republic of Cape Verde)	**Praia** 61 700	4 033	341 000	84	63.0
CENTRAL AFRICAN REPUBLIC (République Centrafricaine)	**Bangui** 597 000	622 436	3 015 000	5	48.0
CHAD (République du Tchad/ Republic of Chad)	**N'djamena** 594 000	1 284 000	5 819 000	4	45.9
COMOROS (République Fédérale Islamique des Comores)	**Moroni** 22 000	1 862	481 000	258	54.0
CONGO (République Populaire du Congo/People's Republic of the Congo)	**Brazzaville** 760 000	342 000	2 346 000	7	52.1
DJIBOUTI (République de Djibouti/ Jumhūrīya Jībutī/ Republic of Djibouti)	**Djibouti** 220 000	23 200	541 000	23	47.4
EGYPT (Jumhūrīyat Mişr al 'Arabīya/ Arab Republic of Egypt)	**Cairo** (Al Qāhirah) 6 069 000	942 247	54 688 000	58	59.0

...SS ...NAL ...UCT ...)	LANGUAGES	RELIGIONS	ECONOMY
)20	Arabic (off.); French; Berber	Muslim	**Agriculture** Supplies processing industry (vines, vegetables, olives, citrus fruit) and satisfies subsistence needs. **Mineral resources** Hydrocarbons. **Industry** Developing gradually; traditional crafts bring in foreign revenue.
520	Portuguese (off.); Bantu languages	Cath. 65%; Animist Protestant	**Agriculture** One of the country's main economic activities; coffee, cotton, tobacco, palm-oil, sugar-cane and sisal are the principal crops. **Mineral resources** Mining (petroleum, diamonds and iron) generates considerable income.
380	French (off.); Fon; Yoruba; Adja	Animist 63%; Cath. 18%; Mus. 15%	**Agriculture** Dominates the economy. Cereals, cassava, cotton and palm-oil are the main products. Animal farming and fishing are widely practiced. **Industry** Limited to the processing of agricultural goods.
590	English (off.); Setswana	Animist; Christian 30%	**Economy** Traditionally based on animal farming (especially cattle) and subsistence agriculture (cereals, legumes, groundnuts, citrus fruit). **Principal resources** Diamonds, coal, copper and nickel are the main mineral exports.
350	French (off.); Mossi; Fulani	Animist; Mus. 30%; Christ. 10%	**Economy** Very poor and with few natural resources. **Agriculture** Cereals, sugar-cane and cotton are the only crops of any importance. Cattle rearing is becoming more widespread.
210	French and Kirundi (both off.); Swahili	Cath. 65%; Animist; Protestant	**Economy** Principally agrarian. **Agriculture** The main source of employment. The most important subsistence crops are sweet potatoes and cassava; coffee, tea and cotton are exported.
)40	French and English (both off.); Fulani; Sao; Bamileke	Animist 40%; Mus. 22%; Cath. 21%	**Agriculture** A major sector of the domestic economy. Crops include cereals, cocoa, coffee, sugar-cane, palm-oil, cotton and bananas. Forests provide timber and caoutchouc. **Industry** The oil industry is of growing importance.
750	Portuguese (off.); Crioulu	Catholic	**Agriculture** Yields a variety of products, but in quantities insufficient to sustain the local population. **Economy** Export trade is boosted by the production of sea salt and fishing (tuna, lobster).
390	French (off.); Sangho (nat.); Sudanese dialects	Animist 57%; Prot. 15%; Mus. 8%	**Agriculture** Cereals, cassava and bananas are cultivated for domestic consumption; cotton, groundnuts, palm-oil and coffee for export. **Principal resources** Diamonds and gold are sold internationally. **Industry** Largely food processing.
220	French and Arabic (off.); other local languages	Muslim 50%; Animist 44%	**Agriculture** Cotton plantations are a highly profitable part of the economy. Cereal crops are also significant, as is fishing (on Chad's internal rivers and lakes). Animal farming is quite advanced. **Industry** Very limited.
500	French and Arabic (both off.); other local languages	Muslim	**Agriculture** The main economic activity, producing vanilla, cloves, ylang-ylang, copra, coffee, cocoa and bananas for export. Some fishing. **Industry** Generally quite undeveloped although the islands are beginning to attract tourists.
120	French (off.); local languages	Animist 47%; Catholic 38%	**Economy** Oil is a major source of foreign revenue, thanks to reserves of petroleum and natural gas. **Agriculture** Well organized (mainly sugar-cane, coffee, cocoa, palm-oil and cassava); the forests provide timber for export.
500	Arabic and French (both off.); other local languages	Muslim	**Economy** Impoverished, largely as the land is so arid and infertile. Relies mainly on service industries, particularly the capital's port and airport. **Agriculture** Low rainfall restricts agriculture to nomadic animal grazing (sheep, goats, camels).
520	Arabic (off.); French and English used commercially	Muslim 90%; Christian 7%	**Agriculture** Concentrated along the banks of the Nile. Main crops: cereals, cotton and sugar-cane. **Mineral resources** Petrol, natural gas, iron, phosphates. **Economy** Tourism and tolls on the Suez Canal bring in foreign currency.

STATE (official name/ English translation)	CAPITAL ① inhabitants	AREA (sq km)	POPULATION	DENSITY (inhab/sq km)	LI EXP AN (in y M
EQUATORIAL GUINEA (República de Guinea Ecuatorial/Republic of Equatorial Guinea)	**Malabo** 30 700	28 051	356 000	13	44.4
ERITREA (Eritrea)	**Asmara** (Āsmera) 331 000	121 143	3 325 000	27	–
ETHIOPIA (Ityopya)	**Addis Ababa** 1 673 000	1 130 139	50 058 000	44	42.4
GABON (République Gabonaise/ Gabonese Republic)	**Libreville** 352 000	267 667	1 350 000	5	49.9
GAMBIA (Republic of the Gambia)	**Banjul** 44 500	11 295	884 000	78	41.4
GHANA (Republic of Ghana)	**Accra** 949 000	238 538	15 509 000	65	52.2
GUINEA (République de Guinée/ Republic of Guinea)	**Conakry** 705 000	245 857	7 052 000	28	42.0
GUINEA-BISSAU (República da Guiné-Bissau/ Republic of Guinea-Bissau)	**Bissau** 125 000	36 125	984 000	27	41.9
IVORY COAST (République de la Côte d'Ivoire/ Republic of the Ivory Coast)	**Yamoussoukro** 120 000	322 463	10 820 000	33	52.8
KENYA (Jamhuri ya Kenya/ Republic of Kenya)	**Nairobi** 1 429 000	582 646	23 183 000	40	56.5
LESOTHO (Muso oa Lesotho/ Kingdom of Lesotho)	**Maseru** 109 400	30 355	1 806 000	59	51.5
LIBERIA (Republic of Liberia)	**Monrovia** 465 000	111 369	2 520 000	23	53.9
LIBYA (Al Jamāhīrīya al 'Arabīya al-Lībīya ash Sha'bīya al-Ishtir ākīya)	**Tripoli** (Tarābulus) 591 000	1 775 500	4 325 000	2	59.1
MADAGASCAR (Repoblika demokratika n'i Madagaskar/République démocratique de Madagascar)	**Antananarivo** (Tananarive) 1 050 000	587 041	11 493 000	19	54.0

GROSS NATIONAL PRODUCT ( )	LANGUAGES	RELIGIONS	ECONOMY
130	Spanish (off.); Bubi; Fang; Pidgin English	Catholic 80%	**Agriculture** Cocoa and coffee are the most common plantation crops, followed by sugar-cane, bananas, palm-oil and coconuts. The country's main resource is its valuable timber (rosewood, ebony). **Industry** Almost none.
–	Tigrinya and Arabic (both off.); Italian	Coptic; Muslim	**Economy** Based on agriculture (cereals, citrus fruits, oilseed, cotton, tobacco, coffee), animal farming (sheep and goats), fishing and extracting sea salt. **Industry** Undergoing reconstruction.
120	Amharic (off.); Arabic; Oromo; other local languages	Coptic 55%; Muslim 35%	**Agriculture** The most profitable sector of the economy (coffee, tobacco, cotton, bananas and sugar-cane). Animals are reared extensively for their skins and leather. **Industry** Food processing and textile manufacture predominate.
780	French (off.); Bantu (Fang)	Christian	**Economy** Depends on the forests, which provide valuable timber. **Agriculture** Practiced only at subsistence level. **Principal resources** Petroleum, natural gas, uranium, manganese and gold are lucratively mined and exported.
360	English (off.); Wolof; Mandinka; Fula	Muslim 95%; Christ. 4%	**Economy** Depends on the cultivation of groundnuts. Other crops include cotton, cereals and palm nuts. **Industry** Manufacturing centres on processing groundnuts. Tourism is a rapidly growing industry.
400	English (off.); Asante; Ewe; Ga	Christ. 52%; Animist 35%; Mus. 13%	**Economy** Ghana is the third leading producer of cocoa, which it exports worldwide. Fishing, forestry and mining (diamonds, gold, bauxite, petroleum and manganese) are also important.
450	French (off.); Sudanese languages	Muslim 85%; Animist 5%	**Economy** Most of the workforce is employed in agriculture. Groundnuts, citrus fruits, bananas, pineapple, coffee and palm-oil are exported. **Mineral resources** Guinea has large reserves of bauxite, which is exported in considerable bulk.
190	Portuguese (off.); Creole; Sudanese languages	Animist 65%; Muslim 30%	**Economy** Agricultural: the main products are groundnuts, palm-nuts, cashew nuts and cotton, which are processed locally and then exported. Cereals are widely cultivated. Many inhabitants engage in fishing and lumbering.
690	French (off.); local languages	Animist 37%; Mus. 34%; Cath. 22%	**Economy** Most revenue comes from agriculture (especially from coffee and cocoa, followed by oil and palm-nuts), lumbering (valuable wood and caoutchouc) and mining (petroleum, diamonds). **Industry** Expanding.
340	Swahili (off.); Kikuyu; Kamba; English	Animist; Cath. 21%; Prot. 15%	**Agriculture** Flourishing: the broad range of crops include cereals, coffee, tea, sugar-cane, pyrethrum, cotton and sisal. Animal farming is widespread. **Industry** Productive, especially food processing. Tourism brings in substantial revenue.
580	English; Sesotho	Christian 90%; Animist 6%	**Economy** Very impoverished. **Agriculture** Barely above subsistence level (cereals, legumes, fruit). Animal farming is widespread; wool and mohair are exported. **Industry** Some mining (precious stones). Tourism is profitable.
400	English (off.); Sudanese languages	Christian; Animist 20%; Mus. 15%	**Agriculture** Coffee, cocoa, rice, citrus fruits and cassava; plantation crops such as palm-oil and caoutchouc are significant. **Mineral resources** Iron ore, diamonds and gold are mined. **Industry** Manufacturing industries are developing.
310	Arabic; other local languages	Muslim	**Economy** Depends on reserves of petroleum and natural gas. **Agriculture** Cereals, olives, grapes, citrus fruits and dates are among the main crops; animal farming is also practiced. **Industry** Centres on oil production.
210	Malagasy; French	Anim. 50%; Cath. 25%; Prot. 20%; Muslim 5%	**Economy** The island depends largely on agriculture; coffee, vanilla, cloves and pepper are the principal exports. Rice and cassava are cultivated for domestic consumption. **Industry** Mainly food processing.

STATE (official name/ English translation)	CAPITAL ① inhabitants	AREA (sq km)	POPULATION	DENSITY (inhab/sq km)	LI EXP AN (in y M
MALAWI (Mfuko la Malaŵi/ Republic of Malawi)	**Lilongwe** 220 000	118 484	8 556 000	72	48.4
MALI (République du Mali/ Republic of Mali)	**Bamako** 646 200	1 240 142	8 299 000	6	45.0
MAURITANIA (Jumhūrīyat Mūrītānīya al-Islāmīya/Islamic Republic of Mauritania)	**Nouakchott** 393 000	1 030 700	2 036 000	2	45.0
MAURITIUS (Republic of Mauritius)	**Port Louis** 143 000	2 045	1 069 000	523	65.0
MOROCCO (Al Mamlakah al Maghribīya/ Kingdom of Morocco)	**Rabat** 556 000	458 730	25 698 000	56	61.6
MOZAMBIQUE (República de Moçambique/ Republic of Mozambique)	**Maputo** 1 070 000	799 380	16 084 000	20	46.9
NAMIBIA (Republic of Namibia/ Republiek van Namibie)	**Windhoek** 115 000	824 292	1 400 000	2	55.0
NIGER (République du Niger/ Republic of Niger)	**Niamey** 399 000	1 186 408	7 984 000	6	42.9
NIGERIA (Federal Republic of Nigeria)	**Abuja** 379 000	923 768	88 500 000	96	50.8
RWANDA (Republika y'u Rwanda/ République Rwandaise)	**Kigali** 234 000	26 338	7 150 000	271	48.8
SAO TOME E PRINCIPE (República Democrática de São Tomé e Príncipe)	**São Tomé** 35 000	964	123 000	127	64.0
SENEGAL (République du Sénégal/ Republic of Senegal)	**Dakar** 1 490 000	196 722	7 433 000	38	54.0
SEYCHELLES (Republic of Seychelles)	**Victoria** 24 300	453	68 000	150	65.3
SIERRA LEONE (Republic of Sierra Leone)	**Freetown** 470 000	71 740	4 260 000	59	41.4

OSS ONAL UUCT ②	LANGUAGES	RELIGIONS	ECONOMY
230	English (off.); Chichewa (nat.); other local dialects	Animist; Catholic 19%	**Economy** Relatively poor. Tobacco, cotton, sugar-cane and tea are cultivated for export; maize is the principal subsistence crop. **Industry** Growing modestly, particularly the food processing, cement manufacture and tobacco sectors.
280	French (off.); Bambara; local languages	Muslim 90%; Animist 9%	**Economy** Extremely poor, and based almost entirely on agriculture. Cotton, rice, cassava and groundnuts are the main crops. Fishing is important, and sheep, goat and cattle farming is well developed (droughts notwithstanding).
510	Arabic (off.); French; Poular; Wolof; Soninke	Muslim	**Agriculture** Severe droughts have hampered arable farming: cereals and dates are almost the only crops. Deep-sea fishing and nomadic animal farming (cattle, sheep) are widespread. **Principal resources** Rich reserves of iron ore.
420	English (off.); French; Creole; Hindi	Christ. 30%; Hindu 52%; Mus. 13%	**Economy** Depends on the production and export of sugar-cane, although there are also large plantations of tea, coffee and coco-palm. Fishing is profitable. **Industry** Mainly manufacturing; tourism is a significant source of revenue.
030	Arabic (off.); Berber; French	Muslim	**Agriculture** Cereals, grapes, vegetables and fruit are cultivated. Animal farming is widespread (sheep, goats, cattle). **Principal resources** Phosphates. **Industry** Food manufacturing, textile and tanning industries.
70	Portuguese (off.); other local languages	Animist 48%; Cath. 14%; Mus. 16%	**Agriculture** The main crops are cotton and sugar-cane; also tea, sisal, cassava, cashew nuts, cereals, bananas. **Mineral resources** Rich but under-exploited deposits of coal, diamonds and bauxite. **Industry** Largely food manufacturing.
120	Afrikaans (off.); English; other local languages	Christian	**Economy** Depends on rich deposits of diamonds and uranium (plus copper, lead, zinc, silver and tin) which are exported internationally. **Agriculture** Animal farming and fishing are practiced widely. **Industry** Mainly food processing.
300	French (off.); Hausa; Tamashek; Poular; Djerma; Kanuri	Muslim; Animist 15%	**Economy** Uranium, the main mineral resource, is mined in substantial quantities, but agriculture employs the bulk of the population. Millet, sorghum, rice and cassava are the chief crops. Animals are farmed for their skins and leather.
290	English (off.); Sudanese languages (Hausa, Ibo, Yoruba)	Muslim 45%; Christian 38%	**Economy** In the past, agriculture predominated (cocoa, palm-oil, coconuts, groundnuts, caoutchouc and bananas), but oil is now the main source of revenue. **Industry** Mining (tin as well as oil) and food processing.
260	French; Kinyarwanda	Catholic 56%; Anim. 17%; Prot. 13%	**Agriculture** Coffee, tobacco, tea, pyrethrum and groundnuts are grown for cash; maize, rice, sorghum, sweet potatoes, cassava and bananas for subsistence. Some animal herding. **Principal resources** Tin, gold and tungsten.
350	Portuguese (off.); Creole	Catholic	**Agriculture** The mainstay of the economy. Cocoa, coffee, walnuts, palm-oil, coconuts, copra and bananas are the most important crops. Fishing is another source of revenue. **Industry** Scarcely developed.
720	French (off.); Sudanese languages (Wolof, nat.)	Muslim 85%	**Economy** Largely agrarian (groundnuts, cotton, cereals). Senegal is a leading producer of groundnuts. Fishing is important. **Principal resources** Phosphates. **Industry** Mainly groundnuts processing, oil production and tourism.
110	Creole (off.); English; French	Catholic	**Agriculture** Coconut palms, cinnamon and vanilla are the principal crops. Fishing is also an important aspect of the economy. **Industry** About a third of the labour force is employed in the highly successful tourist industry.
210	English (off.); Krio; Sudanese languages	Animist 51%; Muslim 39%	**Mineral resources** The chief exports, particularly diamonds, rutile and bauxite. **Agriculture** Mainly at a subsistence level, the principal crops being cocoa, coffee and palm kernels. **Industry** Processing industries.

	STATE (official name/ English translation)	CAPITAL ① inhabitants	AREA (sq km)	POPULATION	DENSITY (inhab/sq km)	LI EXP AN (in y M
★	**SOMALIA** (Jamhuuriyadda Diimoqraadiga Soomaaliya/ Somali Democratic Republic)	**Mogadishu** (Muqdisho) 500 000	637 657	6 760 000	11	43.4
	SOUTH AFRICA (Republic of South Africa/ Republiek van Suid-Afrika)	**Pretoria/Cape Town** (Kaapstad)* 443 000/777 000	1 224 641	38 191 000	31	57.5
	SUDAN (Jamhūrỹat es Sūdān/ Republic of Sudan)	**Khartoum** (Al Kharṭūm) 557 000	2 505 813	25 941 000	10	52.0
	SWAZILAND (Umbuso we Swatini/ Kingdom of Swaziland)	**Mbabane** 38 000	17 364	798 000	46	56.2
	TANZANIA (Jamhuri ya Muungano wa Tanzania/United Republic of Tanzania)	**Dodoma** 204 000	939 470	26 353 000	28	51.3
★	**TOGO** (République Togolaise/ Togolese Republic)	**Lomé** 400 000	56 785	3 643 000	64	51.3
☾	**TUNISIA** (Al Jumhūrīyah at Tūnisīyah/ Republic of Tunisia)	**Tunis** 626 000	163 610	8 293 000	51	64.9
	UGANDA (Republic of Uganda)	**Kampala** 651 000	241 038	16 830 000	70	51.4
	ZAIRE (République du Zaïre/ Republic of Zaïre)	**Kinshasa** 3 741 000	2 344 885	36 672 000	15	50.3
	ZAMBIA (Republic of Zambia)	**Lusaka** 982 000	752 614	8 023 000	10	54.4
	ZIMBABWE (Republic of Zimbabwe)	**Harare** 863 000	390 759	10 130 000	26	57.9

AFRICA   29 981 681   630 136 000   21
AFRICA Total ⓐ   30 249 096   632 915 000   21

SS NAL UCT)	LANGUAGES	RELIGIONS	ECONOMY
50	Somali (off.); Arabic; Italian; English (adm.)	Muslim (Sunni)	**Economy** Depends on animal farming (cattle, sheep, goats, camels) and agriculture (cereals, cotton, sugar-cane, bananas). Both are major sources of employment. Fishing is on the increase.
30	Afrikaans and English (both off.); other local languages	Protestant; Animist; Cath. 8%	**Economy** The most prosperous in Africa. The mining sector (gold, diamonds, uranium, platinum, coal, iron), industry (mechanical, chemical and textile) and agriculture (cereals, vegetables, fruit) are all flourishing.
00	Arabic (off.); other local dialects	Mus. 73%; Animist 17%; Cath. 6%	**Agriculture** Cotton is the most important crop; cereals, dates, sugar-cane and oilseed are also cultivated. Nomadic herding is widespread. Sudan is one of the world's largest producers of gum arabic. **Industry** Relatively undeveloped.
60	English and siSwati	Christian 47%; Animist 40%	**Economy** Arable and animal farming, timber felling and mining are the main activities. **Agriculture** Sugar-cane and citrus fruits are cultivated widely. **Mineral resources** The country is quite rich in asbestos, carbon, diamonds and iron.
00	Swahili; English	Muslim; Christ. 30%; Hindu; Animist	**Agriculture** Coffee, tea, cotton, tobacco, sugar, sisal and cloves are grown for export. Animal farming and fishing are common. **Mineral resources** Diamonds and gold. **Industry** Food processing and textile production.
10	French (off.); Ewe; Poular; Hausa; Gour; Assirelii	Animist; Muslim 17%; Cath. 26%	**Agriculture** The population largely comprises subsistence farmers; coffee, cocoa, cotton, groundnuts and palm-oil are grown for export. **Mineral resources** Phosphates are the main export; iron ore is also mined. **Industry** Modest.
10	Arabic (off.); French; Berber	Muslim	**Economy** Based on agriculture (cereals, olives, grapes, citrus fruits, dates) and mining; phosphates and petrol account for over a third of exports. Fishing is profitable. **Industry** Mainly food processing and metallurgy. Tourism is increasing.
60	English and Swahili (both off.); Luganda	Cath. 40%; Prot. 20%; Muslim 6%	**Agriculture** Coffee, tea, cotton, tobacco, cocoa and sugar-cane are cultivated for export, while maize, millet, sorghum and cassava are the main subsistence crops. **Industry** Well developed in the food and metallurgical fields.
20	French (off.); other local dialects	Cath. 48%; Prot. 29%; Animist	**Agriculture** Cassava, rice, maize and bananas are the chief subsistence crops; coffee, cotton, cocoa, tea, caoutchouc and palm-oil are exported. **Mineral resources** Tin, copper, diamonds, petroleum and zinc are mined for export.
20	English (off.); local languages include Lozi, Nyanja, Tonga	Prot. 34%; Cath. 26%; Animist 27%	**Economy** Depends on mining (copper, cobalt, manganese, lead, zinc, tin) and the related industries of metal and chemical processing. **Agriculture** Limited; maize, cassava, groundnuts and tobacco are the most common crops.
20	English (off.); local languages include Chishona and Sindebele	Animist; Prot. 17%; Cath. 12%	**Agriculture** Wheat, maize, cotton, sugar, coffee, soya and tobacco are the principal crops. **Mineral resources** Gold, asbestos, coal, iron, silver, tin, nickel, copper and cobalt are exported. **Industry** Manufacturing is developing slowly.

cludes Saint Helena, Comoros Is., Réunion I., Madeira,
anary Is., Ceuta, Melilla, Socotra, Western Sahara.

etoria (administrative); Cape Town (legislative)

(1) The local form is given in brackets only when it differs from the English form

(2) Per inhabitant, in US$

	STATE (official name/ English translation)	CAPITAL inhabitants	AREA (sq km)	POPULATION	DENSITY (inhab/sq km)	LI EXP AN (in y M
	AUSTRALIA (Commonwealth of Australia)	**Canberra** 302 500	7 682 300	17 086 000	2	73.3
	FIJI (Matanitu Ko Viti/ Republic of Fiji)	**Suva** 70 000	18 272	736 000	40	68.3
	KIRIBATI (Republic of Kiribati)	**Bairiki** 2 100	849	72 000	85	50.6
	MARSHALL ISLANDS (Republic of the Marshall Islands)	**Dalap-Uliga-Darrit** 17 600	181	44 000	243	61.0
	MICRONESIA (Federated States of Micronesia)	**Palikir** —	707	111 000	157	64.0
	NAURU (Republic of Nauru)	**Yaren** —	21	9 000	428	64.0
	NEW ZEALAND (New Zealand)	**Wellington** 147 800	270 534	3 390 000	12	72.0
	PALAU	**Koror** 10 500	487	15 000	31	—
	PAPUA NEW GUINEA (Papua New Guinea)	**Port Moresby** 152 100	462 840	3 600 000	8	54.0
	SOLOMON ISLANDS (Solomon Islands)	**Honiara** 35 300	28 369	319 000	11	59.9
	TONGA (Pule'anga Tonga/ Kingdom of Tonga)	**Nuku'alofa** 28 900	748	96 000	128	61.0
	TUVALU (The Tuvalu Islands)	**Fongafale** —	24	9 000	375	60.0
	VANUATU (Ripablik Blong Vanuatu/ Republic of Vanuatu)	**Port-Vila** 19 300	12 189	147 000	12	61.1
	WESTERN SAMOA (Malo Tuto'atasi/ Independent State of Western Samoa)	**Apia** 33 200	2 831	164 000	58	64.0

AUSTRALIA AND OCEANIA		8 480 352	25 798 000	3
AUSTRALIA AND OCEANIA Total Ⓐ		8 942 252	29 128 000	3

LANGUAGES	RELIGIONS	ECONOMY
English	Protestant; Catholic 26%	**Economy** Based on agriculture (cereals, fruit, sugar-cane, cotton) and animal farming (sheep, cattle). **Mineral resources** Vast reserves of coal, natural gas, oil, nickel, gold, iron ore and bauxite. **Industry** All sectors expanding.
English, Fijian; Hindi	Methodist; Hindu 38%; Muslim	**Economy** Sustained by agriculture (sugar-cane, bananas, coconuts and potatoes) and fishing. Tourism also generates considerable revenue. **Mineral resources** Subsoil is rich in gold and silver. The island is heavily forested.
English (off.); I-Kiribati	Protestant; Catholic	**Agriculture** Most of the population is involved in agriculture and fishing. The principal crop is the coconut palm. **Industry** The tourist industry is expanding.
English (off.); Marshallese	Protestant; Catholic 8.5%	**Economy** Based on subsistence agriculture and fishing. Main crops are coconuts, copra, cassava and fruit. **Industry** Tourism is well developed.
English	Protestant; Catholic	**Economy** Most islanders are involved in fishing and cultivation (coconuts, copra, sweet potatoes, cassava, bananas). **Industry** The tourist industry is growing fast.
Nauruan (off.); English	Protestant; Catholic 24%	**Economy** Nauru is the wealthiest country in Oceania thanks to its rich phosphate deposits (which cover nearly 75% of the island). Phosphate mining accounts for three-quarters of the country's GDP.
English	Protestant; Catholic 15%	**Economy** Dominated by livestock farming, particularly sheep (for wool and meat) and cattle (dairy products and beef). **Agriculture** Well established. **Industry** Expanding, due in part to inexpensive hydroelectricity.
English; Palauan	Christian	**Economy** At subsistence level. The archipelago relies mainly on agriculture (potatoes, coconuts, cassava and bananas) and fishing. **Industry** Tourism is beginning to develop.
English (off.); Pidgin-English; Motu; other local dialects	Animist; Catholic 27%	**Economy** Essentially agricultural; sweet potatoes, cocoa, coffee and coconuts are the main crops. **Principal resources** Mining (especially gold, silver, copper) generates considerable revenue. The island is richly forested.
English (off.); Pidgin-English; Melanesian and Polynesian languages	Protestant; Catholic 18%	**Economy** The population is largely employed in cultivating coconut palms and sweet potatoes. Timber, fish and copra are the main exports. **Industry** Fishing is a major concern; a modest food processing industry has been established.
English; Tongan	Protestant; Catholic 13%	**Economy** Some 58% of the population is involved in agriculture (coconuts, potatoes, cassava and groundnuts). The chief exports are copra and coconuts. Fishing is also profitable. **Industry** Tourism is well established.
Tuvaluan; English	Protestant	**Economy** The two main sources of income are coconuts and fishing. The country relies on revenue from emigrants and foreign aid.
Bislama; English (off.); French (off.); other local dialects	Animist; Catholic 14%	**Economy** Based on subsistence agriculture and fishing. Main crops are coconut palm, cocoa, groundnuts and maize. The islands are densely forested. **Mineral resources** Primarily manganese.
Samoan (off.); English	Protestant; Catholic 22%	**Economy** Agriculture is the country's main resource, the principal crops being bananas, coconuts and cocoa. Fishing and pig farming are also well developed. **Industry** Confined to the manufacture of agricultural products.

des Norfolk I., Macquarie I., Cook Is, Niue I., Tokelau tcairn Is, New Caledonia, Wallis and Futuna, Po- sia, Clipperton, Guam, Hawaii, Midway Is, American oa, Wake Is, Mariana Is, Irian Jaya, Chilean Is.

① Per inhabitant, in US$1million

ANTARCTICA has an area of 14 107 637 sq km, including the islands and ice-shelf (13 176 727 sq km without the ice-shelf).

STATE (official name/ English translation)	CAPITAL ① inhabitants	AREA (sq km) POPULATION		DENSITY (inhab/sq km)	EX A (in M
ANTIGUA AND BARBUDA (Antigua and Barbuda)	Saint John's 36 000	442	64 000	145	70.
BAHAMAS (The Commonwealth of the Bahamas)	Nassau 172 000	13 939	259 000	18	69.
BARBADOS (Barbados)	Bridgetown 7 600	431	258 000	598	72.
BELIZE (Belize)	Belmopan 3 700	22 965	189 000	8	67.
CANADA (Canada)	Ottawa 300 800	9 970 610	27 300 000	3	73.
COSTA RICA (República de Costa Rica/ Republic of Costa Rica)	San José 297 000	51 100	3 064 000	60	72.
CUBA (República de Cuba/ Republic of Cuba)	Havana (La Habana) 2 119 000	110 922	10 736 000	97	73.
DOMINICA (Commonwealth of Dominica)	Roseau 15 900	751	71 000	94	73.
DOMINICAN REPUBLIC (República Dominicana)	Santo Domingo 1 600 000	48 442	7 313 000	151	63.
EL SALVADOR (República de El Salvador/ Republic of El Salvador)	San Salvador 481 000	21 041	5 392 000	256	63.
GRENADA (State of Grenada)	Saint George's 7 500	344	101 000	293	69.
GUATEMALA (República de Guatemala/ Republic of Guatemala)	Guatemala City 1 114 000	108 889	9 197 000	84	59.
HAITI (République d'Haïti/ Republic of Haiti)	Port-au-Prince 514 000	27 400	6 625 000	242	53.
HONDURAS (República de Honduras/ Republic of Honduras)	Tegucigalpa 608 000	112 088	4 708 000	42	61.

SS NAL UCT	LANGUAGES	RELIGIONS	ECONOMY
70	English (off.); Creole	Protestant	**Economy** Domestic economy relies primarily on tourism and secondarily on agriculture (cotton, sugar-cane, coconuts, vegetables and fruit). Fishing is well developed. **Industry** Limited to the manufacture of agricultural products and rum.
'20	English (off.); Creole	Protestant; Catholic 22%	**Economy** The tourist industry is the main source of revenue. Agriculture (sugar-cane, tomatoes, pineapple), fishing (shellfish and turtles) and the production of sea-salt are also important.
30	English	Protestant; Catholic 5%	**Economy** The island's economy is based entirely on sugar-cane. Maize, potatoes and cassava are produced for domestic consumption. Fishing is profitable. **Industry** Expanding. The tourist industry is highly developed.
)50	English (off.); Spanish; Creole	Catholic 58%; Protestant 28%	**Economy** Agriculture-based; citrus fruits, cereals (rice and maize), coconuts, bananas and sugar-cane are the main cash crops. Other activities include fishing, animal farming and lumbering (cedar, mahogany, pine and rosewood).
'260	English; French	Catholic 46%; Protestant 41%	**Economy** Cereal crops dominate (wheat, oats, rye, barley, maize). Cattle and animal-fur farming are also widely practiced. **Principal resources** The vast forests are a rich asset. **Industry** All sectors are well established.
'30	Spanish	Catholic	**Economy** Primarily plantation agriculture (coffee, bananas, cocoa, sugar-cane, cotton and tobacco). Tuna-fishing and animal farming also generate considerable revenue. **Industry** Food processing is a principal industry.
00	Spanish	Catholic	**Economy** The national wealth depends on sugar-cane (the main export), tobacco, coffee and fruit. Also, animal farming and fishing. **Industry** Nickel-mining, food processing, and the textile and tobacco industries are the chief industries.
40	English (off.); French patois	Catholic	**Economy** Based on agriculture (bananas, citrus fruits, coconuts) and fishing. **Industry** The processing of agricultural products is developing rapidly. Tourism is also growing.
'50	Spanish	Catholic	**Agriculture** Based on plantation crops (cocoa, sugar-cane, coffee, tobacco, coconuts). Also animal farming and fishing. **Mineral resources** Gold, silver and nickel are major exports. **Industry** Tourism brings in foreign revenue.
'70	Spanish; Nahua; Maya	Catholic	**Economy** The main resource of this agricultural country is maize, followed by rice, beans, coffee, sugar-cane, cotton and sesame. Forests yield cedar, mahogany and rosewood. **Industry** Modestly developed.
80	English (off.); Creole; French patois	Catholic; Protestant 34%	**Economy** Agriculturally based. Citrus fruits, bananas, cocoa, coconuts, cotton, sugar-cane and nutmeg are cultivated. Fishing is an important pursuit. **Industry** Tourism is developing.
'30	Spanish (off.); Mayan languages	Catholic; Protestant 25%	**Economy** Depends on plantation agriculture (bananas, coffee, sugar-cane, cotton, tobacco, and cocoa). Forests provide valuable wood, in particular mahogany and cedar. Sheep and cattle farming are profitable.
'70	French; Creole	Catholic	**Economy** Essentially agricultural. The main crops are coffee, bananas and sisal, followed by cotton, sugar-cane, cocoa, citrus fruits and tobacco. **Principal resources** Bauxite is the sole mining resource of any significance.
'70	Spanish (off.); other local languages	Catholic	**Agriculture** Bananas, coconuts, coffee and tobacco. **Principal resources** Timber (mahogany, cedar and pine). Gold, silver, lead, zinc and antimony are mined on a large scale. **Industry** Processing yields a high income.

STATE (official name/ English translation)	CAPITAL ① inhabitants	AREA (sq km)	POPULATION	DENSITY (inhab/sq km)	L EX A (in M
JAMAICA (Jamaica)	**Kingston** 104 100	10 991	2 375 000	216	70.4
MEXICO (Estados Unidos Mexicanos/United Mexican States)	**Mexico City** (Ciudad de México) 8 237 000	1 972 547	82 151 000	41	66.5
NICARAGUA (República de Nicaragua/ Republic of Nicaragua)	**Managua** 682 000	130 682	3 999 000	31	64.8
PANAMA (República de Panamá/ Republic of Panama)	**Panama City** 411 000	77 082	2 466 000	32	70.1
SAINT CHRISTOPHER (KITTS) AND NEVIS (Federation of Saint Christopher and Nevis)	**Basseterre** 18 500	269	44 000	163	65.9
SAINT LUCIA (Saint Lucia)	**Castries** 51 200	616	153 000	248	68.0
SAINT VINCENT AND THE GRENADINES (Saint Vincent and the Grenadines)	**Kingstown** 26 500	389	108 000	277	68.0
UNITED STATES OF AMERICA (United States of America)	**Washington** 607 000	9 355 855	250 928 000	27	72.0

NORTH & CENTRAL AMERICA Ⓐ 22 037 795 417 501 000 19
NORTH & CENTRAL AMERICA Total Ⓐ 24 227 189 422 159 000 17

OSS ONAL DUCT ②	LANGUAGES	RELIGIONS	ECONOMY
380	English	Protestant	**Economy** A leading producer of bauxite. **Agriculture** Plantation agriculture (tobacco, coffee, cocoa, bananas, sugar-cane, spices) is well developed. **Industry** Expanding. Tourism generates substantial foreign currency.
870	Spanish (off.); Nahua; Maya	Catholic 90%	**Economy** Oil, silver, lead, gold and sulphur are the mainstays of the domestic economy. **Agriculture** A third of the population is in agriculture and animal farming. **Industry** Rapidly expanding. Tourism is well developed.
340	Spanish (off.); other local languages	Catholic	**Economy** Principally plantation agriculture (coffee, cotton, cocoa, sugar-cane, and bananas). The forests are rich in valuable wood (mahogany, cedar, rosewood). **Industry** Relatively undeveloped.
180	Spanish (off.)	Catholic	**Economy** Sustained mainly by revenue raised by granting access to the Panama Canal. **Agriculture** Subsistence agriculture is practiced; large plantations growing bananas, coffee and cocoa also exist.
960	English (off.); Creole	Protestant	**Agriculture** The economy's main source of revenue, with cotton and sugar-cane the chief crops. **Industry** Agricultural processing is developing modestly while the tourist industry is undergoing rapid expansion.
500	English (off.); French patois	Catholic	**Agriculture** Domestic economy dominated by agriculture (potatoes, bananas, cocoa, coconuts and copra). Animal farming and fishing are developed. **Industry** Principally food processing and the production of fertilizers.
730	English (off.); Creole	Protestant; Catholic 19%	**Agriculture** Plantation agriculture yields potatoes, bananas, coconuts, cotton and exotic fruit, largely for the overseas market. **Industry** Industry in general is developing; tourism is well established.
560	English	Protestant 53%; Catholic 26%	**Economy** The economy of the United States is the most developed in the world. It is founded on highly specialized agriculture, substantial mineral reserves and power resources, and impressive industrial organization.

udes the Virgin Is, Puerto Rico, Anguilla, Cayman Is, Turks
Caicos, Bermuda, Montserrat, Guadeloupe, Martinique,
Pierre and Miquelon, North American Antilles, Greenland.
ludes the 16 759 sq km and 1 135 000 inhabitants of
vaii, which is included in Oceania.

① The local form is given in brackets only when it differs from the English form

② Per inhabitant, in US$

	STATE (official name/ English translation)	CAPITAL inhabitants	AREA (sq km) POPULATION DENSITY (inhab/sq km)			L EXF A (in y M
	ARGENTINA (República Argentina/ Argentine Republic)	**Buenos Aires** 2 961 000	2 780 092	32 713 000	12	68.0
	BOLIVIA (República de Bolivia/ Republic of Bolivia)	**Sucre (legal); La Paz (admin.)** 101 000/126 000	1 098 581	7 612 000	7	50.9
	BRAZIL (República Federativa do Brasil/Federative Republic of Brazil)	**Brasília** 1 596 000	8 511 996	146 000 000	17	63.5
	CHILE (República de Chile/Republic of Chile)	**Santiago** 5 134 000	756 626	13 386 000	18	68.1
	COLOMBIA (República de Colombia/ Republic of Colombia)	**Santa Fe de Bogotá** 4 922 000	1 141 748	33 613 000	29	66.4
	ECUADOR (República del Ecuador/ Republic of Ecuador)	**Quito** 1 094 000	283 561	9 819 000	34	63.4
	GUYANA (Cooperative Republic of Guyana)	**Georgetown** 200 000	214 970	760 000	3	61.0
	PARAGUAY (República del Paraguay/ Republic of Paraguay)	**Asunción** 608 000	406 752	4 004 000	10	64.4
	PERU (República del Perú/ Republic of Peru)	**Lima** 6 115 000	1 285 216	21 998 000	17	62.9
	SURINAME (Republiek van Suriname/ Republic of Suriname)	**Paramaribo** 67 900	163 820	417 000	2	66.4
	TRINIDAD AND TOBAGO (Republic of Trinidad and Tobago)	**Port of Spain** 50 900	5 123	1 253 000	244	69.7
	URUGUAY (República Oriental del Uruguay/Eastern Republic of Uruguay)	**Montevideo** 1 248 000	176 215	3 112 000	17	68.9
	VENEZUELA (República de Venezuela/ Republic of Venezuela)	**Caracas** 1 290 000	912 050	19 733 000	21	67.0

SOUTH AMERICA			17 736 750	294 420 000	16
SOUTH AMERICA	Total	Ⓐ	17 833 382	294 762 000	16

SS JNAL JUCT)	LANGUAGES	RELIGIONS	ECONOMY
'80	Spanish (off.); Guaraní; Quechua	Catholic 91%	**Economy** Traditionally farming (crops and animals) and the manufacture of pastoral and agricultural goods. **Industry** Petroleum output is rising; iron and steel, mechanical goods, textiles and food also of importance.
350	Spanish; Quechua; Aymará	Catholic 94%	**Principal resources** Minerals, including tin, gold, silver, bismuth, lead, zinc, tungsten, antimony and oil. **Agriculture** Currently at subsistence level, but animal husbandry (cattle, sheep) is developing rapidly.
)20	Portuguese (off.); Carib; Tupí	Catholic 88%	**Economy** Based on plantation crops (coffee, cocoa, sugar-cane, tobacco, cotton). **Industry** Food processing (by large, specialized companies) is the main activity. Industry is prosperous. The country is densely forested.
160	Spanish (off.); Araucanian	Catholic 89%	**Economy** The most profitable sector is mining, particularly of copper, nitrates, oil, gold, silver, iron ore and coal. **Agriculture** Agronomy, animal farming and fishing are booming. **Industry** In a good position to grow.
280	Spanish (off.); other local languages	Catholic 94%	**Economy** Principal export is coffee; other profitable cash crops include tobacco, cotton and sugar-cane. **Mineral resources** Gold, silver, platinum, emeralds and oil. **Industry** Relatively undeveloped.
)20	Spanish (off.); Quechua	Catholic 90%	**Economy** Relies on plantation crops: cocoa, coffee, sugar-cane, bananas, tobacco, cotton. **Mineral resources** Of considerable importance, principally oil, gold, silver and iron. **Industry** Developing modestly.
290	English (off.); Creole; Hindu; Urdu	Hindu 37%; Prot. 31%; Cath. 11%; Mus. 9%	**Agriculture** Mainly cane, rice, coffee, cassava and citrus fruits. **Mineral resources** Large quantities of bauxite (Guyana's main export), as well as gold and diamonds. **Industry** Limited to the production of agricultural goods.
210	Spanish (off.); Guaraní	Catholic	**Economy** Essentially agricultural. Cotton, tobacco and fruit are the main exports, and timber. Cattle ranching also a major concern. **Industry** Growing as a result of inexpensive hydroelectric power.
)20	Spanish, Quechua, Aymará (all off.)	Catholic 92%	**Economy** Agriculture-based. Principal crops are cotton, sugar-cane, coffee and fruit. Animal farming is an important economic activity, and fishing even more so. **Mineral resources** Oil, copper and silver. **Industry** Prosperous.
510	Dutch (off.); Carib; Creole	Hindu 26%; Cath. 22%; Mus. 19%; Prot. 18%	**Economy** Depends on agricultural products (especially rice, sugar-cane, coffee, citrus fruits, bananas and coconuts) and mining (bauxite, gold). **Industry** Limited to the production of agricultural goods.
520	English (off.); Spanish; Hindu; Creole	Cath. 32%; Prot. 28%; Hindu 24%	**Economy** Industry has superseded agriculture as the main source of revenue due to rich deposits of oil, natural gas and asphalt. Other major industrial activities include refining and the production of petrochemicals and fertilizers.
360	Spanish	Catholic	**Economy** Rearing livestock (sheep and cattle) and food processing are the chief economic activities in Uruguay, with wool, meat and hides the principal exports. **Agriculture** Also developing.
510	Spanish (off.); Carib	Catholic 92%	**Economy** Previously relied on plantation crops, but petroleum production and the petrochemical industry now account for most export earnings. Fishing is also profitable. The country has considerable forest resources.

cludes the Falkland Is, South American Antilles, uba and French Guiana

① Per inhabitant, in US$

WORLD MAPS

Earth seen from the Moon
(image taken by astronauts aboard "Apollo 10" in May 1969)

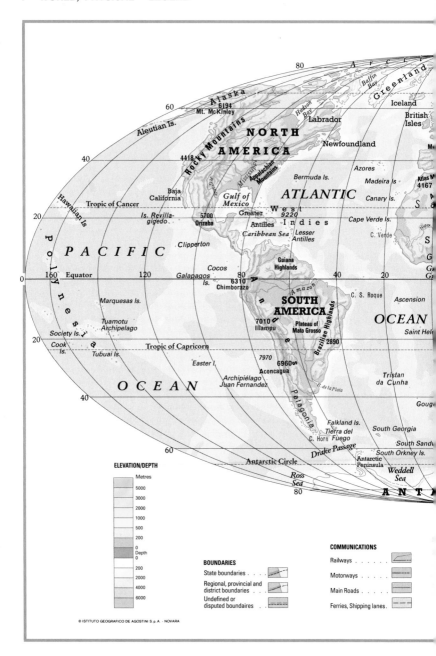

ELEVATION/DEPTH

Metres
- 5000
- 3000
- 2000
- 1000
- 500
- 200
- 0
- Depth 0
- 200
- 2000
- 4000
- 6000

© ISTITUTO GEOGRAFICO DE AGOSTINI S.p.A. · NOVARA

BOUNDARIES

State boundaries . . . .

Regional, provincial and district boundaries . . .

Undefined or disputed boundaires . . .

COMMUNICATIONS

Railways . . . . .

Motorways . . . . .

Main Roads . . . . .

Ferries, Shipping lanes .

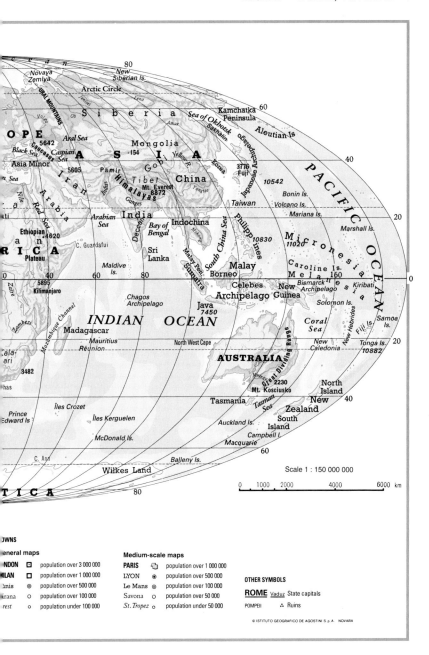

80
Novaya
Zemlya
New
Siberian Is.
Arctic Circle
60
Siberia
Kamchatka
Peninsula
Sea of Okhotsk
Aleutian Is.
URAL MOUNTAINS
Ob
Lena
Yenisei
Amur
O P E
5642
Caucasus
Aral Sea
Mongolia
-154
Gobi
40
Volga
Black Sea
Caspian Sea
A S I A
Yellow R.
Korea
PACIFIC OCEAN
Asia Minor
5605
Pamir
Tibet
China
3776
Fuji
10542
n Sea
Iran
Himalayas
Mt. Everest
8872
Indus
Ganges
Yangtze
Bonin Is.
Japanese Trench
Nile
Red Sea
Arabia
Arabian
Sea
India
Decean
Taiwan
Volcano Is.
Mariana Is.
20
ti
Ethiopian
a n
4620
C. Guardafui
Bay of
Bengal
Indochina
Mekong
Philippines
10830
11020
Micronesia
Marshall Is.
R I C A
Plateau
Sri
Lanka
Malay Pen.
South China Sea
Caroline Is.
Zaire
0
40
60
Maldive
Is.
80
Sumatra
Malay
Borneo
Java
7450
Celebes
Archipelago
New
Guinea
M e l a 160
Bismarck
Archipelago
Kiribati
0
5895
Kilimanjaro
Chagos
Archipelago
Solomon Is.
Zambezi
Mozambique Channel
INDIAN   OCEAN
Coral
Sea
New Hebrides
Fiji Is.
Samoa
Is.
ala-
ari
Madagascar
Mauritius
Réunion
North West Cape
New
Caledonia
Tonga Is.
10882
20
3482
AUSTRALIA
Great Dividing Range
has
Îles Crozet
2230
Mt. Kosciusko
North
Island
Prince
Edward Is
Îles Kerguelen
Tasmania
Tasman Sea
New
Zealand
40
McDonald Is.
Auckland Is.
South
Island
Campbell I.
C. Ann
Balleny Is.
Macquarie
60
Wilkes Land
80
T I C A

Scale 1 : 150 000 000

0   1000   2000   4000   6000 km

43

1 GUYANA
2 SURINAME
3 French Guiana
4 UNITED KINGDOM
5 IRELAND
6 NETHERLANDS
7 BELGIUM
8 FRANCE
9 LUXEMBOURG
10 GERMANY
11 POLAND
12 ESTONIA
13 LATVIA
14 LITHUANIA
15 BELARUS
16 CZECH REPUBLIC
17 SLOVAKIA
18 AUSTRIA
19 HUNGARY
20 MOLDOVA
21 ROMANIA
22 SWITZERLAND
23 ITALY
24 SLOVENIA
25 CROATIA
26 BOSNIA–HERZEGOVINA
27 YUGOSLAVIA
28 MACEDONIA
29 ALBANIA
30 BULGARIA
31 GREECE
32 PORTUGAL
33 SPAIN
34 BURKINA
35 BENIN
36 CENTRAL AFRICAN REPUBLIC
37 CAMEROON
38 EQUATORIAL GUINEA
39 UGANDA
40 RWANDA
41 BURUNDI
42 MALAWI
43 ZIMBABWE
44 DJIBOUTI
45 ERITREA
46 OMAN
47 UNITED ARAB EMIRATES
48 QATAR
49 BAHRAIN
50 ARMENIA
51 GEORGIA
52 AZERBAIJAN
53 TURKMENISTAN
54 UZBEKISTAN
55 TAJIKISTAN
56 KYRGYZSTAN
57 BANGLADESH
58 CAMBODIA
59 British Indian Ocean Territory

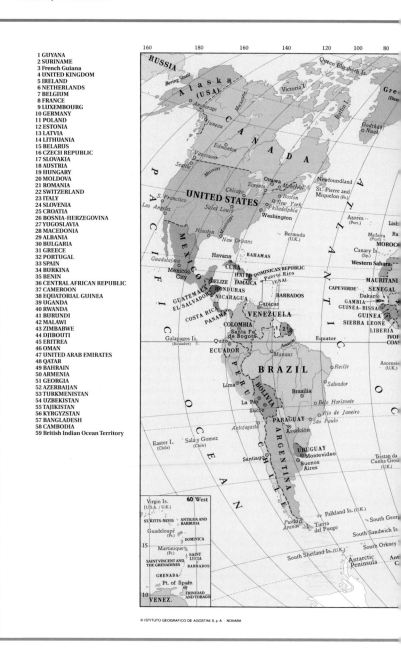

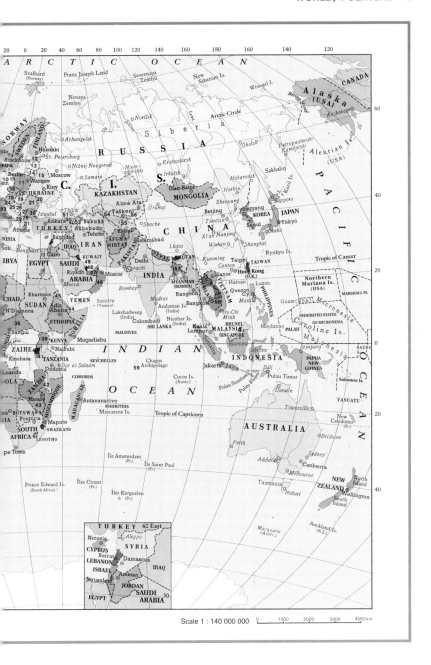

A R C T I C   O C E A N

Svalbard Franz Joseph Land   Severnaya New
(Norway)   Zemlya   Siberian Is.   CANADA
                                                          Wrangel I.   Alaska
                                                                              (USA)
Novaya   Anchorage
Zemlya   Norilsk   Arctic Circle   Bering Strait

NORWAY   Arhangelsk   Lena   60

SWEDEN FINLAND   S i b e r i a   Ohotsk   Petropavlovsk-
lo   Helsinki   Kamčatski   Aleutian Is.
Stockholm St. Petersburg R U S S I A   (USA)
ARK   13   Krasnojarsk   Habarovsk   Sakhalin
Berlin 14 15 Moscow   Novo-   40
10   1 Warsaw   Samara sibirsk   Irkutsk   Harbin   Kuri Is. Sapporo
m   2 Kiev   C. I.   Ulan-Bator Shenyang   Sapporo
18 17 UKRAINE KAZAKHSTAN   MONGOLIA   Beijing P'yongyang KOREA JAPAN
24 25 27 30 Tbilisi Tashkent 54 Ürümqi   Tientsin Seoul Tôkyô
29 26 Istanbul 51 Baku 53 55 56 Shache C H I N A   Osaka
31   Ankara 50 52 Ashabad 57   Xi'an Nanjing
        T U R K E Y Tehrān Kabul   Lhasa   Wuhan Shanghai
NISIA   Baghdad I R A N AFGHA- Islamabad   Ryukyu Is.
oli   Benghazi IRAQ NISTAN PAKISTAN NEPAL BHUTAN Kunming Taipei TAIWAN   Tropic of Cancer
IBYA   Cairo KUWAIT 49   DYPAL   Canton Hong Kong   Northern
        EGYPT SAUDI 48 Kyrachi   Calcutta Hanoi   (U.K.) Mariana Is.
        Riyadh 47 Muscat I N D I A MYANMAR   Hainan   (USA)   MARSHALL IS.
        ARABIA 46   (BURMA) VIETNAM Luzon
CHAD,   Mecca   Bombay   Madras Rangoon THAILAND Manila PHILIPPINES Guam (USA) Micronesia
N'Djamena YEMEN Socotra Lakshadweep Bangkok 58   Quezon Cy.   FEDERATED STATES
        45   (Yemen) (India) Andaman Is.   Ho-Chi   Mindanao PALAU   OF MICRONESIA
36   SUDAN Adis Colombo Nicobar Is. Minh BRUNEI   Caroline Is.
        Abeba 44 SRI LANKA (India) MALAYSIA SINGAPORE   Melanesia
ETHIOPIA   MALDIVES Kuala BRUNEI   Jayapura   NAURU
Bangui 39 KENYA   Lumpur SINGAPORE Borneo   PAPUA
ZAIRE   Nairobi   I N D I A N   Celebes   NEW
Kinshasa TANZANIA SEYCHELLES Chagos Jakarta Java I N D O N E S I A GUINEA
uanda   Dar es Salaam 59 Archipelago   Dili Solomon Is.
        Dodoma COMOROS   Pulau Timor
OLA   ZAMBIA 42   O C E A N Cocos Is. Pulau Sumba VANUATU
        Harare 43 MOZAMBIQUE (Austr.) Pulau Roro Darwin
k   BOTSWANA Antananarivo MAURITIUS   Townsville   New Caledonia
IA   Pretoria Maputo Mascarene Is. Tropic of Capricorn   (Fr.)
        SOUTH SWAZILAND   AUSTRALIA Brisbane
pe Town AFRICA LESOTHO   Perth   Sydney
                                                  Adelaide Canberra
        Île Amsterdam Île Saint Paul   Melbourne
        (Fr.) (Fr.)   NEW North
Prince Edward Is. Îles Crozet   Tasmania ZEALAND Island
(South Africa) (Fr.) Îles Kerguelen   Hobart South Wellington
                b (Fr.)   Island
                                                  Macquarie   40
                                                  (Austr.)
                                          Auckland Is.
                                          (N.Z.)

T U R K E Y 60 East
Nicosia   Aleppo
CYPRUS S Y R I A
        Beirut Damascus
LEBANON   IRAQ
ISRAEL Amman
Jerusalem JORDAN SAUDI
EGYPT   ARABIA 30

Scale 1 : 140 000 000   0   1000   2000   3000   4000 km

Scale 1 : 24 000 000

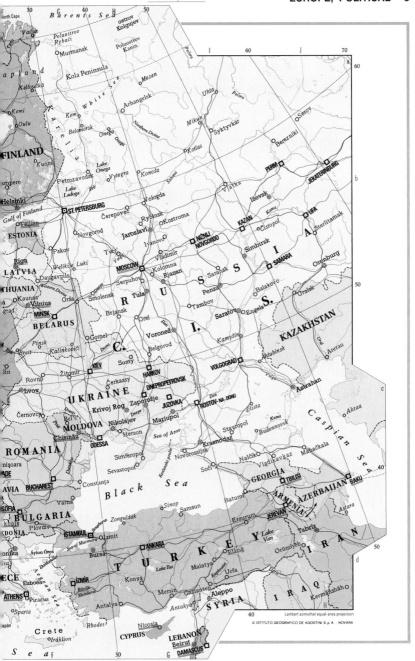

North Cape
Barents Sea
Vadsø
ostrov Kolguev
Poluostrov Rybačí
Murmansk
Poluostrov Kanin
Pečora
Tana
Lapland
Kettoselka
Kola Peninsula
Mezen
Uhta
Pečora
Kemi
White Sea
Arhangelsk
Mikun
Seroy
Oulu
Karelia
Kem
Severnaja Dvina
Syktyvkar
Belomorsk
Onega
Onega
Kotlas
Bereznikí
FINLAND
Kuopio
Lake Onega
Vytegra
Konoša
Suhona
Vjatka
PERM
JEKATERINBURG
Tampere
Petrozavodsk
Vologda
Iževsk
Kama
UFA
Helsinki
Lake Ladoga
Svir
Čerepovec
Rybinsk
Kostroma
KAZAN
Čistopol
Sterlitamak
Gulf of Finland
ST.PETERSBURG
Tallinn
Novgorod
Jaroslavl
Ivanovo
NIŽNIJ NOVGOROD
Simbirsk
SAMARA
Orenburg
ESTONIA
Pskov
Tver
Vladimir
R
U
S
S
I
A
Riga
Welikije Luki
MOSCOW
Kolomna
Sarańsk
LATVIA
Daugavpils
Western Dvina
Serpuhov
Rjazan
Penza
Balakovo
Uralsk
LITHUANIA
Kaunas
Vilnius
Orša
Smolensk
R
Tula
Tambov
S.
S.
R.
Saratov
Engels
grad
MINSK
Brjansk
Orel
Don
Kamyšin
KAZAKHSTAN
BELARUS
Gomel
Desna
Belgorod
Ahtubinsk
Ural
Ateray
Pinsk
Kalinkoviči
C.
Voronež
Brest
KIEV
Sumy
VOLGOGRAD
Žitomir
Čerkassy
HARKOV
Rovno
Don
Astrahan
Lvov
UKRAINE
DNEPROPETROVSK
Krivoj Rog
Zaporožje
JUZOVKA
ROSTOV-NA-DONU
Dnepr
Černovcy
Bela
MOLDOVA
Nikolajev
Mariupol
Elista
Aktau
Prut
Chisinău
Herson
Sea of Azov
Stavropol
Budennovsk
Kuma
Caspian Sea
ROMANIA
ODESSA
Simferopol
Krasnodar
Kerčenski poluostrov
Novorossijsk
Nalčik
Vladikavkaz
Mahačkala
nişoara
Danube
Sevastopol
Sočí
40
ADE
Constanța
Black
Sea
Batumi
GEORGIA
TBILISI
Astara
AVIA
Varna
Erzurum
ARMENIA
AZERBAIJAN
BAKU
SOFIA
Sinop
Samsun
JEREVAN
BUCHAREST
Bosphorus
Zonguldak
Tabriz
50
BULGARIA
Plovdiv
ISTANBUL
Izmit
ANKARA
Elâzığ
Orümiyeh
I
R
A
N
kopje
DONIA
Sea of Marmara
Bursa
Lake Van
onika
IZMIR
Lake Tuz
Malatya
Euphrates
Urfa
Kermanšahõ
ECE
Konya
T
U
R
K
E
Y
Euboea
Büyük Menderes
Mersin
Gaziantep
I
R
A
Q
ATHENS
Piraeus
Antalya
Antakya
Aleppo
SYRIA
Sparta
Rhodes
Nicosia
LEBANON
Crete
Íráklion
CYPRUS
Beirut
Sea
DAMASCUS

Lambert azimuthal equal-area projection
© ISTITUTO GEOGRAFICO DE AGOSTINI S.p.A. - NOVARA

47

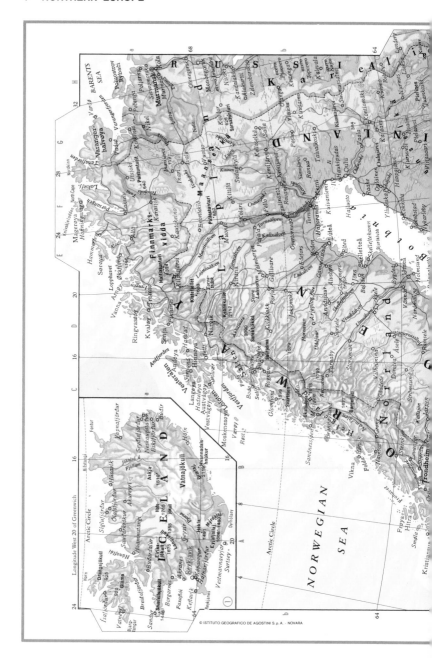

© ISTITUTO GEOGRAFICO DE AGOSTINI S.p.A. · NOVARA

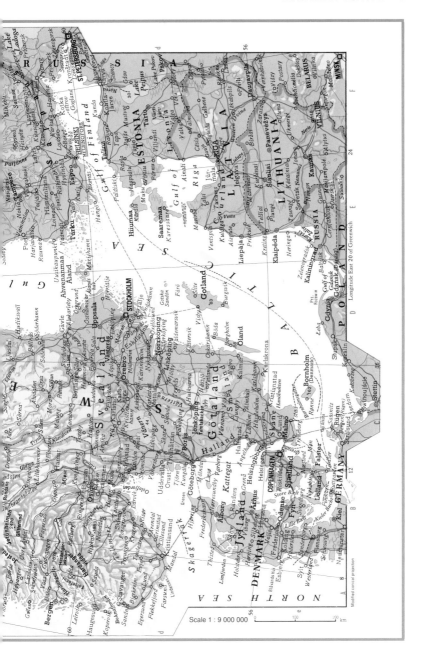

Scale 1 : 9 000 000

Modified conical projection

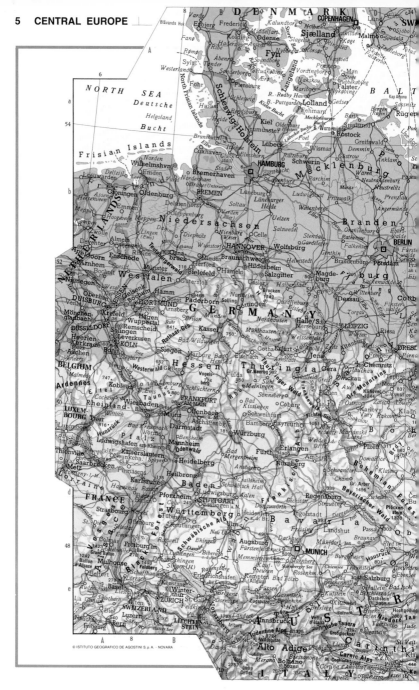

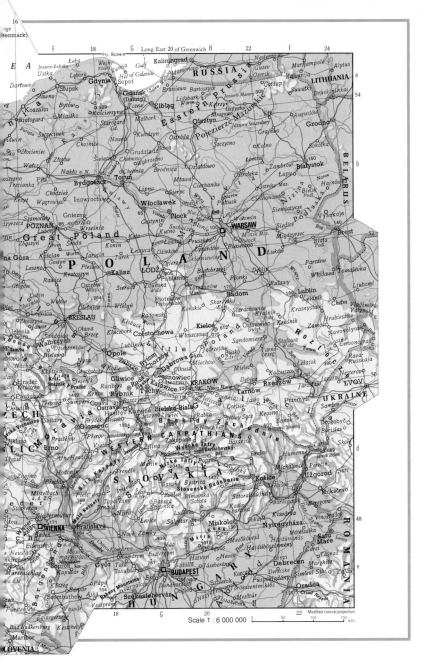

F 18 G Long. East 20 of Greenwich H 22 I 24

E A

Jezioro Łebka Łeba Prz. Rozewie Kaliningrad RUSSIA Nesterov Marijampole Alytus
Ustka Wejka Rumia Gulf of Gdansk Sławkowo Gusev Ozersk Goldap Suwałki Druskininkai LITHUANIA a
Dartowo Lębork Gdynia Hel of Gdansk Braniewo Bartoszyce Jezioro Mamry 309 54
eg Słupsk Sopot Gdansk Lidzbark Warm. Kętrzyn Grzywy Augustów
nia Koszalin Bytów 329 Kościerzyna (Danzig) Elbląg Olsztyn Mrągowo Grodno
a Białogard Miastko Starogard Gd. Malbork Ostróda Pojezierze Mazurskie Sokółka BELARUS
idwin Parpęta Szczecinek Nowe Kwidzyn Szczytno Kolno Grajewo
oszczno Wałcz Złotów Świecie Chełmno Grudziądz Iława Działdowo Łomża Zambrów Białystok 150 b
Trzcianka Piła Nakło n.N. 665 Toruń Chełmża Brodnica Mława Ostrołęka Łapy Hajnówka
zyrzecz Chodzież Bydgoszcz Kujawy Lipno Sierpc Narew Ostrów Maz. Bielsk 140
zin Szamotuły Gniezno Swarzędz Inowrocław Włocławek Płock Nw.Dwór Ciechanów Pułtusk Siemiatycze Wysokie 52
POZNAŃ 85 605 Łęczyca Kutno Sochaczew Błonie WARSAW Wołomin Minsk Maz. Siedlce Podlaski Brest
Great Poland Środa Konin Turek Łowicz Pruszków Żyrardów Piaseczno Międzyrzec Biała Podl.
na Góra Zbąszyn Kościan Jarocin Zgierz Skierniewice Łuków Parczew Włodawa Tomaszówka
Leszno Gostyń Pleszew Kalisz ŁÓDŹ Abianów Białobrzegi Pionki Puławy Lublin 160 Ljuboml
Głogów Rawicz Krotoszyn Ostrów Wlkp. Sieradz Zduńska Wola Piotrków Tryb. Tomaszów Maz. 170 Radom Dęblin Włodawa Chełm Vladimir. Volynski
Lubin Ostrzeszów Wieluń Radomsko Końskie Skarżysko Starachowice Kraśnik Fab. Świdnik Krasnystaw Hrubieszów
Legnica Oleśnica 284 Radomsko Kielce 612 Ostrowiec Świet. Kraśnik Zamość Novovolynsk
BRESŁAU Brzeg Kłobuck Włoszczowa 675 Sandomierz Stalowa Wola Rożno Cervonograd
Świdnica Oława Częstochowa Little Poland Jędrzejów Busko Zdrój Vis. Leżajsk 390 Ravar Russkaja Sokol
Walbrzych Dzierżoniów Nysa Opole Kłodzko Strom Olkusz Miechów Zdrój Kolbuszowa Nesterov
Bielawa Racibórz Zabrze Chorzów Dąbrowa Górn. Mielec Debica Rzeszów Jarosław LVOV
Gliwice Sosnowiec KRAKÓW Nowa Huta Tarnów Przemyśl Sambor
Tychy Oświęcim Jasło UKRAINE
Ostrava Bielsko-Biała Żywiec Beskidy Zach. Nowy Sącz Gorlice Krosno Sanok Drogobyč Borislav
Frýdek-Místek Cieszyn Rabka Nowy Targ 502 Turka Skol
WESTERN CARPATHIANS Zachodnie Zakopane Wysoke Tatry Bardejov Humenné perevai Uzkoi
Martin Nízke Tatry 2043 Poprad Prešov Michalovce Užgorod 677
Banská Bystrica 1477 Spišská 209 Mukačevo
SLOVAKIA Slovenské Rudohorie Rožňava Košice Sárospatak Beregovo
Zvolen Rimavská Sobota Kamenica barádka Kisvárda Vinogradov 48
Nitra Levice Lučenec Tokaj Pokaj Nyíregyháza ROMANIA
VIENNA Bratislava Nové Zámky Salgótarján Miskolc Bükk 130 Satu Mare e
Komárom 939 Vác Mezőkövesd Hajdúnánás Carei Tasnad
Esztergom Mátra 1015 Eger Hajdúböszörmény 121 Debrecen Marghita
Győr Tata Tatabánya 1457 Gödöllő Hatvan Heves Karcag Derecske Simleul Silv. Oradea
BUDAPEST Monor Jászberény Püspökladány Törökszentmiklós Crisul Repede
Székesfehérvár Cegléd HUNGARY Mezőtúr 129

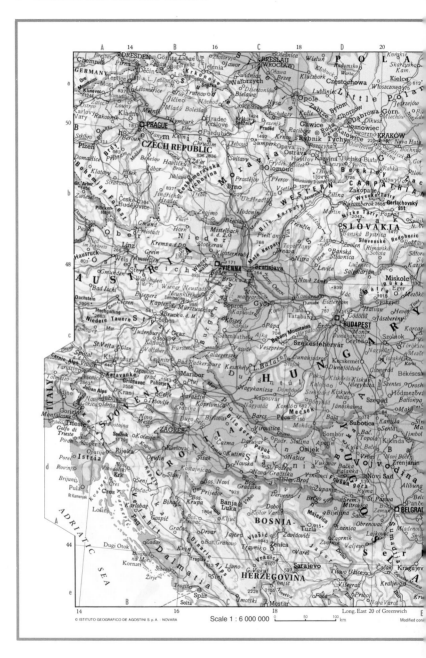

Scale 1 : 6 000 000

Long. East 20 of Greenwich

© ISTITUTO GEOGRAFICO DE AGOSTINI S.p.A. - NOVARA

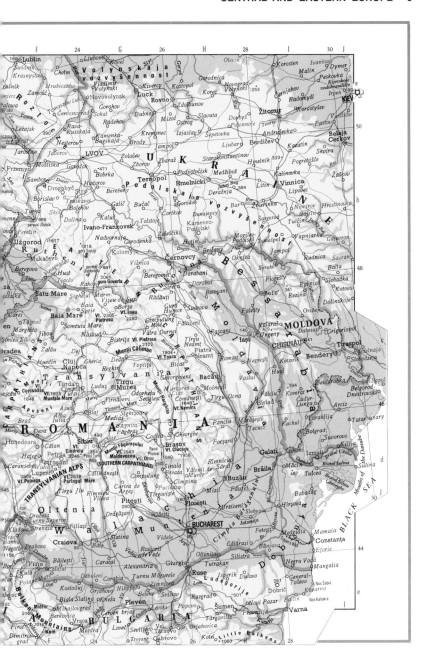

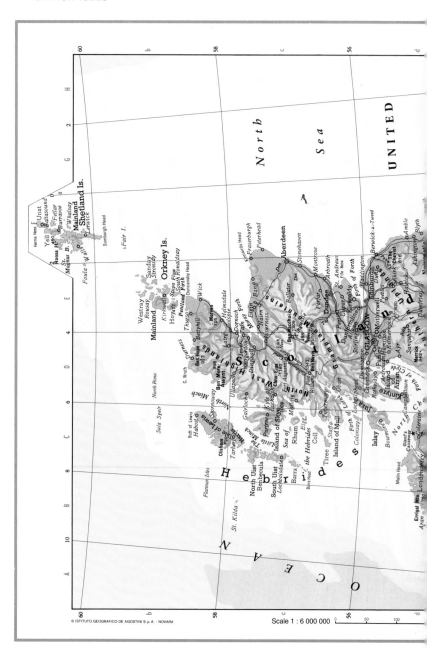

Scale 1 : 6 000 000   0   50   100

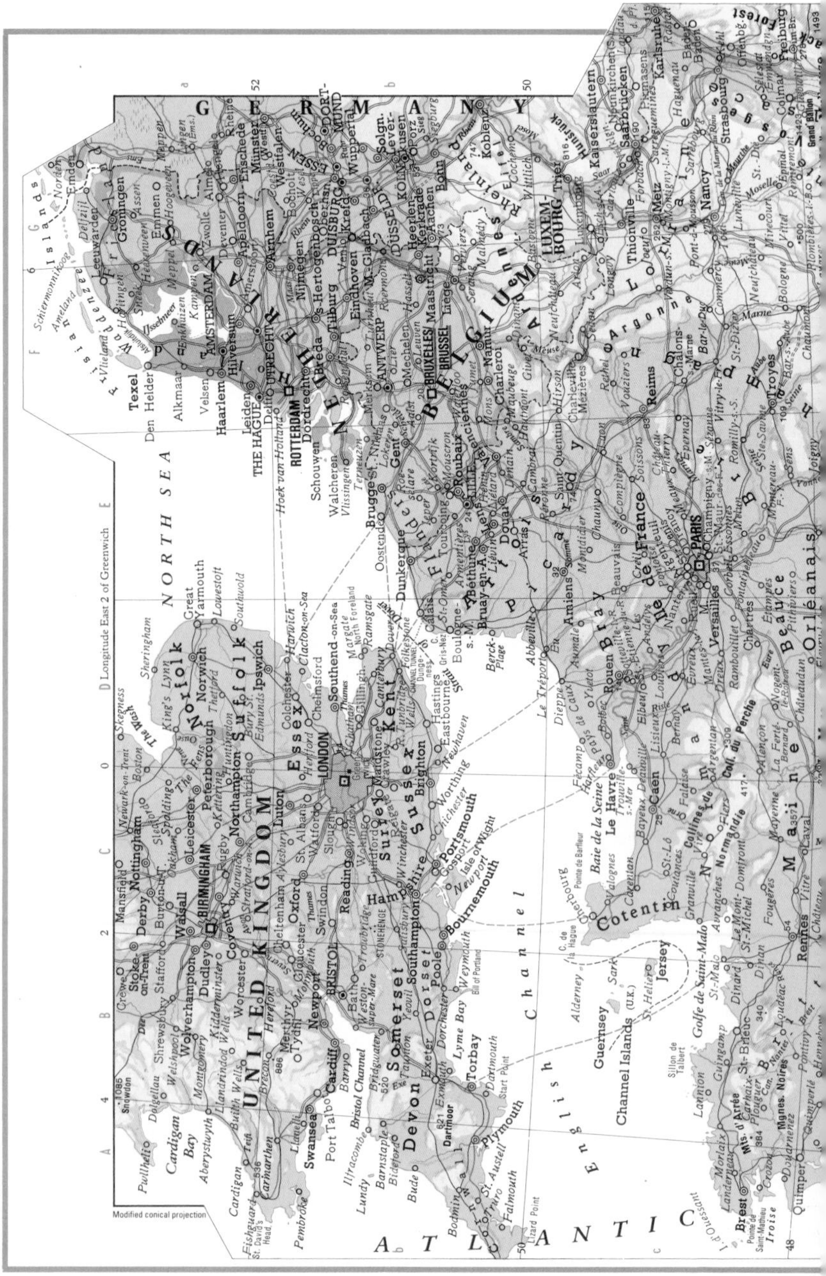
NORTH SEA
ATLANTIC
English Channel
UNITED KINGDOM
NETHERLANDS
BELGIUM
GERMANY
LUXEMBOURG
LONDON
PARIS
AMSTERDAM
THE HAGUE
ROTTERDAM
BRUXELLES/BRUSSEL
BIRMINGHAM
Longitude East 2 of Greenwich
Modified conical projection
Channel Islands (U.K.)
Guernsey
Jersey
Île de France
Normandie
Picardy
Flanders
Brittany
Lorraine
Champagne
Maine
Beauce
Cotentin
Norfolk
Suffolk
Essex
Kent
Sussex
Surrey
Hampshire
Dorset
Somerset
Devon
Cornwall
Frisian Islands
Waddenzee
Ardennes
Vosges
Argonne
Bristol Channel
Cardigan Bay
Baie de la Seine
Golfe de Saint-Malo

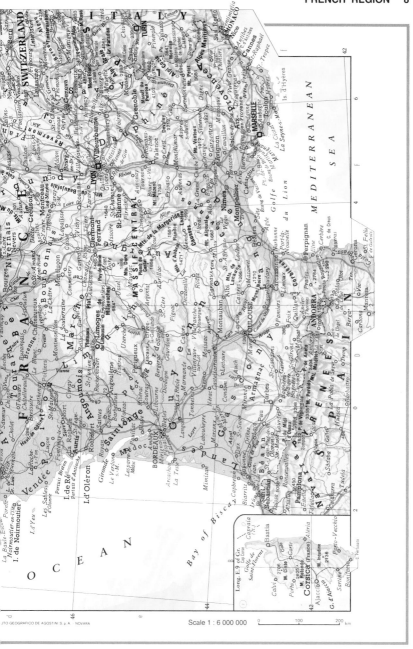

Scale 1 : 6 000 000

0   100   200 km

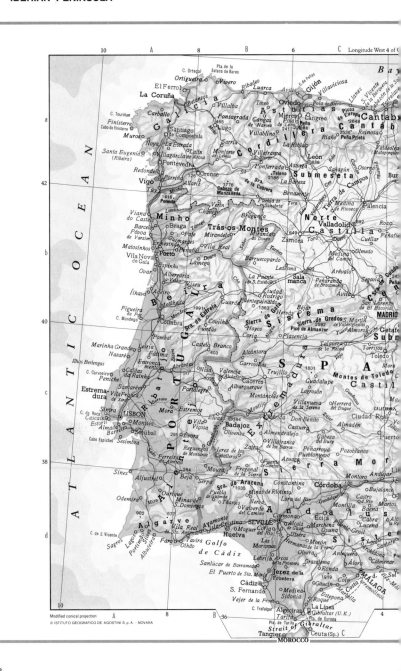

Scale 1 : 6 000 000

0   50   100   150 km

© ISTITUTO GEOGRAFICO DE AGOSTINI S.p.A.

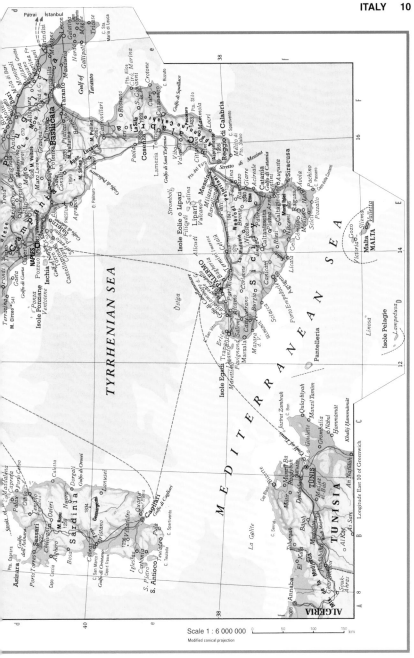

Scale 1 : 6 000 000

Modified conical projection

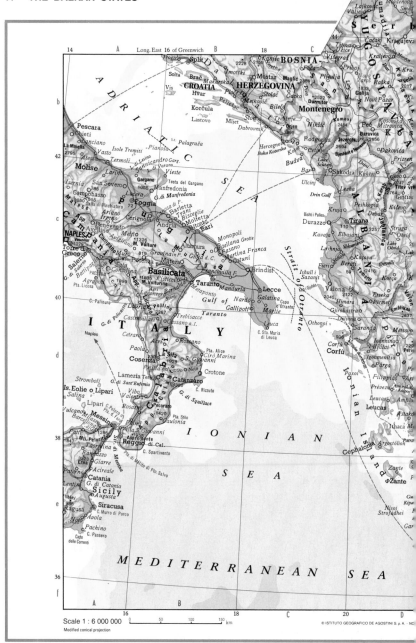

Scale 1 : 6 000 000
0   50   100   150 km
Modified conical projection

© ISTITUTO GEOGRAFICO DE AGOSTINI S.p.A. - NO

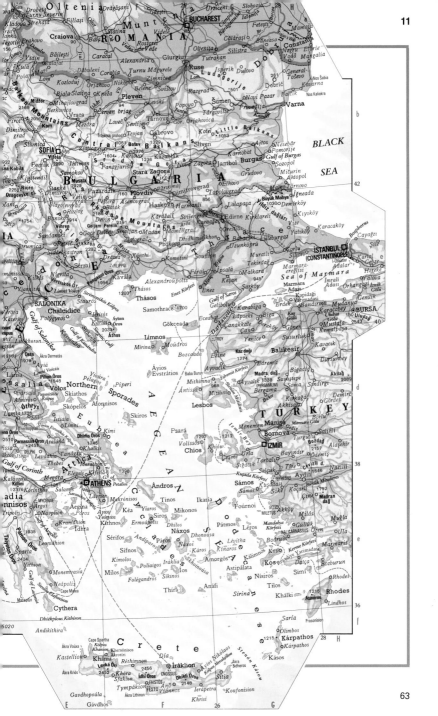

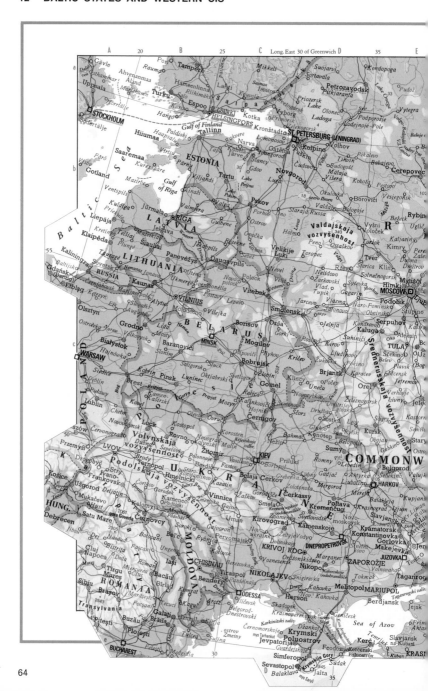

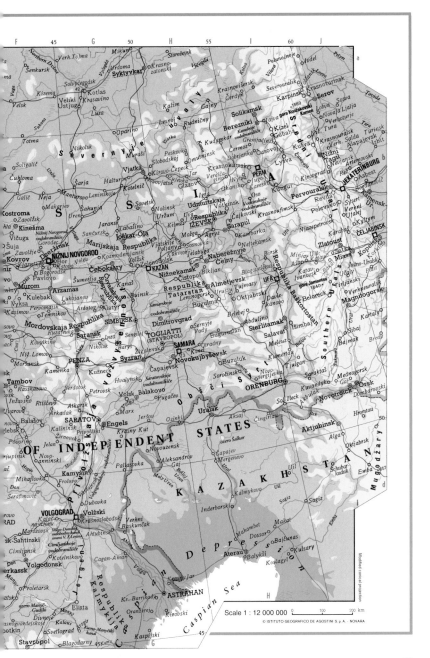

Scale 1 : 12 000 000

© ISTITUTO GEOGRAFICO DE AGOSTINI S.p.A. · NOVARA

Modified conical projection

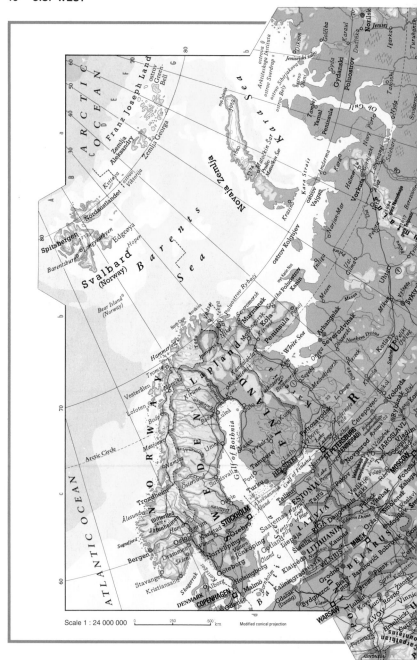

Scale 1 : 24 000 000   0   250   500 km   Modified conical projection

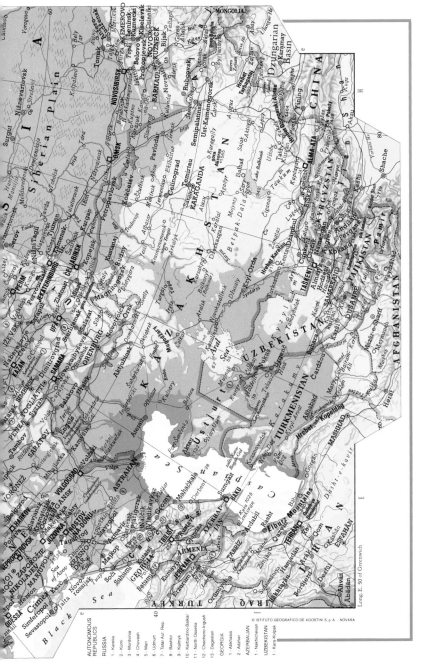

Long. E. 50 of Greenwich

AUTONOMOUS
REPUBLICS

RUSSIA
1 - Karelia
2 - Komi
3 - Mordvinia
4 - Chuvash
5 - Mari
6 - Udmurt
7 - Tatar Aut. Rep.
8 - Bashkir
9 - Kalmyk
10 - Karbardino-Balkar
11 - North Ossetia
12 - Checheno-Ingush
13 - Dagestan

GEORGIA
1 - Abhasia
2 - Adzhar

AZERBAIJAN
1 - Nakhichewan

UZBEKISTAN
1 - Kara-Kalpak

PACIFIC OCEAN

Bering Sea

Sea of

Kamchatka Peninsula

Sredinny Hrebet

Chukchi Peninsula

Ploskogorje

Anadyrskoje

Kolymskoje Nagorje

Chukchi Sea

De Long Strait

ostrov Wrangel

East Siberian Sea

Hrebet Cerskogo

Hrebet Suntar-

Verholjanski Hrebet

New Siberian Islands

ostrova Anžu

ostrov Kotelnyj

Laptev Sea

Lena

ARCTIC OCEAN

Central

ostrov Komsomolec

Severnaja Zemlja

ostrov Oktjabrskoj Revoljucii

ostrov Pioner

ostrov Bolševik

Poluostrov Tajmyr

Gory Byrranga

Norilsk

Plato Putorana

Kara Sea

Jenisej

Modified conical projection

Scale 1 : 24 000 000

0   250   500
km

© ISTITUTO GEOGRAFICO DE AGOSTINI S.p.A. - NOVARA

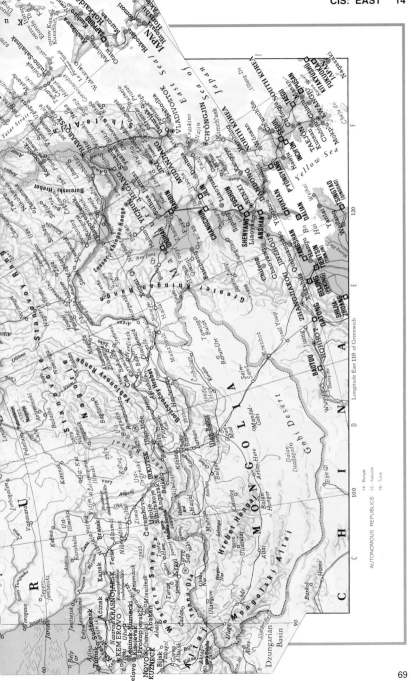

AUTONOMOUS REPUBLICS

14 - Buryat
15 - Yakutsk
16 - Tuva

Longitude East 110 of Greenwich

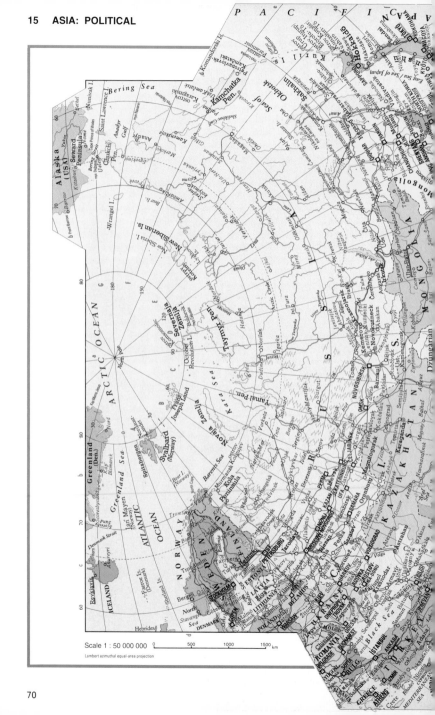

Scale 1 : 50 000 000

0   500   1000   1500 km

Lambert azimuthal equal-area projection

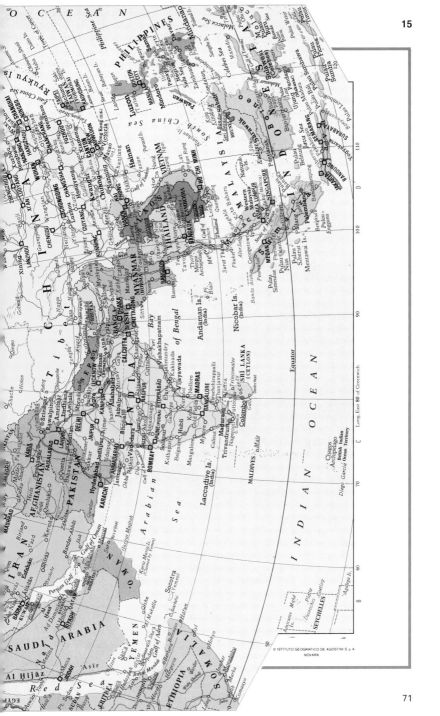

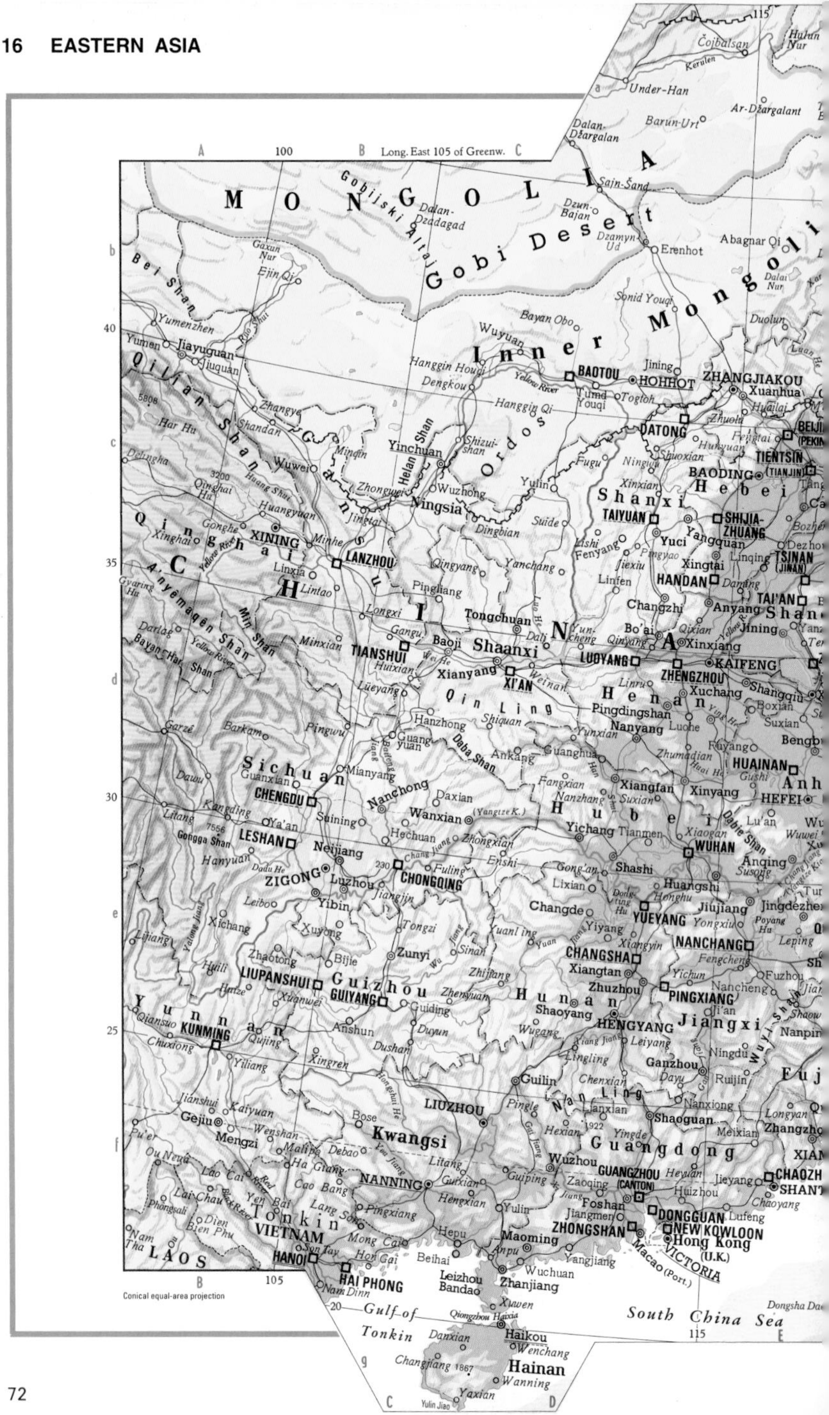

Long. East 105 of Greenw.
MONGOLIA
Gobijski Altaj
Gobi Desert
Inner Mongolia
Čojbalsan
Hulun Nur
Kerulen
Under-Han
Ar-Džargalant
Barun-Urt
Dalan-Džargalan
Sajn-Šand
Dzun-Bajan
Dalan-Dzadagad
Dzamyn-Ud
Erenhot
Abagnar Qi
Dalai Nur
Gaxun Nur
Ejin Qi
Bei Shan
Sonid Youqi
Bayan Obo
Duolun
Yumenzhen
Yumen
Jiayuguan
Jiuquan
Wuyuan
Hanggin Houqi
Dengkou
Yellow River
BAOTOU
HOHHOT
Jining
ZHANGJIAKOU
Xuanhua
Huailai
Tumd Youqi
Togtoh
Hanggin Qi
Ordos
Qilian Shan
5808
Har Hu
Zhangye
Shandan
Gansu
Minqin
Yinchuan
Helan Shan
Shizuishan
DATONG
Fengtai
Hunyuan
BEIJING (PEKING)
TIENTSIN (TIANJIN)
Delingha
3200
Qinghai Hu
Huang Shui
Wuwei
Zhongwei
Wuzhong
Ningsia
Jingtai
Fugu
Ningwu
Shuoxian
Yulin
Xinxian
BAODING
Hebei
Shanxi
Qinghai
Xinghai
Gonghe
Huangyuan
XINING
Minhe
LANZHOU
Dingbian
Suide
TAIYUAN
Yuci
SHIJIAZHUANG
Yangquan
Dezhou
Lishi
Fenyang
Pingyao
Jiexiu
Xingtai
Linqing
TSINAN (JINAN)
Qingyang
Yanchang
Linfen
HANDAN
Daming
Linxia
Lintao
CHINA
Gyaring Hu
A'nyêmaqên Shan
Min Shan
Pingliang
Tongchuan
Changzhi
Anyang
TAI'AN
Shandong
Longxi
Luo He
Darlag
Bayan Har Shan
Minxian
TIANSHUI
Gangu
Baoji
Shaanxi
Dali
Yuncheng
Bo'ai
Qinyang
Qixian
Xinxiang
Jining
Yellow River
Wei He
Huixian
Xianyang
XI'AN
Weinan
LUOYANG
ZHENGZHOU
KAIFENG
Lüeyang
Qin Ling
Linru
Xuchang
Shangqiu
Henan
Boxian
Pingdingshan
Garzê
Barkam
Pingwu
Hanzhong
Shiquan
Nanyang
Luohe
Suxian
Bengbu
Guangyuan
Daba Shan
Ankang
Yunxian
Guanghua
Zhumadian
Fuyang
Sichuan
Mianyang
Guanxian
Huai He
HUAINAN
Gushi
Anhui
Dawu
CHENGDU
Nanchong
Fangxian
Xiangfan
Xinyang
HEFEI
Daxian
Nanzhang
Suxian
Litang
Kangding
Ya'an
Suining
Wanxian
(Yangtze K.)
Hubei
Lu'an
Wuwei
Dabie Shan
7556
Gongga Shan
LESHAN
Neijiang
Hechuan
Zhongxian
Yichang
Tianmen
Xiaogan
WUHAN
Hanyuan
Dadu He
ZIGONG
Luzhou
230
CHONGQING
Fuling
Enshi
Gong'an
Shashi
Anqing
Susong
Lixian
Huangshi
Leibo
Yibin
Jiangjin
Honghu
Changde
Dongting Hu
YUEYANG
Jiujiang
Jingdezhen
Xichang
Yalong Jiang
Xuyong
Tongzi
Yuanling
Yiyang
Yongxiu
Poyang Hu
Lijiang
Zhaotong
Bijie
Zunyi
Sinan
Xiangyin
CHANGSHA
NANCHANG
Leping
Huili
LIUPANSHUI
Guizhou
Zhijiang
Xiangtan
Fengcheng
Huize
Xuanwei
GUIYANG
Zhenyuan
Hunan
Zhuzhou
Yichun
PINGXIANG
Fuzhou
Nancheng
Yunnan
Qiansuo
KUNMING
Guiding
Shaoyang
Ji'an
Jiangxi
Wuyi Shan
Nanping
Chuxiong
Qujing
Anshun
Duyun
Wugang
HENGYANG
Leiyang
Yiliang
Dushan
Xiang Jiang
Lingling
Ganzhou
Ningdu
Xingren
Chenxian
Dayu
Ruijin
Fujian
Guilin
Hongshui He
Nan Ling
Jianshui
Kaiyuan
LIUZHOU
Pingle
Lianxian
Nanxiong
Longyan
Gejiu
Bose
Kwangsi
Hexian
1922
Yingde
Shaoguan
Meixian
Zhangzhou
Pu'er
Wenshan
Mengzi
Malipo
Debao
Gui Jiang
Guangdong
Ou Neua
Ha Giang
Litang
Wuzhou
XIAMEN
Lao Cai
Red River
NANNING
Guixian
Guiping
GUANGZHOU (CANTON)
Heyuan
Jieyang
CHAOZHOU
SHANTOU
Lai Chau
Black River
Yen Bai
Cao Bang
Hengxian
Zaoqing
Huizhou
Chaoyang
Phongsali
Tonkin
Lang Son
Pingxiang
Yulin
Foshan
Jiangmen
DONGGUAN
Lufeng
Dien Bien Phu
Nam Tha
VIETNAM
Mong Cai
Hepu
Maoming
ZHONGSHAN
NEW KOWLOON
Hong Kong (U.K.)
LAOS
HANOI
Son Tay
Hon Gai
Beihai
Anpu
Yangjiang
Macao (Port.)
VICTORIA
HAI PHONG
Nam Dinh
Leizhou Bandao
Wuchuan
Zhanjiang
Gulf of Tonkin
Xuwen
Qiongzhou Haixia
South China Sea
Dongsha Dao
Haikou
Danxian
Wenchang
Changjiang
1867
Hainan
Wanning
Yaxian
Yulin Jiao
A
B
C
D
E
b
c
d
e
f
g
40
35
30
25
20
100
105
115
Conical equal-area projection

Manchuria

Keshan Bel'an Fuyuan Hor Nelma 140
Butha Qi Leninskoje Tongjiang Vjazemski Dolinsk Južno-
Longjiang YICHUN HEGANG Fujin Raohe Bikin RUSSIA Sakhalin Sakhalinsk
QIQIHAR Heilongjiang Shuang- Bira Svetlaja Gornozavodsk Sea
DAQING Suihua Jiamusi yashan Ussuri Sovetskaja mys Aniva of
Tailai Anda Hulan Tonghe Yilan Hulin Mishan Velikaja Kema La Perouse Strait of Okhotsk 45
Ulanhot Zhaodong HARBIN Linkou Dalnerečensk Rebun-Tō Rishiri-Tō Wakkanai
Baicheng Fuyu Shuang- Shangshi 151 JIXI ozero Dahi Arsenjev Nayoro Mombetsu
Tao'an cheng MUDANJIANG Suifenhe Hanka Olga Asahikawa Taketsu-Tan Hokkaido
Nong'an Jiutai Jiaohe Ussurijsk 4230 Ashibetsu Yūbari Obihiro
Tongliao CHANGCHUN JILIN Dunhua Waheqing Artem Rudnaja-Pristan Otaru SAPPORO Kushiro
Shuanglia Yitong Wangqing Yanji VLADIVOSTOK Hakodate Muroran
Xiliao Siping Liaoyuan Hunan Tumen Yenki Nahodka Okushiri-Tō Mutsu
SHENYANG Tieling Linjiang Changbai Shan Najin Peter the Great Bay Aomori Hachinohe
FUXIN FUSHUN Xinmin Tonghua 744 Hyesan CH'ONGJIN Hirosaki Miyako
Xinmin Liaoyang Ji'an Kanggye Kimch'aek East Sea / Akita Noshiro Hanamaki Morioka
BENXI ANSHAN Hamhūng NORTH KOREA Sakata Yokote Ishinomaki 40
Yingkou HAICHENG Sinŭiju Hŭngnam Sea of Japan Yamagata Yonezawa SENDAI
DANDONG Chŏngju Anju Wŏnsan Sado-Shima Niigata Aizu- Fukushima
FUXIAN P'YŎNGYANG Songnim Kaesŏng Kosŏng Toyama Nagaoka wakamatsu Iwaki
Namp'o Sariwŏn Ch'unchŏn Kanazawa Nagano Hitachi
Ongjin Haeju Kangnŭng Ullŭng-Do Matsumoto Ashikaga Utsunomiya
DALIAN (South Korea) Fukui Maebashi KAWASAKI
(LÜDA) INCH'ŎN SEOUL (SŎUL) Komatsu Gifu Kōfu Fuji YOKOHAMA 35
Yantai Weihai Suwŏn Ch'ŏngju KYOTO Tōkyō Yokosuka
Laixi Shidao SOUTH Matsue Tottori NAGOYA Tokyo Odawara
TSINGTAO KOREA TAEJŎN Andŏng Oki-Shotō Tsuyama ŌSAKA SAKAI Toyohashi
(QINGDAO) Yellow Chinju P'ohang Himeji KŌBE Taichi Shizuoka
Kunsan TAEGU ULSAN Fukuyama Okayama Wakayama HAMAMATSU
Yangyang (Xinpu) Sea Chŏnju Masan PUSAN HIROSHIMA Inland Takamatsu Hachijō-Jima
Mokp'o Yŏsu (Huang hai) Shimonoseki Kure Sea Tokushima
YANCHENG Tsushima KITAKYŪSHŪ Kōchi
Cheju-Haehyŏp FUKUOKA Kurume Matsuyama
CHANGSHU Cheju-do Cheju Saga Ōita Shikoku
Nantong Sasebo Goto- Nobeoka
SUZHOU Haimen Retto KUMAMOTO Kyūshū
SHANGHAI Nagasaki Miyazaki
Songjiang KAGOSHIMA Miyakonojō
Jiaxing Ōsumi-Kaikyō
NINGBO Zhenhai Ōsumi-Shotō Tane-ga-Shima
Linhai East Yaku-Shima
Haimen China
Hongyan Sea
WENZHOU Tokara-Rettō Amami Ōshima
Ruian Naze Kikai-Jima
Tokuno-shima
Okinoerabu-Jima PACIFIC
Yoron-Jima Kita-Daitō-Jima
Senkaku-Shotō Iheya- Naha Minami-Daitō-Jima
TAIPEI Keelung 2720 Kume-Jima Jima Okinawa-Jima Daito Is.
Hsinchu Suao Kerama-Rettō 7500 Oki-Daitō-Jima
TAICHUNG Hualien Miyako-Jima
TAIWAN Tropic of Cancer
(FORMOSA) Tarama-Jima
3997 Ishigaki-Jima
Yushan Iriomote-Jima
Taitung
Pingtung Lan Hsu OCEAN
(Hungtuo Yu)

East Sea / Sea of Japan

HONSHŪ

JAPAN

Yellow Sea

East China Sea

RYUKYU IS. (Nansei-Shotō)

PACIFIC OCEAN

125 G 130 H 135 I
Scale 1 : 18 000 000 0 100 200 km
© ISTITUTO GEOGRAFICO DE AGOSTINI S.p.A. - NOVARA

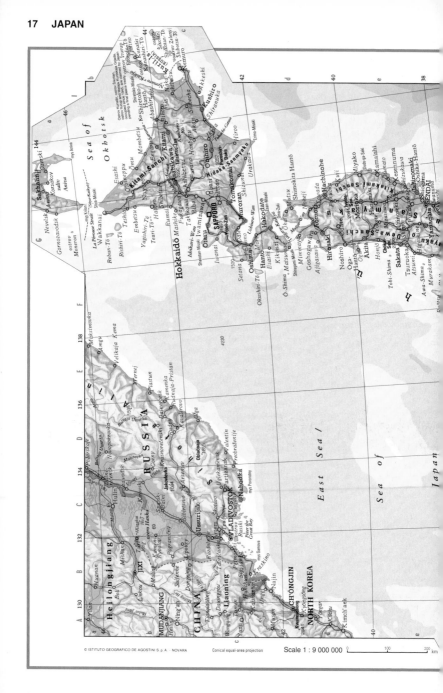

Conical equal-area projection

Scale 1 : 9 000 000

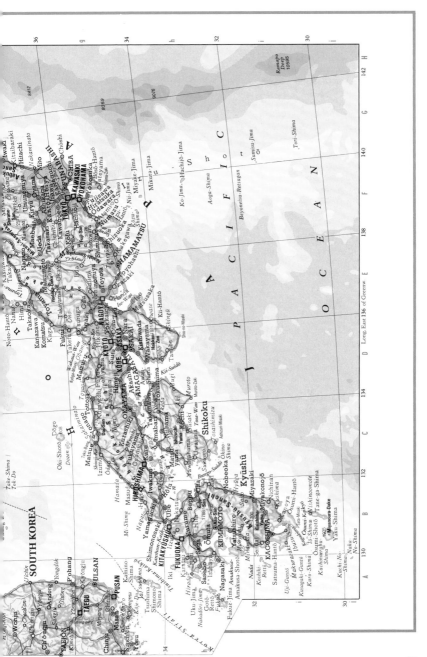

Scale 1 : 18 000 000

© ISTITUTO GEOGRAFICO DE AGOSTINI S.p.A. - NOVARA

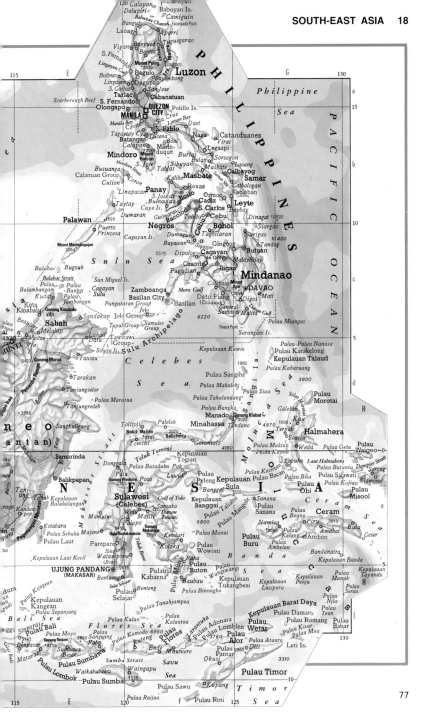

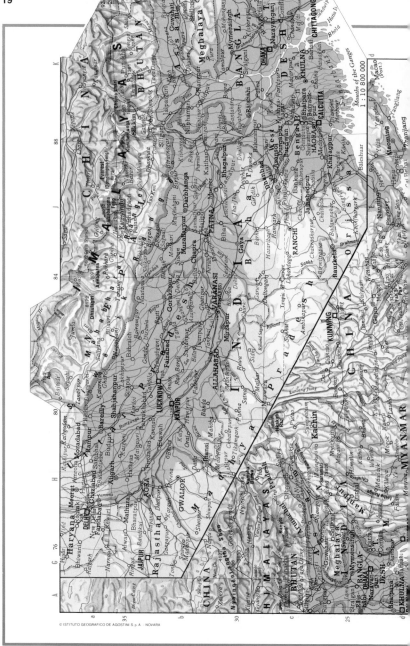

© ISTITUTO GEOGRAFICO DE AGOSTINI S.p.A. · NOVARA

1 : 10 800 000

Mouths of the Ganges

Scale 1 : 18 000 000

0   250   500 km

Modified conical projection

Long. East 90 of Greenwich

N. = Nagaland
T. = Tripura
M. = Mizoram

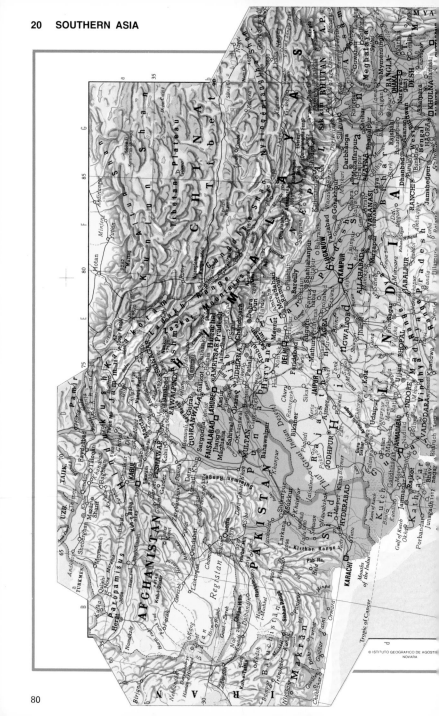

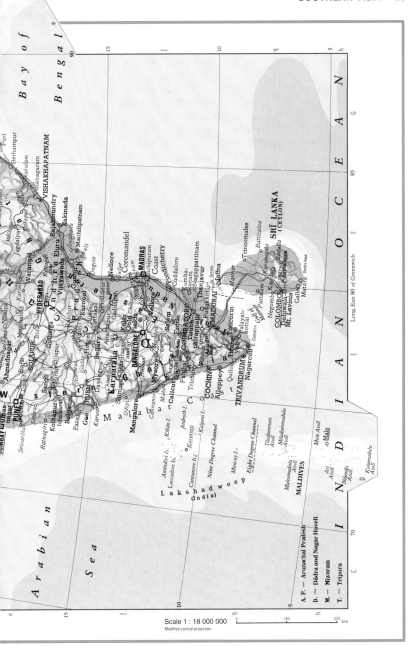

(BURMA)

Bay of Bengal

Arabian Sea

I N D I A N   O C E A N

Long. East 80 of Greenwich

SRI LANKA
(CEYLON)

Puri
Berhampur
Srikakulam
Vizianagaram
VISHAKHAPATNAM
Rajahmundry
Kakinada
Machilipatnam
Eluru
Vijayawada
Warangal
HYDERABAD
Andhra Pradesh
Coromandel Coast
Nellore
MADRAS
Pondicherry
Cuddalore
Kumba-konam
Nagappattinam
Thanjavur
Tiruchirappalli
Salem
COIMBATORE
Erode
Karnataka
BANGALORE
Mysore
Tamil Nadu
MADURAI
Trincomalee
Batticaloa
Negombo
COLOMBO
Dehiwala
Mt. Lavinia
Galle
Matara
TRIVANDRUM
Nagercoil
COCHIN
Alleppey
Quilon
Mangalore
Kerala
Calicut
Goa
Panaji
Belgaum
HUBLI
Kolhapur
Ratnagiri
SOLAPUR
Ahmadnagar
PUNE
POONA
BOMBAY
Ulhas-nagar

Mule Atoll
Male
Thiladummati Atoll
Miladummadulu Atoll
Malosmadulu Atoll
Ari Atoll
Nilandu Atoll
Kolumadulu Atoll
MALDIVES

L a k s h a d w e e p
(India)

Aminidivi Is.
Kiltan I.
Amindivi Is.
Androth I.
Kavaratti
Laccadive Is.
Kalpeni I.
Nine Degree Channel
Minicoy I.
Eight Degree Channel

A.P. = Arunachal Pradesh
D. = Dadra and Nagar Haveli
M. = Mizoram
T. = Tripura

Scale 1 : 18 000 000
Modified conical projection
0   250   500 km

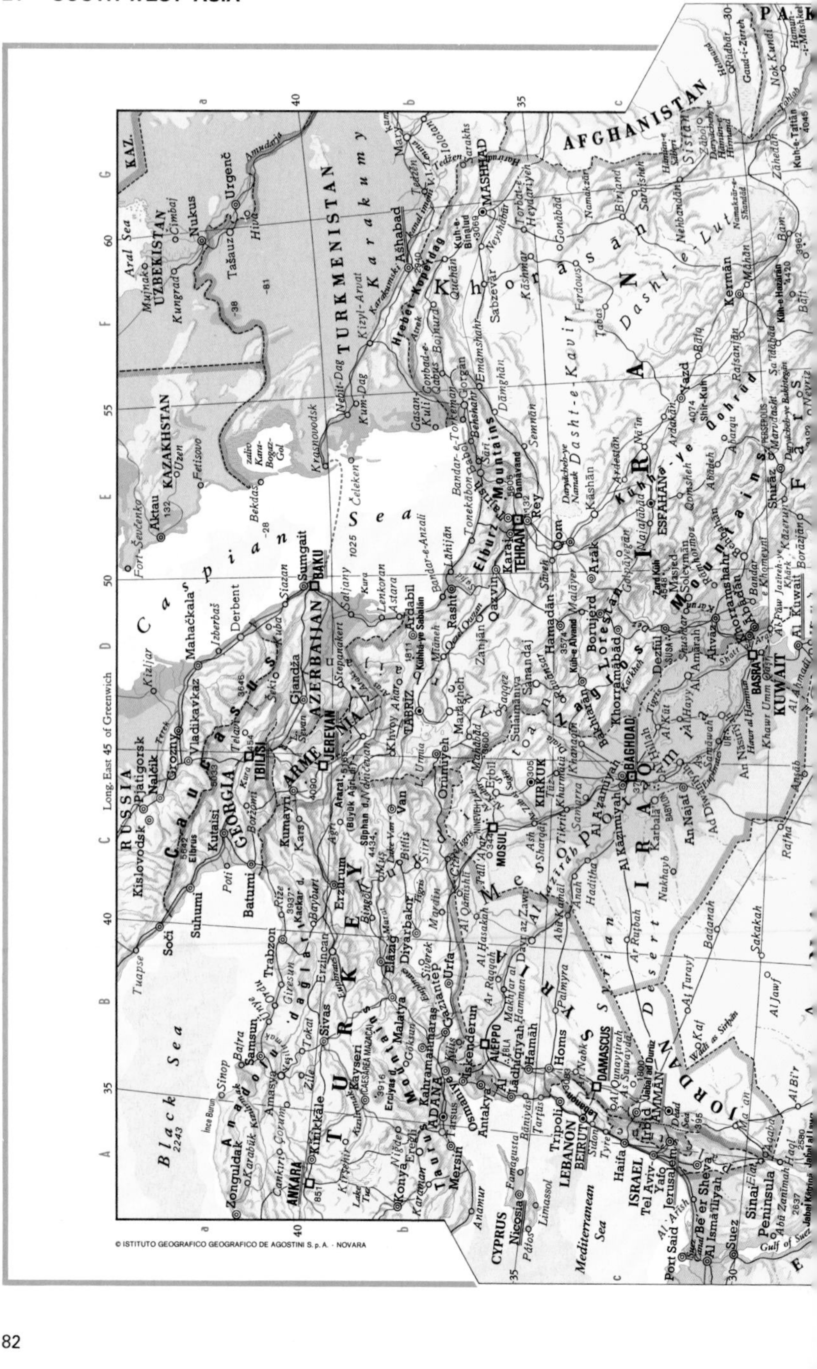
KAZ.
KAZAKHSTAN
UZBEKISTAN
TURKMENISTAN
AFGHANISTAN
RUSSIA
GEORGIA
AZERBAIJAN
TURKEY
KUWAIT
CYPRUS
LEBANON
ISRAEL
Aral Sea
Black Sea
Caspian Sea
Mediterranean Sea
Long. East 45 of Greenwich
ANKARA
TEHRAN
BAGHDAD
DAMASCUS
AMMAN
BEIRUT
BAKU
TBILISI
JEREVAN
BASRA
ESFAHAN
MOSUL
KIRKUK
ALEPPO
ADANA
MASHHAD
Aškhabad
Nicosia
Elburz Mountains

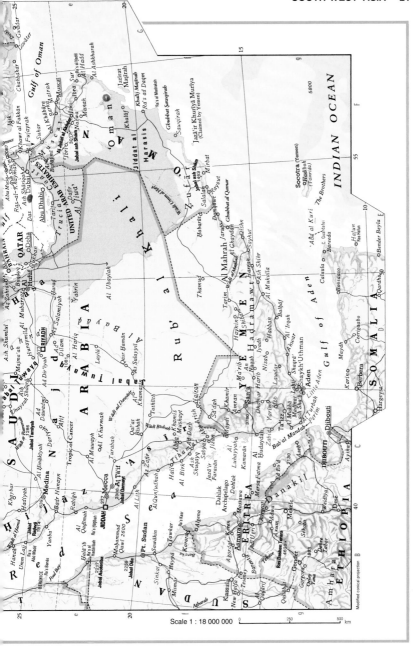

Gulf of Oman

'Omán

Gulf of Oman

Jazirat Maṣírah

INDIAN OCEAN

5800

Jazā'ir Khūriyā Mūrīyā
(Claimed by Yemen)

Socotra (Yemen)
(Suqutrā)

The Brothers

'Abd al Kūri
C. Guardafui
Ras Hafun

Hadiboh

Bender Beyla

UNITED ARAB EMIRATES

Abu Dhabi

Trucial Coast

QATAR

Doha

BAHRAIN

Al Mahrah

Jiddat al Harāsis

Rub' al Khali

Gulf of Aden

SOMALIA

Bosaso

Qardho

Karin

Berbera

S A U D I   A R A B I A

Y E M E N

Hadramaw

Aden

DJIBOUTI

Tropic of Cancer

Mecca

JIDDA

Medina

H I J A Z

Port Sudan

S U D A N

E R I T R E A

Asmara

ETHIOPIA

Danakil

Amhara

Kassala

INDIAN OCEAN

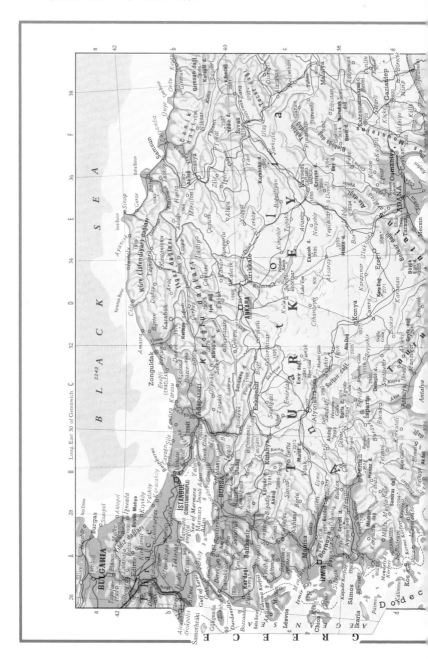

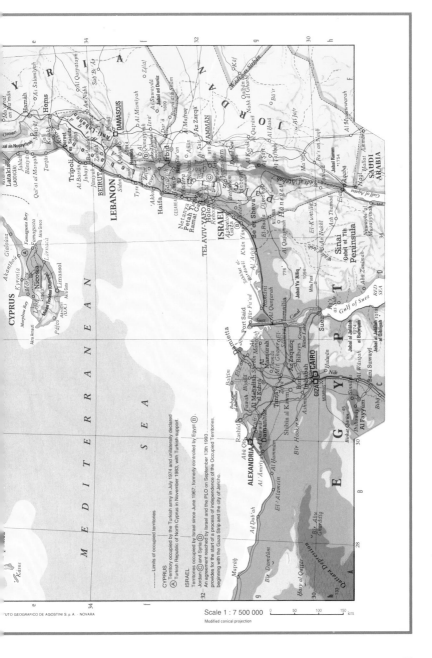

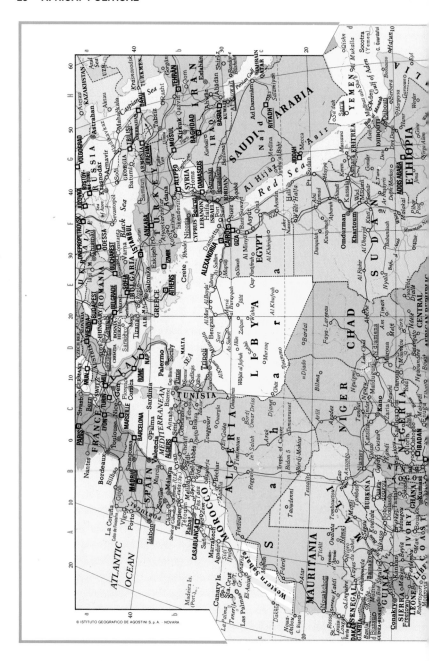

© ISTITUTO GEOGRAFICO DE AGOSTINI S.p.A. - NOVARA

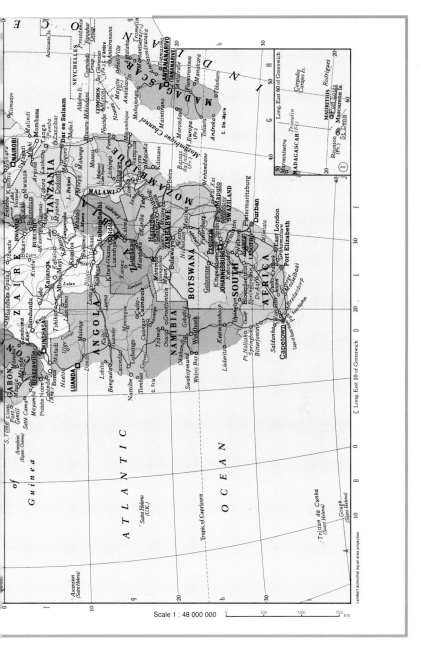

Scale 1 : 48 000 000

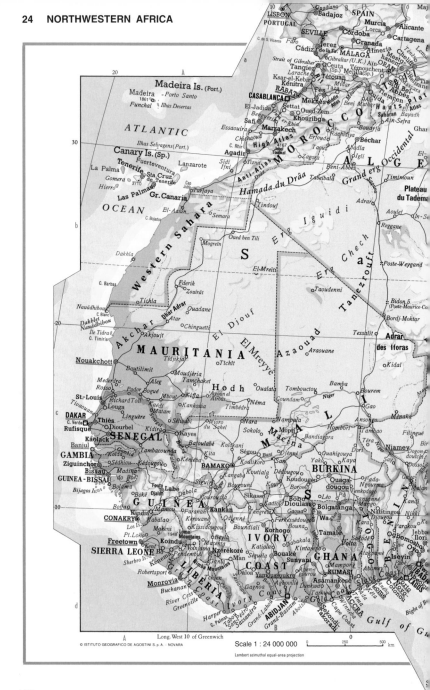

Scale 1 : 24 000 000
Lambert azimuthal equal-area projection

© ISTITUTO GEOGRAFICO DE AGOSTINI S.P.A. - NOVARA

Long. West 10 of Greenwich

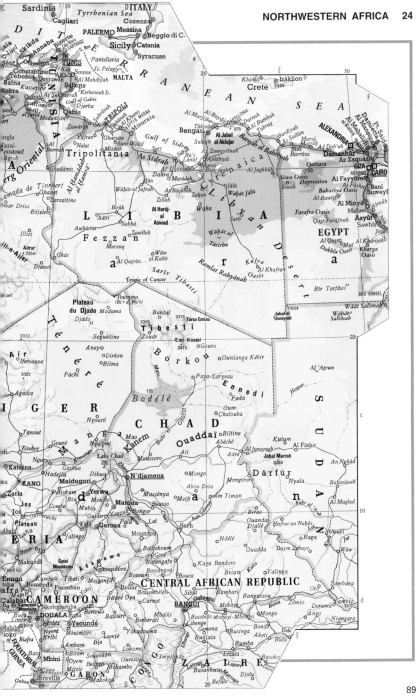

Sardinia
Cagliari
Tyrrhenian Sea
ITALY
Cosenza
PALERMO   Messina
Reggio di C.
Sicily   Catania
Syracuse

Skikda
Annaba
Bizerte
CARTHAGE
TUNIS
C. Bon
Pantelleria
Is. Pelagie
MALTA

Constantine
Tébessa
Qayrawan
Sousse
Safaqis
Al Mahdiyah
Kerkennah Is.

Batna
Kasserine
Gafsa
Shatt al Jarid
Gulf of Gabès
Djerba
Qabis
Madaniyin
Zuwarah
Sabratah
TRIPOLI
Al Khums
LEPTIS MAGNA
Misurata

Khania
Crete
2456
Iráklion

MEDITERRANEAN SEA

Al Marj
Tukrah   Barce   APOLLONIA   Darnah
Bengasi   Al Bayda   875   Al Bumbah
Tubruq
Bardiyah
Marsá Sallúm
Al Sallúm
Sidi Barráni
Marsá Matrúh
Ad Dab'ah
ALEXANDRIA
Al Iskandariyah
Al Mansúrah
Pt. Said
Damietta

Al Jabal al Akhdar
Sulúq
Barqah
Ajdabiyah
Al Bahrayn
Az Zaqaziq
Damanhúr
GIZA
CAIRO

Ghadámis
Al Burmah
Nalut
Mizdah
Bani Walid
Gharyán
Surt
Ra's Lanúf
As Sidrah
Marsá al Burayqah
Zuwaytinah

Hamáda de Tinrhert
Ohanet
Zarzaitine
Adiri
Birák
Al Haruj al Aswad
Waha
Sarir

Siwa Oasis
Siwah
Qattara
Depression
-133
Baharíya Oasis
Al Bawiti
Al Fayyúm
Bani Suwayf

Djanet
Adrar
2254
Ghát
Sabhá
Murzuq
Zawilah
Awbári
Fezzan

Wáhát al Tazirbú
Farafra Oasis
Qasr Faráfirah
Al Minya
Asyút
Mallawi
Al Minya

Al Qatrún
Wáw al Kabir
Sarir Tibasti
Ramlat Rabyánah
Kufra
Al Khufrah
Oasis
Al Qasr
Dakhla Oasis
Mut
Al Khárijah
Kharga Oasis

Tropic of Cancer

Plateau du Djado
Djado
Seguédine
Zouar
Toummo
(Bi'r al Wa'r)
Madama
Bardai
Tarso Emisu
3376
Tibesti
3265
Emi Koussi
3415
Gouro

Bír Tarfáwi
Jabal al 'Uwaynát
1934
Wáhát Salimah
Wáhát Salimah
ABU SIMBEL

Aïr
Iferouane
2022
Fachi
Aneyo
Dirkou
Bilma
Borkou
Faya-Largeau
Ennedi
Fada
Ouniana Kébir
Al 'Atrun

Agadez
Ténéré
Bodélé
155'
Maro
Oum Chalouba
Hoggar
SUDAN

NIGER
Tanout
Zinder
Ngourti
Mao
Nguigmi
Lake Chad
Moussoro
Ati
Biltine
Abéché
Adré
Kutum
Al Fáshir
An Nuhúd

Katsina
KANO
Zaria
Jos
Plateau
Hadejia
Gashua
Dikwa
N'djamena
CHAD
Kanem
Ouaddai
Jabal Marrah
3088
Nyala
Babanúsah
Darfúr

Maiduguri
Potiskum
Biu
Mubio
Mokolo
Yerwa
Guidero
Kagou
Bongor
Maroua
Massénya
Bousso
Melfi
Am Timan
Birao
Ouandi Djallé
Hufrat an Nahás
Al Muglad

Yola
Garoua
Pala
Laï
Sarh
Moundou
Ndélé
Ouadda
Raga
Daym Zubayr
Uwayl
Jur
Wáw

Makurdi
Jalingo
Adamawa
Gotel Mountains
Ngaoundéré
Baïbokoum
Goré
Batangafo
Bossangoa
Bozoum
Bouca
Kaga Bandoro
Briao
Yalinga
Kato
Tamboura

Enugu
Bamenda
Foumban
Tibati
Meiganga
Bouar
Bassembelé
Sibút
Bambari
Bangassou
Obo
CENTRAL AFRICAN REPUBLIC

CAMEROON
Calabar
Cameroon Mountains
4070
Nkongsamba
Bertoua
Bétaré Oya
Carnot
Ubanqui
BANGUI
Mobaye
Bosobolo
Mobayi-Mbongo
Bomu
Zémio
Doruma
Zambio
Niangara

DOUALA
Yaoundé
Batá
Mbalmayo
Lomié
Yokadouma
Berbérati
Mbaïki
Libenge
Gemena
Businga
Bondo
Aketi
Bula
Uele

EQUATORIAL GUINEA
Mbini
Bitam
Oyem
Souanké
Ambam
Dja
Lokomo
Ouesso
Impfondo
Lisala
Lopori
Basoko

GABON
Libreville
Cogo
Mitzic
Makokou
Bélinga
Mékambo
Sangha
Befale
Djolu
Basankusu

ZAIRE
CONGO

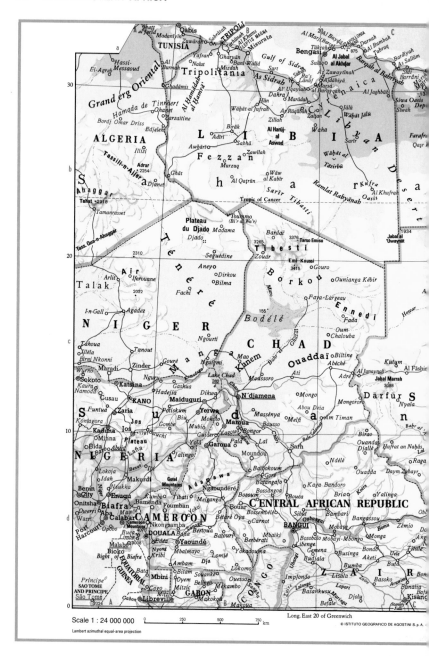

Scale 1 : 24 000 000

Long. East 20 of Greenwich

© ISTITUTO GEOGRAFICO DE AGOSTINI S.p.A.

Lambert azimuthal equal-area projection

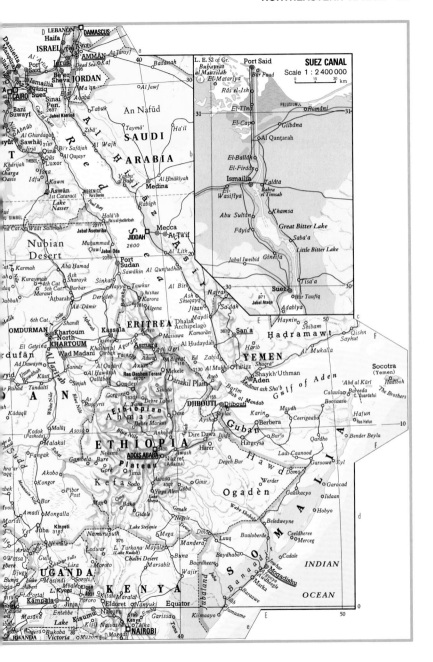

SUEZ CANAL
Scale 1 : 2 400 000

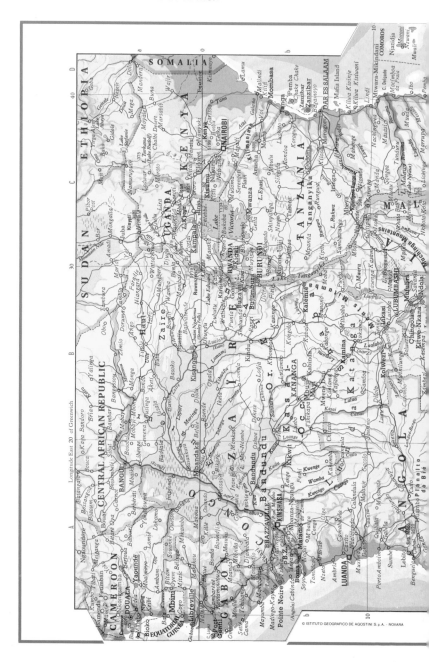

© ISTITUTO GEOGRAFICO DE AGOSTINI S.p.A. - NOVARA

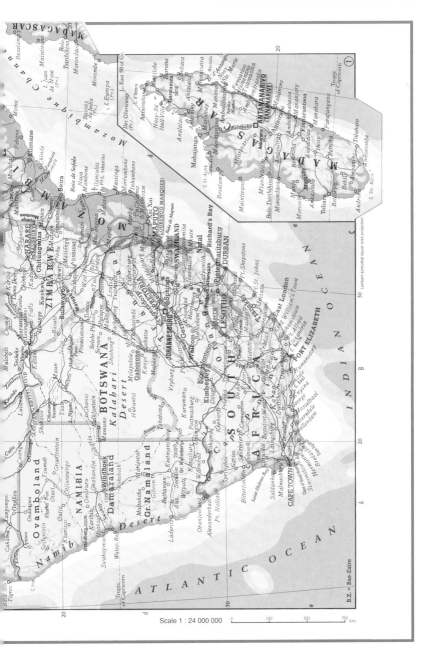

Scale 1 : 24 000 000

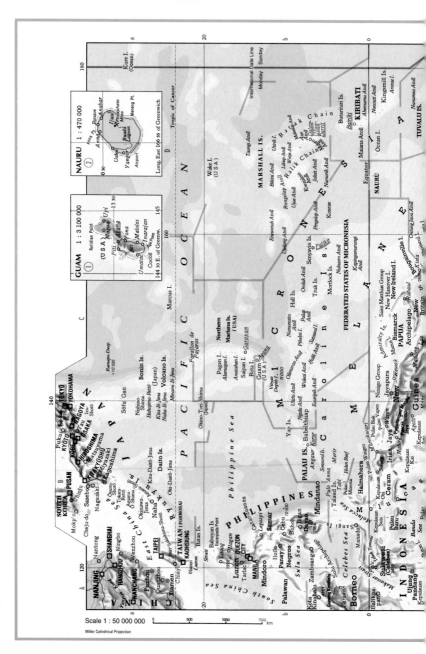

NAURU 1 : 470 000

GUAM 1 : 3 100 000

Scale 1 : 50 000 000

Miller Cylindrical Projection

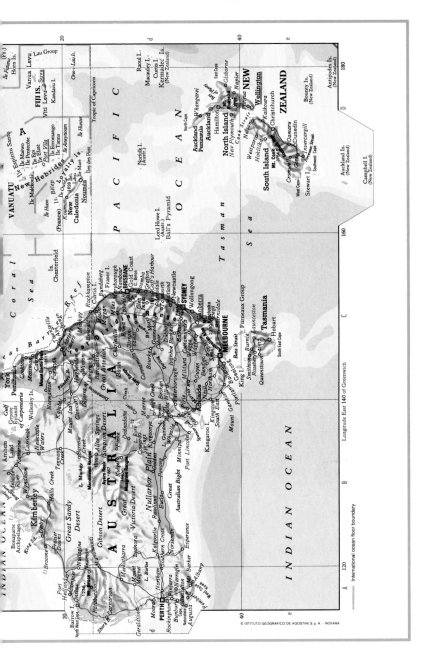

International ocean floor boundary

© ISTITUTO GEOGRAFICO DE AGOSTINI S.p.A. - NOVARA

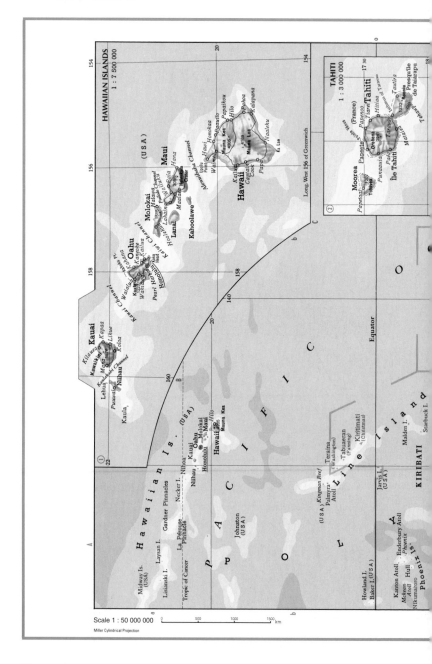

HAWAIIAN ISLANDS
1 : 7 500 000

(USA)

Molokai

Oahu

Maui

Hawaii

Kauai

Niihau

TAHITI
1 : 3 000 000

(France)

Moorea

Île Tahiti

Scale 1 : 50 000 000

0   500   1000   1500 km

Miller Cylindrical Projection

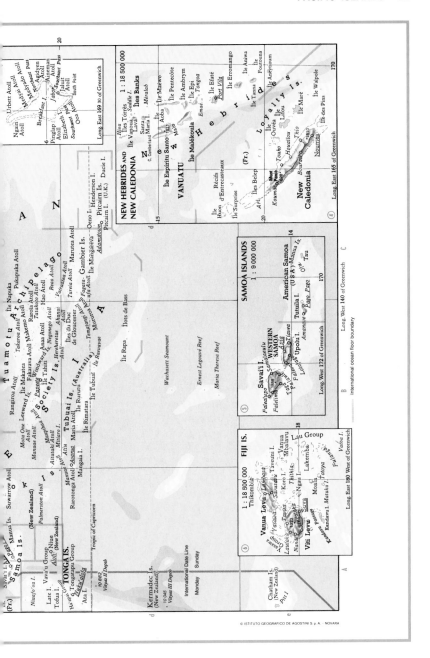

Long. East 169 30 of Greenwich

NEW HEBRIDES AND
NEW CALEDONIA
1 : 18 500 000

Îles Torrès Saddle I.
Hiou
Île Vapoua. Santa Lava Merelab
C. Cumberland Maria I.

Île Espiritu Santo Aoba Île Maewo
Mao Île Pentecôte
Île Malékoula Île Ambrym
Île Epi
Emaɐ Tongoa
VANUATU Port Vila
Île Éfaté

H e b r i d e s

Île Erromango
Île Aniwa
Île Tanna Île Foutouna
Île Anéityoum

Récifs
Île d'Entrecasteaux
Île Belep (Fr.) L o y a l t y   I s.
Île Surprise Île Ouvéa Lifou
Art Îles Belep Toutho Île Maré
Huon Mont Koumac Pamié Houaïlou Thio Île Walpole
Île Panié Canala
New Bourail Noumea Île des Pins
Caledonia
Long. East 165 of Greenwich

SAMOA ISLANDS
1 : 9 000 000

Savai'i I. Matautu Apia
Fatelupo pass Falealupo Faleolo O Leava
Falelima Sagone Upolu I. Tau
WESTERN Faleolo Aleipata
SAMOA Apia Amanave Ot Tutuila I. Manu'a Is.
Loto'opa Pago Pago
American Samoa
Tutuila I. (U.S.A) Ot Tau
Page Pago
Long. West 172 of Greenwich Long. West 170 of Greenwich

International ocean floor boundary

FIJI IS.
1 : 18 500 000
Thikombia

Vanua Levu Lambasa
Yasawa Sawusawa Taveuni I.
Group Koro I. Vanua
Naviti I. Koro I. Mbalavu
Thithia.
Lautoka Tavua Koro I. Ngau I.
Nandi Mba Lakemba
Ovalau Moala
Suva
Viti Levu
Kandavu I. Matuku Totoya Vatoa I.
Kandavu passage Fulanga
Vatoa I.
Long. East 180 West of Greenwich Lau Group

Kermadec Is.
(New Zealand)
10 045
Vityaz III Depth
Raoul I.
Phil I.

Chatham Is.
(New Zealand)
Pitt I.

International Date Line
Monday Sunday

Tropic of Capricorn

10 882
Vityaz II Depth

TONGA IS.
Ha'apai Gr. Tongatapu Group
Nuku'alofa
Ata I.

Niuafo'ou I.
Late I. Vava'u Group
Tofua I. Atolu (New Zealand)

Samoa Is.
(Fr.)
Savai'i I. Apia Manua Is. Suwarrow Atoll
Samoa Is.
Palmerston Atoll
(New Zealand)

Rarotonga Atoll Mangaia Atoll Maria Atoll
Manuae Atoll Atiu Maria Atoll
Mangaia I. Mitiaro I.
Aitutaki Atoll
Mauke Atoll Manuae Atoll
I s Tubuai Is. (Austral Is.)
C o o k Île Rurutu
Manuae Atoll Maria Atoll
Île Rimatara Île Tubuai Île Raivavae

Î l e s   S o c i e t y   I s.
Motu One Leeward Is. Île Tahiti
Atoll
Manuae Atoll Windward Pa'ea
Mauahua Atoll Île Makatea

Rangiroa Atoll Île Napuka
Takaroa Atoll Île Makata Pukapuka Atoll
Fakarava Atoll Makemo Atoll Raroia Atoll
Windward Anaa Atoll Takaroa Atoll Hao Atoll
T u a m o t u   A r c h i p e l a g o
Heretheretua Nengopo Atoll Ahunu
Îles du Duc Atoll Marutea Atoll
de Gloucester Turéia Atoll
Temataŋi Atoll Fagataufa Atoll Gambier Is.
Murutoa Atoll ʻufa Atoll Île Mangaréva

Oeno I. Henderson I.
Adamstown Pitcairn Is. Ducie I.
Pitcairn I. (U.K.)

Île Rapa Îlots de Bass

Wachusett Seamount

Ernest Legouvé Reef

Maria Theresa Reef

Urbett Atoll
Ngain Mejayo Atoll Mejayo pass
Atoll Mejadjo Atoll Northeast Pass
Breakfast I. Agidyen Ailinglap
Atoll Aterman Pass
Pinglap Jabot Southeast Pass
Atoll Elizabeth I. Jaluit
Southwest Atoll Atoll
Oca South Point

© ISTITUTO GEOGRAFICO DE AGOSTINI S.p.A. · NOVARA

20

170

15

14

170

C

Long. West 140 of Greenwich

B

20

4

18

5

6

A

D

97

Arafura

130 E
10

Melville I. Milikapiti Dundas Str. Cobourg Pen
Bathurst I. Van Diemen Gulf Go
Clarence Str
Rum Jungle Darwin
Adelaide River Batchelor Arn
Joseph Bonaparte Gulf Port Keats Fine Creek Land
C. Londonderry Katherine
Admiralty Gulf Kalumburu Pine Creek Mataranka
Cartier I. Daly R.

B 120 C 125 D

INDIA N

a Scott Reef Browse I. Bonaparte Archipelago King Edward R. Drysdale R. Wyndham Kununurra Victoria Riv. Birdum
Adele I. Kuri Bay Mt. Hann 776 Downs Daly Waters
15 Collier B. Kimberley Ord River
OCEAN Yampi Sd. Mt. Ord 936 Kimberley 900 Victoria Riv. Downs
C. Lévêque King Sound King Leopold Range Plateau Ord River Wave Hill
Lacepede Is. Derby Fitzroy Halls Creek Nort
Rowley Shoals Broome Crossing
b Roebuck B. Fitzroy R. Margaret River
Frazier Downs Lagrange Tanami
Eighty Mile Beach Desert Tenn Cre
Shay Gap Tanami The Granites Lande R
Port Hedland De Grey R. Gregory L. Bars
Dampier Archipelago Wickham Great Sandy Desert Percival Lakes
Monte Bello Is. Dampier Roebourne Marble Bar L. Waukarly- carly Yuendumu Terri
Barrow I. Pannawonica Fortescue R. Nullagine L. Dora L. Auld L. Mackay
Exmouth Gulf North West Cape Onslow Wittenoom Roy Hill Macdonnell
Exmouth Mt. Bruce 1226 L. Disappointment L. Macdonald Haasts Bluff Mt. Ziel 1510
Learmouth Hamersley Range Mt. Brockman 1118 Tom Price Newman Mundiwindi L. Neale
c Ashburton R. Uaroo Paraburdoo Western L. Hopkins L. Amadeus Erldunda
Tropic of Capricorn Gibson Desert Petermann Range 867
L. Mc Leod Minilya Mt. Augustus 1106 Carnegie Ayers Rock Kulge
Carnarvon Gascoyne AUSTR Warburton Mission Musgrave Ranges Mt. Woodroffe 1440
Geographe Channel Gascoyne Junction Peak Hill L. Gregory L. Carnegie Mt. Olga De Re
Naturaliste Channel Shark Bay Wooramel R. Wiluna L. Wells
Cape Inscription Bay Meekatharra Australia L. Yeo
Dirk Hartog Denham Cue Sandstone Agnew Great Victoria Desert Serpentine Lakes
d L. Austin Mount Magnet Leonora Laverton Rason L.
Gascoyne Channel Northampton Yalgoo Sandstone L. Raeside L. Carey L. Minigwal South
Houtman Geraldton Mullewa Morawa Payne's Find L. Barlee Menzie L. Rebecca
Abrolhos Dongara Three Springs L. Moore Kalgoorlie Zanthus Haig Forrest Yalata
Walheroo Dalwallinu Nullarbor Plain Ooldea T
30 Milling Mukinbudin Bullfinch Coolgardie Kambalda Rawlinna Cocklebiddy Eucla Fowler's Bay Penc
Moora Lancelin Goomalling Southern Cross Widgiemooltha L. Cowan Nuyts Archipelago Streaky B
Kalamunda Meredin Norseman Balladonia Great
PERTH Northam Kondinin Lake Johnston L. Dundas Investigator
Rockingham Beverley Brookton Newdegate
e Mandurah Pinjarra Narrogin Ravensthorpe Esperance Australian Bight
Bunbury Wagin 565
Geographe Bay Collie Katanning Gnowangerup Hopetoun C. Arid Archipelago of the Recherche
Cape Naturaliste Busselton Bridgetown Stirling Range
Augusta Blackwood Pemberton Mount Barker Albany
C. Leeuwin Flinders Range Denmark King George Sound
Pt d'Entrecasteaux West Cape Howe

115 B 120 C 125 D Long. East 130 of Greenwich E

Scale 1 : 18 000 000 0 250 500 km
Conical equal-area projection
© ISTITUTO GEOGRAFICO DE AGOSTINI S.p.A.

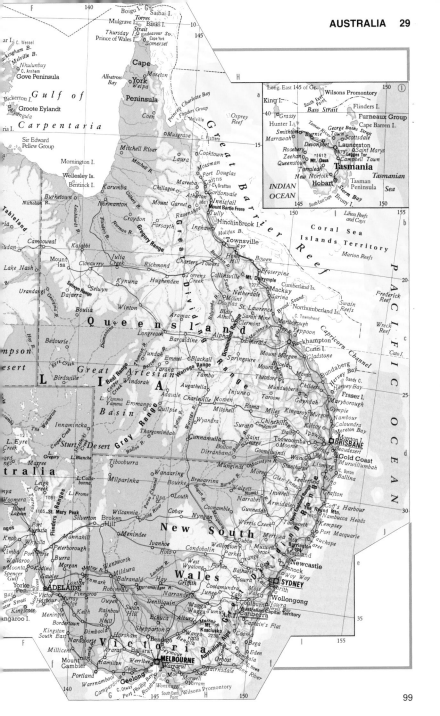

© ISTITUTO GEOGRAFICO DE AGOSTINI S.p.A. - NOVARA

Scale 1 : 48 000 000

Lambert azimuthal equal-area projection

A 140 B 130 C 120 D 110 E 100 F 90

Mackenzie Bay

Banks I.

Sachs Harbour

Prince Albert Peninsula

Stefansson I.

Somerset I.

Prince of Wales I.

C. Bathurst

C. Parry

Holman

Amundsen Gulf

Prince Albert Sound

Victoria I.

McClintock Channel

Franklin Strait

District of Boothia Peninsula

Porcupine

Fort Yukon

Old Crow

Rampart House

Dawson

Paulatuk

Wollaston Peninsula

Coronation Gulf

Coppermine

Cambridge Bay

Kent Peninsula

Maud Gulf

King William I.

Gjoa Haven

Spence Bay

Alaska

U.S.A.

Yukon Territory

Mackenzie Mountains

Northwest

District

Mt. St. Elias Mountains

Mt. Fairweather

Keele Peak 2917

Norman Wells

Fort Good Hope

Fort Franklin

Echo Bay

Great Bear Lake

Bathurst Inlet

Arctic Circle

Terr

District of Keewatin

Baker Lake

Chesterfield

Yathkyed Lake

Whitehorse

Haines Junction

Watson Lake

Fort Simpson

Fort Norman

Wrigley

L. Grandin

Fort Rae

Yellowknife

District of Mackenzie

Reliance

Snowdrift

L. Garry

Thelon

Dubawnt Lake

Alexander Archipelago

Juneau

Sitka

Admiralty I.

Atlin

Stikine Ranges

Churchill Peak 2819

Fort Liard

Fort Providence

Great Slave Lake

Hay River

Pine Point

Fort Resolution

Fort Smith

Ennadai

Kasba Lake

Prince of Wales I.

Dixon Entrance

Graham I.

Prince Rupert

Hazelton

Terrace

Fort Nelson

Fort Vermilion

Uranium City

L. Athabasca

Wollaston Lake

Kazan

Nueltin Lake

British Columbia

Queen Charlotte Is.

Moresby I.

Kitimat

Prince George

Dawson Creek

Fort St. John

Peace River

Fort McMurray

Lake Athabasca

L. Claire

Fort Chipewyan

Cree Lake

Reindeer Lake

Lynn Lake

Southern Indian Lake

Churchill

York

Ocean Falls

Mt. Waddington

Williams Lake

McLennan

Grande Prairie

Lesser Slave Lake

Lac la Biche

La Ronge

Flin Flon

Sherridon

Thompson

Nelson

Wabowden

Pacific Ocean

Vancouver I.

Strait of Juan de Fuca

Mt. Robson 3954

Mt. Jasper

Mt. Columbia 3747

Alberta

Edmonton

Camrose

Saskatchewan

North Saskatchewan

North Battleford

Prince Albert

Big River

Meadow Lake

Manitoba

The Pas

Norway House

Lake Winnipeg

Kamloops

Golden

Red Deer

Calgary

Hanna

Rosetown

Saskatoon

South Saskatchewan

Winnipegosis

Gypsumville

Bissett

Nanaimo

Vancouver

New Westminster

Penticton

Kelowna

Merritt

High River

Brooks

Swift Current

Moose Jaw

Watrous

Yorkton

Melville

Manitoba

Portage la Prairie

St. Boniface

Winnipeg

Victoria

Seattle

Tacoma

Olympia

Bremerton

Mt. Olympus 2424

Mt. Rainier 4392

Trail

Cranbrook

Lethbridge

Medicine Hat

Regina

Weyburn

Brandon

Emerson

Astoria

Portland

Salem

Eugene

Spokane

Mt. Cleveland 3190

Shelby

Havre

Glasgow

Williston

Minot

Grand Forks

Crookston

Pacific Ocean

Columbia

Yakima

Pasco

Lewiston

Great Falls

Helena

Glendive

Miles City

Bismarck

Fargo

Jamestown

Moorhead

Saint

Springfield

Bend

Burns

Nampa

Boise

McCall

Salmon R.

Butte

Bozeman

Yellowstone

Billings

Sheridan

Buffalo

Mobridge

Aberdeen

Minneapolis

Roseburg

Klamath Falls

Twin Falls

Idaho Falls

Pocatello

Snake R.

Mackay

Gannett Peak 4202

Thermopolis

Black Hills 2207

Rapid City

Cheyenne

Newcastle

Pierre

Sioux Falls

Mankato

Mt. Shasta 4317

Redding

Winnemucca

Elko

Great Salt Lake

Ogden

Casper

Alliance

Valentine

Niobrara

Yankton

Mitchell

Sioux City

United States

UNITED STATES

Long. West 100 of Greenwich

Scale 1 : 24 000 000

0 250 500 750 km

Lambert azimuthal equal-area projection

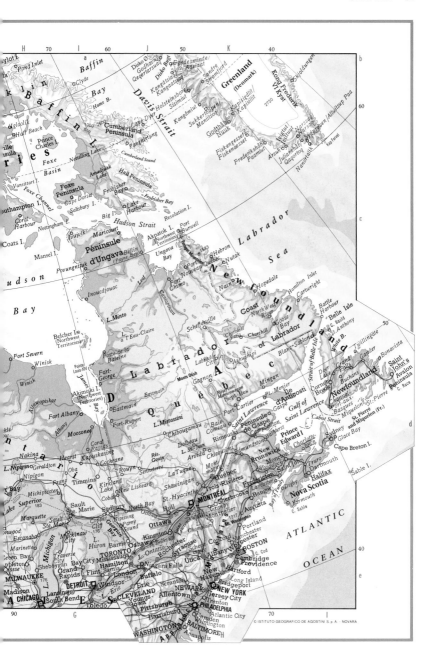

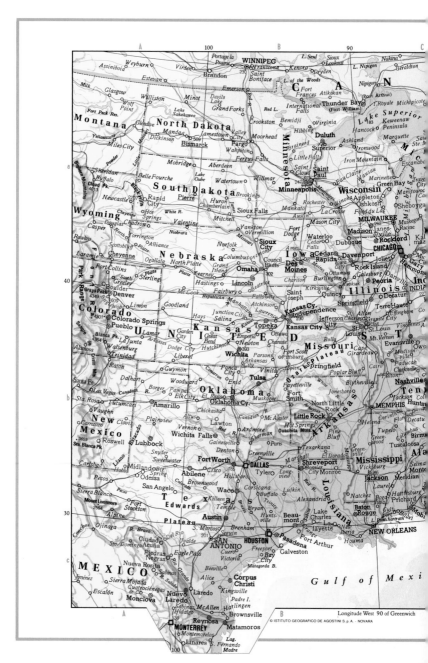

Longitude West 90 of Greenwich
© ISTITUTO GEOGRAFICO DE AGOSTINI S.p.A. - NOVARA

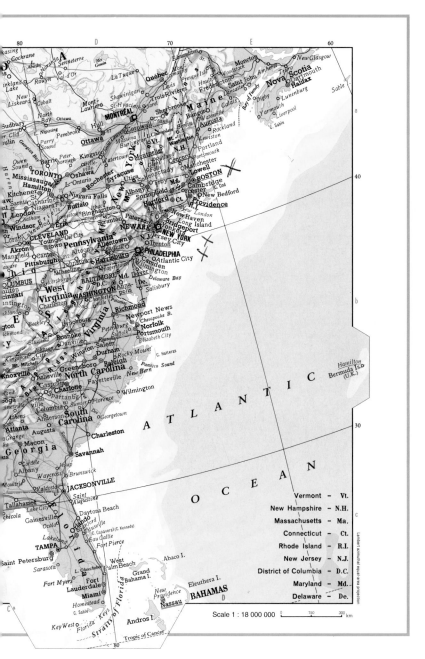

Vermont	– Vt.
New Hampshire	– N.H.
Massachusetts	– Ma.
Connecticut	– Ct.
Rhode Island	– R.I.
New Jersey	– N.J.
District of Columbia	– D.C.
Maryland	– Md.
Delaware	– De.

Scale 1 : 18 000 000

Lambert azimuthal equal-area projection

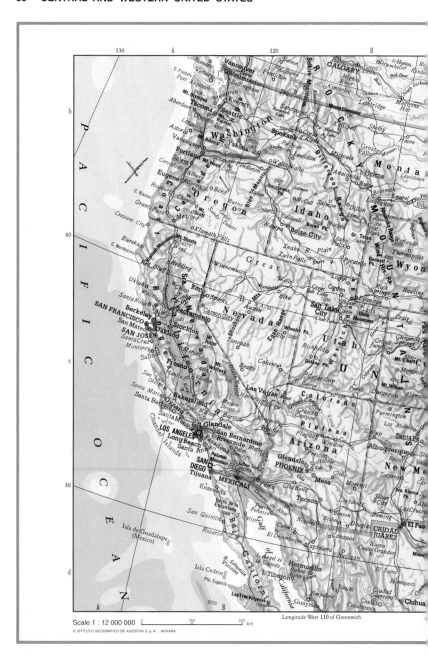

Scale 1 : 12 000 000

0   250   500 km

© ISTITUTO GEOGRAFICO DE AGOSTINI S. p. A. · NOVARA

Longitude West 110 of Greenwich

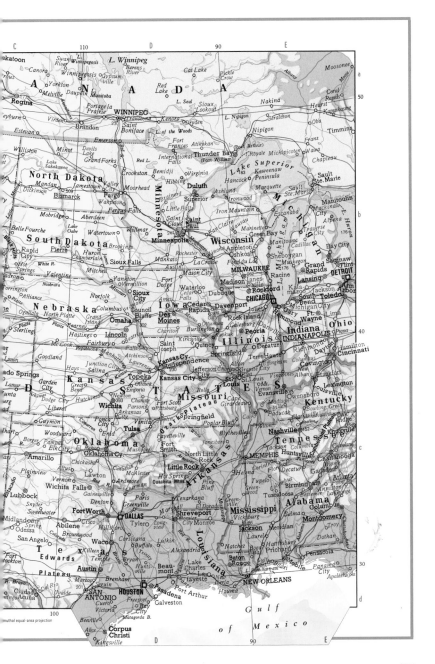

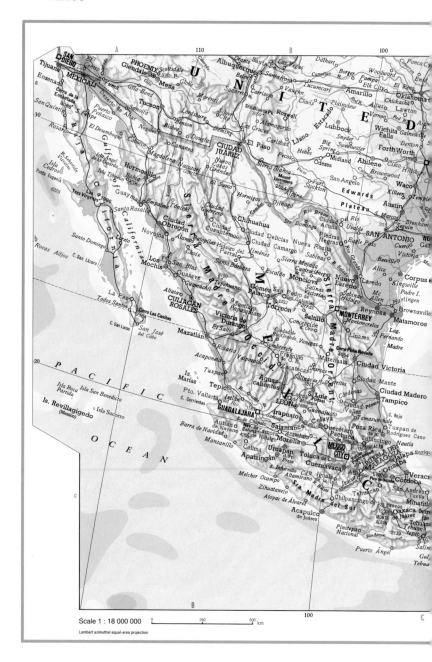

Scale 1 : 18 000 000

0   250   500 km

Lambert azimuthal equal-area projection

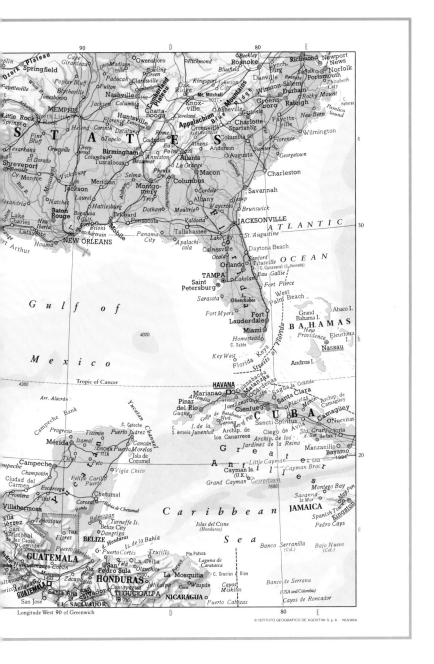

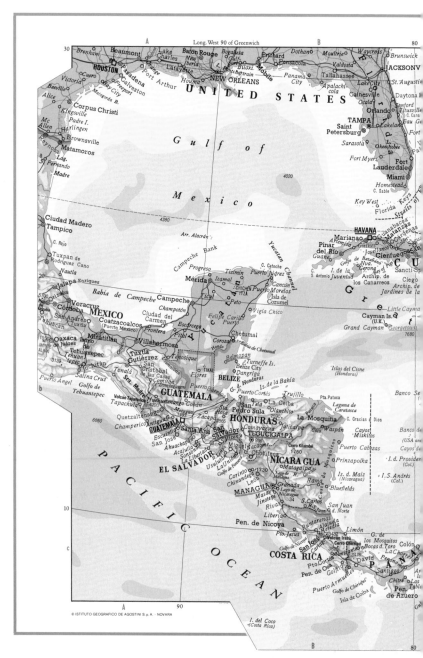

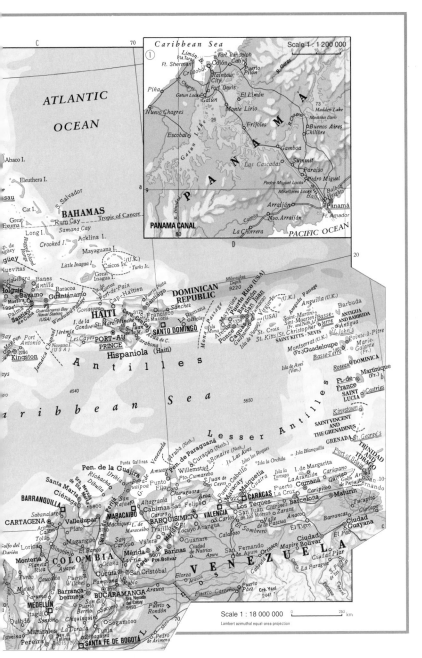

ATLANTIC
OCEAN

Abaco I.

Eleuthera I.

nassau

Cat I.

Great
Exuma I.

BAHAMAS

Long I.

Rum Cay   Tropic of Cancer

Samana Cay

Crooked I.   Acklins I.

Mayaguana I.

Little Inagua I.   Caicos Is.   (U.K.)

Great
Inagua I.   Turks Is.

Caribbean Sea   Scale 1 : 1 200 000

① Limón
Pta Toro   Ft. Randolph
Fort Sherman   Colón   Catino
Cristóbal   Puerto   R. Gatún
Rainbow   Pilón
City
Piña   Chagres   Fort Davis   El Limón

Nuevo Chagres   Gatún Locks   Gatún   Monte Lirio   73
Madden Lake
Escobal   26   Frijoles   Madden Dam

Gatún Lake   Buenos Aires   Chilibre

Gamboa

Summit
Las Cascadas   Paraíso

Pedro Miguel Locks   Pedro Miguel

Miraflores Locks   Balboa   Balboa
Arraiján   Heights

PANAMA CANAL   Nvo. Arraiján   Panamá   Ft. Amador

80   La Chorrera   **PACIFIC OCEAN**

güey
Maestra   Gibara   Banes
Holguin   Antilla
1994   Bayamo   Baracoa   Port-de-Paix   Puerto Plata
Palma   Guantánamo   Cap-Haïtien   Santiago
Santa   Guantánamo Bay   Gonaïves   **DOMINICAN**   Sánchez
de Cuba   Naval Station   St-Marc   **REPUBLIC**
(USA)   Windward   Hinche   Moca   **Milwaukee**
Bay   Pen. Port   Jérémie   I. de la   San Francisco   Bonao   **Depth**
Antonio   Les Cayes   Gonâve   de Macorís   **9220**
HAITI   **SANTO DOMINGO**
2286   Barahona

PORT-AU-
PRINCE
Kingston   Hispaniola (Haiti)

A   n   t   i   l   l   e   s

4540

Anegada Passage
Puerto Rico (USA)   Anguilla (U.K.)
Mayagüez   Bayamón   Barbuda
Aguadilla   San Juan   Saint-Martin   Basse-
Isla de   Ponce   Caguas   (Fr. and Neth.)   Terre   **ANTIGUA**
Mona   Humacao   St. Croix   Sint-Maarten   **AND BARBUDA**
Isla de Vieques   (USA)   St. Kitts/St. Christopher   **ANTIGUA**
St. Croix   **SAINT KITTS - NEVIS**   St. John's
Montserrat (U.K.)   Pointe-à-Pitre
Marie-
Isla de Aves   (Fr.)**Guadeloupe**   Galante
(Ven.)   (Fr.)

Basse-Terre

Roseau   **DOMINICA**

C   a   r   i   b   b   e   a   n   S   e   a   Fort-de-   Martinique
5650   France   (Fr.)
SAINT   Castries
LUCIA

Kingstown
SAINT VINCENT
AND
THE GRENADINES
GRENADA   St. George's

L   e   s   s   e   r   A   n   t   i   l   l   e   s   **TRINIDAD**
AND
TOBAGO   Port of Spain
Punta Gallinas
Pen. de Paraguaná   Isla Blanquilla

Aruba (Neth.)   Bonaire (Neth.)
Willemstad   Is. Las Aves
Pen. de la Guajira   Curaçao (Neth.)   Islas los Roques   Isla la Orchila
Santa Marta   Uribia   Pto. Cumarebo   Islas los Roques
Ríohacha   Punto   San Juan   La Tortuga   I. de Margarita
Maicao   Filo   de los Cayos   La Asunción   Carúpano
Ciénaga   Coro   Puerto Cabello   Maiquetía   Cumaná   Güiria   Aruba
BARRANQUILLA   San Rafael   Churuguara   Aroa   **CARACAS**   Puerto La Cruz   Carúpano   Golfo de Paria   Fernando
Sabanalarga   Altagracia   San Felipe   Los Teques   Barcelona   Maturín
CARTAGENA   Valledupar   Cabimas   **VALENCIA**   San Juan   Clarines   Anaco   Tucupita
Machiques   **MARACAIBO**   **BARQUISIMETO**   San Carlos   de los Morros   Zaraza   Curiapa
Magangué   5800   de   Trujillo   Ocumare   Valle   Pascua   El Tigre   Barrancas   Ciudad
Arjona   Plato   Maracaibo   Machiques   Tocuyo   Acarigua   de la Pascua   Guayana
Golfo del   Loricaro   El Banco   San   Valera   Guanare   Sombrero   El Pao
Darién   Sinceleio   Carlos   Mérida   Barinas   Cd. de Nutrias   San Fernando   Mapire   Ciudad   El Pao
Montería   Ayapel   Ocaña   La   5007   Pco. Bolívar   de Apure   Orinoco   Bolívar
Planeta   El   Fría   Puerto   Ciudad Pjar
Rica   Caucasia   Cúcuta   San Cristóbal   **V E N E Z U E L A**   Caicara   La Paragua
Turbo   Puerto   Pamplona   1018   Elorza   Puerto   Cro. Yavi
Mutatá   Wilches   Rubio   Arauca   Páez   2441
Yarumal   Barranca   San Gil   Puerto Carreño
bermeja   Berrío   Sra. Nevada   Puerto
MEDELLÍN   del Cocuy   Rondón
Itagüí   Puerto   5493
Quibdó   Sonsón   Chiquinquirá   Sogamoso
Manizales   La Dorada   Tunja   Pedro
Pereira   Nev. d.   Zipaquirá   de Arimena
Tolima   **SANTA FE DE BOGOTÁ**
5215

70   Scale 1 : 18 000 000   0   250 km
Lambert azimuthal equal-area projection

111

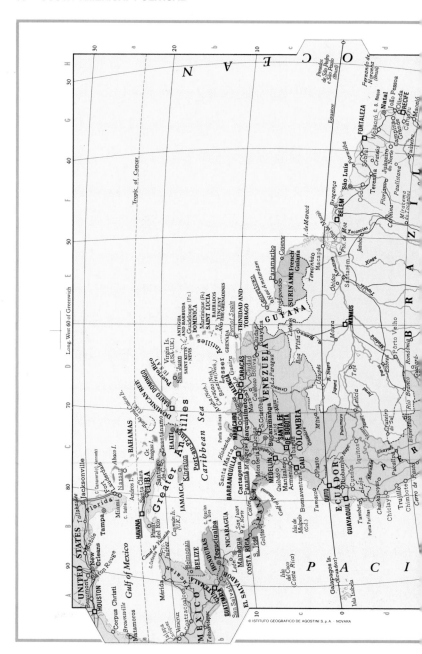

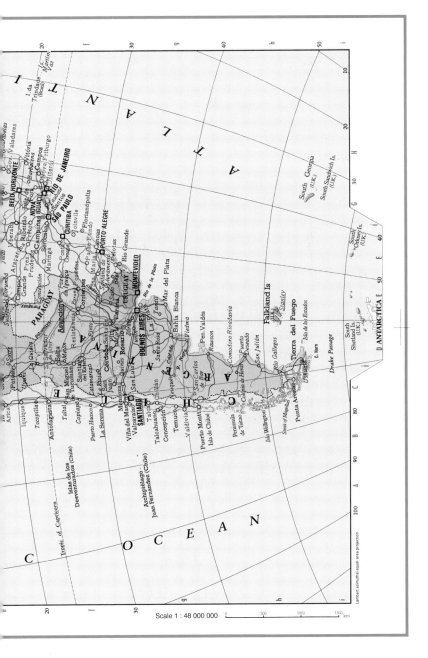

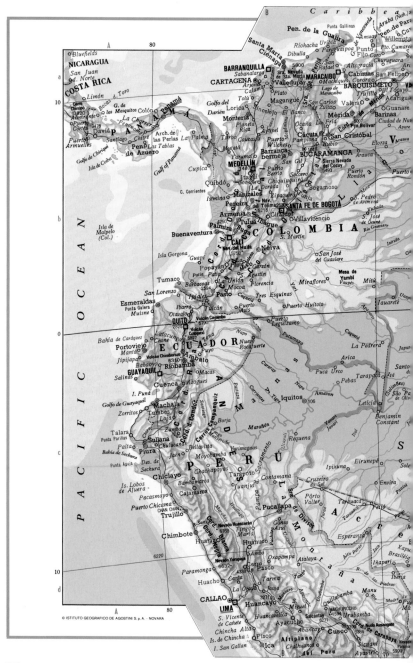

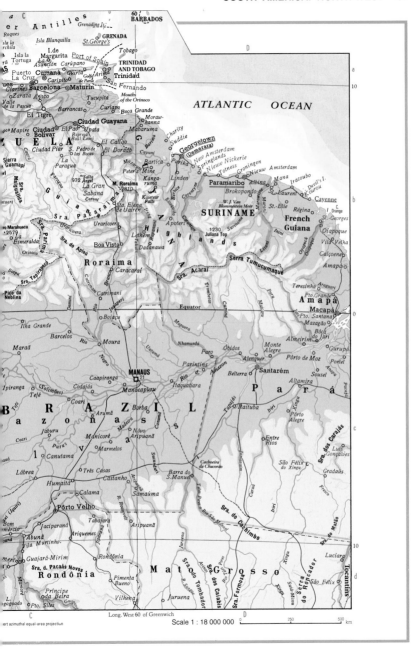

er Antilles

BARBADOS

Grenadine Is.

GRENADA

Roques

Isla Blanquilla

St.George's

Tobago

Isla la
chila

I.de
Margarita

Port of Spain

Puerto
La Cruz

Cumaná

Asunción Carúpano

Güiria

TRINIDAD
AND TOBAGO

Trinidad

Golfo
de Paria

Barcelona Maturín

San Fernando

Clarines

Zaraza Anaco

Tucupita

Mouths
of the Orinoco

ATLANTIC   OCEAN

El Tigre

Barrancas

Curiapo

Boca Grande

Mora-
hanna

Valle
de la Pascua

UELA

Ciudad
Bolívar

El Pao

Upata

Represa
Raúl Leoni

Ciudad Guayana

Charity

Suddie

Georgetown

(Demerara)

New Amsterdam

Ciudad Piar

La
Paragua

El Callao

S. Pedro de
las Bocas

El Dorado

Cuyuní

Mazaruni

Parika

Springlands

Nieuw Nickerie

Springlands

Nieuw Amsterdam

Sierra
Guampí

972

Salto
Ángel

La Gran
Sabana

M. Roraima
2810

Caroní

Bartica
Peter's Mine

Kanga-
ruma

Linden

Corentyn

Totness

Groningen

Paramaribo

Nieuw Amsterdam

Albina

Mana

Iracoubo

Devil's I.

Cayenne

ro Marahuaca
2579

La
Esmeralda

Sra. Pacaraima

Sta. Elena
de Uairén

Kaieteur
Falls

HIGHLANDS

SURINAME

W. J. Van
Blommestein Meer

St.-Laurent

Maroni

St.-Élie

Régina

French
Guiana

St.-Georges

Orange

Oiapoque

uari

Sra. Parima

Uraricoera

Apoteri

1230
Juliana Top

Sra. Tapirapeco

Orinoco

Pico da
Neblina

Uraricoera

Lethem

Dadanawa

Roraima

Caracaraí

Serra Acarai

Serra Tumucumaqué

Calçoene

Amapá

Siapa

Demini

Catrimani

Igarapé

Equator

Teresinha

Pto. Grande

Amapá

Macapá

Ilha Grande

Boiaçu

Maguera

Pto. Santana

Mazagão

Bôch
do Jari

Barcelos

Rio

Moura

Nhamundá

Faro

Óbidos

Monte
Alegre

Almeirim

Pôrto de Moz

Gurupá

Pontei

Marã

Negro

Uatumã

Parintins

Amazon

Belterra

Santarém

Sousel

Ipiranga

(Solimões)

MANAUS

Caapiranga

Codajás

Itaquatiara

Rio

Tapajós

Altamira

Pará

Teje

Manacapuru

Coari

Arumã

Borba

Novo
Aripuanã

BRAZIL

zo

n

a

Manicoré

Marmelos

Madeira

Canumã

Entre
Rios

São Félix
do Xingu

Sra. dos Carajás

Luís
Gonçalves

Jaburu

Puru

Coari

Canutama

Três Casas

Castanho

Barra do
S.Manuel

Cachoeira
da Chacorão

Gradaús

Lábrea

Humaitá

Calama

Samaúma

Roosevelt

Sucunduri

Teles Pires

Sra. do Cachimbo

Pôrto Velho

Tabajara

Aripuanã

Jiparaná

Guajará-Mirim

Jaciparaná

Ariquemes

Rondônia

Luciara

Sra. d. Pacaás Novos

Rondônia

Pimenta
Bueno

Mato   Grosso

São Félix

Príncipe
da Beira

Vilhena

Juruena

Sra. do Tombador

Sra. Formosa

Rio dos Caiabis

Xingu

Serra
do
Roncador

Tocantins

Pto. Sites

Long. West 60 of Greenwich

ert azimuthal equal-area projection

Scale 1 : 18 000 000

250   500
km

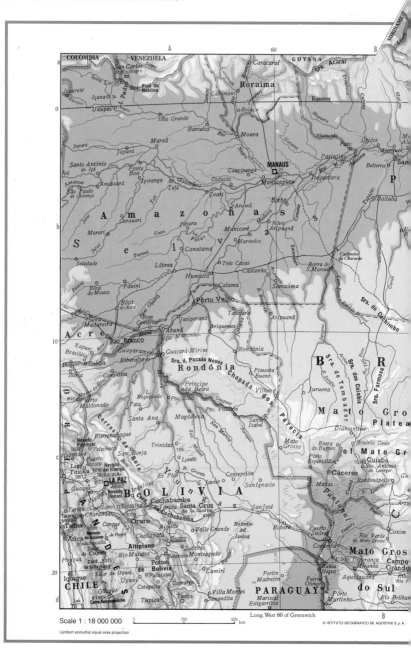

Scale 1 : 18 000 000

Long. West 60 of Greenwich

Lambert azimuthal equal-area projection

© ISTITUTO GEOGRAFICO DE AGOSTINI S.p.A.

C. Orange
Georges
Tappoue
Vila Velha
Calçoene
mapáo
I. de Maracá
C. Norte
Pta. Grande
Caciana
Mexiana
Mouths of the Amazon
Chaves
Soure
Salinópolis
Ilha
Mosqueiro Vigia Capanema
de Marajó
Breves
Belém
Guamá
Portel
Abaetetuba
Cametá
Baião
Tucuruí

D

40

(i) Disputed border between the states of Piauí and Ceará.

d

A T L A N T I C

O C E A N   4356

Tutóia
Alcântara
S. LUIS
Humberto de Campos
Pinheiro
Rosário
Viana
Axará
Chapa-
Baço dinha
Coroatá
Codó
Campo
Maior
Caxias

b

Ilha
de Noronha
Atol das
Rocas
Fernando
Ilha

Maranhão
Imperatriz
Araguatins
Grajaú
Pres.
Dutra
Colinas
Teresina
Castelo
do Piauí
Quixadá
Crateús
Ceará
Senador
Pompeu

Fortaleza
Itapipoca
Sobral
Caucaia
Baturité
Ipu
Aracati
Canindé

Marabá
Tocantinópolis
Pau
d'Arco
Carolina
Loreto
Amarante
Valença
do Piauí
Floriano
Oeiras
Juazeiro do Norte
Iguatu
Picos

Russas
Mossoró
Areia Branca
Macau
Camara
C. S. Roque
Rio Grande
do Norte
Natal
Nova Cruz

Filadélfia
Balsas
Uruçuí
Bertolínia
Paulistana
Araripina
Crato
Seabra

Rio Tinto
Cabedelo
João Pessoa
Paraíba
Campina
Grande
Paulista
Olinda
Recife
Escada

Conceição
do Araguaia
Pedro
Afonso
Bom Jesus
Raimundo
Nonato
São Raimundo
Petrolina

Pernambuco
Caruaru
Barreiros

Tocantins
Pôrto
Nacional
Natividade
Dianópolis
Barra
Xique-
Xique
Jacobina

Alagoas
Maceió
Arapiraca
Sergipe
Aracaju

Luciara
Felix
Gurupi
Paranã
Barreiras
Bahia
Feira de
Santana
Serrinha
Alagoinhas

Estância

Bandeirante
Uruaçu
Aruanã
Ceres
Goiás
Iporá

Mique-
lândia
Arraias
Sta. Maria
da Vitória
Sítio do
Abadia
Carinhanha
Caetité
Brumado
Urandi

Bom Jesus
da Lapa

Santo
Amaro
Salvador
Nazaré
B. de Todos os Santos

Divisões
Anápolis
BRASÍLIA
Distr. Fed.

Formosa

Vitória
da Conquista
Poções

Maraú
Ubaitaba
Ilhéus
Itabuna

Goiânia
Hires
Caraçu
Cristalina

Januária
Monte
Azul

Pedra
Azul
Canavieiras
Belmonte

Rio
Verde
Ipameri
Catalão
Patos
de Minas

Montes
Claros
Salinas
Araçuaí
Pôrto Seguro

São
Simão
Uberlândia
Uberaba
Patrocínio
Araxá
Pico do
Itambé
2033
Teófilo
Otoni
Monte Pascoal
Caravelas

Minas Gerais
Diamantina
Curvelo

Governador
Valadares
São Mateus

São José
do Rio Prêto
Barretos
Franca
Divinópolis
Formiga
Lagoa
Santa
BELO
HORIZONTE
Itabira
Catinga
Colatina
Linhares

Catanduva
Ribeirão
Prêto
Araçatuba
Aiuruoca
Lavras
Barbacena
Vila Velha
Vitória
Domingos-Martins

S. Paulo
Bauru
Limeira
Guaratinguetá
Pico das
Agulhas Negras
Juiz de Fora
Campos
Cachoeiro de Itapemirim

Rio Claro
Piracicaba
CAMPINAS
Taubaté
Rio de Janeiro
Friburgo

Sorocaba
Jundiaí
NITERÓI
RIO DE JANEIRO
SÃO PAULO
SANTO ANDRÉ
Santos
São Sebastião
Tropic of Capricorn

40

50

0

10

20

c

d

117

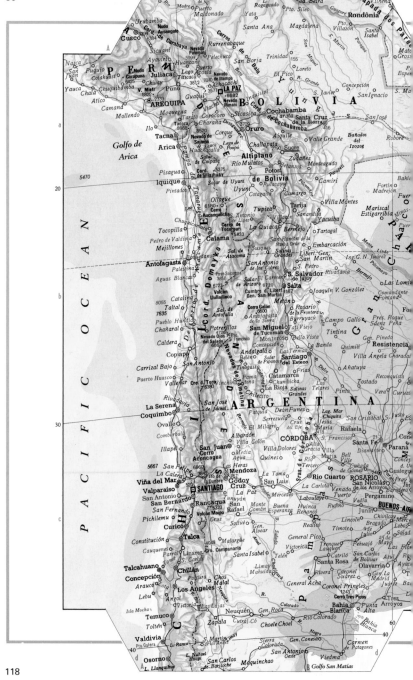

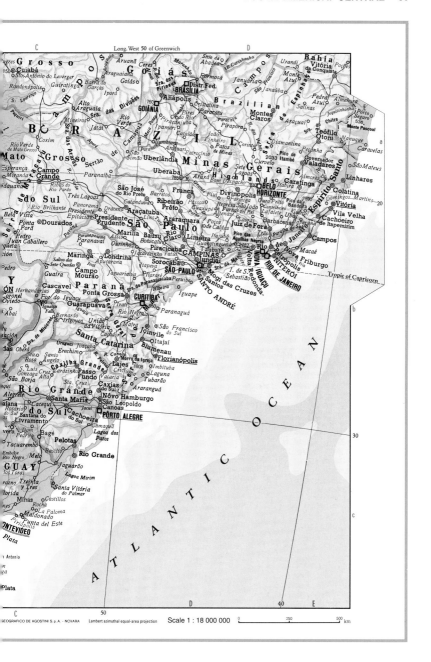

Long. West 50 of Greenwich

Scale 1 : 18 000 000

GEOGRAFICO DE AGOSTINI S.p.A. - NOVARA   Lambert azimuthal equal-area projection

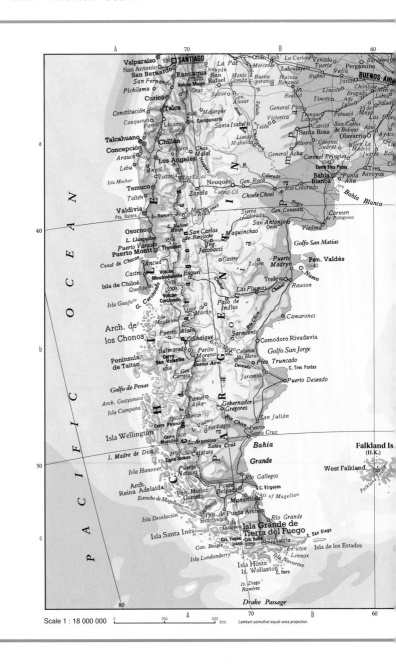

Scale 1 : 18 000 000

0   250   500 km

Lambert azimuthal equal-area projection

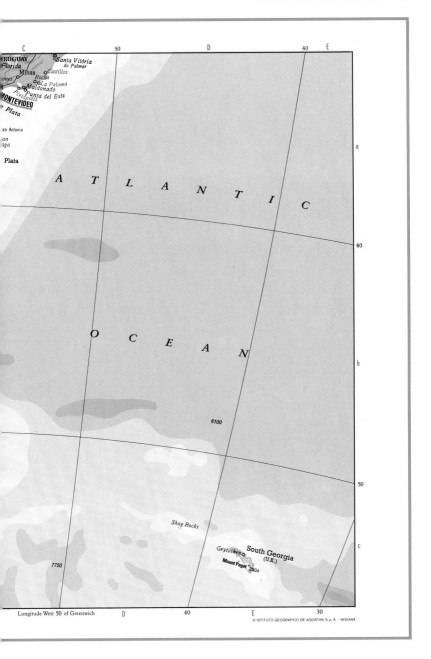

URUGUAY
Florida
Santa Vitória
do Palmar
Minas
Castillos
Rocha
La Paloma
Maldonado
Punta del Este
Piriápolis
MONTEVIDEO
Plata

an Antonio
aga

Plata

A T L A N T I C

O C E A N

6100

Shag Rocks

Grytviken
Mount Paget 2934
South Georgia
(U.K.)

7750

Longitude West 50 of Greenwich

© ISTITUTO GEOGRAFICO DE AGOSTINI S. p. A. - NOVARA

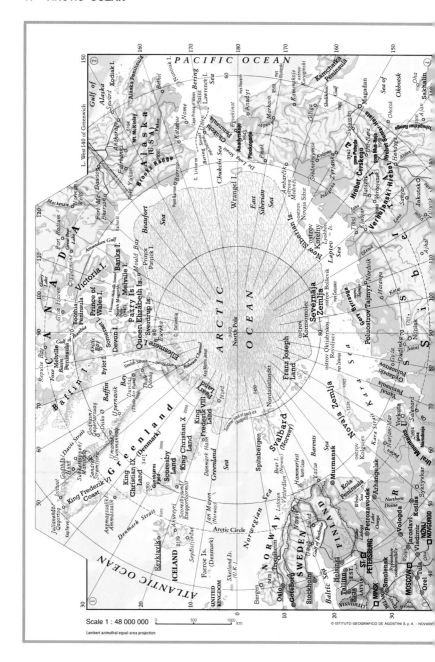

Scale 1 : 48 000 000

Lambert azimuthal equal-area projection

0   500   1000 km

© ISTITUTO GEOGRAFICO DE AGOSTINI S.p.A. - NOVARA

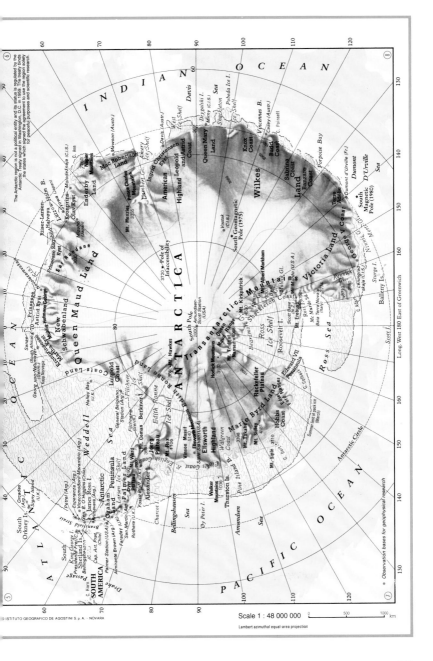

Scale 1 : 48 000 000

Lambert azimuthal equal-area projection

© ISTITUTO GEOGRAFICO DE AGOSTINI S.p.A. - NOVARA

* Observation bases for geophysical research

INDEX

All the names shown on the maps are only listed once in the index and normally, the reference given is to the principle map on which they appear.

The individual maps in numerical order are divided by the lines of the meridian and the parallels into grid squares marked from left to right with upper case letters and from top to bottom with lower case letters.

The names which refer to the map inserts are followed by the words "map no."; those refering to the maps of the polar region are followed by the words "grid square no.".

The names referred to on The World Political map are followed only by the number of the map.

In general, names are listed in the index in full even if they are abbreviated on the maps.

All the names are listed in alphabetical order according to their international form, not taking into account any diacritic letter forms (e.g. ā, æ, ö, œ, ū, etc.).

Physical features composed of a proper name and a description are listed alphabetically by the proper name, followed by the description.

To ease understanding for physical features and administrative divisions, an abbreviation of the type of feature is shown in brackets in the index after its name.

In the case of two places with the same name, the political identity is shown in square brackets.

Abbreviations used in the index

at.	atoll
Aut. Reg.	Autonomous Region
Aut. Rep.	Autonomous Republic
b.	bay
c.	cave
can.	canal
cap.	cape
co.	County
Dep.	Dependency, Colony
des.	desert
g.	gulf
gl.	glacier
hist. reg.	historical region
i.	island
Ind. St.	Independent State
is.	islands
l.	lake
lag.	lagoon
mt.	mountain
mts.	mountains
p.	pass
pen.	peninsula
phys. reg.	physical region
plat.	plateau, upland
prov.	Province
r.	ruins
reg.	Region
res.	reservoir
rf.	reef
riv.	river
riv. m.	river mouth
sal. l.	salt lake
sc. stat.	scientific station
s. m.	salt marsh
str.	strait
sw.	swamp, marsh
v.	valley
volc.	volcano
w.	wadi
wf.	waterfall

© ISTITUTO GEOGRAFICO DE AGOSTINI - Novara

Ak.-U.S.	Alaska, U.S.	I.C.	Ivory Coast	Nor.	Norway
Al.-U.S.	Alabama, U.S.	Id.-U.S.	Idaho, U.S.	Nv.-U.S.	Nevada, U.S.
Alta.-Can.	Alberta, Canada	Il.-U.S.	Illinois, U.S.	N.Y.-U.S.	New York, U.S.
Ant.	Antarctica	In.-U.S.	Indiana, U.S.	N.Z.	New Zealand
Ar.-U.S.	Arkansas, U.S.	Indon.	Indonesia	Oh.-U.S.	Ohio, U.S.
Arg.	Argentina	Ire.	Ireland	Ont.-Can.	Ontario, Canada
Atg.	Antigua and Barbuda	It.	Italy	Or.-U.S.	Oregon, U.S.
Aus.	Austria	Jam.	Jamaica	Pa.-U.S.	Pennsylvania, U.S.
Austl.	Australia	Jap.	Japan	Pak.	Pakistan
Az.-U.S.	Arizona, U.S.	Jor.	Jordan	Pan.	Panama
Bah.	Bahamas	Kaz.	Kazakhstan	Par.	Paraguay
Bel.	Belgium	Ky.-U.S.	Kentucky, U.S.	Phil.	Philippines
Bela.	Belarus	Kyrg.	Kyrgyzstan	Pol.	Poland
Bngl.	Bangladesh	La.-U.S.	Louisiana, U.S.	Port.	Portugal
Bol.	Bolivia	Lbr.	Liberia	Reu.	Reunion
Braz.	Brazil	Leb.	Lebanon	Rom.	Romania
Bul.	Bulgaria	Lib.	Libya	S. Afr.	South Africa
Ca.-U.S.	California, U.S.	Ma.-U.S.	Massachusetts, U.S.	S. Amer.	South America
Can.	Canada	Mala.	Malaysia	S.C.-U.S.	South Carolina, U.S.
C.A.R.	Central African Republic	Me.-U.S.	Maine, U.S.		
Cay. Is.	Cayman Islands	Mex.	Mexico	Scot.-U.K.	Scotland, U.K.
Co.-U.S.	Colorado, U.S.	Mi.-U.S.	Michigan, U.S.	S.D.-U.S.	South Dakota, U.S.
Col.	Colombia	Mn.-U.S.	Minnesota, U.S.		
C.R.	Costa Rica	Mo.-U.S.	Missouri, U.S.	Sp.	Spain
Cyp.	Cyprus	Mold.	Moldova	Sud.	Sudan
Czech Rep.	Czech Republic	Moz.	Mozambique	Sur.	Suriname
De.-U.S.	Delaware, U.S.	Ms.-U.S.	Mississippi, U.S.	Swe.	Sweden
Dom. Rep.	Dominican Republic	Mt.-U.S.	Montana, U.S.	Tn.-U.S.	Tennessee, U.S.
		Mtna.	Mauritania	Trin.	Trinidad and Tobago
Ec.	Ecuador	Mya.	Myanmar (Burma)		
Eg.	Egypt	N. Amer.	North America	Tun.	Tunisia
El Sal.	El Salvador	Nb.-U.S.	Nebraska, U.S.	Tur.	Turkey
Eng.-U.K.	England, U.K.	N.B.-Can.	New Brunswick, Canada	Tx.-U.S.	Texas, U.S.
Eth.	Ethiopia			U.K.	United Kingdom
Fl.-U.S.	Florida, U.S.	N.C.-U.S.	North Carolina, U.S.	Ukr.	Ukraine
Fr.	France			Ur.	Uruguay
Fr. Gui.	French Guiana	N.D.-U.S.	North Dakota, U.S.	U.S.	United States
Fr. Poly.	French Polynesia	Nep.	Nepal	Va.-U.S.	Virginia, U.S.
Ga.-U.S.	Georgia, U.S.	Neth.	Netherlands	Ven.	Venezuela
Ger.	Germany	Newf.-Can.	Newfoundland, Canada	Vt.-U.S.	Vermont, U.S.
Grc.	Greece			Wa.-U.S.	Washington, U.S.
Guat.	Guatemala	N.H.-U.S.	New Hampshire, U.S.		
Hi.-U.S.	Hawaii, U.S.	Nic.	Nicaragua	Wi.-U.S.	Wisconsin, U.S.
H.K.	Hong Kong	Nig.	Nigeria	W.V.-U.S.	West Virginia, U.S.
Hond.	Honduras	N.Ire.-U.K.	Northern Ireland, U.K.	Wy.-U.S.	Wyoming, U.S.
Ia.-U.S.	Iowa, U.S.	N.M.-U.S.	New Mexico, U.S.	Yugo.	Yugoslavia
				Zimb.	Zimbabwe

A

Aachen 5 Ac
Aaiún, El– 24 Ab
Aalen 5 Cd
Aalst 8 EFb
Äänekoski 4 Fc
Aansaríyé, Gebel– (mt.) 22 Fe
Aarau 5 Be
Aasiaat / Egedesminde 31 JKb
Aba 24 Cd
Abaco Island 32 Dc
Ābādān 21 Dc
Abādeh 21 Ec
Abaetetuba 38 Cb
Abagnar Qi 16 DEb
Abai 39 Cb
Abakan 14 BCd
Abalakova 14 Cd
Abancay 37 Bd
Abano Terme 10 Cb
Abarqu 21 Ec
Abashiri 16 Jb
Abaya, Lake– 25 Dd
Abaza 14 BCd
Abbeville 8 Db
Abbottabad 20 Db
Abd al Kuri (i.) 21 Eg
Abdulino 12 Hc
Abéché 25 Cc
Abemama Atoll 27 Db
Abengourou 24 Bd
Ábenrå 5 Ba
Abeokuta 24 Cd
Abercorn → Mbala 26 Cb
Aberdeen [S.D.–U.S.] 32 Ba
Aberdeen [U.K.] 7 EFc
Aberdeen [Wa.–U.S.] 33 Ab
Aberystwyth 7 De
Abez 13 Fc
Abha 21 Cf
Abidjan 24 Bd
Abilene 33 CDc
Abitibi Lake 32 Ca
Abkhasia (Aut. Rep.) 13 De
Abminga 29 EFd
Abnûb 25 Db
Aboisso 24 Bd
Abomey 24 Cd
Abou Deïa 25 BCc
Abrántes 9 ABc
Abruzzo (reg.) 10 DEcd
Absaroka Range 33 BCb
Abu 20 Dd
Abū ʿAlī 21 DEd
Abu Arish 21 Cf
Abu Dhabi 21 Ee
Abu Gharādiq, Bïr– 22 Bgh
Abū Ḩamad 25 Dc
Abuja 24 Cd
Abū Kamāl 21 Cc
Abū Madd, Raʾs– 21 Be
Abu Musa (i.) 21 EFd
Abuná (riv.) 37 Ccd
Abuná 37 Cc
Abū Qïr 22 BCg
Abu Simbel (r.) 25 CDb
Abu Sultân 25 map no.1
Abū Zanïmah 21 Ad
Acajutla 35 ABb

Acámbaro 34 Bbc
Acaponeta 34 Bb
Acapulco de Juárez 30 Hlh
Acaraí, Serra– (mts.) 38 Ba
Acaraú 38 CDb
Acarigua 37 Cb
Accra 24 BCd
Achacachi 39 Ba
Achill Island 7 ABe
Acıgöl 22 BCd
Ačinsk 14 Cd
Acireale 10 Ef
Acklins Island 35 Ca
Aconcagua, Cerro– (mt.) 39 ABc
Acqui Terme 10 Bb
Acre 39 Ba
Acre (State) 37 BCc
Acri 10 Fe
Acsu (riv.) 22 Cd
Açu 38 Db
Ada 24 Cd
Adabïya 25 map no.1
Adalar (is.) 11 Hc
Adama 25 DEd
Adamawa 24 Dd
Adamello (mt.) 10 Ca
Adams, Mount– 33 Ab
Adamstown 28 Cd
Adana 22 Ed
Adapazarı 22 Cb
Adare, Cape– 42 grid square no.4
Adavale 29 GHd
Adda (riv.) 10 Bb
Ad Dirʿïyah 21 De
Addis Ababa 25 Dd
Adelaide 29 FGef
Adelaide River 29 Ea
Adele Island 29 Cb
Adélie, Terre– 42 grid square no.4
Aden 21 Dg
Aden, Gulf of– 25 EFc
Adige (riv.) 10 Ca
Adigrat 25 DEc
Adīrī 24 Db
Adirnaz (riv.) 22 Bc
Adi Ugri 21 Bg
Adıyaman 22 FGd
Admiralty (i.) 31 Bc
Admiralty Gulf 29 CDa
Admiralty Islands 27 Cc
Adonara, Pulau– (i.) 18 Ff
Adoni 20 Ee
Adour (riv.) 8 Cf
Adra [India] 19 Ik
Adra [Sp.] 9 Dd
Adrar 22 Bb
Adrar (mt.) 24 Db
Adrar, Dhar– (mts.) 24 Ab
Adré 25 Cc
Adria 10 Db
Adriatic Sea 10 Ec
Adwa 25 Dc
Adzhar (Aut. Rep.) 13 De
Aegean Sea 11 FGde
Aegina (i.) 11 Ee
Ærø 5 Ca
Afghanistan (Ind. St.) 15 Cf
Afgooye 25 Ed
ʿAfif 21 Ce
Afyonkarahisar 22 Cc

Agadez 24 Cc
Agadir 24 ABab
Agadyr 13 Ge
Agalega Islands 15 BCk
Agaña 27 map no.1
Aga Point (cap.) 27 map no.1
Agartala 19 Bd
Agats 27 Bc
Agboville 24 Bd
Agde 8 Ef
Agen 8 De
Agidyen Atoll 28 map no.3
Aginskoje 14 Ed
Agnew 29 Cd
Agnita 6 Gcd
Agordat 25 Dc
Agout (riv.) 8 DEf
Agra 15 Cg
Agreb, El– 24 Ca
Agrigento 10 Df
Agrinion 11 Dd
Agropoli 10 Ed
Agryz 12 Hb
Aguas Blancas 39 ABb
Aguascalientes 34 Bb
Águilas 9 Ed
Aguja, Punta– (cap.) 37 Ac
Agulhas, Cape– 26 ABe
Agulhas Negras, Pico das– (mt.) 39 Db
Ahaggar (mts.) 24 Cb
Ahar 21 Db
Ahmadabad 15 Cg
Aḩmadï, Al– 21 Dd
Ahmadnagar 20 DEe
Ahmar (hist. reg.) 25 Dc
Ahtopol 11 GHb
Ahtuba (riv.) 13 De
Ahtubinsk 3 Hc
Ahtyrka 12 Ec
Ahuachapán 35 ABb
Ahunui Atoll 28 Bc
Åhus 5 Ea
Ahvāz 21 Dc
Ahvenanmaa / Åland (is.) 4 DEc
Ahwar 21 Dg
Aigoual, Mont– (mt.) 8 Ee
Aigues (riv.) 8 Fe
Aihui 16 Ga
Aim 14 Gd
Aimorés 39 Da
Ain (riv.) 8 Fd
Ainaži 4 EFd
Aïn–Beni Mathar 24 Ba
Aïn–Defla 9 FGd
Aineman Atoll 28 map no.3
Aïn–Sefra 24 BCa
Aïn–Témouchent 24 Ba
Aiquile 39 Ba
Aïr (mt.) 24 Cc
Aitutaki Atoll 28 ABc
Aiud 6 Fc
Aix–en–Provence 8 FGf
Aix–les–Bains 8 FGe
Aiyion 11 Ed
Āizawl 19 Bd
Aizpute 4 Ed
Aizuwakamatsu 16 IJc
Ajaccio 8 map no.1
Ajaccio, Golfe d'– 8 map no.1
Ajaguz 13 GHe
Ajan 14 Gd

Ajanta (r.) 20 Ed
Ajdäbiyä 24 DEa
Ajhal 14 Ec
Ajigasawa 17 FGd
Ajka 6 Cc
ʿAjlūn 22 EFf
Ajmer 20 Dc
Ajon, ostrov– (i.) 14 Jbc
Ajtos 11 Gb
Akademgorodok, Novosibirsk– 13 GHd
Akan 17 Hlc
Akanthoú 22 De
Akapatok Island 31 Ib
Akashi 17 Dg
Akbulak 12 Ic
Akçakoca 22 Cb
Akchar (hist. reg.) 24 Abc
Akdağ [Tur.] (mt.) 22 Bd
Akdağ [Tur.] (mt.) 22 Eb
Akdağ [Tur.] (mt.) 22 BCc
Aketi 25 Cd
Akhḑar, Al Jabal al– (mts.) 24 Ea
Akhdar, Gebel al– (mt.) 21 Fe
Akheloos (riv.) 11 Dd
Akhisar 22 ABc
Aki 17 CDh
Akimiski Island 31 GHc
Akita 16 IJc
Akjoujt 24 Abc
Akkajaure (l.) 4 Cb
Akkeshi 17 Ic
ʿAkko 22 Ef
Akköy 11 Ge
Aklavik 31 Bb
Akmol (Temirtau) 13 Gd
Akobo 25 Dd
Akola 20 Ed
Akranes 4 map no.1
Akritas, Ákra– 11 De
Akron 32 Ca
Akrotiri 22 De
Akrotíri, Kersónisos– 11 Ff
Aksaj 12 Hc
Aksaray 22 DEc
Akşehir 22 Cc
Akşehir Gölü 22 CDc
Akseki 22 CDd
Aksenovo–Zilovskoje 14 Ed
Aksoran, gora– (mt.) 13 Ge
Aksu [China] 15 He
Aksu [Kaz.] 13 Gd
Aktaš 13 Hd
Aktau (Ševčenko) 13 Ec
Aktjubinsk 13 Ede
Aktogaj 13 Ge
Akureyri 4 map no.1
Akyab → Sittwe 19 Bde
Alabama (riv.) 32 Cb
Alabama (State) 32 Cb
Alaca 22 Ed
Alacahan 22 FGc
Alacrán, Arrecife– (rf.) 34 CDb
Ala Dağ (mt.) 22 Dcd
Ala dağları (mts.) 22 Ed
Alagoas (State) 38 Db
Alagoinhas 38 Dc
Alagón 9 Eb
Alagón (riv.) 9 Bbc
Alajuela 35 Bbc

Iakol, ozero– (l.) **13** He
Iakurtti **4** Gb
Iamagan Island **27** Cb
Iamein, El– **22** Bg
Iamogordo **33** Cc
Iamos **34** Bb
Iamos, Los– **33** Cc
Iamosa **33** Cc
Iaska (State) **30** CDc
Iaska, Gulf of– **41** grid
square no.2
Iaska Peninsula **41** grid
square no.2
Iassio **10** Bbc
Iatri **10** Dd
Iatyr **13** Dd
Iavus **4** Ec
Iba **10** Bb
Ibacete **9** DEc
Iba Iulia **6** Fcd
Ibania (Ind. St.) **3** EFc
Ibany (riv.) **31** Db
Ibany [Austl.] **29** Bef
Ibany [Ga.–U.S.] **32** Cb
Ibany [N.Y.–U.S.] **32** Da
Ibany [Or.–U.S.] **33** Ab
Ibardón **39** Bc
Ibarracin, Sierra de– (mts.)
9 Eb
Ibatross Bay **29** Ga
Ibenga **10** Bb
Iberche (riv.) **9** Cb
Ibergaria–a–Velha **9** ABb
Ibert, Lake– **25** Dd
Iberta (prov.) **31** Dc
Ibert Markham, Mount– **42**
grid square no.4
Ibert Nile (riv.) **26** Ca
Ibertville **8** FGe
Ibi **8** Ef
Ibina **37** Db
Ibino **10** Bb
Iborg **4** Bd
Ibufeira **9** Ad
Ibuquerque **33** Cc
Ibuquerque **9** Bc
Ibury **29** Hf
Icalá de Chivert **9** EFb
Icalá de Guadaira **9** Cd
Icalá de Henares **9** Db
Icalá la Real **9** Dd
Icamo **10** Df
Icañiz **9** EFb
Icántara **38** Cb
Icántara **9** Bc
Icaraz, Sierra de– (mts.) **9**
Dc
Icarria, La– (hist. reg.) **9** Db
Icázar de San Juan **9** Dc
Ičeusk **12** EFd
Icira **9** Ec
Icoy **9** Ec
Icudia **9** Gc
Idabra Islands **23** Gf
Idan **14** Fd
Idan (riv.) **14** Gc

Alderney (i.) **8** Bc
Aleg **24** Ac
Alegrete **39** Cb
Alejsk **13** Hd
Aleksandrov **12** EFb
Aleksandrov Gaj **13** DEde
Aleksandrovsk–Sahalinsk **14**
Hd
Aleksandry, Zemlja– **13** CDa
Aleksin **12** Ec
Aleksinac **6** EFe
Alençon **8** Dc
Alenquer **38** Bb
Alentejo (phys. reg.) **9** ABcd
Alenuihaha Channel **28** map
no.1
Aleppo **21** Bb
Aléria **8** map no.1
Alès **8** EFe
Alessandria **10** Bb
Ålesund **4** Ac
Aleutians Islands **30** Bd
Alexander Archipelago **31** Bc
Alexanderbaai **26** Ad
Alexander Island **42** grid
square no.1
Alexandria [Austl.] **29** Fb
Alexandria [Eg.] **25** Ca
Alexandria [La.–U.S.] **32** Bb
Alexandria [Rom.] **6** Gde
Alexandria [S. Afr.] **26** Be
Alexandroúpolis **11** Fc
Alfambra **9** Eb
Alfenas **39** Db
Alföld (phys. reg.) **6** DEc
Alga **12** Id
Algarve (phys. reg.) **9** ABd
Algeciras **9** Cd
Algemesí **9** Ec
Algena **25** Dc
Algeria (Ind. St.) **23** Cbc
Alghero **10** Bd
Algiers **24** Ca
Al Harūj–al Aswad (mts.) **24**
Db
Aliákmōn (riv.) **11** DEcd
Alibunar **6** Ed
Alicante **9** EFc
Alice **32** Bc
Alice, Punta– (cap.) **10** Fe
Alice Springs **29** EFc
Alicudi (i.) **10** Ee
Aligarh **20** Ec
Aliwal North **26** Be
Aljustrel **9** Ad
Alkmaar **8** Fa
Al Kuwait **21** Dd
Allahabad **15** Cg
Allah–Jun **14** GHc
Allariz **9** ABa
Allegheny Mountains **32**
CDab
Allen, Lake– **7** Bd
Allentown **32** Da
Alleppey **20** Eg
Aller (riv.) **5** BCb
Alliance **33** Cb
Allier (riv.) **8** Ee
Alloa **7** DEc
Alluitsup Paa / Sydprøven **31**
Kb
Alma–Ata **13** Ge
Almada **9** Ac

Almadén **9** Cc
Almalyk **13** Fe
Almansa **9** Ec
Almanzor, Pico de– (mts.) **9**
Cb
Almas, Rio das– (riv.) **39** Da
Almazán **9** Db
Almeirim **38** Bb
Almelo **8** Ga
Almenara **39** DEa
Almendralejo **9** BCc
Almería **9** Dd
Almería, Golfo de– **9** DEd
Almetjevsk **12** Hbc
Älmhult **4** Cd
Almirante **35** Bc
Almirante Brown **42** grid
square no.1
Almirós **11** Ed
Almorox **9** Cb
Almuñécar **9** Dd
Alofi **28** Ac
Alonnisos (i.) **11** EFd
Alor, Pulau– (i.) **18** FGf
Álora **9** Cd
Alor Setar **19** CDg
Alpena **32** Ca
Alpes Maritimes **10** Ab
Alpha **29** Hc
Alpi Carniche **10** Da
Alpi Cozie **10** Ab
Alpi Graie **10** Ab
Alpine **33** Cc
Alpi Retiche **10** BCa
Als (i.) **5** Ba
Alsace (hist. reg.) **8** Gcd
Alsasua **9** DEa
Alta **4** Ea
Altafjord (g.) **4** Ea
Alta Gracia **39** Bc
Altagracia **37** Ba
Altaj **14** Ce
Altaj (mts.) **13** Hde
Altamira **38** Bb
Altamura **10** Fd
Altata **34** Bb
Altay **13** He
Altdorf **10** Ba
Altenburg **5** Dc
Altinova **22** Ac
Alto Araguaia **38** Bc
Alton **32** BCb
Altoona **32** Da
Alto Parnaíba **38** Cb
Altos **38** Cb
Altun Shan (mts.) **20** FGb
Altus **33** CDc
Alvand, Kū– e– (mt.) **21** Dc
Alvdalen **4** Cc
Älvkarleby **4** Dc
Älvsbyn **4** Eb
Alwar **20** Ec
Alyangula **29** Fa
Alytus **4** EFe
Alzamaj **14** CDd
Amadeus, Lake– **29** Ecd
Amadi **25** Dd
Amadjuak Lake **31** Hlb
Amador, Fort– **35** map no.1
Amagasaki **16** Hlcd
Amahai **18** Ge
Amakusa–Nada **17** Ah
Amakusa–Shotō **17** Ah

Åmål **4** Cd
Amaliás **11** De
Amami–Shotō (is.) **16** GHe
Amanave **28** map no.5
Amanus Mountains **22** EFd
Amapá (State) **38** Ba
Amapá **38** Ba
'Amārah, Al– **21** Dc
Amarante **38** Cb
Amarillo **33** Cc
Amasra **22** CDb
Amasya **22** EFb
Amatiaurá **37** Cc
Amazon (riv.) **38** Bb
Amazon, Mouths of the– **38**
Ca
Amazonas (State) **37** CDc
Ambala **15** Cf
Ambalavao **26** map no.1
Ambam **24** Dd
Ambarčik **14** Jc
Ambato **37** Bc
Ambatondrazaka **23** GHg
Ambelau, Pulau– (i.) **18** Ge
Amberg **5** CDd
Ambès **8** Ce
Ambikapur **20** Fd
Ambilobe **26** map no.1
Amble **7** Fd
Ambo **37** Bcd
Ambodifototra **26** map no.1
Ambohimahasoa **26** map
no.1
Ambon **18** Ge
Ambositra **26** map no.1
Ambovombe **26** map no.1
Ambre, Cap d'– **23** GHg
Ambriz **26** Ad
Ambriz **23** Ad
Ambrym, Île– (i.) **28** map no.4
Amderma **13** Fbc
American Highland **42** grid
square no.2
American Samoa (is.) **28** map
no.5
Amersfoort **8** FGa
Amery Ice Shelf **42** grid
square no.2
Ames **32** Ba
Amfilokhia **11** Dd
Ámfissa **11** DEd
Amga (riv.) **14** Fd
Amga **14** Gc
Amgu **17** Eb
Amgun (riv.) **14** Gd
Amherst **32** Ea
Amiata, Monte– **10** Cc
Amiens **8** DEc
Amik Gölü **22** Fd
Amīndivi Islands **20** Df
Amirante Islands **15** Bj
'Āmiriyah, Al– **22** Bg
Amlekhganj **19** Ij
'Ammān **22** Fg
Ammassalik / Angmagssalik
30 Oc
Ammersee **5** Cde
Amnok–Kang (riv.) **16** FGb
Amorgós (i.) **11** FGe
Ampanihy **26** map no.1
Amposta **9** Fb
'Amran **21** Cf
Amrāvati **20** Ed
Amritsar **15** Cf

Amroha 20 Ec
Amsterdam 8 Fa
Amsterdam, Île– (i.) 2
Amstetten 5 Ed
Am Timan 25 Cc
Amuay 37 Ba
Amudarja (riv.) 13 Ff
Amundsen Gulf 31 CDab
Amundsen Scott 42 grid square no.2
Amundsen Sea 42 grid square no.3
Amur (riv.) 14 Fd
Amvrakikós, Kólpos– 11 Dd
Anaa Atoll 28 Bc
Anabar 27 map no.2
Anabar (riv.) 14 Eb
Anaco 37 Cb
Anaconda 33 Bb
Anadolu Dağlari 21 ACa
Anadyr (riv.) 14 Kc
Anadyr 14 Kc
Anadyr Gulf 14 Lc
Anadyrskoje Ploskogorje 14 Kc
Anáfi (i.) 11 FGe
'Ánah 21 Cc
Anai Mudi (mt.) 20 Efg
Analalava 26 map no.1
Anambas, Kepulauan– 18 Cd
Anamur 22 Dd
Anamur Burun 22 Dde
Anantapur 20 Ef
Anantnag 20 DEb
Anapa 12 Ee
Anápolis 39 Da
Anapu (riv.) 38 Bb
Anatahan Island 27 Cb
Anatolia (phys. reg.) 22 BFc
Añatuya 39 Bb
Ancenis 8 Cd
Anchorage 30 CDc
Ancona 10 Dc
Ancud 40 Ab
Anda 16 FGa
Andalgalá 39 Bb
Andalsnes 4 ABc
Andalusia (phys. reg.) 9 CDd
Andaman and Nicobar 19 Bfg
Andaman Islands 19 Bf
Andaman Sea 19 Cfg
Andara 26 Bc
Andelys, Les– 8 Dc
Andermatt 10 Ba
Anderson (riv.) 31 Cb
Anderson 32 Cb
Andes 37 Bcd
Andfjorden (g.) 4 CDa
Andhra Pradesh (State) 20 EFe
Andikíthira (i.) 11 Ef
Andíparos (i.) 11 Fe
Andiria Burun 22 Ee
Andirlangar 20 Fa
Andižan 13 Gef
Andkhoy 20 BCa
Andöng 16 Gc
Andorra (Ind. St.) 9 FGa
Andøya (i.) 4 CDa
Andria 10 Fd
Androka 26 map no.1
Ándros (i.) 11 Fe
Andros Island 32 Dc

Androth Island 20 Df
Andruševka 6 Iab
Andújar 9 CDc
Anegada Passage (str.) 35 Db
Aného 24 Cd
Aneto, Pico de– (mt.) 9 Fa
Aney 24 Dc
Aneytioum, Île– (i.) 28 map no.4
Angara (riv.) 14 Dd
Angarsk 14 Dd
Angaur (i.) 27 Bb
Ånge 4 Cc
Angel, Salto– (wf.) 37 Cb
Ángel de la Guarda, Isla– 34 Ab
Ángeles, Los– 39 Ac
Angeles, Los– 33 ABc
Angeles–Hollywood, Los– 33 ABc
Ångelholm 4 BCd
Ångermanälven (riv.) 4 Dbc
Angermünde 5 Db
Angers 8 Cd
Angkor (r.) 19 Df
Anglesey (i.) 7 De
Angmagssalik / Ammassalik 30 Oc
Ango 25 Cd
Angoche 26 CDc
Angol 39 Ac
Angola (Ind. St.) 23 DEg
Angoulême 8 De
Angoumois 8 CDde
Angren 13 Ge
Anguilla (i.) 35 Db
An Hoa 19 Ee
Anhui (prov.) 16 Ed
Anina 6 EFd
Aniva 17 GHa
Aniva, mys– 16 Ja
Aniva, zaliv– 17 Ha
Aniwa, Île– (i.) 28 map no.4
Anjou (hist. reg.) 8 Cd
Anju 16 Gc
Ankang 16 Cd
Ankara 22 Dc
Ankara (riv.) 22 Dbc
Ankaratra 26 map no.1
Ankazoabo 26 map no.1
Anklam 5 Db
Ankober 25 Dcd
An Loc 19 Ef
Ann, Cape– 42 grid square no.2
Anna [Nauru] 27 map no.2
Anna [Russia] 12 EFc
Anna, Pulo– (i.) 27 Bb
Annaba 24 Ca
An Najaf 21 Cc
Annam (phys. reg.) 19 Eef
Anna Point 27 map no.2
Annapolis 32 Db
Annapurna (mt.) 20 Fc
Ann Arbor 32 Cb
An Nāsiriyah 21 Dc
Annecy 8 FGe
Anniston 32 Cb
Annobón (i.) 23 Cf
Annonay 8 Fe
An Nuqub 21 Dfg
Ánō Viánnos 11 Ff

Anpu 16 CDf
Anqing 16 Ed
Anşāb 21 Cd
Ansbach 5 Cd
Anshan 16 Fb
Anshun 16 Ce
Ansongo 24 BCc
Antakya 22 Fd
Antalaha 26 map no.1
Antalya 22 Cd
Antalya Körfezi 22 Cd
Antananarivo (Tananarive) 23 GHgh
Antarctica 42 grid square no.1
Antarctic Peninsula 42 grid square no.1
Antequera 9 Cd
Anti–Atlas (mts.) 24 Bab
Antibes 8 Gf
Antibes, Cap d'– (cap.) 8 Gf
Anticosti, Île d'– (i.) 31 Icd
Antigua (i.) 35 Db
Antigua and Barbuda (Ind. St.) 35 Db
Antigua Guatemala 35 Ab
Antilebanon (mts.) 22 Fef
Antilla 35 Ca
Antioche, Pertuis d'– (str.) 8 Cd
Antipodes Islands 27 DEe
Ántissa 11 Fd
Antofagasta 39 Ab
Antofagasta de la Sierra 39 Bb
Antofalla, Salar de– (s. m.) 39 Bb
Antongil, Baie d'– 26 map no.1
Antsirabe 23 GHgh
Antsiranana 23 GHg
Antsohihy 26 map no.1
Antwerp 8 Fb
An Uaimh / Navan 7 CDe
Anxi 15 Def
Anyang 16 DEc
A'nyêmaqên Shan (mts.) 16 ABcd
Anžero–Sudžensk 13 Hld
Anzio 10 Dd
Anžu, ostrova– 14 GHb
Aoba, Île– (i.) 28 map no.4
Aoga–Shima (i.) 17 Fh
Aomori 16 IJb
Aosta 10 Ab
Aoulef 24 Cc
Apalachicola 32 Cc
Apaporis (riv.) 37 Bbc
Aparri 18 Fa
Apatin 6 Dd
Apatzingán 34 Bc
Api (mt.) 20 Fbc
Apia 28 Ac
Apiaú, Serra do– (mts.) 37 Cb
Apo, Mount– 18 FGc
Apolda 5 Cc
Apollonia 24 Ea
Aporé (riv.) 39 Ca
Apoteri 37 Db
Appalachian Mountains 32 CDab
Appennino Abruzzese 10 Dc
Appennino Calabro 10 Fe

Appennino Ligure 10 Bb
Appennino Lucano 10 EFde
Appennino Tosco–Emiliano 10 Cbc
Appleton 32 BCa
Apucarana 39 Cb
Apure (riv.) 37 Cb
Apurimac (riv.) 37 Bd
Apuseni, Munţii– 6 Fc
'Aqaba 21 Bd
Aqaba, Gulf of– 22 Fh
Aquidauana 39 Cb
Aquila, L'– 10 Dc
'Arab, Baḥr al– (riv.) 25 Ccd
'Arabab, Wādī al– (riv.) 22 E
Arabian Sea 20 BCef
Araç 22 De
Aracaju 38 Dc
Aracati 38 Db
Araçatuba 39 CDb
Aracena, Sierra de– (mts.) 9 Bd
Araçuaí 39 Da
Arad 6 Ec
Arafura Sea 27 Bc
Aragón (phys. reg.) 9 Eab
Aragón (riv.) 9 Ea
Araguacema 38 BCb
Araguaia (riv.) 38 Bc
Araguaiana 39 Ca
Araguari 39 Da
Araguari (riv.) 38 Ba
Araguatins 38 Cb
Araioses 38 Cb
Arak 24 Cb
Arāk 21 DEc
Arakan Yoma 19 Bde
Araks (riv.) 21 Db
Aral Sea 13 EFe
Aralsk 13 Fe
Aramac 29 GHc
Aranda de Duero 9 Db
Aran Island (i.) 7 Bd
Aran Isles 7 ABe
Aranjuez 9 Dbc
Aranyaprathet 19 Df
Araouane 24 Bc
Arapiraca 38 Dc
Araranguá 39 Db
Araras, Serra das– (mts.) 39 Ca
Ararat 29 Gf
Ararat (Büyük Ağri daği) (mt.) 13 De
Arari 38 Cb
Araripe, Chapada do– (mts.) 38 CDb
Araripina 38 CDb
Aras (riv.) 21 Db
Arauca (riv.) 37 Cb
Arauca 37 Bb
Arauco 39 Ac
Arawalli Range 20 Dcd
Araxá 39 Dab
Arba, L'– 9 Gd
Arbaj–Here 14 Dc
Arboga 4 Cd
Arbroath 7 EFc
Arcachon 8 Ce
Arcadia (hist. reg.) 11 DEe
Archidona 9 CDd
Arciz 6 Icd
Arco 10 Cb

rcos de la Frontera **9** BCd
rctic Bay **31** Ga
rda (riv.) **11** Fc
rdabīl **21** Db
rdakān **21** Ec
rdatov **12** Gc
rderin (mt.) **7** BCe
rdestān **21** Ec
rdmore **32** Bb
rdrossan **7** Dd
recibo **35** Db
reia Branca **38** Db
rendal **4** Bd
requipa **39** Aa
révalo **9** Cb
rezzo **10** Cc
rgens (riv.) **8** Gf
rgentat **8** CDc
rgentat **8** Ee
rgenteuil **8** Ec
rgentina (Ind. St.) **36** Dgh
rgentino, Lago– **40** Abc
rgenton–sur–Creuse **8** Dd
rgeş (riv.) **6** GHd
rghandab (riv.) **20** Cb
rgolis, Gulf of– **11** Ee
rgonne (mts.) **8** Fc
rgos **11** Ee
rgostólion **11** Dd
rgun (riv.) **16** Ea
rhangelsk **3** Ha
rhus **4** Bd
riano Irpino **10** Ed
ri Atoll **20** Dh
rica [Chile] **39** Aa
rica [Col.] **37** Bc
rica, Golfo de– **39** Aa
rid, Cape– **29** Ce
riège (riv.) **8** Df
rima **37** Ca
rinos (riv.) **38** Bc
ripuanã (riv.) **37** CDc
ripuanã **37** CDc
riquemes **37** Ccd
rīsh, Al– **25** Da
rish, Wādī al– (riv.) **22** Dgh
rizaro, Salar de– (s. m.) **39** 3b
rizona (State) **33** Bc
rjeplog **4** Db
rjona **37** Bab
rkadak **12** Fc
rkalyk **13** Fde
rkansas (riv.) **33** Cc
rkansas (State) **32** Bb
rkansas City **32** Bb
rklow **7** CDe
rkona, Kap– **5** Da
rkonam **20** EFf
rkticeskoga Instituta, strova– **13** GHb
rlberg (p.) **5** Ce
rles **8** Ef
rlon **8** Fc
rmagh **7** Cd
rmagnac (hist. reg.) **8** Df
rmavir **13** De
rmenia **37** Bb
rmenia (Ind. St.) **13** Def
rmentières **8** Eb
rmidale **29** Ie
rmu (riv.) **17** DEab
rnauti, Akra– **22** CDe

Arnedillo **9** DEa
Arnhem **8** FGb
Arnhem, Cape– **29** Fa
Arnhem Land **29** Ea
Arno (riv.) **10** Cc
Arnøy (i.) **4** DEa
Arnsberg **5** Bc
Arnstadt **5** Cc
Aroa **37** Ca
Aroab **26** ABd
Arorae Island **27** Dc
Ar–Rachidiya **24** Ba
Arrah **20** Fc
Arraias **38** Cc
Arraiján **35** map no.1
Arran, Island of– **7** Dd
Arras **8** Eb
Arrée, Monts d'– (mts.) **8** ABc
Arsenjev **14** Ge
Arsenjevka (riv.) **17** Cbc
Arsuk **31** JKb
Art (i.) **28** map no.4
Árta **11** Dd
Artá **9** Gc
Artawiyah, Al– **21** Dd
Artem **14** Ge
Artemisa **35** Ba
Artemovsk [Russia] **14** Cd
Artemovsk [Ukr.] **12** Ed
Artemovski [Russia] **12** Jb
Artemovski [Russia] **14** Jb
Artic Ocean **41** grid square no.4
Artigas **39** Cc
Artois (hist. reg.) **8** DEb
Aru, Kepulauan– **27** Bc
Arua **26** Ca
Aruanã **39** CDa
Aruba (i.) **37** Ca
Arumã **37** Cc
Arunachal Pradesh (State) **19** BCc
Arusha **26** Cb
Aruwimi (riv.) **26** Ba
Arvida **31** Hd
Arvidsjaur **4** Db
Arvika **4** Cd
Arys **13** Fe
Arzamas **13** Dd
Arzgir **12** Fd
Aša **12** Ib
Asadābād **20** CDab
Asahikawa **16** Jb
Asamankese **24** Bd
Asansol **20** Gd
Asbest **13** Fd
Ascension (i.) **23** Af
Aschaffenburg **5** Bd
Ascó **9** Fb
Ascoli Piceno **10** Dc
Aseb **25** Ec
Åsele **4** Db
Asenovgrad **11** Fbc
Aşgabat (Ašhabad) **15** Bf
Ašhabad → Aşgabat **15** Bf
Ashburton River **29** Bc
Asheville **32** Cb
Ashibetsu **16** Jb
Ashikaga **16** Ic
Ashington **7** EFd
Ashizuri–Misaki **17** Ch
Ashkharah, Al– **21** FGe
Ashland [Ky.–U.S.] **32** Cb

Ashland [Wi.–U.S.] **32** BCa
Ashmūn **22** Cg
Ashqelon **22** Eg
Ashuanipi **31** Ic
Asinara **10** Bd
Asinara, Golfo dell'– **10** Bd
Asino **13** Hd
'Asīr (hist. reg.) **21** Cef
Asker **4** Bd
Askersund **4** Cd
Askja (mt.) **4** map no.1
Asmara **25** Dc
Asnam, El– **24** BCa
Asosa **25** Dcd
Aso–San (mt.) **17** Bh
Asoteriba, Jabal– (mt.) **25** Db
Aspres–sur–Buëch **8** Fe
Aspromonte (mts.) **10** Ee
Assam (State) **19** BCc
Assen **8** Ga
Assens **5** BCa
Assiniboia **33** Cb
Assiniboine (riv.) **33** Cab
Assis **39** Cb
Assisi **10** Dc
Astakós **11** Dd
Astara **21** Db
Asti **10** Bb
Astipálata (i.) **11** Ge
Astorga **9** BCa
Astoria **33** Ab
Astrahan **13** De
Asturias (phys. reg.) **9** BCa
Asunción **39** Cb
Asunción, La– **37** Ca
Aswān **25** Db
Asyût **25** CDb
Atacama, Desierto de– **39** ABb
Atacama, Salar de– (sal. l.) **39** Bb
Atafu Atoll **28** Ac
Ata Island **28** Ad
Atakpamé **24** Cd
Atalándi **11** Ed
Atalaya **37** Bc
Atami **17** Fg
Ataqa, Jabal– (mt.) **25** map no.1
Atar **24** Abc
Atasu **13** Ge
Atauat, Phou– (mt.) **19** Ee
Atauro, Pulau– (i.) **18** Gf
Atáviros (mt.) **11** GHe
'Aţbarah **25** Dc
'Aţbarah (riv.) **25** Dc
Atbasar **13** Fd
Atchinson **32** Bb
Aterau (Gurjev) **13** DEe
Athabasca (riv.) **31** Dc
Athabasca **31** Dc
Athabasca, Lake– **31** Ec
Athenry **7** Be
Athens [Ga.–U.S.] **32** Cb
Athens [Grc.] **11** EFe
Atherton **29** GHb
Athi Galana **26** Cb
Athlone **7** BCe
Áthos (mt.) **11** Fc
Ati **25** Ec
Atico **39** Aa
Atikokan **32** Ba

Atiu (i.) **28** Bcd
Atka **14** Ic
Atkarsk **12** FGc
Atlanta **32** Cb
Atlantic City **32** Db
Atlantic Ocean **2**
Atlin, Lake– **31** Bc
Atlixco **34** Cc
Atoyac, Río– (riv.) **34** Cc
Atoyac de Álvarez **34** Bc
Atrato (riv.) **37** Bb
Atrek (riv.) **21** Fb
'Aţrun, Al– **25** Cc
Atsumi **17** Fe
Attapu **19** Eef
Attawapiskat (riv.) **31** Db
Attica (hist. reg.) **11** Ed
Atuel (riv.) **39** Bc
Aubagne **8** FGf
Aube (riv.) **8** Fc
Aubenas **8** Fe
Aubrac, Monts d'– (mts.) **8** Ee
Aubusson **8** Ee
Aucanquilcha, Cerro– (mt.) **39** Bb
Auch **8** Df
Auckland **27** Dd
Auckland Islands **27** De
Auckland Peninsula **27** Dd
Aude (riv.) **8** Ef
Audincourt **8** Gd
Aue **5** Dc
Augathella **29** Hd
Augila **24** Eb
Augsburg **5** Cd
Augusta [Austl.] **29** ABe
Augusta [Ga.–U.S.] **32** Cb
Augusta [It.] **10** Ef
Augusta [Me.–U.S.] **32** Ea
Augustów **5** Ib
Augustus, Mount– **29** Bc
Auki **27** Dc
Auld, Lake– **29** Cc
Aumale **8** Dc
Aunis (hist. reg.) **8** Cd
Aurangabad **20** DEde
Aur Atoll **27** Db
Aurillac **8** Ee
Aus **26** Ad
Ausangate, Nudo– (mt.) **39** ABa
Austin [Mn.–U.S.] **32** Ba
Austin [Nv.–U.S.] **33** Bc
Austin [Tx.–U.S.] **32** Bb
Austin, Lake– **29** Bd
Australia (Ind. St.) **29** CGd
Australian Alps **29** Hf
Australian Capital Territory (State) **29** Hf
Australian Capital Territory → A.C.T. **29** Hf
Austria (Ind. St.) **3** Ec
Austvågøy (i.) **4** Ca
Autlán de Navarro **34** Bc
Autun **8** EFd
Auvergne (hist. reg.) **8** Ee
Auxerre **8** Ee
Avallon **8** Ed
Avalon Peninsula **31** JKd
Avanos **22** Ec
Avarua **28** Bd
Aveiro **9** Ab
Avellino **10** Ed

Aves, Isla de– (i.) **35** Db
Avesta **4** Dc
Aveyron (riv.) **8** Def
Avezzano **10** Dc
Avignon **8** Ff
Ávila **9** Cb
Avilés **9** BCa
Avlağı **22** Eb
Avola **10** Ef
Avon (i.) **27** Ccd
Avon (riv.) **7** EFe
Avranches **8** Cc
Awaji–Shima **17** Dg
Awash **25** DEd
Awash (riv.) **25** Ecd
Awa–Shima (i.) **17** Fe
Awbārī **24** Db
Awdheegle **25** Ed
Ax–les–Thermes **8** DEf
Axum **25** Dc
Ayacucho [Arg.] **39** Cc
Ayacucho [Peru] **37** Bd
Ayakkum Hu (l.) **16** Dc
Ayamonte **9** Bd
Ayancık **22** Eab
Ayapel **37** Bb
Ayaviri **39** Aa
Aydın **22** Ad
Aydıncık **22** Dde
Ayers Rock **27** Bd
Ayiá **11** Ed
Áyion Óros (pen.) **11** Fc
Áyios Evstrátios (i.) **11** Fd
Áyios Yeóryios (i.) **11** EFe
Aylesbury **7** Fef
Aylmer Lake **31** Eb
'Ayoûn el 'Atroûs **24** Bc
Ayr [Austl.] **29** Hb
Ayr [U.K.] **7** Dd
Aysha **25** Ec
Ayutthaya **19** CDf
Ayvacık **11** Gd
Ayvalık **22** Ac
Azamgarh **19** Hj
A'zamīyah, Al– **21** Cc
Azaouad (phys. reg.) **24** Bbc
Azaouak **24** Cc
A'zāz **22** Fd
Azerbaijan (Ind. St.) **13** Def
Azerbaijan (phys. reg.) **21** Dab
Azogues **37** Bc
Azores (is.) **2**
Azov **3** Gc
Azov, Sea of– **13** Ce
Azua de Compostela **35** CDb
Azuaga **9** Cc
Azuero, Peninsula de– (pen.) **35** BCc
Azul **39** BCc
Azur, Côte d'– (coast) **8** Gf
Az Zāb Al Kabīr (riv.) **21** Cb
Az Zāb aş Saghīr (riv.) **21** Cb
Az Zuwaytīnah **24** DEa

B

Baardheere **25** Ed
Bāb, Al– **22** Fe
Baba Burun **22** Ac
Babadag **6** Id

Babaeski **11** Gc
Babahoyo **37** ABc
Babajevo **12** Eb
Bab al Mandab (str.) **25** Ec
Babanūsah **25** Cc
Babar, Pulau– (i.) **18** GHf
Babelthuap (i.) **27** Bb
Bābol **21** Eb
Babuškin **14** Dd
Babuyan (i.) **18** Fa
Babuyan Channel **18** Fa
Babuyan Islands **15** Eh
Babylon (r.) **21** Cc
Bacabal **38** Cb
Bacan, Pulau– (is.) **18** Ge
Bacău **6** Hc
Bačka (phys. reg.) **6** Dd
Bačka Palanka **6** Dd
Bačka Topola **6** DEd
Back River **31** Fb
Bacolod **18** Fb
Badajoz **9** Bc
Badalona **9** Gb
Badampahar **19** Ik
Badanah **21** Cc
Bad Ems **5** ABc
Baden **5** Fd
Baden–Baden **5** ABd
Baden–Württemberg (State) **5** BCd
Badgastein **5** De
Bad Hersfeld **5** Bc
Bad Ischl **5** DEe
Bad Kissingen **5** Cc
Bad Kreuznach **5** ABd
Bad Mergentheim **5** BCd
Bad Reichenhall **5** De
Badr Hunayn **21** BCe
Bad Tölz **5** Ce
Badulla **20** Fg
Bad Wildungen **5** Bc
Baena **9** Cd
Bærun **4** Bcd
Baeza **9** Dcd
Baffin Bay **41** grid square no.1
Baffin Island **31** Glab
Bafia **24** Dd
Bafing (riv.) **24** Ac
Bafoulabé **24** ABc
Bāfq **21** Fc
Bafra **22** EFb
Bafra Burun **22** EFb
Bāft **21** Fd
Bafwasende **25** Cd
Bagamoyo **26** CDb
Bagan Siapiapi **18** Bd
Bagdarin **14** Ed
Bagé **39** Cc
Baghdad **21** CDc
Bagheria **10** De
Baghlan **20** Ca
Bagnères–de–Bigorre **8** Df
Bagnères–de–Luchon **8** Df
Bagnols–sur–Cèze **8** Fe
Bagrationovsk **5** Ha
Baguıo **18** Fa
Bagur, Cabo– (cap.) **9** Gab
Bahamas (Ind. St.) **32** Dc
Baharampur **20** Gd
Bahariya Oasis **25** Cb
Bahawalpur **20** Dc
Bahia (State) **38** Cc

Bahía, Islas de la– (is.) **35** Bb
Bahía Blanca **39** Bc
Bahía de Caráquez **37** Ac
Bahía Grande (b.) **40** Bc
Bahía Negra **39** Cb
Bahmač **12** Dc
Bahraich **20** Fc
Bahrain (Ind. St.) **21** Ed
Baía dos Tigres **26** Ac
Baia Mare **6** Fc
Baião **38** Cb
Baia Sprie **6** FGc
Baïbokoum **25** Bd
Baicheng **16** Fa
Baidoa **25** Ed
Baie–Comeau **31** HIcd
Baikal, Lake– **14** Dd
Baile Átha Cliath → Dublin **7** CDe
Băileşti **6** Fd
Bailong Jiang (riv.) **16** Cd
Bailundo **26** Ac
Bä'ir **22** Fg
Bairiki **27** Db
Bairin Zuoqi **16** Eb
Bairnsdale **29** Hf
Baïse (riv.) **8** Df
Baitadi **19** Hi
Baja **6** Dc
Baja California (pen.) **30** Gfg
Bäjah **10** Bf
Bajan–Hongor **14** CDe
Bajčunas **12** Hd
Bajkal **14** Dd
Bajkonur → Bajkonyr **13** Fe
Bajkonyr (Bajkonur) **13** Fe
Bajmak **12** Ic
Bajo Nuevo (i.) **35** Cb
Bajram–Ali **13** Ff
Bakal **12** Ic
Baker **33** Bc
Baker Island **28** Abc
Baker Lake **31** GHb
Bakersfield **33** Cc
Bakır (riv.) **11** Gd
Bako **25** Dd
Bakony Mountains **6** CDc
Bak Tegän, Daryācheh–ye– **21** Ed
Baku **13** DEef
Bala, Cerros de– (mt.) **38** Ac
Balabac (i.) **18** Ec
Balabac Strait **18** Ec
Ba'labakk **22** EFef
Balabálagan, Kepulauan– **18** Ee
Balaghat **20** Fd
Balaklava **12** De
Balakleja **12** Ed
Balakovo **13** DEd
Balambangam Pulau (i.) **18** Ec
Balašov **12** Fd
Balaton, Lake– **6** CDc
Balboa Heights **35** Cc
Balcarce **39** Cc
Balčik **11** GHb
Balearic Islands **9** FGbc
Balej **14** Ed
Bäleshuar **20** Gd
Balḩāf **21** Dg
Balhaš **13** Ge
Bali, Pulau– (i.) **18** Ef

Bali, Selat– **18** Df
Balıkesir **22** Ac
Balikpapan **15** Dj
Bali Sea **18** DEf
Balkan Mountains **11** Eb
Balkans, Little– (mts.) **11** Gb
Balkhash, Lake– **13** Ge
Balladonia **29** Ce
Ballah, El– **25** map no.1
Ballarat **29** Gf
Ballater **7** Ec
Balleny Islands **42** grid square no.4
Ballia **20** Fc
Ballina [Austl.] **29** Id
Ballina [Ire.] **7** Bd
Ballon d'Alsace (mt.) **8** Gd
Ball's Pyramid (i.) **27** CDd
Ballymena **7** CDd
Balmaceda **40** Ab
Balonne River **29** Hd
Balrampur **19** Hj
Balranald **29** Ge
Balş **6** Gd
Balsas **38** Cb
Balsas, Río– (riv.) **34** BCc
Balta **6** Ibc
Baltasar Brum **39** Cc
Baltasound **7** Fa
Baltic Sea **4** DEde
Baltijsk **5** Ga
Balţīm **22** Cg
Baltimore **32** Db
Baltit **20** Da
Baluchistān (phys. reg.) **21** FGd
Balygyčan **14** Ic
Balykši **12** Hd
Bam **21** Fd
Bamako **24** Bc
Bamba **24** Bc
Bambamarca **37** Bc
Bambari **25** Cd
Bamberg **5** Ccd
Bamenda **24** CDd
Bämiān **20** Cab
Bampur (riv.) **21** FGd
Bampur **21** FGd
Banaadir (phys. reg.) **25** Ed
Banalia **25** Cd
Bananal, Ilha do– (i.) **38** BCc
Banas (riv.) **20** DEc
Banâs, Ra's– **25** Db
Banat (phys. reg.) **6** Ed
Banaz (riv.) **22** Bc
Ban Ban **19** De
Banco, El– **37** Bb
Banda **19** Hj
Banda, Kepulauan– **18** GHe
Banda, La– **39** Bb
Banda Aceh **18** ABc
Bandama (riv.) **24** Bcd
Bandanaira **18** GHe
Bandar–Abbās **21** Fd
Bandar–e–Anzali **21** DEb
Bandar–e Khomeynī **21** DE
Bandar–e–Langeh **21** EFd
Bandar–e–Torkamam **21** EF
Bandar Seri Begawan **15** Di
Banda Sea **18** FGef
Bandeira, Pico da– (mt.) **39** Db
Bandeirantes **38** BCc

Bandiagara 24 Bc
Bandikui 19 Gi
Bandırma 22 ABb
Bandundu 26 Ab
Bandundu (reg.) 26 ABb
Bandung 15 Dj
Băneasa 6 Hd
Banes 35 Ca
Bañeza, La– 9 BCa
Banff [Can.] 31 Dc
Banff [U.K.] 7 Ec
Bangalore 15 Ch
Bangassou 25 Cd
Banggai (i.) 18 Fe
Banggai, Kepulauan– 18 Fe
Banggi, Pulau– (i.) 18 Ec
Bangil 18 Df
Bangka, Pulau– [Indon.] (i.)
    18 FGd
Bangka, Pulau– [Indon.] (i.)
    18 Ce
Bangkalan 18 Df
Bangkinang 18 ABd
Bangko 18 Be
Bangkok 15 Dh
Bangladesh (Ind. St.) 15 CDg
Bangor [N. Ire.–U.K.] 7 Dd
Bangor [U.S.] 32 DEa
Bangor [Wales–U.K.] 7 DEe
Bangriposi 19 Ik
Bangued 18 Fa
Bangui [C.A.R.] 25 Bd
Bangui [Phil.] 18 EFa
Bangweulu, Lake– 26 BCc
Banhã 22 Cg
Bani (riv.) 24 Bc
Bani Suwayf 25 Db
Banī Walīd 24 Da
Bāniyās 22 EFe
Banja Luka 6 Cd
Banjarmasin 18 De
Banjul 24 Ac
Banks, Îles– 28 map no.4
Banks Island 31 CDa
Banks Strait 29 map no.1
Bankura 20 Gd
Ban Mae Sariang 19 Ce
Bann (riv.) 7 Cd
Bannu 20 CDb
Banská Bystrica 5 GHd
Banská Stiavnica 5 Gd
Bansko 11 Ec
Bantaeng 18 Ef
Bantry 7 Bf
Bantry Bay 7 ABf
Banyak Islands 18 Ad
Banyuwangi 18 Df
Banzare Coast 42 grid square
    no.4
Bao'an 16 Df
Baoding 16 DEc
Baoji 15 Df
Baoshan 19 Ccd
Baotou 16 CDb
Baquedano 39 Bb
Bar [Ukr.] 6 Hb
Bar [Yugo.] 11 Cb
Baraawe 25 Ed
Barabinsk 13 GHd
Baracaldo 9 Da
Baracoa 35 Ca
Baradero 39 BCc
Bărăganului, Cîmpia– 6 Hd

Barahona 35 Cb
Baraka (riv.) 25 Dc
Baraki 20 Cb
Baramula 20 DEb
Baranof Island 31 Bc
Baranoviči 13 Bd
Barat Daya, Kepulauan– 18
    Gf
Barbacena 39 Db
Barbacoas 37 Bb
Barbados (i.) 35 Db
Barbados (Ind. St.) 30 Lh
Barbar 25 Dc
Barbas, Cabo– 24 Ab
Barbastro 9 Fa
Barbezieux 8 CDe
Barbuda (i.) 35 Db
Barcaldine 29 GHc
Barce → Al Marj 24 DEa
Barcellona 10 Ee
Barcelona [Sp.] 9 Gb
Barcelona [Ven.] 37 Cab
Barcelonnette 8 FGe
Barcelos [Braz.] 37 Cc
Barcelos [Port.] 9 Ab
Barcoo River 29 Gcd
Barcs 6 Ccd
Bardaï 25 Bb
Bardawīl, Sabkhet el– (l.) 22
    Dg
Bardejov 5 Hd
Bardīyah 24 Ea
Bareeda 25 Fc
Bareilly 20 EFc
Barentsburg 13 Ab
Barents Sea 41 grid square
    no.3
Barentù 21 Bfg
Barfleur, Pointe de– (cap.) 8
    Cc
Barga 20 Fb
Barhi 20 Gd
Bari 10 Fd
Barīm 25 Ec
Barima (riv.) 37 Db
Baripada 19 Ik
Barisal 20 GHd
Barisan, Pegunungan– 18 Be
Barito (riv.) 18 Df
Barka 21 Fe
Barkam 16 Bd
Barkly Tableland 29 Fb
Barkol 14 Cf
Barla dağı (mt.) 22 Ccd
Bar–le–Duc 8 Fc
Barlee, Lake– 29 Bd
Barletta 10 Fd
Barmer 20 Dc
Barnaul 13 Hd
Barnstaple 7 Df
Baro 24 Cd
Barqah al Bahrīyah (phys.
    reg.) 24 Ea
Barquisimeto 37 BCab
Barra 38 Cc
Barra (is.) 7 BCc
Barrackpur 19 Jk
Barra de Navidad 34 Bc
Barra do Bugres 39 Ca
Barra do Garças 39 Ca
Barra do São Manuel 38 Bb
Barra Head 7 BCc

Barrancabermeja 37 Bb
Barrancas 37 Cb
Barranquilla 36 Cb
Barreiras 38 Cc
Barreiro 9 Ac
Barreiros 38 Db
Barretos 39 Db
Barrie 31 GHd
Barrington Tops (mt.) 29 Ie
Barrow 30 CDb
Barrow (riv.) 7 Ce
Barrow, Point– 41 grid square
    no.2
Barrow Creek 29 Ec
Barrow–in–Furness 7 Ed
Barrow Island 29 ABc
Barruecopardo 9 Bb
Barry 7 Ef
Barsi 20 Ee
Barstow 33 Bc
Bar–sur–Aube 8 Fc
Barth 5 Da
Bartica 37 Db
Bartin 22 Db
Bartle Frere, Mount– 29 Hb
Bartoszyce 5 Ha
Barun–Urt 14 Ee
Barwon River 29 Hde
Baryš 12 Gc
Basankusu 25 BCd
Basel 5 Ae
Bashi Haixia (str.) 16 Ff
Bashkir (Aut. Rep.) 13 Ed
Basilan (i.) 18 Fc
Basilan City 18 Fc
Basilicata (reg.) 10 EFde
Basilio 39 Cc
Basoko 25 Cd
Basque Provinces (phys.
    reg.) 9 Da
Basra 21 Dc
Bass, Îlots de– 28 BCd
Bassano del Grappa 10 Cb
Bassein 15 Dh
Basseterre 35 Db
Bass Strait 29 map no.1
Bastak 21 EFd
Basti 19 Hj
Bastia 8 map no.1
Bastogne 8 FGbc
Basuto 26 Bc
Bas Zaïre (reg.) 26 Ab
Bata 24 CCd
Batabanó, Golfo de– 35 Ba
Batagaj 14 Cc
Bataisk 12 EFd
Batak 11 Fc
Batala 20 Eb
Batan (i.) 18 Fa
Batang 15 Df
Batanga 24 Ce
Batangafo 25 Bd
Batangas 18 EFb
Batanghari (riv.) 18 Be
Batan Islands 15 Eg
Batanta, Pulau– (i.) 18 GHe
Batchelor 29 Ea
Bâtdâmbâng 19 Df
Bath 7 Ef
Bathinda 20 Eb
Bathurst [Austl.] 29 He
Bathurst [Can.] 31 Id
Bathurst, Cape– 31 BCa

Bathurst Inlet 31 DEb
Bathurst Island [Austl.] 29 Da
Bathurst Island [Can.] 30 Hlb
Bātin, Wādī al– 21 Dd
Batna 24 Ca
Baton Rouge 32 BCb
Batopilas 34 Bb
Batouri 24 Dd
Batrūn, Al– 22 Ee
Batticaloa 20 Fg
Battle Harbour 30 Md
Battonya 6 Cc
Batu, Kepulauan– 18 Ade
Batudaka, Pulau– (i.) 18 Fe
Batumi 21 Ca
Baturaja 18 BCe
Baturité 38 Db
Bau 18 Dd
Baubau 18 Ff
Bauchi 24 CDcd
Baudh 16 Cf
Bauld, Cape– 31 Jc
Baule–Escoublac, La– 8 Bd
Bauru 39 Db
Bautzen 5 Ec
Bavaria (State) 5 CDd
Bawean, Pulau– (i.) 18 Df
Bawīţī, Al– 25 CDb
Bayamo 35 Ca
Bayamón 35 Db
Bayana 19 Gj
Bayan Har Shan (mts.) 16
    ABd
Bayan Obo 16 CDb
Bayawan 18 Fc
Baybay 18 FGb
Bayburt 21 Ca
Bay City [Mi.–U.S.] 32 Ca
Bay City [Tx.–U.S.] 32 Bc
Bayḑā', Al– 24 DEa
Bayerischer Wald (mts.) 5 Dd
Bayeux 8 Cc
Bayındır 22 Ac
Bayombong 18 Fa
Bayonne 8 Cf
Bayreuth 5 Ccd
Baza 9 Dd
Beagle, Canal– 40 Ac
Beal Range 29 Gcd
F ardmore Glacier 42 grid
    ͵quare no.4
ear Island 41 grid square
    no.3
Béarn (hist. reg.) 8 Cf
Beas (riv.) 20 DEb
Beatrice 32 Ba
Beatty 33 Bc
Beauce (phys. reg.) 8 DEc
Beaudesert 29 Id
Beaufort 18 Ec
Beaufort Sea 41 grid square
    no.2
Beaufort West 26 Be
Beaujolais, Monts du– (mts.)
    8 Fde
Beaumont 32 Bb
Beaune 8 Fd
Beauvais 8 Ec
Beawar 20 Dc
Bečej 6 Cb
Béchar 24 Ba
Beckley 32 Cb
Bedford 7 FGe

Bedourie **29** Fc
Be'er Sheva **22** Eg
Beeville **32** Bc
Befale **26** Ba
Bega **29** Hlf
Bègles **8** Ce
Behbahán **21** Ec
Behshahr **21** Eb
Beihai **16** Cf
Beijing (Peking) **16** Ebc
Beira (hist. reg.) **9** ABb
Beira **26** Cc
Beirut **22** Ef
Bei Shan (mts.) **16** Ab
Beitbridge **26** Cd
Beiuş **6** EFc
Beja **9** Bcd
Béjaïa **24** Ca
Béjar **9** Cb
Bejneu **13** Ee
Békés **6** Ec
Békéscsaba **6** Ec
Bekily **26** map no.1
Bela [India] **20** Fc
Bela [Pak.] **20** Cc
Bela Crkva **6** Ed
Belaja (riv.) **13** Ed
Belaja Cerkov **6** IJb
Bel'an **16** Ga
Belarus (Ind. St.) **13** BCd
Bela Vista **39** Cb
Bel'c' **13** Be
Belcher Islands **31** GHc
Belebej **12** Hc
Beledweyne **25** Ed
Belém **38** Cb
Belen **33** Cc
Belén **39** Bb
Belene **11** Fb
Bélep, Iles– **27** Dc
Belev **12** Ec
Belfast **7** Dd
Belfort **8** Gd
Belgaum **20** De
Belgium (Ind. St.) **3** Db
Belgorod **13** Cd
Belgorod–Dnestrovski **6** IJc
Belgrade **6** Ed
Belgrade–Zemun **6** Ed
Bélinga **26** Aa
Belitung, Pulau– (i.) **15** Dj
Belize (Ind. St.) **30** Jh
Belize City **35** Bb
Belkovski, ostrov– **14** Gb
Bellac **8** Dd
Bellary **20** Eef
Bellavista **37** Bc
Bella Vista [Arg.] **39** Cb
Bella Vista [Arg.] **39** Bb
Belle Fourche **33** Cb
Bellegarde–sur–Valserine **8** FGde
Belle–Ile (i.) **8** Bd
Belle Isle (i.) **31** Jc
Belle Isle, Strait of– **31** IJcd
Belleville **31** Hd
Bellin (Payne Bay) **31** Hlbc
Bellingham **33** Ab
Bellingshausen **42** grid square no.1
Bellingshausen Sea **42** grid square no.1
Bellinzona **10** Ba

Belluno **10** Da
Bell Ville **39** Bc
Belmonte **38** Dc
Belmopan **35** Bb
Belo **26** map no.1
Belogorsk **14** FGd
Belo Horizonte **39** Dab
Beloje ozero **12** Ea
Belomorsk **13** Cc
Belopolje **12** DEc
Beloreck **13** EFd
Belovo **13** Hd
Belozersk **12** Eab
Belterra **38** Bb
Beluha, gora– (mt.) **13** Hde
Bely, ostrov– **13** FGb
Belyando River **29** Hc
Bely Jar **13** Hd
Bemidji **32** Ba
Benalla **29** Hf
Benares → Varanasi **20** Fcd
Benavente **9** BCab
Benbecula (i.) **7** BCc
Bend **33** Ab
Bender (Bendery) **6** Ic
Bender Beyla **25** Fd
Bendery → Bender **6** Ic
Bendigo **29** GHf
Benešov **5** Ed
Benevento **10** Ed
Bengal (phys. reg.) **20** Gd
Bengal, Bay of– **20** Gef
Bengasi **24** DEa
Bengbu **16** Ed
Bengkulu **18** Be
Benguela **23** Dg
Benguerir **24** Ba
Ben Hope (mt.) **7** Db
Beni (riv.) **37** Cd
Beni–Abbès **24** Bab
Benicarló **9** Fb
Benidorm **9** Fc
Benin (Ind. St.) **23** Cde
Benin, Bight of– **24** Cd
Benin City **24** Cd
Benjamin Constant **37** BCc
Ben Macdhui (mt.) **7** DEc
Ben More Assynt (mt.) **7** Db
Bennet, ostrov– **14** Hb
Ben Nevis (mt.) **7** Dc
Benoni **26** Bd
Bensheim **5** Bd
Benson **33** BCc
Bent **21** Fd
Benteng **18** Ff
Bentinck (i.) **19** Cf
Bentinck Island **29** FGb
Benue (riv.) **24** Cd
Benxi **16** Fb
Beppu **17** Bh
Berati **11** CDc
Berbera **25** Ec
Berberati **25** Bd
Berbice (riv.) **37** Db
Berchtesgaden **5** De
Berck–Plage **8** Db
Berčogur **12** Id
Berdičev **12** Ccd
Berdjansk **12** Ed
Beregomet **6** Gb
Beregovo **5** Id
Berenice (r.) **25** Db
Bereza **5** Jb

Berežany **6** Gb
Berezina (riv.) **12** Cc
Berezniki **13** Ed
Berezovka **12** Dd
Berezovo **13** Fc
Berga **9** Fa
Bergama (Pergamum) **22** Ac
Bergamo **10** Bb
Bergen **4** Ac
Bergen (Rügen) **5** Da
Bergerac **8** De
Berhampur **20** FGe
Beringa, ostrov– **14** Jd
Beringovski **14** Kc
Bering Sea **41** grid square no.2
Bering Strait **41** grid square no.2
Berit daği (mt.) **22** Fcd
Berja **9** Dd
Berkeley **33** Ac
Berkner Island **42** grid square no.1
Berkovica **11** Eb
Berlengas, Ilhas– **9** Ac
Berlin [Ger.] **5** DEb
Berlin [U.S.] **32** Da
Bermejo **39** Bb
Bermejo, Río– [Arg.] (riv.) **39** Bbc
Bermejo, Río– [Bol.] (riv.) **39** Bb
Bermeo **9** Da
Bermuda Islands **30** Lf
Bern **5** Ae
Bernalda **10** Fd
Bernardo de Irigoyen **39** Cb
Bernay **8** Dc
Bernburg **5** CDc
Berner Alpen **10** ABa
Bernina (mt.) **10** Ba
Beroroha **26** map no.1
Beroun **5** Ed
Berounka (riv.) **5** Dcd
Berre, Étang de– (sw.) **8** Ff
Berre–l'Étang **8** Ff
Berrouaghia **9** Gd
Berry (hist. reg.) **8** DEd
Berry, Canal de– **8** Ed
Bertolínia **38** Cb
Bertoua **24** Bd
Berwick–upon–Tweed **7** EFd
Besalampy **26** map no.1
Besançon **8** Gd
Beskidy Zachodnie (mts.) **5** GHd
Besna Kobila (mt.) **11** Eb
Besni **22** Fd
Bessarabia (phys. reg.) **6** Hlbc
Bessarabka **6** Ic
Bessemer **32** Cb
Betanzos [Bol.] **39** Ba
Betanzos [Sp.] **9** ABa
Bétaré Oya **24** Bd
Bethanien **26** Ad
Bethel **30** Bc
Bethlehem [Jor.] **22** Eg
Bethlehem [S. Afr.] **26** Bd
Béticos, Sistema– (mts.) **9** CEcd
Betioky **26** map no.1

Betpak–Dala **13** FGe
Betroka **26** map no.1
Bet She'an **22** Ef
Betsiboka (riv.) **26** map no.1
Bettiah **19** Hlj
Bettyhill **7** Fe
Betul **20** Ed
Betwa (riv.) **20** Ec
Beverley [Austl.] **29** Be
Beverley [U.K.] **7** FGe
Beycuma **22** CDb
Bey daği (mt.) **22** EFc
Bey daǧları (mts.) **22** BCd
Beyla **24** Bd
Beyoneisu–Retsugan **17** Fi
Beypazarı **22** CDb
Beyşehir **22** CDd
Beyşehir Gölü **22** Cd
Bežeck **12** Eb
Béziers **8** Ef
Bhabua **19** Hj
Bhadgaon **20** Gc
Bhadrak **20** Gd
Bhadravati **20** Ef
Bhagalpur **15** CDg
Bhamo **19** Cd
Bharatpur **20** Ec
Bharuch **20** Dd
Bhatpara **20** Gd
Bhavnagar **20** Dd
Bhawanipatna **20** Fe
Bheri (riv.) **19** Hi
Bhilai **20** Fd
Bhima (riv.) **20** DEe
Bhind **20** Ec
Bhiwani **19** Gi
Bhola (i.) **19** Jk
Bhopal **20** Ed
Bhubaneswar **20** FGde
Bhuj **20** Cd
Bhusawal **20** Ed
Bhutan (Ind. St.) **15** Dg
Biafra (phys. reg.) **24** Cd
Biafra, Bight of– **24** Ccd
Biak, Pulau– **27** Bc
Biała Podlaska **5** Ibc
Białobrzegi **5** Hc
Białogard **5** Fab
Białystok **5** Ib
Biarritz **8** Cf
Bibà **22** Ch
Bibai **17** Gc
Biberach an der Riss **5** BCde
Bicaz **6** GHc
Biçer **22** Cc
Bickerton Island **29** Fa
Bida **24** Cd
Bidar **20** Ee
Bideford **7** Df
Bidon 5 → Poste–Maurice–Cortier **24** Cb
Bié, Planalto do– **26** Ac
Biel **5** Ae
Bielawa **5** Fc
Bielefeld **5** Bbc
Biella **10** Bb
Bielsko–Biała **5** Gd
Bielsk Podlaski **5** Ib
Bien Hoa **19** Ef
Biga **22** Ab
Biğadiç **22** Bc
Biggar **33** Ca
Bighorn (riv.) **33** Cb

horn Mountains 33 Cb
Island 31 Hb
River 31 Ec
Spring 33 Cc
ac 6 Bd
ar (State) 20 FGc
ar 20 Gcd
aramulo 26 Cb
oro 17 Ic
a (riv.) 13 Hd
agos Islands 24 Ac
apur 20 Ee
auri 19 Hi
aljina 6 Dd
e 16 Ce
sk 13 Hd
aner 20 Dc
'n (riv.) 16 Hla
n 14 Ge
ini Atoll 27 Db
ljan 12 Hb
oro 26 Ab
aspur 20 Fd
auktaung Range 19 Cf
ao 9 Da
ays 22 Cg
eca 11 Cb
ecik 22 BCb
ě Karpaty (mts.) 5 FGd
n 19 Ce
ings 33 Cb
of Portland 7 EFf
ma 24 Dc
ela 29 Hlc
o gora (mts.) 6 Ccd
oxi 32 Cb
ine 25 Cc
a 20 Ed
alud, Kuh– e– (mt.) 21 Fb
aboğa dağ (mts.) 22 Fcd
gen 5 ABcd
ghamton 32 Da
göl 21 Cb
hai 16 EFd
jai 18 Ad
ongko, Pulau– (i.) 18 Ff
atuhan 18 Be
atulu 18 Dd
Bio, Rio– (riv.) 39 Ac
grad na Moru 6 Bde
ko 24 Cd
iă', Al– (phys. reg.) 22 Fef
, Al– 21 Bd
äk 24 Db
al Wa'r 24 Db
ao 25 Ccd
atnagar 19 Ij
Damdūm 22 Ag
dsville 29 FGd
dum 29 Eb
ecik 22 Gd
euen 18 Ac
ganj 20 FGc
iand 21 FGc
iusa (riv.) 14 Cd
k, Al– 21 Cf
kenhead 7 Ee
lad 6 Hlc
lad (riv.) 6 Hcd
mingham [U.K.] 7 Fe
mingham [U.S.] 32 Cb
mitrapur 19 Ik

Birnin Kebbi 24 Cc
Birni Nkonni 24 Cc
Birobidžan 14 Ge
Birpur 19 Ij
Birr 7 BCe
Bi'r Safäjah 25 Db
Birsk 13 Ed
Bîr Tarfâwi 25 Cb
Biržai 4 Fd
Bisa, Pulau– (i.) 18 Ge
Bisbee 33 BCc
Biscay, Bay of– 8 BCef
Bisceglie 10 Fd
Bischofshofen 5 De
Bïshah, Wädï– 21 Cf
Bishnupur 19 Ik
Biškek (Frunze) 13 Ge
Biskra 24 Ca
Bismarck 33 CDb
Bismarck Archipelago 27 Cc
Bissau 24 Ac
Bissett 31 Fc
Bistriţa 6 Gc
Bistriţa (riv.) 6 Gc
Bitam 24 Dd
Bitlis 21 Cb
Bitola 11 Dc
Bitonto 10 Fd
Bitterfontein 23 Di
Bitterroot Range 33 Bb
Biu 24 Dc
Biwa–Ko 16 Ic
Biyad, Al– (phys. reg.) 21 De
Biyalä 22 Cg
Bizerte 24 CDa
Bjala Slatina 11 Eb
Bjargtangar (cap.) 4 map no.1
Bjelovar 6 Ccd
Bjerkreim 4 Ad
Bjuröklubb (cap.) 4 Eb
Blackall 29 Hc
Blackburn 7 Ee
Black Forest (mts.) 5 ABde
Black Hills 33 Cb
Blackpool 7 Ee
Black River 19 Dd
Black Sea 13 De
Black Volta (riv.) 24 Bcd
Blackwater (riv.) 7 Be
Blackwood River 29 Be
Blagodarny 12 Fd
Blagoevgrad 11 Ebc
Blagoveščensk [Russia] 14 FGd
Blagoveščensk [Russia] 12 Hlb
Blair Athol 29 Hc
Blaj 6 FGc
Blanc, Cap– [Mtna.] 24 Ab
Blanc, Cap– [Tun.] 24 CDa
Blanc, Le– 8 Dd
Blanc, Mont– 10 Ab
Blanca, Bahía– (b.) 39 BCcd
Blanca, Cordillera– (mts.) 37 Bc
Blanca, Costa– 9 Ec
Blanca Peak 33 Cc
Blanche, Lake– 29 FGd
Blanco, Cape– 33 Ab
Blanc–Sablon 31 IJc
Blanquilla, Isla– (i.) 35 Db
Blantyre 26 Cc
Blåvands Huk (cap.) 5 ABa

Blaye 8 Ce
Bloemfontein 23 Eh
Blois 8 Dd
Błonie 5 Hb
Bluefield 32 Cb
Bluefields 35 Bb
Blue Mountains 33 Bb
Blue Nile 25 Dc
Blue Ridge 32 Cb
Blumenau 39 Db
Blyth 7 Fd
Blythe 33 Bc
Blytheville 32 BCb
Bo 24 Ad
Boac 18 Fb
Bo'ai 16 Dc
Boano, Pulau– (i.) 18 Ge
Boa Vista 37 Cb
Bobbio 10 Bb
Bobo Dioulasso 24 Bc
Bóbr (riv.) 5 Ec
Bobriki (Novomoskovsk) 13 CDd
Bobrka 6 Gb
Bobrujsk 13 BCd
Bôca do Acre 37 Cc
Bôca do Jari 38 Bb
Bôca do Moaco 37 Cc
Boca Grande (riv. m.) 37 CDb
Bocas del Toro 35 Bc
Bochnia 5 Hd
Bocholt 5 Ac
Bochum 5 Ac
Bocşa 6 Ed
Böda 4 Dd
Bodajbo 14 Ed
Bodélé (phys. reg.) 25 Ac
Boden 4 Eb
Bodmin 7 Df
Bodø 4 Cc
Bodrum 22 ABd
Boende 25 Cde
Boffa 24 Acd
Bogalusa 32 BCb
Bogan River 29 He
Bogatynia 5 Ec
Boğazlıyan 22 Ec
Bogdanovič 12 Hb
Bogor 18 Cf
Bogorodick 12 Fd
Bogorodsk 12 Fb
Bogra 19 Jj
Bogué 24 Ac
Bo Hai (b.) 16 EFc
Bohemia (phys. reg.) 5 DEcd
Bohemian Forest (mts.) 5 DEd
Bohol (i.) 18 Fbc
Boiaçu 37 Cc
Bois (riv.) 39 CDa
Boise 33 Bb
Bojador, Cabo– 24 Ab
Bojnürd 21 Fb
Boké 24 Ac
Boknafjorden (b.) 4 Ad
Bokspits 26 Bd
Bolama 24 Ac
Bolbec 8 Dc
Bolehov 6 FGb
Bolesławiec 5 Ec
Bolgatanga 24 Bcd
Bolgrad 6 Id
Boli 16 Ha

Boliden 4 DEb
Bolinao 18 Ea
Boliohertu (mt.) 18 Fd
Bolívar, Pico– (mt.) 37 Bb
Bolivia (Ind. St.) 36 De
Bolivia, Altiplano de– 38 Acd
Bolkar dağları (mts.) 22 Ed
Bollnäs 4 Dc
Bollon 29 Hd
Boločanka 14 Cb
Bologna 10 Cb
Bologne 8 Fc
Bologoje 12 Db
Bolšaja Ussurka (riv.) 16 Hla
Bolsena, Lago di– 10 Cc
Bolševik, ostrov– 41 grid square no.4
Bolsöj Anjuj (riv.) 14 Jc
Bolšoj Begičev, ostrov– 14 Eb
Bolsoj Jenisej (riv.) 14 Cd
Bolsoj Ljahovski, ostrov– (i.) 14 Hlb
Bolšoj Uzen (riv.) 12 Gd
Bolton 7 Ee
Bolu 22 Cb
Bolzano 10 Ca
Boma 26 Ab
Bombala 29 Hlf
Bombay 15 Ch
Bom Comércio 37 Cc
Bom Despacho 39 Da
Bomili 26 Ba
Bom Jesus 38 Cc
Bom Jesus da Lapa 38 Cc
Bon, Cape– 24 Da
Bonaire (i.) 35 Db
Bonaparte Archipelago 29 CDa
Bonavista 31 Jd
Bonda 26 Ab
Bondo 25 Cd
Bondowoso 18 Df
Bone → Watampone 18 EFe
Bone, Teluk– 18 Fef
Bongor 25 Bcd
Bonifacio 8 map no.1
Bonifacio, Strait of– 10 Bd
Bonin Islands 27 Ca
Bonn 5 Ac
Bontoc 18 Fa
Bonyhád 6 Dc
Boosaaso 25 EFc
Boothia Gulf 31 FGab
Boothia Peninsula 31 Fa
Booué 26 Aab
Bophuthatswana (hist. reg.) 26 Bd
Bor [Russia] 12 Fb
Bor [Sud.] 25 Dd
Bor [Tur.] 22 Ed
Bor [Yugo.] 6 Fd
Borah Peak 33 Bb
Borås 4 Cd
Boräzjän 21 DEd
Borba 37 CDc
Borcea, Bratul– (riv.) 6 Hd
Bordeaux 8 Ce
Borden Peninsula 31 Ga
Bordertown 29 FGf
Bordj Omar Driss 24 Cb
Borgå 4 Fc
Borgarnes 4 map no.1
Børgefjell (mt.) 4 Cb

Borger 33 Cc
Borgholm 4 Dd
Borgomanero 10 Bb
Borislav 5 Id
Borisoglebsk 13 Dd
Borisov 5 Ka
Borispol 12 Dc
Borja 37 Bc
Borkou (phys. reg.) 25 BCc
Borlänge 4 Cc
Borlu 22 Bc
Borneo (Kalimantan) (i.) 18 DEd
Bornholm (i.) 4 CDe
Bornholmsgatten (str.) 4 Ce
Bornova 22 Ac
Boromo 24 Bc
Boroviči 12 Db
Borroloola 29 EFb
Borşa 6 Gc
Borščovočny, Hrebet– 14 DEde
Borujerd 21 Dc
Borzja 14 Ed
Bosa 10 Bd
Bosanska Gradiška 6 Cd
Bosanska Krupa 6 Cd
Bosanski Novi 6 Cd
Bosanski Petrovac 6 Cd
Bosansko Grahovo 6 Cd
Bose 16 Cf
Boshan 16 Ec
Bosna (riv.) 6 CDd
Bosnia (phys. reg.) 6 CDd
Bosnia–Herzegovina (ind. St.) 6 CDde
Bosobolo 26 ABa
Bōsō–Hantō 17 Gg
Bosphorus (str.) 22 Bb
Bossangoa 25 Bd
Bossembélé 25 Bd
Bossier City 32 Bb
Bostan 20 Cb
Boston [U.K.] 7 FGe
Boston [U.S.] 32 DEa
Botev (mt.) 11 Fb
Bothnia, Gulf of– 4 DEbc
Botletle (riv.) 26 Bd
Botoşani 6 Hc
Botswana (Ind. St.) 23 Eh
Botucatu 39 Db
Bouaké 24 Bd
Bouar 25 Bd
Bouârfa 24 Ba
Bouca 25 Bd
Boudouaou 24 Ca
Boufarik 9 Gd
Bougainville Island 27 Cc
Bougouni 24 Bc
Bouguenais 8 Cd
Boulder 33 Cbc
Boulia 29 FGc
Boulogne–sur–Mer 8 Db
Bouna 24 Bd
Boundiali 24 Bd
Boundji 24 De
Bountiful 33 Bb
Bounty Islands 27 DEe
Bourail 28 map no.4
Bourbonnais (hist. reg.) 8 Ed
Bourem 24 BCc
Bourg–en–Bresse 8 Fd
Bourges 8 Ed

Bourg–lès–Valence 8 Fe
Bourgogne, Canal de– 8 Fd
Bourg–Saint–Maurice 8 Ge
Bourke 29 GHde
Bournemouth 7 Ff
Bou–Saada 24 Ca
Bousso 25 Bc
Boutlimit 24 Ac
Bow (riv.) 33 Ba
Bowen 29 Hbc
Bowling Green 32 Cb
Bowmore 7 Cd
Boxian 16 Ed
Bozburun 11 He
Bozcaada (i.) 22 Ac
Bozdağ (mt.) 22 Bc
Bozeman 33 BCb
Bozhen 16 Ec
Bozkır 22 Dd
Bozoum 25 Bd
Bozüyük 22 Cbc
Bra 10 Ab
Brač (i.) 11 Bb
Bracciano, Lago di– 10 Dc
Bräcke 4 CDc
Brad 6 Fc
Bradford 7 EFe
Braga 9 Ab
Bragado 39 Bc
Bragança [Braz.] 38 Cb
Bragança [Port.] 9 Bb
Brahmani (riv.) 20 FGd
Brahmaputra (Maquan He) (riv.) 20 GHc
Brahmaputra (Yarlung Zangbo Jiang) 20 GHc
Brăila 6 Hd
Brainerd 32 Ba
Brake 5 Bb
Branco, Rio– (riv.) 37 Cbc
Brandberg (mt.) 26 Ad
Brandenburg 5 Db
Brandenburg (hist. reg.) 5 Db
Brandon 31 EFcd
Braniewo 5 GHa
Bransfield Strait 42 grid square no.1
Brasiléia 37 Cd
Brasília 39 Da
Braşov 6 GHd
Bratislava 5 Fd
Bratsk 14 CDd
Bratskoje vodohranilišče 14 Dd
Braunau am Inn 5 Dd
Braunschweig 5 BCb
Brava, Costa– 9 Gb
Bravo, Rio– (riv.) 34 Bb
Bray (hist. reg.) 8 DEc
Brazil (Ind. St.) 36 DFde
Brazilian Highlands 39 Da
Brazos (riv.) 32 Bb
Brazzaville 26 Ab
Brčko 6 Dd
Brdy (mt.) 5 Dd
Breakfast Island 28 map no.3
Breaza 6 Gd
Břeclav 5 Fd
Brecon 7 Ef
Breda 8 Fb
Bredasdorp 23 Ei
Brødy 12 Jc
Bregalnica (riv.) 11 Ec

Bregenz 5 BCe
Breidafjördur (g.) 4 map no.1
Bremen 5 Bb
Bremerhaven 5 Bb
Bremerton 33 Ab
Brenham 32 Bbc
Brenne (phys. reg.) 8 Dd
Brennero (p.) 10 Ca
Breno 10 Cb
Brenta (riv.) 10 Cab
Brescia 10 Cb
Breslav 5 Fc
Bressanone / Brixen 10 Ca
Bressuire 8 CDd
Brest [Bela.] 5 IJb
Brest [Fr.] 8 Ac
Breton, Pertuis– (str.) 8 Cd
Breueh, Pulau– (i.) 18 Ac
Breves 38 BCb
Brewarrina 29 Hde
Bria 25 Cd
Briançon 8 Ge
Briare 8 Ed
Bričany 6 Hb
Bridgeport 32 Da
Bridgetown 29 Be
Bridgwater 7 Ef
Bridlington 7 FGd
Brie (phys. reg.) 8 Ec
Brig 10 ABa
Brighton 7 FGf
Brijuni 6 Ad
Brilon 5 Bc
Brindisi 10 Fd
Brisbane 29 Id
Bristol 7 Ef
Bristol Channel 7 DEf
British Columbia (prov.) 31 Cc
Brittany (phys. reg.) 8 BCcd
Brive–la–Gaillarde 8 De
Briviesca 9 Da
Brixen / Bressanone 10 Ca
Brixlegg 5 CDe
Brjansk 13 Cd
Brno 5 Fd
Broad Sound 29 HIc
Brocken (mt.) 5 Cc
Brockman, Mount– 29 Bc
Brodeur Peninsula 31 Ga
Brodnica 5 Gb
Brody 12 BCcd
Broken Hill 29 Ge
Broken Hill → Kabwe 26 Bc
Brokopondo 37 Db
Bron 8 Fe
Brønnøysund 4 Cb
Bronte 10 Ef
Brookings 32 Ba
Brooks Range 41 grid square no.2
Brookton 29 Be
Broome 29 Cb
Brothers, The– (i.) 21 Eg
Brownsville 32 Bc
Brownwood 32 Bb
Browse Island 29 Ca
Bruay–en–Artois 8 Eb
Bruce, Mount– 29 Bc
Bruck an der Leitha 5 Fde
Bruck an der Mur 5 Ee
Brugge 8 Eb
Brumado 39 Da
Brunei (Ind. St.) 15 Di

Brunsbüttel 5 Ba
Brunswick 32 CDb
Brunswick, Península de– 41 Ac
Bruny Island 29 map no.1
Brussel / Bruxelles 8 Fb
Bruxelles / Brussel 8 Fb
Bryan 32 Bb
Brza Palanka 6 Fd
Brzeg 5 Fc
Buada Lagoon 27 map no.2
Buala 27 Cc
Bučać 6 Gb
Bucak 22 Cd
Bucaramanga 36 CDc
Buchanan 24 ABd
Buchans 31 Jd
Bucharest 6 Hd
Buckingham Bay 29 Fa
Budapest 6 Dc
Budardalur 4 map no.1
Budaun 20 Efc
Budd Coast 42 grid square no.4
Bude 7 Df
Budennovsk 3 Hc
Búdir 4 map no.1
Budjala 25 BCd
Budogošč 12 Db
Budva 11 Cb
Buea 24 Cd
Buena Esperanza 39 Bc
Buenaventura 36 BCc
Buenos Aires [Arg.] 39 BCci
Buenos Aires [Pan.] 35 map no.1
Buenos Aires, Lago– 40 ABi
Buffalo [N.Y.–U.S.] 32 Da
Buffalo [Tx.–U.S.] 32 Bb
Buffalo [Wy.–U.S.] 33 Cb
Bug (riv.) 5 Jc
Buga 37 Bb
Bugsuk (i.) 18 Ec
Bugulma 12 Hc
Buguruslan 12 Hc
Buhara 13 Ff
Buhayrat al–Assad (l.) 22 Fl
Builth Wells 7 Ee
Buinsk 12 Gbc
Buir–Nur (l.) 16 Ea
Buj 13 Dd
Bujalance 9 CDd
Bujumbura 26 Bb
Bukačača 14 Ed
Bukama 26 Bb
Bukavu 26 Bb
Bukit Mertajam 19 Dgh
Bukittinggi 18 ABde
Bükk 6 Ebc
Bukoba 25 De
Bukovina (hist. reg.) 6 GHb
Bula 18 He
Bulan 18 Fb
Bulandshahr 19 Gi
Bulawayo 23 Egh
Buldan 22 Bc
Bulgan 14 De
Bulgaria (Ind. St.) 3 Fc
Bullfinch 29 Be
Bulloo River 29 Gd
Bumba 25 Cd
Bumbah, Al– 24 Ea
Buna 26 CDa

Bunbury 29 ABe
Bundaberg 29 Icd
Bundoran 7 Bd
Bungo–Suidō 17 BCh
Bunguran (i.) 18 Cd
Bunja 25 CDd
Buon Me Thuot 19 Ef
Buqayq 21 DEd
Buraydah 21 Cd
Buraymī, Al– 21 Fe
Burdekin River 29 Hbc
Burdur 22 BCd
Burdur Gölü 22 BCd
Burdwan 20 Gd
Bure 25 Dd
Bureinski Hrebet 14 Gde
Bureja (riv.) 14 Gd
Bureja 14 FGe
Būr Fuad 25 map no.1
Burgas 11 Gb
Burgas, Gulf of– 11 GHb
Burgenland (phys. reg.) 5 Fe
Burghausen 5 Dd
Burgio 10 Df
Burgos 9 Da
Burgsvik 4 Dd
Burgundy (phys. reg.) 8 EFd
Burias (i.) 18 Fb
Burjasot 9 EFc
Burketown 29 Fb
Burkina (Ind. St.) 23 BCd
Burlington [Ia.–U.S.] 32 Ba
Burlington [Vt.–U.S.] 32 Da
Burmah, Al– 24 CDa
Burne 29 map no.1
Burnley 7 Ee
Burns 33 Bb
Bur'o 25 Ed
Burra 29 Fe
Burravoe 7 Fa
Burriana 9 EFc
Burruyacú 39 Bb
Bursa 22 Bb
Būr Taufiq 25 map no.1
Burton–upon–Trent 7 Fe
Buru, Pulau– (i.) 18 Ge
Burullus, Buḩayrat al– 22 Cg
Burundi (Ind. St.) 26 BCb
Bururi 26 BCb
Buryat (Aut. Rep.) 14 Dd
Bury Saint Edmunds 7 Ge
Businga 26 Ba
Busko Zdrój 5 Hc
Buşrá ash Shām 22 Ff
Busselton 29 ABe
Busto Arsizio 10 Bb
Busuanga (i.) 18 Eb
Buta 25 Cd
Butaritari Islands 27 Db
Butha Qi 16 Fa
Butte 33 Bb
Butuan 18 Gc
Butung (i.) 18 Fef
Buuloberde 25 Ed
Büyük Ağrı dağı → Ararat (mt.) 21 Cb
Büyük Egri dağ (mt.) 22 Dd
Büyük Mahya (mt.) 22 ABb
Büyük Menderes (riv.) 22 ABd
Buzançais 8 Dd
Buzău 6 Hd
Buzuluk 13 Ed

Bydgoszcz 5 FGb
Bygdeå 4 DEb
Byhov 12 Dc
Bylot Island 30 Kb
Byrd Glacier 42 grid square no.4
Byron, Cape– 29 Id
Byrranga Gory 14 CDb
Bytom 5 Gc
Bytów 5 Fa
Bzura (riv.) 5 Gb

C

Ca (riv.) 19 DEe
Caanood, Laas– 25 Ed
Caapiranga 37 Cc
Caatinga 38 Cbc
Cabanatuan 18 Fa
Cabedelo 38 Db
Cabeza del Buey 9 Cc
Cabezón de la Sal 9 Ca
Cabimas 37 Ba
Cabinda 26 Ab
Caborca 34 Aa
Cabot Strait 31 IJd
Cabra 9 Cd
Cabras 10 Be
Cabrera, Isla– (i.) 9 Gc
Cabrera, Sierra de la– (mts.) 9 Ba
Cábriel (riv.) 9 Ec
Cabruta 37 Cb
Caçador 39 Cb
Čačak 6 Ede
Caccia, Capo– 10 Bd
Cacequí 39 Cbc
Cáceres [Braz.] 39 Ca
Cáceres [Sp.] 9 Bc
Cachimbo, Serra do– (mts.) 38 Bb
Cachoeira 38 Dc
Cachoeira do Sul 39 Cbc
Cachoeiro de Itapemirim 39 DEb
Cacolo 26 Abc
Caconda 26 Ac
Cadale 25 Ed
Čadan 14 BCd
Cadillac 32 Ca
Cádiz 9 Bd
Cadiz 18 Fb
Cádiz, Golfo de– 9 Bd
Čadyr–Lunga 6 Ic
Caen 8 CDc
Caernarvon 7 De
Caetité 38 Cc
Cagan–Aman 12 Gd
Cagayan (riv.) 18 Fa
Cagayan de Oro 18 Fc
Cagayan Islands 18 Ec
Cagayan Sulu (i.) 18 Ec
Čagda 14 Gd
Cagliari 10 Be
Cagliari, Golfo di– 10 Be
Caguas 35 Hd
Cahama 26 Ac
Cahersiveen 7 Af
Cahora Bassa, Lago de– 26 Cc
Cahors 8 De

Caia 26 Cc
Caiabis, Serra dos– (mts.) 38 Bc
Caicó 38 Db
Caicos Islands 32 Dc
Caimito (riv.) 35 map no.1
Cairns 29 Hb
Cairo [Eg.] 25 Dab
Cairo [Il.–U.S.] 32 Cb
Cajamarca 37 Bc
Cajázeiras 38 Db
Čajkovski 12 Hlb
Çal 22 Bcd
Calabar 24 Cd
Calabozo 36 Dc
Calabria (reg.) 10 EFef
Calafat 6 Fde
Calafate 40 Ac
Calahorra 9 Ea
Calais [Fr.] 8 Db
Calais [U.S.] 32 Ea
Calama [Braz.] 37 Cc
Calama [Chile] 39 Bb
Calamar 37 Bab
Calamian Group 18 EFb
Calamocha 9 Eb
Călan 6 Fd
Calandula 26 Ab
Calapan 18 Fb
Călăraşi 6 Hd
Calatayud 9 Eb
Calayan (i.) 18 Fa
Calbayog 18 FGb
Calçoene 38 BCa
Calcutta 15 Cg
Caldas da Rainha 9 Ac
Caldera 39 Ab
Caldwell 33 Bb
Caledon (riv.) 26 Bde
Caledonian Canal 7 Dc
Calera, La– 39 Ac
Caletta 10 Bd
Calgary 30 Gde
Cali 36 Cc
Calicut 20 DEf
Caliente 33 Bc
California (State) 33 ABc
California, Gulf of– 33 Bcd
Căliman, Munţii– 6 Gc
Călimăneşti 6 Gd
Callabonna, Lake– 29 Gde
Callao 36 Ce
Callao, El– 37 Cb
Caloundra 29 Id
Calpe 9 Fc
Caltagirone 10 Ef
Caltanissetta 10 Ef
Caluire–et–Cuire 8 Fe
Caluula 25 EFc
Calvi 8 map no.1
Calvinia 26 ABe
Calw 5 Bd
Camabatela 26 Ab
Camacupa 26 Ac
Camagüey 35 Ca
Camagüey, Archipiélago de– (is.) 35 Ca
Camaná 39 Aa
Campapuã, Sertão de– (steppe) 39 CDa
Camaquã 39 Cc
Camargo 39 Bb

Camargue (phys. reg.) 8 Ff
Camarones 40 Bb
Ca Mau Point 19 Dg
Cambodia (Ind. St.) 15 Dh
Cambrai 8 Eb
Cambrian Mountains 7 DEef
Cambridge [U.K.] 7 FGe
Cambridge [U.S.] 32 DEa
Cambridge Bay 31 Eb
Çam Burun 22 FGb
Camden 32 Db
Cameroon (Ind. St.) 23 CDe
Cameroon Mountains 24 CDd
Cametá 38 BCb
Camiguin (i.) 18 Fa
Camiri 39 Bb
Camocim 38 CDb
Camooweal 29 Fbc
Camorta (i.) 19 Bg
Campagna 10 Ed
Campana, Isla– (i.) 40 Ab
Campanario, Cerro– (mt.) 39 ABc
Campania (reg.) 10 DEd
Campanquiz, Cerros– (mt.) 37 Bc
Campbell Island 27 De
Campbell River 31 Cc
Campbellton 31 Id
Campbell Town 29 map no.1
Campbeltown 7 Dd
Campeche 34 Cc
Campeche, Bahía de– 34 Cc
Campeche Bank 34 CDb
Camperdown 29 Gf
Campina Grande 38 Db
Campinas 39 Db
Campobasso 10 Ed
Campo Formoso 38 Cc
Campo Gallo 39 Bb
Campo Grande 39 Cab
Campo Maior 38 Cb
Campo Mourão 39 Cb
Campos 39 Db
Campos [Braz.] (phys. reg.) 38 Cc
Campos [Braz.] (phys. reg.) 38 Bc
Campos, Tierra de– (phys. reg.) 9 Cab
Cam Ranh 19 Ef
Camrose 31 Ab
Çan 22 Bb
Canada (Ind. St.) 30 GKcd
Cañada de Gómez 39 Bc
Canadian River 32 Bb
Çanakkale 22 Ab
Canal du Centre (can.) 8 Fd
Cananea 33 BCc
Canarreos, Archipiélago de los– (is.) 35 Bb
Canary Islands 24 Aab
Canaveral, Cape– (Kennedy, Cape–) 32 CDc
Canavieiras 38 Dc
Canberra 29 Hlf
Cancún 34 Db
Çandır 22 Db
Canelones 39 Cc
Cangamba 26 ABc
Cangas de Narcea 9 Ba
Cangzhou 16 Ec
Caniapiscau (riv.) 31 Ic

Can - Cer

Canicattì **10** Df
Canik dağları (mts.) **22** Fb
Çankırı **22** Db
Cannanore **20** DEf
Cannanore Islands **20** Df
Cannes **8** Gf
Cann River **29** Hf
Canoas **39** CDbc
Canoas, Rio– (riv.) **39** Cb
Canora **33** Ca
Canta **37** Bd
Cantabria (phys. reg.) **9** CDa
Cantal, Plomb du– (mts.) **8** Ee
Canterbury **7** Gf
Can Tho **19** Efg
Canton **32** CDa
Canton (Guangzhou) **15** Dg
Canumã (riv.) **37** Dc
Canutama **37** Cc
Cao Bang **19** Ed
Cap, El– **25** map no.1
Čapajev **12** Hc
Čapajevsk **13** DEd
Capanema **38** Cb
Capbreton **8** Cf
Cape Barren Island **29** map no.1
Cape Breton Island **31** IJd
Cape Coast **24** BCd
Cape Dorset **31** Hb
Cape Dyer **31** IJb
Cape Girardeau **32** BCb
Capelongo **26** Ac
Cape Province (prov.) **26** ABde
Cape Town **26** Ae
Cape Verde (Ind. St.) **2**
Cape York Peninsula **29** Ga
Cap–Haïtien **35** Cab
Capim (riv.) **38** Cb
Capitano Arturo Prat (sc. stat.) **42** grid square no.1
Čaplygin **12** EFc
Capraia **10** Bc
Caprara, Punta– (cap.) **10** Bd
Caprera **10** Bd
Capri **10** Ed
Capricorn Channel **29** Ic
Caprivi Strip (phys. reg.) **26** Bc
Captain Cook **28** map no.1
Captain's Flat **29** Hlf
Caquetá (riv.) **37** Bb
Čara (riv.) **14** Ed
Carabaya, Cordillera de– (mts.) **39** ABa
Caracal **6** Gd
Caracaraí **37** CDb
Caracas **37** Ca
Carajás, Serra dos– (mts.) **38** Bb
Caransebeş **6** Fd
Caratasca, Laguna de– **35** Bb
Caratinga **39** Da
Carauari **37** Cc
Caravaca **9** DEc
Caravelas **39** Ea
Carázinho **39** Cb
Carballo **9** Aa
Carbonia **10** Be
Carcassonne **8** Ef

Cárdenas [Cuba] **35** Ba
Cárdenas [Mex.] **34** Cb
Cardiff **7** Ef
Cardigan **7** De
Cardigan Bay **7** De
Cardona **9** Fb
Čardžev (Čardžou) **13** Ff
Čardžou → Čardžev **13** Ff
Carei **6** Fc
Carentan **8** Cc
Carey, Lake– **29** Cd
Cargados Carajos Islands **23** map no.1
Carhaix–Plouguer **8** Bc
Cariñena **9** Eb
Carinhanha **38** Cc
Carinhanha, Rio– (riv.) **39** Da
Carinthia (reg.) **5** DEe
Caripito **37** Ca
Carlisle **7** Ed
Carlota, La– **39** Bc
Carlow **7** Ce
Carlsbad **33** Cc
Carmarthen **7** Df
Carmaux **8** Ee
Carmelo **39** Cc
Carmen, El– **39** Bb
Carmen de Patagones **40** Bb
Carmona **9** BCd
Carnac **8** Bd
Carnarvon [Austl.] **29** Acd
Carnarvon [S. Afr.] **26** Be
Carnegie **29** Cd
Carnegie, Lake– **29** Cd
Carn Eige (mt.) **7** Dc
Car Nicobar (i.) **19** Bg
Carnot **25** Ed
Carnsore Point **7** CDe
Carolina **38** Cb
Carolina, La– **9** Dc
Caroline Atoll **28** Bc
Caroline Islands **27** BDb
Caroní (riv.) **37** Cb
Carora **37** Ba
Carpentaria, Gulf of– **29** FGa
Carpentras **8** Fe
Carrantuohill **7** Bef
Carrara **10** Cb
Carribean Sea **35** CDb
Carrión (riv.) **9** Ca
Carrizal Bajo **39** Ab
Carrizozo **33** Cc
Çarşamba **22** Fb
Čarsk **13** GHe
Carson City **33** Bc
Cartagena [Col.] **36** Cb
Cartagena [Sp.] **9** Ed
Cartago **35** Bc
Carthage (r.) **24** Da
Cartier Island **29** Ca
Cartwright **31** Jc
Caruaru **38** Db
Carúpano **37** Ca
Carvoeiro, Cabo– **9** Ac
Casablanca **24** ABa
Casale Monferrato **10** Bb
Casarea Mazaca → Kayseri **22** EFc
Cascadas, Las– **35** map no.1
Cascade Range **33** Ab
Cascais **9** Ac
Cascavel [Braz.] **38** Db
Cascavel [Braz.] **39** Cb

Caserta **10** Ed
Casey **42** grid square no.4
Casino **29** Id
Casiquiare (riv.) **37** Cb
Caspe **9** EFb
Casper **33** Cb
Caspian Depression **12** GHd
Caspian Sea **13** DEef
Cassai (riv.) **26** Bb
Cassino **10** Dd
Castanho **37** Cc
Castelfranco Veneto **10** Cb
Castellammare, Golfo di– **10** De
Castellammare del Golfo **10** De
Castellammare di Stabia **10** Ed
Castellana Grotte **10** Fd
Castellane **10** Ac
Castellón de la Plana **9** EFbc
Castelnaudary **8** DEf
Castelo Branco **9** Bc
Castelo do Piauí **38** Cb
Castelsarrasin **8** De
Castelvetrano **10** Df
Castilla–La Mancha (phys. reg.) **9** CDbc
Castilla–León (phys. reg.) **9** Cab
Castillos **39** Cc
Castlebar **7** Be
Castres **8** Ef
Castries **35** Db
Castro **40** Ab
Castro del Río **9** Cd
Castro Urdiales **9** Da
Castrovillari **10** Fe
Castuera **9** Cc
Catalão **39** Da
Catalina **33** Ab
Catalonia (phys. reg.) **9** Fb
Catamarca **39** Bb
Catanduanes **18** FGb
Catanduva **39** CDb
Catania **10** Ef
Catania, Golfo di– **10** Ef
Catanzaro **10** Fe
Catarroja **9** EFc
Catastrophe, Cape– **29** EFef
Catbalogan **18** FGb
Cat Island **32** Dc
Cativá **35** map no.1
Catoche, Cabo– **34** Cb
Cato Island **29** Jc
Catriló **39** Bc
Catrimani **37** Cb
Catrimani (riv.) **37** Cb
Catwick, Îles– **19** Eg
Cauca (riv.) **37** Bb
Caucaia **38** Db
Caucasia **37** Bb
Caucasus (mts.) **13** De
Caungula **26** ABb
Cauquenes **39** Ac
Caura (riv.) **37** Cb
Cauvery (riv.) **20** Ef
Cava, La– **9** Fb
Cavaillon **8** Fe
Cavally (riv.) **24** Bd
Cavan **7** Ce
Caviana, Ilha– **38** BCa

Cavite **18** Fb
Caxias **38** Cb
Caxias do Sul **39** CDb
Caxito **26** Ab
Cayağzi (Riva) **22** Bb
Cayambe, Volcán– (mt.) **37** Bbc
Cayenne **37** Db
Cayes, Les– **35** Cb
Cayman Brac (is.) **35** Cb
Cayman Islands **35** Bab
Cayo, El– **35** Bb
Čazma **6** Cd
Cazombo **26** Bc
Cazorla **9** Dd
Cea (riv.) **9** Ca
Ceará (State) **38** CDb
Ceará Mirim **38** Db
Čeboksary **13** Dd
Cebu **18** Fbc
Cebu (i.) **15** Ehi
Cecerleg **14** De
Cecina **10** Cc
Cedar City **33** Bc
Cedar Falls **32** Ba
Cedar Rapids **32** Ba
Cedros, Isla– (i.) **34** Ab
Ceduna **29** Ee
Ceeldheree **25** Ed
Ceerigaabo **25** Ec
Cefalù **10** Ee
Čegdomyn **14** Gd
Cegléd **6** Dc
Čehov **14** He
Ceiba, La– **35** Bb
Čekerek (riv.) **22** Fbc
Cela **26** Ac
Celaya **34** BCb
Celebes → Sulawesi (i.) **18** EFe
Celebes Sea **18** Fd
Čeleken **21** Eb
Celinograd **13** Gd
Čeljabinsk **13** Fd
Celje **6** Bc
Čelkar **13** EFe
Celle **5** Cb
Celtic Sea **7** BCf
Čeljuskin, mys– **41** grid square no.4
Cenis, Mont– (p.) **10** Ab
Central, Sistema– (mts.) **9** BDb
Central African Republic (Ind St.) **23** DEe
Central Balkans (mts.) **11** EFb
Central Siberian Uplands **14** CDc
Centro, El– **33** Bc
Cephalonia (i.) **11** CDd
Ceram (i.) **18** GHe
Ceram Sea **18** GHe
Cerbère **8** Ef
Čerdyn **12** Ia
Čeremhovo **14** CDd
Čerepovec **3** Gb
Ceres **38** BCc
Cergy–Pontoise **8** Ec
Cerignola **10** Ed
Čerkassy **13** BCe
Çerkeş **22** Db
Čerkessk **13** De

Čerlak 13 Gd
Čermoz 12 Hlb
Černiahov 6 Ia
Černigov 13 BCd
Černjahovsk 12 Bc
Černogorsk 14 Cd
Černomorskoje 12 Dd
Černovcy 6 GHb
Černyševski 14 Ec
Cerritos 34 BCb
Cerro de Pasco 37 Bd
Čerski 14 Jc
Čerskogo Hrebet 14 GHc
Červen brjag 11 Fb
Cervera 9 Fb
Červonograd 6 FGa
Cesarea (r.) 22 Ef
Cesena 10 Db
Cēsis 4 Fd
České–Budějovice 5 Ed
Ceskomoravská Vrchovina
(mts.) 5 EFd
Çeşme 22 Ac
Cessnock 29 Ie
Cettigne 11 Cb
Ceuta 24 Ba
Cévennes (mts.) 8 EFef
Cevizli dağı (mt.) 22 ABc
Ceyhan 22 EFd
Ceyhan (riv.) 22 Ed
Ceylon → Sri Lanka (Ind.
St.) 15 Ci
Chacao, Canal de– (str.) 40
Ab
Chachapoyas 37 Bc
Chacorão, Cachoeira– 38 Bb
Chad (Ind. St.) 23 DEd
Chad, Lake– 25 Bc
Chadileuvú (riv.) 39 Bc
Chadron 33 Cb
Chägai Hills 20 Bc
Chaghcharān 20 BCb
Chagos Archipelago 15 Ci
Chahbahar 21 FGde
Chaibasa 19 Ik
Chake Chake 26 CDb
Chakradharpur 19 Ik
Chala 39 Aa
Chalbi Desert 26 Ca
Chalcidice 11 Ec
Chalhuanca 37 Bd
Challapata 39 Ba
Chalna 19 Jk
Châlons–sur–Marne 8 Fc
Châlon–sur–Saône 8 Fd
Cham 5 Dd
Chamalières 8 Ee
Chaman 20 Cb
Chamba 16 Bd
Chambal (riv.) 20 Ec
Chamberlain 32 Ba
Chambéry 8 Fe
Chambeshi (riv.) 26 Cbc
Champagne (hist. reg.) 8
EFcd
Champagne (phys. reg.) 8
EFcd
Champerico 35 Ab
Champigny–sur–Marne 8 Ec
Champlain, Lake– 32 Da
Champotón 34 Cc
Chan, Ko– (i.) 19 Cg
Chañaral 39 Ab

Chan Chan (r.) 37 Bc
Chanda 20 EFde
Chandigarh 20 Eb
Chandil 19 Ik
Chandpur 20 Hd
Chang, Ko– (i.) 19 Df
Changbai Shan (mts.) 16 Gb
Changchun 16 FGb
Changde 16 De
Changhua 16 EFf
Changjiang 16 Cg
Changli 16 EFc
Changsha 15 Dg
Changzhi 16 Dc
Changzhou 16 EFd
Channel Islands [U.K.] 8 Bc
Channel Islands [U.S.] 33
ABc
Channel–Port–aux–Basques
31 Jd
Channel Tunnel (dam) 7 GHf
Chanthaburi 19 Df
Chanute 32 Bb
Chao'an 16 Ef
Chao Phraya (riv.) 19 Def
Chaor He (riv.) 16 Fa
Chaoyang [China] 16 Ef
Chaoyang [China] 16 EFb
Chapadinha 38 Cb
Chapala, Lago de– 34 Bb
Chapleau 32 Ca
Chapra 20 Fc
Charadai 39 BCb
Charaña 39 Ba
Charcas 34 Bb
Charcot Island 42 grid square
no.1
Charente (riv.) 8 CDe
Chari (riv.) 25 Bc
Charikar 20 CDab
Charité–sur–Loire, La– 8 Ed
Chariton 32 Ba
Charity 37 Db
Charleroi 8 Fb
Charleston [S.C.–U.S.] 32
CDb
Charleston [W.V.–U.S.] 32
CDb
Charleville 29 Hd
Charleville–Mézières 8 EFc
Charlotte 32 CDb
Charlottesville 32 Db
Charlottetown 31 Id
Charters Towers 29 GHc
Chartres 8 Dc
Chascomús 39 Cc
Châteaubriant 8 Cd
Château–du–Loir 8 Dd
Châteaudun 8 Dc
Château–Gontier 8 Cd
Château–Renault 8 Dd
Châteauroux 8 DEd
Château–Thierry 8 Ec
Châtellerault 8 CDd
Chatham [N.B.–Can.] 32 Ea
Chatham [Ont.–Can.] 32 Ca
Chatham [U.K.] 7 Gf
Chatham Island (i.) 27 Ee
Chatham Islands 28 Ae
Châtillon–sur–Seine 8 Fd
Châtre, La– 8 DEd
Chattahoochee (riv.) 32 Cb
Chattanooga 32 Cb

Chaumont 8 Fc
Chauny 8 Ec
Chaux–de–Fonds, La– 5 Ae
Chaves [Braz.] 38 BCb
Chaves [Port.] 9 Bb
Cheb 5 Dcd
Checheno–Ingush (Aut. Rep.)
13 De
Cheduba (i.) 19 Be
Cheju 16 Gd
Cheju–Do (i.) 16 FGd
Cheju–Haehyöp 16 Gd
Cheliff 24 BCa
Chełm 5 Ic
Chełmno 5 Gb
Chełmża 5 Gb
Cheltenham 7 EFf
Chemnitz 5 Dc
Chemult 33 Ab
Chenab (riv.) 20 Eb
Chengde 16 Eb
Chengdu 16 Bd
Chenxian 16 De
Chepo 35 Cc
Cher (riv.) 8 Ede
Cherbourg 8 Cc
Cherchell 9 FGd
Chesapeake Bay 32 Db
Chester 7 Ee
Chesterfield 7 Fe
Chesterfield, Iles– 27 Cc
Chesterfield Inlet 31 FGb
Chesterfield Inlet (str.) 31 Fb
Chetumal 34 Dc
Chetumal, Bahía de– 34 Dc
Cheviot, The– (mt.) 7 EFd
Cheyenne (riv.) 33 Cb
Cheyenne 33 Cb
Chhatarpur 19 Gj
Chi (riv.) 18 Ba
Chiang Mai 19 Ce
Chiang Rai 19 CDde
Chianje 26 Ac
Chiari 10 Bb
Chiavari 10 Bb
Chiavenna 10 Ba
Chiayi 16 EFf
Chiba 17 Gg
Chibougamau 31 Hcd
Chicago 32 Ca
Chichagof Island 31 Bc
Chichaoua 24 ABa
Chichén Itzá (r.) 34 Db
Chichester 7 Ff
Chichibu 17 Ffg
Chickasha 32 Bb
Chiclayo 36 BCd
Chico 33 Ac
Chico, Río– (riv.) 40 Bb
Chicomo 26 Cd
Chicoutimi 31 Hld
Chiemsee 5 Dde
Chieti 10 Ec
Chifeng 16 Eb
Chifre, Serra do– (mts.) 39
Da
Chihuahua 30 Hg
Chilas 20 Da
Childers 29 Id
Chile (Ind. St.) 36 CDfg
Chilecito 39 Bb
Chilia, Bratul– (riv.) 6 Id

Chilibre 35 map no.1
Chilivani 10 Bd
Chillagoe 29 Gb
Chillán 39 Ac
Chiloé, Isla de– 40 Ab
Chilpancingo de los Bravos
34 Cc
Chimanimani 26 Ccd
Chimborazo, Volcán– (mt.) 37
Bc
Chimbote 37 Bc
Chimoio 26 Cc
Chin (State) 19 Bd
China (Ind. St.) 15 Df
Chinandega 35 Bb
Chincha, Islas de– (is.) 37 Bd
Chincha Alta 37 Bd
Chinchilla 29 Hld
Chinchilla de Monte Aragón 9
Ec
Chinde 26 Cc
Chindwin (riv.) 19 Bd
Chingola 26 Bc
Chinguetti 24 Ab
Chinhae 17 Ag
Chinhoyi 26 BCc
Chiniot 20 Eb
Chinju 16 Gc
Chinmen Quemoy 16 Ef
Chinon 8 CDd
Chinsura 19 IJk
Chioggia 10 Db
Chios (i.) 22 Ac
Chipata 26 Cc
Chiquinquirá 37 Bb
Chira (riv.) 37 Ac
Chiriquí, Golfo de– 35 Bc
Chirripó, Cerro– (mt.) 35 Bc
Chişinău (Kišinev) 13 BCe
Chitato 26 Ab
Chitipa 26 Cb
Chitorgarh 20 DEcd
Chitose 17 GHc
Chitral 20 Da
Chitré 35 Bc
Chittagong 15 CDg
Chittoor 20 Ef
Chivasso 10 Ab
Chivay 39 Aa
Chivhu 26 Cc
Chivilcoy 39 BCc
Chodzież 5 Fb
Choele Choel 39 Bc
Choix 34 Bb
Chojnice 5 Fb
Chojnów 5 EFc
Chōkai–San (mt.) 17 FGe
Cholet 8 Cd
Cholseul Island 27 Cc
Choluteca 35 Bb
Choma 26 Bc
Chomo Lhari (mt.) 19 Jij
Chomutov 5 DEc
Chone 37 ABc
Ch'öngjin 14 FGe
Chŏngju 16 FGc
Ch'ŏngju 16 Gc
Chongqing 15 Dg
Chŏnju 16 Gc
Chonos, Archipiélago de los–
(is.) 40 Ab
Chorrera, La– 35 BCc

137

Chorzów 5 Gc
Chōshi 16 Jc
Chos Malal 39 ABc
Choszczno 5 EFb
Christchurch 27 De
Christmas → Kiritimati 28 Bb
Christmas Island 18 Cg
Chrudim 5 EFd
Chubut (riv.) 40 Bb
Chūgoku–Sanchi 17 BDg
Chukchi Peninsula 14 Lc
Chukchi Sea 14 Lc
Chulucanas 37 ABc
Chumbicha 39 Bb
Chumphon 19 CDf
Ch'unchŏn 16 Gc
Ch'ungmu 17 Ag
Chuŏr Phnum Krăvanah 19 Df
Chuquibamba 39 Aa
Chuquicamata 39 ABb
Chur 5 Be
Churchill 31 Fc
Churchill [Alta.–Can.] (riv.) 31 Ec
Churchill [Newf.–Can.] (riv.) 31 Ic
Churchill Peak 31 Cc
Churk 19 Hj
Churu 20 Dc
Churuguara 37 BCa
Chuvash (Aut. Rep.) 13 Dd
Chuxiong 16 Bef
Cianjur 18 Cf
Cide 22 Db
Ciechanów 5 Hb
Ciechanowiec 5 Hlb
Ciego de Ávila 35 BCa
Ciénaga 37 Ba
Cienfuegos 35 Ba
Cieszyn 5 Gd
Cieza 9 Ec
Čiganak 13 Ge
Ciguela (riv.) 9 Dc
Cihanbeyli 22 Dc
Cilacap 18 Cf
Cilician Gates (p.) 22 Ed
Cimarron (riv.) 32 Bb
Čimbaj 13 EFe
Čimkent → Šimkent 13 FGe
Cimljansk 12 Fd
Cimljanskoje vodohranilišče 12 Fd
Cimone, Monte– 10 Cb
Cimpia Turzii 6 Fc
Cîmpina 6 GHd
Cîmpulung 6 Gd
Cîmpulung Moldovenesc 6 Gc
Cinca (riv.) 9 Fb
Cincinnati 32 Cb
Cindrelu, Vîrful– (mt.) 6 Fd
Çine 11 GHe
Čingirlau 12 Hc
Cinto, Monte– 8 map no.1
Ciotat, La– 8 Ff
Circeo, Monte– 10 Dd
Čirčik 13 FGe
Circle 31 Ab
Cirebon 18 Cf
Cirò Marina 10 Fe
Čirpan 11 Fb
C.I.S. → Commonwealth of Independent States 15 BDd
Cisa, Passo della– 10 Bb

Cisco 32 Bb
Ciskei (hist. reg.) 26 Be
Cisnădie 6 Gd
Cisne, Islas del– 35 Bb
Čistopol 13 Ed
Čita 14 Ed
Citlaltépetl (mt.) 34 Cc
Citrusdal 26 ABe
Cittanova 10 Fe
Ciucaşu, Vîrful– (mt.) 6 GHd
Ciudad Acuña 34 Bb
Ciudad Altamirano 34 Bc
Ciudad Bolívar 37 Cb
Ciudad Camargo 34 Bb
Ciudad Cuauhtémoc 34 Bb
Ciudad del Carmen 34 Cc
Ciudad Delicias 34 Bb
Ciudad de Río Grande 34 Bb
Ciudadela 9 GHbc
Ciudad Guayana 37 Cb
Ciudad Guerrero 34 Bb
Ciudad Juárez 34 Ba
Ciudad Madero 34 Cb
Ciudad Mante 34 Cb
Ciudad Obregón 34 ABb
Ciudad Piar 37 Cb
Ciudad Real 9 CDc
Ciudad Rodrigo 9 Bb
Ciudad Valles 34 Cb
Ciudad Victoria 34 Cb
Civita Castellana 10 Dc
Civitanova Marche 10 Dc
Civitavecchia 10 Cc
Civray 8 Dd
Çivril 22 Bc
Cizre 21 Cb
Clacton–on–Sea 7 GHf
Claire, Lake– 31 Dc
Clamecy 8 Ed
Claremorris 7 Be
Clarence Strait 29 DEa
Clarines 37 Cb
Clarión (i.) 30 Gh
Clark Fork (riv.) 33 Bb
Clarksville 32 Cb
Clearwater, Lake– 31 Hc
Clermont 29 Hc
Clermont–Ferrand 8 Ee
Cleveland [Oh.–U.S.] 32 CDa
Cleveland [Tn.–U.S.] 32 Cb
Cleveland, Mount– 33 Bb
Cleveland Hills 7 Fd
Clifden 7 ABe
Clipperton, Île– (i.) 30 Hhi
Clisham (mt.) 7 Cb
Clonakilty 7 Bf
Cloncurry 29 FGc
Clonmel 7 Ce
Cloppenburg 5 Bb
Clorinda 39 Cb
Cloud Peak 33 Cb
Clovis 33 Cc
Cluj Napoca 6 Fc
Cluny 8 EFd
Clyde 31 Ia
Clyde (riv.) 7 Ed
Clyde, Firth of– (b.) 7 Dd
Cna (riv.) 12 Fc
Cnossus (r.) 11 Ff
Côa (riv.) 9 Bb
Coari (riv.) 37 Cc
Coari 37 Cc
Coast Mountains 31 BCab

Coast Ranges 33 Abc
Coats Island 30 la
Coats Land 42 grid square no.1
Coatzacoalcos (Puerto México) 34 Cc
Cobalt 31 GHd
Cobán 35 ABb
Cobar 29 He
Cobh 7 Bf
Cobija 37 Cd
Cobourg Peninsula 29 Ea
Coburg 5 Cc
Cochabamba (mts.) 39 Ba
Cochabamba, Cordillera de– 39 Ba
Cochem 5 Ac
Cochim 20 DEfg
Cochin China (phys. reg.) 19 Efg
Cochrane 31 GHd
Cocklebiddy 29 De
Coco (riv.) 35 Bb
Coco, Isla del– (i.) 30 Ji
Cocos (i.) 27 map no.1
Cocos Islands [Austl.] 2
Cocos Islands [Mya.] 19 Bf
Cod, Cape– 32 DEa
Codajás 37 Cc
Codlea 6 Gd
Codó 38 Cb
Coen 29 Ga
Coesfeld 5 Abc
Coetivy (i.) 15 Bj
Cœur d'Alene 33 Bb
Coff's Harbour 29 IJe
Cognac 8 Ce
Cogo 26 Aa
Coiba, Isla de– (i.) 35 Bc
Coihaique 40 Ab
Coimbatore 20 Ef
Coímbra 9 Ab
Coín 9 Cd
Coipasa, Salar de– (s. m.) 39 Ba
Čojbalsan 14 Ee
Čokurdah 14 Hlb
Colac 29 Gf
Colatina 39 DEab
Colbeck, Cape– 42 grid square no.3
Colchester 7 Gf
Coleraine 7 Cd
Coleroon (riv.) 20 Ef
Colima 34 Bc
Colima, Nevado de– (mt.) 34 Bbc
Colinas 38 Cb
Coll (i.) 7 Cc
Collie 29 Be
Collier Bay 29 Cb
Collinsville 29 Hc
Colmar 8 Gc
Colmenar 9 CDd
Colmenar Viejo 9 Db
Colômbia 39 Dab
Colombia (Ind. St.) 36 CDc
Colombo 15 Ci
Colón [Cuba] 35 Ba
Colón [Pan.] 35 BCc
Colonia del Sacramento 39 Cc
Colonia las Heras 40 Bb
Colonsay (i.) 7 Cc

Colorado (State) 33 Cc
Colorado [Co.–U.S.] (riv.) 33 Bc
Colorado [Tx.–U.S.] (riv.) 33 CDc
Colorado, Río– [Arg.] (riv.) 39 Bb
Colorado, Río– [Arg.] (riv.) 39 Bc
Colorado Plateau 33 BCc
Colorado Springs 33 Cc
Columbia (riv.) 33 ABb
Columbia [S.C.–U.S.] 32 Cb
Columbia [Tn.–U.S.] 32 Cb
Columbia, Cape– 41 grid square no.2
Columbia, District of– (State) 32 Db
Columbretes, Islas– 9 Fbc
Columbus [Ga.–U.S.] 32 Cb
Columbus [In.–U.S.] 32 Cb
Columbus [Nb.–U.S.] 32 Ba
Columbus [Oh.–U.S.] 32 Cb
Colwyn Bay 7 Ee
Comacchio 10 Db
Comacchio, Valli di– (lag.) 10 Db
Coman, Mount– 42 grid square no.1
Comandante Fontana 39 BCb
Comănești 6 GHc
Comayagua 35 Bb
Combarbalá 39 Ac
Comilla 20 Hd
Còmiso 10 Ef
Comitán de Dominguez 34 Cc
Commentry 8 Ed
Commercy 8 Fc
Commonwealth of Independent States (C.I.S.) 15 BDd
Como 10 Bb
Como, Lago di– 10 Bab
Comodoro Rivadavia 36 DEh
Comorin, Cape– 20 Eg
Comoros (Ind. St.) 23 Gg
Compiègne 8 Ec
Čona (riv.) 14 Ec
Conakry 24 Ad
Concarneau 8 ABd
Conceição do Araguaia 38 BCb
Concepción [Arg.] 39 Bb
Concepción [Bol.] 39 Ba
Concepción [Chile] 39 Ac
Concepción [Par.] 39 Cb
Concepción del Oro 34 Bb
Concepción del Uruguay 39 BCc
Conchos (riv.) 34 Bb
Concord 32 Da
Concordia 39 Cc
Condamine River 29 Hld
Conde 38 Dc
Condoboln 29 He
Condom 8 Df
Condor, Cordillera del– (mts.) 37 Bc
Congo (Ind. St.) 23 Def
Congo (riv.) 26 Ab
Cong Tum → Kontum 19 Ef
Conn, Lake– 7 Bde
Connaught (prov.) 7 Be

Connecticut (State) **32** Da
Conquista **37** Cd
Conselheiro Lafaiete **39** Db
Con Son (i.) **19** Eg
Constanța **6** Id
Constantina **9** BCd
Constantinople → İstanbul **22** Bb
Constitución **39** Ac
Consuegra **9** Dc
Contamana **37** Bc
Contas, Rio de– (riv.) **38** CDc
Contwoyto Lake **31** DEb
Coober Pedy **29** Ed
Cook, Mount– **27** De
Cook Islands **28** ABc
Cook Strait **27** Dde
Cooktown **29** Hb
Coolgardie **29** Ce
Cooma **29** Hlf
Coonamble **29** He
Cooper Creek **29** Fd
Cootamundra **29** He
Cop **5** Id
Copenhagen **4** BCe
Copiapó **39** Ab
Copper Cliff **31** Gd
Coppermine **30** FGc
Coquimbo **39** Abc
Corabia **6** Ge
Coral Harbour **31** Gb
Coral Rapids **31** GHcd
Coral Sea **27** Cc
Coral Sea Islands Territory **29** Hlb
Corantijn (riv.) **37** Db
Corbeil–Essonnes **8** Ec
Corbières (mts.) **8** Ef
Corcovado, Golfo– **40** Ab
Corcovado, Volcán– (mt.) **40** Ab
Cordele **32** Bc
Cordillera Cantábrica (mts.) **9** BDa
Cordillera Central [Col.] (mts.) **37** Bb
Cordillera Central [Dom. Rep.] (mts.) **35** Cb
Cordillera Occidental (mts.) **37** Bb
Cordillera Oriental (mts.) **37** Bb
Córdoba [Arg.] **39** Bc
Córdoba [Mex.] **34** Cc
Córdoba [Sp.] **9** Cd
Córdoba, Sierras de– (mts.) **39** Bbc
Cordova **30** DEc
Corentyne **37** Db
Corfù **11** Cd
Corfù (i.) **11** Cd
Coria **9** Bbc
Coria del Rio **9** Bd
Coringa Islets **29** Hb
Corinth **32** Cb
Corinth, Gulf of– **11** Cd
Corinto [Braz.] **39** Da
Corinto [Nic.] **35** Bb
Cork **7** Bf
Corleone **10** Df
Çorlu **22** ABb
Corner Brook **31** Jd
Cornwall (co.) **7** Df
Cornwall **31** Hd

Coro **37** BCa
Coroatá **38** Cb
Corocoro **39** Ba
Coromandel Coast **20** Fef
Coron **18** Fb
Coronation Gulf **31** DEb
Coronel Oviedo **39** Cb
Coronel Pringles **39** Bc
Coronel Suárez **39** Bc
Coropuna, Nudo– (mt.) **39** Aa
Corozal **35** Bb
Corpus Christi **32** Bc
Corque **39** Ba
Corrente, Rio– (riv.) **38** Cc
Correnti, Capo delle– (cap.) **10** Ef
Corrib, Lake– **7** Be
Corrientes **39** Cb
Corrientes (riv.) **37** Bc
Corrientes, Cabo– [Col.] **37** Bb
Corrientes, Cabo– [Mex.] **34** Bb
Corse, Cap– **8** map no.1
Corsica (i.) **8** map no.1
Corsicana **32** Bb
Corte **8** map no.1
Cortina d'Ampezzo **10** Da
Çortkov **6** GHb
Cortona **10** Cc
Çorum **22** Eb
Corumbá (riv.) **39** Ca
Corumbá **39** Ca
Coruña, La– **9** Aa
Corvallis **33** Ab
Cosenza **10** Fe
Cosmoledo Group **23** GHfg
Cosne–sur–Loire **8** Ed
Costantine **24** Ca
Costa Rica (Ind. St.) **30** Jhi
Costero Catalana, Cadena– **9** FGb
Cotabato **18** Fc
Cotagaita **39** Bb
Cotahuasi **39** Aa
Côte d'Or (mt.) **8** Fd
Cotentin (hist. reg.) **8** Cc
Cotonou **24** Cd
Cotopaxi, Volcán– (mt.) **37** Bc
Cottbus **5** DEc
Couëron **8** BCd
Council Bluffs **32** Ba
Courland (phys. reg.) **4** Ed
Coutances **8** Cc
Coutras **8** CDe
Coventry **7** EFe
Covilhã **9** Bb
Covington **32** Cb
Cowan, Lake– **29** Ce
Coward Springs **29** Fd
Cowra **29** He
Coxilha Grande (mts.) **39** Cb
Coxim **39** Ca
Cox's Bāzār **20** Hd
Cradock **26** Be
Craig **33** Cb
Crailsheim **5** Cd
Craiova **6** Fd
Crateús **38** CDb
Crato **38** CDb
Crawley **7** FGf
Cree Lake **31** Ec
Creil **8** Ec

Crema **10** Bb
Cremenea, Bratul– (riv.) **6** Hd
Cremona **10** Cb
Cres **(i.) 6** Bd
Cres **6** Bd
Crescent City **33** Ab
Crest **8** Fe
Crete (i.) **11** Ff
Creus, Cabo de– (cap.) **9** Ga
Creuse (riv.) **8** Dd
Creusot, Le– **8** EFd
Crewe **7** Ee
Criciúma **39** CDb
Crikvenica **10** Bb
Crimea (pen.) **3** Gc
Cristalina **39** Da
Cristóbal **35** map no.1
Crişu Alb (riv.) **6** EFc
Crişu Negru (riv.) **6** EFc
Crişu Repede (riv.) **6** Fc
Crna reka (riv.) **11** DEc
Croatia (Ind. St.) **6** BCd
Croisic, Le– **8** Bd
Cromwell **27** De
Crooked Island **32** Dc
Crookston **32** Ba
Crosse, La– **32** Ba
Crotone **10** Fe
Croydon **29** Gb
Crozet, Îles– (is.) **2**
Crozon **8** Ac
Cruces, Las– [Mex.] **34** Cc
Cruces, Las– [U.S.] **33** Cc
Cruz, Cabo– **32** Dd
Cruz, La– **39** ABc
Cruz Alta **39** Cb
Cruz del Eje **39** Bc
Cruzeiro **39** Bc
Cruzeiro do Sul **37** Bc
Csongrád **6** DEc
Ču **13** Ge
Ču (riv.) **13** Ge
Cuamba **26** Cc
Cuando (riv.) **26** Bc
Cuangar **26** ABc
Cuango (riv.) **26** Ab
Cuanza (riv.) **26** Abc
Cuatrociénegas de Carranza **34** Bb
Cuba (Ind. St.) **30** Kg
Cubal **26** Ac
Cubango (riv.) **26** Ac
Çubuk **22** Db
Cucuí **37** Cb
Cúcuta **36** Cc
Cuddalore **20** EFf
Cuddapah **20** Ef
Čudovo **12** Db
Cue **29** Bd
Cuéllar **9** Cb
Cuenca [Ec.] **36** Cd
Cuenca [Sp.] **9** DEbc
Cuenca, Serranía de– (mts.) **9** DEbc
Cuernavaca **34** BCc
Cuero **32** Bc
Cuevas del Almanzora **9** Ed
Čuhloma **12** Fb
Cuiabá (riv.) **39** Ca
Cuiabá **39** Ca
Cuilo (riv.) **26** Ab
Cuíto (riv.) **26** Ac

Cuíto Cuanavale **23** DEg
Čuja **14** Ed
Cu Lao Hon (i.) **19** EFf
Cullacán Rosales **34** Bb
Culion (i.) **18** EFb
Čulkovo **14** BCc
Cullera **9** EFc
Čulym (riv.) **14** Bd
Cumaná **37** Ca
Cumberland (co.) **7** Ed
Cumberland (i.) **32** Cb
Cumberland, Cap– **28** map no.4
Cumberland Islands **29** Hlc
Cumberland Peninsula **31** Ib
Cumberland Plateau **32** Cb
Cumberland Sound **31** Ib
Cumbre, Paso de la– (p.) **39** ABc
Cumbrian Mountains **7** Ed
Čumikan **14** Gd
Cuminá (riv.) **38** Bab
Cummins **29** EFe
Çumra **22** Dd
Čuna (riv.) **14** Cd
Cuneo **10** Ab
Čunja (riv.) **14** Dc
Cunnamulla **29** Hd
Cupar **7** Ec
Cupica **37** Bb
Čuprija **6** Ee
Curaçao (i.) **35** Db
Curaray (riv.) **37** Bc
Curcubăta, Vîrful– (mt.) **6** Fc
Curiapo **37** Db
Curicó **39** Ac
Curitiba **39** Cb
Currais Novos **38** Db
Curtea de Arges **6** Gd
Curtis Island [Austl.] **29** Ic
Curtis Island [N.Z.] **27** DEd
Curuá (riv.) **38** Bb
Curuzú Cuatiá **39** BCb
Curvelo **39** Da
Cusco **39** Aa
Čusovaja (riv.) **12** Ib
Čusovoj **13** Ed
Cusset **8** Ed
Cutral–Có **39** Bc
Cutro **10** Fe
Cuttack **15** Cgh
Cuxhaven **5** Bb
Cuyo Islands **18** Fb
Cuyuni (riv.) **37** Db
Cuzumel, Isla– **34** Cbc
Cyclades (is.) **11** Fe
Cyprus (Ind. St.) **15** ABf
Cyrenaica (phys. reg.) **24** DEab
Cyrene (r.) **24** Ea
Cythera (i.) **11** Ee
Czech Republic (Ind. St.) **3** EFc
Częstochowa **5** Gc

D

Dab'ah, Aḍ– **25** Ca
Dabakala **24** Bd
Daba Shan (mts.) **16** Cd
Dabbah, Ad– **25** CDc
Dabie Shan (mts.) **16** DEd

Dab - Dew

Dabola 24 Ac
Dąbrowa Górnicza 5 GHc
Dābuleni 6 FGe
Dachau 5 Cd
Dachstein (mt.) 5 De
Dadanawa 37 Db
Daday 22 Db
Dādra and Nagar Haveli 20 Dd
Dadu 20 Cc
Dadu He (riv.) 16 Be
Daet 18 Fb
Dafir 21 Ee
Dagestan (Aut. Rep.) 13 De
Dagupan 18 Fa
Dahlak (i.) 21 Cf
Dahna', Ad– (phys. reg.) 21 CDde
Dahra 24 Db
Dahra (phys. reg.) 9 Fd
Daimiel 9 Dc
Dai–Sen 17 Cg
Daitō Islands 16 He
Dajarra 29 FGc
Dakar 24 Ac
Dakhla 24 Ab
Dakhla Oasis 25 Cb
Đakovica 11 Db
Dalai Nur (l.) 16 Eb
Dalälven (riv.) 4 Dc
Dalaman (riv.) 22 Bd
Dalan–Dzadagad 14 De
Dalan–Džargalan 16 CDa
Dalap–Uliga–Darrit 27 Db
Da Lat 19 Ef
Dalbandin 20 Bc
Dalby 29 Id
Dale 4 Ac
Dalhart 33 Cc
Dali [China] 19 CDc
Dali [China] 16 CDcd
Dalian (Lüda) 16 Fc
Dalías 9 Dd
Dallas 32 Bb
Dalles, The– 33 Ab
Dalmatia (phys. reg.) 6 BDde
Dalmatovo 12 Jb
Dalnegorsk 14 Ge
Dalnerečensk 14 Ge
Daloa 24 Bd
Dalrymple, Mount– 29 Hc
Daltonganj 20 Fd
Dalupiri (i.) 18 Fa
Dalwallinu 29 Be
Daly River 29 Ea
Daly Waters 29 Eb
Daman 20 Dd
Damanhûr 25 CDa
Damar, Pulau– (i.) 18 Gf
Damaraland (hist. reg.) 26 Ad
Damâs 22 Cg
Damascus 22 Ff
Damāvand (mt.) 21 Eb
Dāmghān 21 EFb
Damietta 25 Da
Daming 16 DEc
'Dāmir, Ad– 25 Dc
Dammām, Ad– 21 Ed
Damme 5 ABb
Damodar (riv.) 19 Ik
Damoh 20 EFd
Dampier 29 Bc
Dampier Archipelago 29 ABbc

Dampier Strait 18 He
Damqawt 21 Ef
Danakil Plain (phys. reg.) 25 DEc
Da Nang 19 Ee
Dandong 16 Fbc
Daneborg 31 Ma
Dangjin Shankou 16 Ec
Dangriga 35 Bb
Danilov 12 Fb
Dankov 12 Ec
Danmark Havn 30 PQb
Danube (riv.) 6 Fd
Danube, Mouths of the– 6 Id
Danville [Il.–U.S.] 32 Ca
Danville [Va.–U.S.] 32 CDb
Danxian 16 Cg
Danzig → Gdańsk 5 Ga
Dar' ā 22 Ff
Dārāb 21 EFd
Darabani 6 Hb
Đaravica (mt.) 11 Db
Darb, Ad– 21 Cf
Darbhanga 20 Gc
Dardanelles (str.) 11 Gcd
Darende 22 Fc
Dar es Salaam 23 FGf
Dārfūr (State) 25 Cc
Darhan 15 De
Darién, Golfo de– 37 Bb
Dariyah 21 Ce
Darjeeling 20 Gc
Darlag 16 Ad
Darling Range 29 Be
Darling River 29 Ge
Darlington 7 EFd
Darłowo 5 EFa
Darmstadt 5 Bd
Darnah 24 Ea
Daroca 9 Eb
Dart, Cape– 42 grid square no.3
Dartmoor (mt.) 7 DEf
Dartmouth [Can.] 31 Id
Dartmouth [U.K.] 7 Ef
Daru 27 Cc
Daruvar 6 Cd
Darwin 29 Ea
Das (i.) 21 Ede
Dašhovuz (Tašauz) 13 Ee
Dasht (riv.) 20 Bc
Dasht–e–Kavir (des.) 21 EFc
Dasht–e–Lut (des.) 21 Fc
Datca 22 Ad
Date 17 Gc
Datia 19 Gj
Datong 16 Dbc
Datu Piang (Dulawan) 18 Fc
Daugavpils 13 Bd
Dauphin 33 CDa
Dauphiné (hist. reg.) 8 FGe
Davangere 20 DEf
Davao 15 Ei
Davao Gulf 18 Gc
Davenport 32 BCa
David 35 Bc
Davis 42 grid square no.2
Davis, Fort– 35 map no.1
Davis Sea 42 grid square no.2
Davis Strait 31 Jb
Davlekanovo 12 Hlc
Davos 5 BCe

Dawadmi, Ad– 21 Ce
Dawāsir, Wādī ad– 21 Ce
Dawei 18 Ab
Dawson 30 Ec
Dawson, Isla– (i.) 40 ABc
Dawson Creek 31 Cc
Dawson River 29 Hlcd
Dawu 16 Bd
Dax 8 Cf
Daxian 16 Cd
Daxinggou 17 ABc
Daym Zubayr 25 Cd
Dayr az Zawr 21 BCb
Dayton 32 Cb
Daytona Beach 32 CDc
Dayu 16 De
De Aar 23 Ei
Dead Sea 22 EFg
Deán Funes 39 Bc
Dease Strait 31 Eb
Death Valley 33 Bc
Deauville 8 CDc
Debao 16 Cf
Debar 11 Dc
Debica 5 Hc
Dębno 5 Eb
Debrecen 6 EFc
Debre Markos 25 Dcd
Debre Tabor 25 Dc
Decatur [Il.–U.S.] 32 Cab
Decatur [U.S.] 32 Cb
Decazeville 8 Ee
Deccan 20 Eef
Děčín 5 Ec
Decize 8 Ed
Deda 6 Gc
Dedegül dağ (mt.) 22 Cd
Dédougou 24 Bc
Dee [Scot.–U.K.] (riv.) 7 Ec
Dee [Wales–U.K.] (riv.) 7 Ee
Deer Lake 31 Jd
Degeh Bur 25 Ed
Deggendorf 5 Dd
De Grey River 29 BCc
Dehiwala–Mount Lavinia 20 Eg
Dehra Dun 20 Ebc
Dehri 19 Hlj
Dej 6 Fc
Dekese 26 Bb
Delano Peak 33 Bc
Delaware 32 Ca
Delaware Bay 32 Db
Delft 8 Fb
Delfzijl 8 Ga
Delgado, Cape– 26 Dc
Delhi 20 Ec
Delice (riv.) 22 Ec
Delingha 16 Ac
Deljatin 12 Bd
Delmenhorst 5 ABb
Delmiro Gouveia 38 Db
De Long Islands 14 Hlb
De Long Strait 41 grid square no.4
Delphi (r.) 11 Ed
Del Rio 33 CDd
Delvina 11 CDd
Demanda, Sierra de la– (mts.) 9 Da
Demerara → Georgetown 37 Db

Deming 33 Cc
Demini (riv.) 37 Cbc
Demirci 11 Hd
Demirköy 11 GHc
Demjanskoje 13 FGd
Demmin 5 Db
Dempo, Gunung– (mt.) 18 Be
Denain 8 Eb
Dengkou 16 Cb
Denham 29 Ad
Den Helder 8 EFa
Denia 9 Fc
Deniliquin 29 GHf
Denizli 22 Bd
Denmark (Ind. St.) 3 DEb
Denmark 29 Bef
Denmark Strait 30 OPc
Denpasar 18 Ef
Denton 32 Bb
D'Entrecasteaux Islands 27 Cc
Denver 33 Cc
Deoghar 19 Ij
Deo Mu Gia (p.) 19 Ee
Deoria 19 Hj
Deputatski 14 GHc
Dera Ghazi Khan 20 CDbc
Dera Ismail Khan 20 CDb
Deražnja 6 Hb
Derbent 13 De
Derby [Austl.] 29 Cb
Derby [U.K.] 7 Fe
Derecske 6 Ec
Dereköy 22 Ab
Derg, Lake– 7 Be
Dermatás, Ákra– 11 Ed
De Rose Hill 29 Ed
Derudeb 25 Dc
Derventa 6 CDd
Derwent (riv.) 7 Fde
Desaguadero [Arg.] (riv.) 39 Bc
Desaguadero [Bol.] (riv.) 39 Ba
Dese 25 DEc
Deseado (riv.) 40 Bb
Desemboque, El– 34 Aa
Desenzano del Garda 10 Cb
Desertas, Ilhas– (is.) 24 Aa
Des Moines (riv.) 32 Ba
Des Moines 32 Ba
Desna (riv.) 12 Dc
Desolación, Isla– (i.) 40 Ac
Desroches (i.) 15 Bi
Dessau 5 Dc
Detroit 32 Ca
Deutsche Bucht (b.) 5 Aa
Deva 6 Fd
Develi 22 Ec
Deventer 8 FGa
Devil's Island 37 Db
Devils Lake 32 Ba
Devin 11 Fc
Devolli (riv.) 11 Dc
Devoluy (mt.) 8 Fe
Devon (co.) 7 DEf
Devon Island 41 grid square no.1
Devonport 29 map no.1
Devrek 22 CDb
Devrez (riv.) 22 Db
Dewa (riv.) 25 Dd
Dewas 20 Ed

ewa–Sanchi (mts.) 17 Gde
ez (riv.) 21 Dc
ezfül 21 Dc
ezhou 16 Ec
ežneva, mys– 14 LMc
naka 15 CDg
halak Archipelago 25 DEc
halli Rajhara 20 Fde
hamar 21 Cg
hamtari 20 Fd
hanbad 20 Gd
hangarhi 19 Hi
hankuta 19 Ij
harwar 20 DEe
haulagiri (mt.) 20 Fc
hidhimótikhon 11 FGc
hikti Óros (mt.) 11 Ff
hilos (i.) 11 Fe
hirfis Óros (mt.) 11 Ed
holpur 19 Gj
hond 20 DEe
hone 20 Ee
honoúsa (i.) 11 FGe
horaji 20 Dd
hubri 19 ABc
hule 20 DEd
hulian 19 IJj
huri 20 Eb
ía (i.) 11 Ff
iala (riv.) 21 Dbc
iamante 39 Bc
iamantina 39 Da
iamantina, Chapada– (plat.)
38 Cc
iamantina River 29 Gc
iamantino 38 Bc
iamond Harbour 19 Jk
ianópolis 38 Cc
ibrugarh 19 BCc
ibulla 37 Ba
ickinson 33 Cb
iefenbaker, Lake– 33 Ca
iego Garcia (i.) 15 Cj
iego Ramírez, Islas– 40 ABc
ien Bien Phu 19 Dd
iepholz 5 Bb
ieppe 8 Dc
igby 31 Id
igne 8 Ge
igoin 8 Ed
igos 18 Gc
ijon 8 Fd
ikson 13 Hb
ikwa 24 Dc
ilam, Ad– 21 De
ili 15 Ej
illon 33 Db
ilolo 23 Efg
imboola 29 Gf
imboviţa (riv.) 6 Gd
imitrovgrad [Bul.] 11 FGb
imitrovgrad [Russia] 13 DEd
imitrovgrad [Yugo.] 11 Eb
imona 22 Eg
inagat (i.) 18 GGbc
inajpur 19 Jj
inan 8 BCc
inant 8 Fb
inapur 19 Ij
inard 8 Bc
inaric Alps 6 Cde
indigul 20 Efg

Dingbian 16 Cc
Dingle Bay 7 Aef
Dingwall 7 Dc
Diourbel 24 Ac
Dipolog 18 Fc
Dir 20 Da
Dire Dawa 25 Ecd
Dirk Hartog Island 29 Ad
Dirkou 24 Dc
Dirranbandi 29 Hd
Disappointment, Lake– 29 Cc
Disko Bugt 31 Jb
Disko Ø (i.) 41 grid square no.1
Dispur 19 Bc
Distrito Federal 39 Da
Diu 20 Dd
Divinópolis 39 Db
Divisões, Serra das– (mts.)
39 Ca
Divisor, Sierra de– (mts.) 37
Bc
Divnoje 12 Fd
Divriği 22 FGc
Dīwānīyah, Ad– 21 CDc
Dixon Entrance 31 Bc
Diyarbakır 21 BCb
Diz (r.) 20 Bc
Dja (riv.) 26 Aa
Djado 24 Db
Djado, Plateau du– (plat.) 24
Db
Djambala 26 Ab
Djanet 24 CDb
Djedeïda 10 Bf
Djelfa 24 Ca
Djénné 24 Bc
Djerba (i.) 24 Da
Djibouti (Ind. St.) 25 Ec
Djibouti 23 Gd
Djolu 26 Ba
Djougou 24 Ccd
Djugu 26 BCa
Dmitrijev–Lgovski 12 DEc
Dmitri Laptev Strait 14 GHb
Dmitrov 12 Eb
Dnepr (riv.) 13 Ce
Dneprodzeržinsk →
Kamenskoje 12 Dd
Dnepropetrovsk →
Jekaterinoslav 13 Ce
Dnestr (riv.) 13 Be
Dno 12 CDb
Dobbiaco / Toblach 10 Da
Doboj 6 CDd
Dobrič (Tolbuhin) 11 GHb
Dobrjanka 12 Hlb
Dobruja (phys. reg.) 6 Hlde
Doce, Rio– (riv.) 39 Da
Doda Betta (mt.) 20 Ef
Dodecanese (is.) 11 Gde
Dodge City 33 CDc
Dodoma 23 Ff
Dogai Coring 19 Ab
Döğer 22 Cc
Dōgo (i.) 17 Cf
Dogondoutchi 24 Cc
Doha 21 Ed
Dohad 20 Dd
Dokšicy 4 Fe
Dolak, Pulau– 27 Bc
Dolbeau 31 Hd
Dole 8 Fd
Dolgellau 7 DEe

Dolina 6 FGb
Dolinsk 14 He
Dolinskaja 12 Dd
Dolinskoje 6 Ic
Dolo 25 Ed
Dolomites (mts.) 10 CDa
Dolores 39 Cc
Domaniç 22 BCc
Domažlice 5 Dd
Dombarovski 13 Ed
Dombas 4 Bc
Dombóvár 6 CDc
Domeyko, Cordillera– (mts.)
39 Bb
Domfront 8 Cc
Domingos Martins 39 DEab
Dominica (Ind. St.) 36 DEb
Dominican Republic (Ind. St.)
30 KLgh
Domo 25 Ed
Domodossola 10 Ba
Dom Pedrito 39 Cc
Don [Russia] (riv.) 13 De
Don [U.K.] (riv.) 7 Ec
Donaueschingen 5 Bde
Donauwörth 5 Cd
Don Benito 9 Cc
Doncaster 7 Fe
Dondo 26 Abc
Dondra Head 20 Fg
Donec (riv.) 12 Ed
Doneck → Juzovka 13 Ce
Donegal 7 BCd
Donegal Bay 7 Bd
Dongara 29 ABd
Donggala 18 EFe
Dong Hoi 19 Ee
Dongliao He (riv.) 16 Fb
Dongning 17 Bb
Dong Rak, Phanom– 19 Df
Dongsha Dao (i.) 16 Ef
Dongting Hu (l.) 16 De
Dora, Lake– 29 Cc
Dora Baltea (riv.) 10 Ab
Dorada, La– 37 Bb
Dorado, El– [U.S.] 32 Bb
Dorado, El– [Ven.] 37 Cb
Dorchester 7 Ef
Dordogne (riv.) 8 De
Dordrecht 8 EFb
Dore, Monts– (mts.) 8 Ee
Dorgali 10 Bd
Dori 24 BCc
Dornbirn 5 BCe
Dornoch 7 DEc
Dorohoi 6 Hc
Dorotea 4 Db
Dorset (co.) 7 Ef
Dortmund 5 ABc
Doruma 26 Ba
Dosatuj 16 Ea
Dos Hermanas 9 BCd
Dosso 24 Cc
Dossor 13 Ee
Dothan 32 Cb
Douai 8 Eb
Douala 24 CDd
Douarnenez 8 ABc
Douglas [Ak.–U.S.] 31 Bc
Douglas [Az.–U.S.] 33 Cc
Douglas [S. Afr.] 26 Bd
Douglas [U.K.] 7 Dd
Douglas [Wy.–U.S.] 33 Cb

Dourada, Serra– (mts.) 38
BCc
Dourados 39 Cb
Douro (riv.) 9 Bb
Dovbyš 6 Ha
Dover [U.K.] 7 Gf
Dover [U.S.] 32 Db
Dover, Strait of– 8 Db
Dovrefjell (mts.) 4 Bc
Downpatrick 7 Dd
Dozen (i.) 17 Cf
Dråa 24 Bab
Dråa, Hamada du– (des.) 24
Bb
Dracena 39 Cb
Drăgăşani 6 Gd
Draguignan 8 FGf
Drakensberg 26 BCde
Drake Passage 40 ABc
Dráma 11 Fc
Drammen 4 Bd
Drancy 8 Ec
Drangajökull (mt.) 4 map no.1
Dravograd 6 Bc
Drawsko Pomorskie 5 Eb
Dresden 5 DEc
Dreux 8 Dc
Drevsjø 4 BCc
Drina (riv.) 6 Dd
Drin Gulf 11 Cc
Drini (riv.) 11 Db
Drogheda 7 Ce
Drogobyč 5 Id
Drôme (riv.) 8 Fe
Dronne (riv.) 8 De
Drontes (riv.) 22 Fe
Drumheller 33 Ba
Drummond Range 29 Hc
Drumochter, Pass of– 7 DEc
Druskininkai 5 IJab
Družba (i.) 12 Dc
Družba 13 He
Družina 14 Hc
Drvar 6 Cd
Dryden 31 Fd
Drygalski Island 42 grid
square no.4
Drysdale River 29 Dab
Dubai 21 EFde
Dubawnt (riv.) 31 Eb
Dubawnt Lake 31 Eb
Dubbo 29 He
Dubesar 6 Ic
Dublin (Baile Átha Cliath) 7
CDe
Dubna 12 Eb
Dubno 12 Cc
Dubovka 12 FGd
Dubrovnik 11 BCb
Dubuque 32 Ba
Duc de Gloucester, Îles du–
28 Bd
Ducie Island 28 Cd
Dudinka 13 Hc
Dudley 7 Ee
Duero (riv.) 9 Cb
Dugi Otok 6 Bd
Dugo Selo 6 BCd
Duisburg 5 CDc
Dukhan 21 Ede
Dukielska, Przełęcz– 5 HId
Dulawan → Datu Piang 18 Fc
Dulce, Rio– (riv.) 39 Bb

Dulovo 11 Gb
Duluth 32 Ba
Dûmā 22 Ff
Dumaguete 18 Fc
Dumaran (i.) 18 EFb
Dumbarton 7 Dcd
Dumfries 7 Ed
Dumka 19 Ij
Dumond d'Urville 42 grid
square no.4
Dumont D'Urville Sea 42 grid
square no.4
Dunaföldvár 6 Dc
Dunaharaszti 6 Dc
Dunajevcy 6 Hb
Dunántúl (phys. reg.) 6 CDc
Dunaújváros 6 Dc
Duncansby Head 7 Eb
Dundalk 7 Cde
Dundalk Bay 7 CDe
Dundas, Lake– 29 Ce
Dundas Strait 29 Ea
Dundee 7 Ec
Dunedin 27 De
Dunfermline 7 DEc
Dungarpur 20 Dd
Dungarvan 7 Cef
Dungeness (cap.) 7 Gf
Dunhua 16 Gb
Dunkerque 8 Eb
Dunkwa 24 Bd
Dún Laoghaire / Dunleary 7
CDe
Dunleary / Dún Laoghaire 7
CDe
Dunqulah 25 CDc
Duns 7 Ed
Duolun 16 Eb
Durance (riv.) 8 Ge
Durango 33 Cc
Durazno 39 Cc
Durazzo 11 Cc
Durban 23 Fhi
Durg 20 Fd
Durgapur 19 IJk
Durham [U.K.] 7 EFd
Durham [U.S.] 32 Db
Durmitor (mt.) 11 Cb
Durness 7 Db
Dursunbey 11 Hd
Durūz, Jabal al– (mt.) 22 Ff
Dušanbe 13 Ff
Dushan 16 Ce
Düsseldorf 5 CDc
Dutch Harbor 31 Bc
Duwaym, Ad– 25 Dc
Duyun 16 Ce
Düzce 22 Cb
Dyer Plateau (plat.) 42 grid
square no.1
Dymer 6 IJa
Dyrhólaey (cap.) 4 map no.1
Džalal–Abad 13 Ge
Džalinda 14 Fd
Džambul 13 Ge
Dzamyn–Ud 16 Db
Džankoj 12 Dd
Džardžan 14 Fc
Džargalant, Ar– 16 DEa
Dzeržinsk 13 Fd
Džetygara 13 Fd
Džezkazgan → Žezkazgan
13 Fe

Dzhugdzhur Range 14 Gd
Działdowo 5 Hb
Dzierżoniów 5 Fc
Dzun–Bajan 16 CDb
Dzungarian Basin (phys. reg.)
14 Be
Džungarski Alatau, Hrebet–
(mts.) 13 GHe
Dzun–Mod 14 Db
Džusaly 13 Fe

E

Eagle 31 Ab
Eagle Pass 33 CDd
Eastbourne 7 Gf
East Cape 27 Dd
East China Sea 16 FGde
Easter Island 2
Eastern Carpathians (mts.) 6
FHbc
Eastern Ghats (mts.) 20 EFef
Eastern Malaysia 18 DEcd
Eastern Prussia (hist. reg.) 5
Glab
East Falkland (i.) 40 Cc
East London 26 Be
Eastmain (riv.) 31 Eb
Eastmain 31 Hc
East Point 32 Cb
East Saint Louis 32 BCb
East Sea / Japan, Sea of– 16
Hibc
East Siberian Sea 41 grid
square no.4
Eau Claire 32 BCa
Eau Gallie 32 CDc
Eauripik Atoll 27 Je
Ebensee 5 DEe
Eber Gölü 22 Cc
Eberswalde 5 Db
Ebla (r.) 21 Bb
Eboli 10 Ed
Ebro (riv.) 9 Da
Eceabat 22 Ab
Echigo–Sanmyaku (mts.) 17
FGef
Echo Bay 30 GHc
Echuca 29 GHf
Écija 9 Cd
Ecuador (Ind. St.) 36 BCd
Ed 25 Ec
Edéa 24 CDd
Edefors 4 Eb
Eden 29 HIf
Edgeoya 13 Bb
Edhessa 11 DEc
Edinburgh 7 Ed
Edirne 11 Gc
Edith Ronne Ice Shelf 42 grid
square no.1
Edith Ronne Land 42 grid
square no.1
Edjeleh 24 Cb
Edmonton 30 Gd
Edmundston 31 Id
Edremit 22 Ac
Edremit Körfezi 22 Ac
Edsel Ford Ranges 42 grid
square no.3
Edward, Lake– 25 Ce

Edwards Creek 29 Ee
Edwards Plateau 33 CDcd
Edward VII Peninsula 42 grid
square no.1
Efaté, Île– (i.) 28 map no.4
Effingham 32 Cb
Eforie 6 Id
Egadi, Isole– 10 Df
Egan Range 33 Bbc
Egedesminde / Aasiaat 31
JKb
Eger 6 Ec
Egersund 4 Ad
Eğnar 22 Ed
Eğridir 22 Cd
Eğridir Gölü 22 Ccd
Eğrigöz dağı (mt.) 22 Bc
Egvekinot 14 KLc
Egypt (Ind. St.) 23 EFc
Ehingen 5 Bd
Eiao, Île– (i.) 28 Bc
Eibar 9 Da
Eichstätt 5 Cd
Eifel (mt.) 5 Ac
Eigg (i.) 7 Cc
Eight Degree Channel 20 Dg
Eights 42 grid square no.1
Eights Coast 42 grid square
no.1
Eighty Mile Beach 29 Cb
Eindhoven 8 Fb
Eiriksjökull (gl.) 4 map no.1
Eirunepé 37 BCc
Eisenach 5 BCc
Eisenerz 5 Ee
Eisenhüttenstadt 5 Eb
Eisenstadt 5 Fe
Eisleben 5 Db
Ejin Qi 16 Bb
Ekecek dağı (mt.) 22 DEc
Ekenäs 4 EFcd
Ekibastuz 13 Gd
Ekonda 14 Dc
El Affroun 9 Gd
Elafonísou, Stenón– (str.) 11
Ee
Elassōn 11 Ed
Elat 22 Eh
Elâzığ 21 BCb
Elba (i.) 10 Cc
Elbasani 11 CDc
El–Bayadh 24 Ca
Elbe (riv.) 5 Cb
Elbert, Mount– 33 Cc
Elbeuf 8 Dc
Elbistan 22 Fc
Elbląg 5 Ga
El Boulaïda 24 Ca
Elbrus (mt.) 21 Ca
Elburz Mountains 21 DEb
Elche 9 Ec
Elda 9 Ec
Eldoret 25 Dde
Elektrostal 12 EFb
Eleusís 11 Ee
Eleuthera Island 32 Dc
Elgin 7 Ec
Elgon (mt.) 25 Dd
Elhovo 11 Gb
Elista 13 Fe
Elizabeth City 32 Db
Elizabeth Island 28 map no.3
Elk 5 Ib

Elk City 33 CDc
Elko 33 Bb
Ellesmere Island 41 grid
square no.1
Elliston 29 EFe
Ellora (r.) 20 Ed
Ellsworth Highland 42 grid
square no.3
Ellsworth Mountains 42 grid
square no.1
Elmalı 22 BCd
Elmira 32 Da
Elmshorn 5 BCb
Elne 8 Ef
Elorza 37 BCb
El Salvador (Ind. St.) 30 IJh
Eluru 20 Fe
Elvas 9 Bc
Elverum 4 BCc
Ely 33 Bc
Emaé (i.) 28 map no.4
Emâmshahr 21 Fb
Emba 13 Ee
Emba (riv.) 13 Ee
Embarcación 39 Bb
Embetsu 17 Gb
Embu 26 Cb
Emden 5 Ab
Emerald 29 Hc
Emerson 31 Fd
Emet 22 Bc
Emi Koussi (mt.) 25 Bbc
Emilia–Romagna (reg.) 10
BCb
Emine, Nos– 22 ABa
Emirdağ 22 Cc
Emir dağları (mts.) 22 Cc
Emmen 8 Ga
Emmendingen 5 ABd
Emmet 29 Dc
Empalme 34 ABb
Émpoli 10 Cc
Emporia 32 Bb
Ems (riv.) 5 Ab
Encantada, Cerro de la– (mt.)
34 Aa
Encarnación 39 Cb
Ende 18 Ff
Endeavour Strait 29 Ga
Enderbury Atoll 28 Ac
Enderby Land 42 grid square
no.2
Enewetak Atoll 27 Db
Enez 11 Gc
Enez Körfezi 11 Fc
Engaru 17 Hb
Engels 13 Dd
Enggano, Pulau– (i.) 18 Bf
England (reg.) 7 EFde
Englewood 33 Cc
English Channel 8 ACbc
Enid 32 Bb
Enkhuizen 8 Fa
Enköping 4 Dd
Enna 10 Ef
Ennadai 31 Eb
Ennedi (plat.) 25 Cc
Ennis 7 Be
Enniscorthy 7 CDe
Enniskillen 7 Cd
Enns (riv.) 5 DEe
Enontekiö 4 EFa
Enschede 8 Ga

nsenada **34** Aa
nshi **16** Cde
ntebbe **25** Dde
ntinas, Punta– (cap.) **9** Dd
ntrecasteaux, Point d'– **29** ABef
ntrecasteaux, Récifs d'– **28** map no.4
ntre Rios **38** Bb
ntroncamento **9** Ac
nugu **24** Cd
nvira **37** BCc
olie o Lipari, Isole– **10** Ee
pernay **8** EFc
phesus (r.) **22** Ad
pi, Île– (i.) **27** Dc
pinal **8** Gc
quateur (reg.) **26** ABab
quatorial Guinea (Ind. St.) **23** CDe
raclea → Ereğli **22** Cb
rbîl **21** CDb
rciyas dağ (mt.) **22** EFc
rd **6** Dc
rdek **11** Gc
rebus, Mount– **42** grid square no.4
reğli **22** DEd
reğli (Eraclea) **22** Cb
renhot **16** Db
rexim **39** Cb
rfoud **24** Ba
rfurt **5** Cc
rg Chech (des.) **24** Bb
rgene (riv.) **11** Gc
rg Iguidi (des.) **24** Bb
rice **10** De
rie **32** CDa
rie, Lake– **32** CDa
rimo–Misaki **17** Hd
ritrea (Ind. St.) **25** DEc
rlangen **5** Cd
rldunda **29** Ed
rmenek **22** Dd
rmesinde **9** Ab
rmoúpolis **11** Fe
rmest Legouvé Reef **28** Bd
rode **20** Ef
romanga **29** Gd
rrigal Mountain **7** Bd
rris Head **7** ABd
rromango, Île– (i.) **28** map no.6
rseka **11** Dc
rtix He (riv.) **13** He
rzincan **21** Bab
rzurum **21** Cb
san–Misaki **17** Gd
sashi [Jap.] **17** Hb
sashi [Jap.] **17** FGd
sbjerg **4** ABe
scada **38** Db
scalón **34** Bb
scanaba **32** Ca
scárcega **34** CDc
scarpada Point **18** Fa
scatrón **9** Eb
sch–sur–Alzette **8** FGc
schwege **5** Cc
scobal **35** map no.1
scuintla **35** Ab
sfahān **21** Ec
skifjörður **4** map no.1

Eskilstuna **4** Dd
Eskimo Point **31** Fb
Eskişehir **22** Cc
Esla (riv.) **9** Ca
Eslöv **5** Da
Eşme **22** Bc
Esmeralda, La– **37** Cb
Esmeraldas **37** ABb
Esperance **29** Ce
Esperanza [Ant.] **42** grid square no.1
Esperanza [Peru] **37** Bc
Espichel, Cabo– (cap.) **9** Ac
Espinhaço, Serra do– (mts.) **39** Da
Espinho **9** Ab
Espíritu Santo (State) **39** Dab
Espíritu Santo, Île– (i.) **28** map no.4
Espoo **4** EFc
Esquel **40** Ab
Essaouira **24** ABa
Essen **5** Ac
Essequibo (riv.) **37** Db
Essex (co.) **7** FGf
Esslingen am Neckar **5** Bd
Estaca de Bares, Punta de la– (cap.) **9** Ba
Estados, Isla de los– **40** Bc
Estância **38** Dc
Estella **9** Da
Estepona **9** Cd
Estevan **33** Cb
Estonia (Ind. St.) **4** Fd
Estoril **9** Ac
Estrada, La– **9** Aa
Estrela, Serra da– (mts.) **9** Bb
Estremoz **9** Bc
Estrondo, Serra do– (mts.) **38** Cb
Esztergom **6** Dc
Étampes **8** DEc
Etawah **20** EFc
Ethiopia (Ind. St.) **23** FGe
Ethiopian Plateau **25** Ed
Etna, Monte– (Mongibello) **10** Ef
Etorofu Tō / Iturup, ostrov– (i.) **14** He
Etosha Pan (sw.) **26** Ac
Eu **8** Dbc
Euboea (i.) **11** EFd
Eucla **29** De
Eugene **33** Ab
Eugenia, Punta– (cap.) **34** Ab
Euphrates (riv.) **22** FGd
Eure (riv.) **8** Dc
Eureka [Can.] **41** grid square no.1
Eureka [U.S.] **33** Ab
Europa, Ile– **26** Dd
Europa, Picos de– (mts.) **9** Ca
Europa, Punta de– (cap.) **9** Cd
Evans, Lake– **32** Da
Evanston **33** BCb
Evansville **32** Cb
Everard, Lake– **29** Ee
Everest (Qomolangma Feng) (mt.) **20** Gc
Everett **33** Ab
Evje **4** Ad

Évora **9** Bc
Evreux **8** Dc
Exe (riv.) **7** Ef
Exeter **7** Ef
Exmouth [Austl.] **29** Ac
Exmouth [U.K.] **7** Ef
Exmouth Gulf **29** Ac
Extremadura (phys. reg.) **9** Ac
Eyasi, Lake– **26** Cb
Eyjafjallajökull (gl.) **4** map no.1
Eyl **25** EFd
Eymoutiers **8** DEe
Eyre, Lake– **29** Fd
Eyre Creek **29** Fd
Eyre Peninsula **29** Fe
Ezcaray **9** Da
Ezine **22** Ac
Ezraa **22** Ff

F

Fabriano **10** Dc
Fachi **24** Dc
Fada **25** Cc
Fada–Ngourma **24** Cc
Faddejevski, ostrov– (i.) **14** Hb
Faenza **10** Cb
Faeroe Island **3** BCa
Fafe **9** ABb
Făgăraş **6** Gd
Făgăraşului, Munţii– **6** Gd
Fagataufa Atoll **28** Cd
Fagernes **4** Bc
Fagersta **4** CDcd
Fairbanks **30** CDc
Fairbury **32** Bab
Fair Island **7** Fb
Fairview **31** Dc
Fairweather Mount **31** ABc
Faisalabad **20** Db
Faistós (r.) **11** Ff
Faizabad **20** Fc
Fakaofo Atoll **28** Ac
Fakarava Atoll **28** Bc
Falaise **8** CDc
Falakrón Óros (mts.) **11** EFc
Falam **19** Bd
Fălciu **6** Hc
Falealupo **28** map no.5
Falelima **28** map no.5
Falémé (riv.) **24** Ac
Falešty **6** Hc
Falevai **28** map no.5
Falkensee **5** Db
Falkland Islands **36** DFi
Falkland Sound **40** BCc
Falköping **4** Cd
Falls City **32** Bab
Falmouth **7** Df
Falso, Cabo– **34** Ab
Falster **5** Da
Falterona, Monte– **10** Cc
Fálticeni **6** Hc
Falun **4** CDc
Famagusta **22** DEe
Famagusta Bay **22** DEe
Famatina **39** Bb
Famatina, Nevados de– **39** Bb

Fang **19** Ce
Fangak **25** Dd
Fangxian **16** Dd
Fangzheng **17** Ab
Fangzi **16** Ec
Fanning (i.) **28** Bb
Fanning → Tabuaeran **28** Bb
Fano **10** Dc
Fanø (i.) **5** ABa
Fan Si Pan (mt.) **19** Dd
Faraday **42** grid square no.1
Faradje **26** Ba
Farafangana **26** map no.1
Farafra Oasis **25** Cb
Farah **20** Bb
Farah rud (riv.) **20** Bb
Faranah **24** ABcd
Farasān, Jazā'ir– **21** Cf
Fargo **32** Ba
Faridabad **20** Ec
Faridpur **19** Jk
Farmington **33** Cc
Fårö (i.) **4** Dd
Faro [Braz.] **38** Bb
Faro [Port.] **9** ABd
Faro, Punta del– → Peloro, Capo– **10** Ee
Farquhar Group **23** GHg
Farrukhabad **20** EFc
Färs (phys. reg.) **21** Ed
Fársala **11** Ed
Farsund **4** Ad
Farvel, Kap– **31** Kc
Fasã **21** Ed
Fasano **10** Fd
Fāshir, Al– **25** Cc
Fashn, Al– **25** CDb
Fashoda → Kodok **25** Dcd
Fastov **5** Ia
Fataka Island **27** Dc
Fatehpur **19** Hj
Fátima **9** Ac
Fatu Hiva, Île– (i.) **28** Cc
Făurei **6** Hd
Fauske **4** CDb
Favignana (i.) **10** Df
Fäw, Al– **21** Dcd
Faxaflói **4** map no.1
Faya–Largeau **25** BCc
Faydzābād **20** Da
Fayetteville [Ak.–U.S.] **32** Bb
Fayetteville [N.C.–U.S.] **32** Db
Fâyid **25** map no.1
Fayyūm, Al– **25** CDb
Fderick **24** Ab
Fécamp **8** CDc
Federal **39** Cc
Federated States of Micronesia (Ind. St.) **27** CDb
Fehmarn (i.) **5** Ca
Feijó **37** BCc
Feira de Santana **38** CDc
Feke **22** EFcd
Felanitx **9** Gc
Feldberg (mt.) **5** Be
Feldkirch **5** Be
Felipe Carillo Puerto **34** Dc
Feltre **10** Cb
Femund (l.) **4** Bc
Fengcheng **16** DEe
Fengtai **16** Dc
Fenoarivo Atsinanana **26** map no.1

Fen - Fru

Fens, The– (phys. reg.) 7 FGe
Fenyang 16 Dc
Feodosija 12 DEde
Férai 11 FGc
Ferdows 21 Fc
Fergana 13 Gef
Fergus Falls 32 Ba
Ferkéssédougou 24 Bcd
Fermo 10 Dc
Fermoy 7 Be
Fernando de Noronha (i.) 36 GHd
Ferrara 10 Cb
Ferreira do Alentejo 9 ABc
Ferrol del Caudillo, El– 9 Aa
Ferté–Bernard, La– 8 Dc
Fès 24 Ba
Feshi 26 Ab
Feteşti 6 Hd
Fethiye 22 Bd
Fethiye Körfezi 22 Bd
Fetlar (i.) 7 Fa
Fezzan (phys. reg.) 24 Db
Fianarantsoa 23 GHh
Fichtel–Gebirge (mts.) 5 CDc
Fidenza 10 Cb
Fieri 11 Cc
Fife Ness (cap.) 7 Ec
Fifth Cataract 25 Dc
Figeac 8 DEe
Figueira da Foz 9 Ab
Figueras 9 Ga
Fiji Islands (Ind. St.) 27 Dc
Filabres, Sierra de los– (mts.) 9 DEd
Filadélfia 38 Cb
Filchner 42 grid square no.1
Filchner Ice Shelf 42 grid square no.1
Filiasi 6 Fd
Filiátai 11 Dd
Filiatrá 11 De
Filicudi (i.) 10 Ee
Filingué 24 Cc
Filippiás 11 Dd
Filippoi (r.) 11 Fc
Filipstad 4 Cd
Fimi (riv.) 26 Ab
Finike 22 Cd
Finisterre 9 Aa
Finisterre, Cabo de– (cap.) 9 Aa
Finke 29 Ed
Finke River 29 Ec
Finland (Ind. St.) 3 Fa
Finland, Gulf of– 4 EFd
Finnmarksvidda (mts.) 4 EFa
Finnsnes 4 Da
Finsteraarhorn (mt.) 10 Aa
Finsterwalde 5 Dc
Firdân, El– 25 map no.1
Firminy 8 EFe
Firozabad 20 EFc
Firozpur 20 Db
First Cataract 25 Db
Fishguard 7 Def
Fiskenæsset / Fiskengesset 31 Jb
Fiskengesset / Fiskenæsset 31 Jb
Fitzroy Crossing 29 Db

Fitzroy River [Austl.] 29 CDb
Fitzroy River [Austl.] 29 Hlc
Fizi 26 Bb
Flagstaff 33 Bc
Flamborough Head 7 FGd
Fläming (mts.) 5 Dbc
Flanders (phys. reg.) 8 Eb
Flannan Isles 7 BCb
Flathead Lake 33 Bb
Flattery, Cape– [Austl.] 29 Hab
Flattery, Cape– [U.S.] 33 Ab
Flèche, La– 8 CDd
Flekkefjord 4 Ad
Flensburg 5 BCa
Flers 8 Cc
Fleury–les–Aubrais 8 Dcd
Flinders Bay 29 ABef
Flinders Group 29 GHa
Flinders Island 29 map no.1
Flinders Ranges 29 Fe
Flinders Reefs (is.) 29 Hb
Flinders River 29 Gb
Flin Flon 31 Bb
Flint 32 Ca
Flint Island 28 Bc
Florac 8 Ee
Florence [It.] 10 Cc
Florence [Al.–U.S.] 32 Cb
Florence [S.C.–U.S.] 32 Db
Florencia 37 Bb
Flores 35 ABb
Flores, Las– 39 BCc
Flores, Pulau– (i.) 15 Ej
Flores Sea 18 EFf
Floreşty 6 Ic
Floriano 38 Cb
Florianópolis 39 Db
Florida 39 Cc
Florida (State) 32 Cbc
Florida, Straits of– 32 CDc
Florida Keys (is.) 32 Cc
Flõrīna 11 Dc
Florø 4 Ac
Foča 6 De
Focşani 6 Hd
Foggia 10 Ed
Föhr (i.) 5 Ba
Foix 8 Df
Fokino 12 DEc
Folda (b.) 4 Cb
Folda (i.) 4 Bb
Folégadros (i.) 11 Fe
Folgefonni (gl.) 4 Acd
Foligno 10 Dc
Folkestone 7 Gf
Fond du Lac 32 BCa
Fondi 10 Dd
Fonsagrada 9 Ba
Fonseca, Golfo de– 35 Ba
Fontainebleau 8 DEc
Fonte Boa 37 Cc
Fontenay–le–Comte 8 Cd
Fontur (cap.) 4 map no.1
Forbach 8 Fc
Forbes 29 He
Forest Lawn 31 Dc
Forfar 7 Ec
Forli 10 Db
Formentera (i.) 9 FGc
Formentor, Cabo de– (cap.) 9 Gbc
Formiga 39 Db

Formosa [Arg.] 39 Cb
Formosa [Braz.] 39 Da
Formosa → Taiwan (Ind. St.) 15 Eg
Formosa, Serra– (mts.) 38 Bc
Forrest 29 De
Forsayth 29 Gb
Forssa 4 Ec
Forst 5 Ec
Fort Albany 31 Db
Fortaleza 38 Db
Fort Augustus 7 Dc
Fort Chimo 30 KLd
Fort Chipewyan 31 DEc
Fort Collins 33 Cb
Fort–de–France 35 Db
Fort Dodge 32 Ba
Fortescue River 29 Bc
Fort Frances 31 Fd
Fort Franklin 31 Cb
Fort George 31 Eb
Fort Good Hope 31 Cb
Forth, Firth of– (b.) 7 Ec
Fortín Madrejón 39 BCb
Fort Lauderdale 32 Cc
Fort Liard 31 CDbc
Fort Mc Pherson 31 Bb
Fort Myers 32 Cc
Fort Nelson 31 Cc
Fort Norman 31 Cb
Fort Peck Reservoir (l.) 33 Cb
Fort Pierce 32 CDc
Fort Portal 25 Dd
Fort Providence 31 CDb
Fort Reliance 31 Eb
Fort Resolution 31 DEb
Fort–Rupert 31 Hc
Fort Saint James 31 Cc
Fort Saint John 30 Fd
Fort Sandeman 20 Cb
Fort Saskatchewan 31 Dc
Fort Scott 32 Bb
Fort Ševčenko 13 Ee
Fort Severn 31 Gc
Fort Simpson 31 Cb
Fort Smith [Can.] 31 Dbc
Fort Smith [U.S.] 32 Bb
Fort Stockton 33 Dc
Fort Vermilion 31 Dc
Fort Wayne 32 Ca
Fort William 7 CDc
Fort William → Thunder Bay 31 FGd
Fort Worth 32 Bb
Fort Yukon 30 Dc
Fos 8 Ff
Foshan 16 Df
Fossano 10 Ab
Fossil Bluff 42 grid square no.1
Fougères 8 Cc
Foula (i.) 7 Ea
Foul Bay 25 Dc
Foumban 24 Dd
Foúrnoi (i.) 11 Ge
Fourth Cataract 25 Dc
Fouta Djalon (mt.) 24 Ac
Foutouna, Île– (i.) 28 map no.4
Foveaux Strait 27 De
Fowler's Bay 29 Ee
Foxe Bassin 31 Hb
Foxe Channel 31 GHb

Foxe Peninsula 31 Hb
Foz do Iguaçu 39 Cb
Fraga 9 EFb
Franca 39 Db
Francavilla Fontana 10 Fd
France (Ind. St.) 3 CDc
Franche–Comté (hist. reg.) 8 FGcd
Francistown 26 Bd
Franconia (hist. reg.) 5 BCd
Frankenwald (mts.) 5 Cc
Frankfort 32 Cb
Frankfurt am Main 5 Bc
Frankfurt an der Oder 5 Eb
Frankische Alb (mts.) 5 Cd
Franklin, District of– 31 DHai
Franklin Strait 31 Fa
Franz 31 Gd
Franz Joseph Land 41 grid square no.3
Frasca, Capo della– 10 Be
Frascati 10 Dd
Fraser (riv.) 33 Aa
Fraserburgh 7 Fc
Fraser Island 29 IJd
Fray Bentos 39 Cc
Frazier Downs 29 Cb
Fredericia 4 Be
Frederick Reef (i.) 29 IJc
Fredericton 31 Id
Frederikshåb / Paamiut 31 JKb
Frederikshavn 4 Bd
Fredrikstad 4 BCd
Freeport 32 Bc
Freetown 24 Ad
Fregenal de la Sierra 9 Bc
Freiberg 5 Dc
Freiburg im Breisgau 5 ABd
Freising 5 Cd
Freistadt 5 Ed
Fréjus 8 Gf
Fremont 32 Ba
French Guiana (Dep.) 36 Ec
French Polynesia 28 BCc
Fresco (riv.) 38 Bb
Fresnillo de Gonzáles Echeverría 34 Bb
Fresno 33 ABc
Fria, Cape– 26 Ac
Fria, La– 37 Bb
Frías 39 Bb
Fribourg 5 Ae
Fridtjof Nansen, Mount– 42 grid square no.3
Friedrichshafen 5 BCe
Friesland (phys. reg.) 8 FGa
Frijoles 35 map no.1
Frio, Cabo– 38 Cd
Frisian Islands 5 CDb
Friuli–Venezia Giulia (reg.) 11 CDab
Frobisher Bay (b.) 31 Ib
Frobisher Bay 31 HIb
Frohavet 4 Bbc
Frolovo 12 Fd
Frome, Lake– 29 FGe
Frontera 34 Cc
Front Range 33 Cbc
Frosinone 10 Dd
Frøya (i.) 4 ABc
Frunze → Biškek 13 Ge
Fruška gora (mt.) 6 Dd

rýdek–Místek **5** FGd
uente de Cantos **9** BCc
uente de San Esteban, La– **9** Bb
uenteguinaldo **9** Bb
uerte (riv.) **34** Bb
uerte Olimpo **39** Cb
uerteventura (i.) **24** Ab
ugu **16** Dc
ujayrah, Al– **21** Fde
ujian (prov.) **16** Ee
ujin **16** Ha
uji–San (mt.) **16** Ic
ujisawa **17** Fg
ukagawa **17** GHc
ukuchiyama **17** Dg
ukue **17** Ah
ukue–Jima (i.) **17** Ah
ukui **16** Ic
ukuoka **16** GHd
ukushima **16** Jc
ukuyama **16** Hcd
ulanga (i.) **28** map no.6
ulda **5** Bc
ulda (riv.) **5** Bc
uling **16** Ce
ulton **32** Cb
unabashi **17** FGg
unafuti (i.) **27** DEc
unchal **24** Aa
undão **9** Bb
undy, Bay of– **31** Id
untua **24** Cc
urancungo **26** Cc
urano **17** Hc
urmanov **12** EFb
urnas, Rêpresa de– (l.) **39** Db
urneaux Group **29** map no.1
ürstenfeld **5** EFe
ürstenfeldbruck **5** Cd
ürstenwalde **5** Eb
ürth **5** Cd
urukawa **17** Ge
ushun **14** Fe
üssen **5** Ce
utuna, Île– (i.) **27** DEc
uwah **22** Cg
u Xian **16** Fc
uxin **16** Fb
uyang **16** DEd
uyu **16** FGa
uyuan **16** Ha
uzhou [China] **16** EFe
uzhou [China] **16** Ee
yn (i.) **4** Be

G

Gaalkacyo **25** Ed
Gabela **26** Ac
Gabès, Gulf of– **24** Da
Gabon (riv.) **24** Cde
Gabon (Ind. St.) **23** CDef
Gaborone **26** Bd
Gabrovo **11** Fb
Gacko **11** Cb
Gadag **20** Ee
Gäddede **4** Cb
Gadjač **12** Dc
Gádor **9** Dd

Gadsden **32** Cb
Gáeşti **6** Gd
Gaeta **10** Dd
Gaeta, Golfo di– **10** Dd
Gagarin **12** DEb
Gagnoa **24** Bd
Gagnon **31** Ic
Gaïdouronésion → Chrysé (i.) **11** Ff
Gainesville [Fl.–U.S.] **32** Cc
Gainesville [Ga.–U.S.] **32** Cb
Gainesville [Tx.–U.S.] **32** Bb
Gairdner, Lake– **29** Fe
Gairloch **7** CDc
Gaj **12** Ic
Gajny **12** Ha
Gajsin **6** Ib
Gajvoron **6** Ib
Galán, Cerro– **39** Bb
Galapagos Islands **36** ABcd
Galaţi **6** HId
Galatina **10** Gd
Galela **18** Gd
Galera, Punta– [Chile] (cap.) **39** Ac
Galera, Punta– [Ec.] (cap.) **37** Ab
Galesburg **32** BCa
Galič [Russia] **12** Fb
Galić [Ukr.] **6** Gb
Galicia [Pol.] (phys. reg.) **5** HId
Galicia [Sp.] (phys. reg.) **9** ABa
Galilee, Sea of– → Tiberias, Lake– **22** EFf
Galite, La– (i.) **10** Bf
Galle **15** Ci
Gállego (riv.) **9** Ea
Gallinas, Punta– (cap.) **37** Ba
Gallipoli **10** Gd
Gallipoli → Gelibolu **22** Ab
Gällivare **4** Eb
Galloway, Mull of– (cap.) **7** Dd
Gallup **33** Cc
Gallur **9** Eb
Galveston **30** Ig
Galway **7** Be
Galway Bay **7** Be
Gambela **25** Dd
Gambia (Ind. St.) **23** Ad
Gambia (riv.) **24** Ac
Gambier Islands **28** Cd
Gamboa **35** map no.1
Gamboma **26** Ab
Gambos **26** Ac
Gammelstad **4** Eb
Gamova, mys– **17** Bc
Ganda **26** Ac
Gandak (riv.) **19** HIj
Gander **31** Jd
Gandhinagar **20** Dd
Gandía **9** EFc
Ganganagar **20** Dc
Gangapur **19** Gj
Gangdisê Shan **20** FGbc
Ganges (riv.) **20** Gcd
Ganges, Mouths of the– **20** GHd
Gangtok **15** Cg
Gangu **16** Cd
Gan Jiang (riv.) **16** DEe

Gannat **8** Ed
Gannett Peak **33** BCb
Ganso Azul **37** Bc
Gansu (prov.) **16** Bc
Ganzhou **16** DEe
Gao **24** Cc
Gaoua **24** Bcd
Gaoyou **16** Ed
Gap **8** FGe
Garacad **25** EFd
Garanhuns **38** Db
Garapan **27** Cb
Garda **10** Cb
Garda, Lago di– (l.) **10** Cb
Gardanne **8** FGf
Gardelegen **5** Cb
Garden City **32** Bb
Gardez **20** Cb
Gardner Pinnacles (i.) **28** Aa
Gargaliánoi **11** De
Gargano, Monte– **10** Ed
Garies **26** Ae
Garissa **26** Cb
Garmisch–Partenkirchen **5** Ce
Garonne (riv.) **8** CDe
Garoowe **25** Ed
Garoua **24** Dd
Garrovillas **9** Bc
Garrucha **9** Ed
Garry, Lake– **31** EFb
Garut **18** Cf
Garwa **19** Hj
Gary **32** Ca
Garyarsa **20** Fb
Garzê **16** ABd
Garzón **37** Bb
Gasan–Kuli **21** Eb
Gascony (hist. reg.) **8** CDf
Gascoyne Junction **29** Bd
Gascoyne River **29** ABcd
Gashua **24** Dc
Gaspé **31** Id
Gaspé, Péninsule de– **31** Id
Gastonia **32** Cb
Gastre **40** Bb
Gata, Akra– **22** De
Gata, Cabo de– (cap.) **9** DEd
Gata, Sierra de– (mts.) **9** Bb
Gatčina **4** Gd
Gateshead **7** EFd
Gâtine, Hauteurs de la– (mts.) **8** Cd
Gatton **29** Id
Gatún **35** map no.1
Gatún, Río– (riv.) **35** map no.1
Gatun Lake **35** map no.1
Gatun Locks **35** map no.1
Gaucín **9** Cd
Gaud–i–Zirreh (l.) **21** Gd
Gauja (riv.) **4** Fd
Gavdhopoúla (i.) **11** Ef
Gávdhos (i.) **11** EFf
Gave de Pau (riv.) **8** Cf
Gävle **4** Dc
Gawahati **19** Bc
Gawler **29** Fe
Gawler Ranges **29** EFe
Gaxun Nur (l.) **16** ABb
Gaya [India] **20** FGcd
Gaya [Niger] **24** Cc
Gayndah **29** Id

Gaza **22** Eg
Gaziantep **21** Bb
Gazipaşa **22** CDd
Gdańsk (Danzig) **5** Ga
Gdańsk, Gulf of– **5** Ga
Gdov **4** FGd
Gdynia **5** FGa
Gebe, Pulau– (i.) **18** Gde
Gebze **11** Hc
Gediz (riv.) **22** ABc
Gediz **22** Bc
Gedser **4** BCe
Geelong **29** Gf
Geelvink Channel **29** Ad
Geesthacht **5** Cb
Geita **26** Cb
Gejiu **16** Bf
Gela **10** Ef
Gelegra **22** CDbc
Gelibolu (Gallipoli) **22** Ab
Gelsenkirchen **5** Ac
Gemena **26** ABa
Gemlik **22** Bb
Genale (riv.) **25** DEd
General Acha **39** Bc
General Alvear **39** Bc
General Belgrano Station **42** grid square no.1
General Bernardo O'Higgins **42** grid square no.1
General Carrera, Lago– **40** Ab
General Conesa **40** Bab
General Juan Madariaga **39** Cc
General La Madrid **39** Bc
General Paz **39** Cb
General Pico **39** Bc
General Pinedo **39** Bb
General Roca **39** Bc
General Santos **18** FGc
General Toševo **11** GHb
Geneva **5** Ae
Geneva, Lake– (Leman, Lac–) **10** Aa
Geničesk **12** DEd
Gennargentu (mts.) **10** Bde
Genoa **10** Bb
Genoa, Gulf of– **10** Bb
Genrietty, ostrov– **14** IJb
Gent **8** Eb
Genthin **5** CDb
Geographe Bay **29** ABe
Geographe Channel **29** Acd
Georga, Zemlja– **13** DEab
George **26** Be
George Town **29** map no.1
Georgetown [Cay. Is.] **35** BCb
Georgetown [Mala.] **19** CDgh
Georgetown [U.S.] **32** Db
Georgetown (Demerara) **37** Db
George V Coast **42** grid square no.4
Georgia (State) **32** Cb
Georgia (Ind. St.) **13** Dc
Georgian Bay **31** GHd
Georgina River **29** Fc
Georg von Neumayer **42** grid square no.1
Gera **5** CDc
Geral, Serra– (mts.) **39** CDb
Geral de Goiás, Serra– (mts.) **38** Cc

Geraldton [Austl.] **29** Ad
Geraldton [Can.] **31** Gd
Gereshk **20** Bb
Gerlachovský štít (mt.) **5** Hd
Germany (Ind. St.) **3** DEbc
Germiston **26** Bd
Gerona **9** Gab
Gers (riv.) **8** Df
Gerze **22** Eb
Geser **18** He
Getafe **9** CDb
Geteina, El– **25** Dc
Gevgelija **11** Ec
Geyik dağ (mt.) **22** Dd
Geysir **4** map no.1
Ghadāmis **24** CDab
Ghaghara (riv.) **20** Fc
Ghana (Ind. St.) **23** BCe
Ghanzi **26** Bd
Ghardaïa **24** Ca
Ghardimaou **10** Bf
Gharyān **24** Da
Ghāt **24** CDb
Ghatsila **19** Ik
Ghaydah, Al– **21** Ef
Ghazāl, Baḥr al– (riv.) **25** CDd
Ghazālah, Al– **21** Cd
Ghaziabad **19** Gi
Ghazipur **19** Hj
Ghazni **20** Cb
Gheorghe Gheorghiu–Dej **6** Hc
Gheorghieni **6** GHc
Gherla **6** FGc
Ghor, El– **22** Efg
Ghugri (riv.) **19** Ij
Ghurdaqah, Al– **25** Db
Gialoúsa **22** DEe
Giandža (Kirovabad) **13** De
Giant's Causeway **7** Cd
Giarre **10** Ef
Gibara **35** Ca
Gibraltar **9** Cd
Gibraltar, Strait of– **24** Ba
Gibson Desert **29** CDc
Gidole **25** Dd
Gien **8** Ed
Gießen **5** Bc
Gifu **16** Ic
Giglio (i.) **10** Cc
Gijón **9** Ca
Gila (riv.) **33** Bc
Gila Bend **33** Bc
Gilbâna **25** map no.1
Gilbert River **29** Gb
Gilgit **20** Da
Gillingham **7** Gf
Gineifa **25** map no.1
Gingoog (mt.) **18** FGc
Ginir **25** Ed
Gioia del Colle **10** Fd
Gióna Óros (mt.) **11** Ed
Giovi, Passo dei– (p.) **10** Bb
Girardot **37** Bb
Giresun **21** Ba
Giresun dağları (mts.) **22** FGb
Giridih **19** Ij
Gironde (riv. m.) **8** Ce
Gisborne **27** Dd
Giulianova **10** DEc
Giurgiu **6** Gde

Givet **8** Fb
Givors **8** Fe
Giza **25** CDab
Gižiga **14** IJc
Giżycko **5** Hab
Gjirokastra **11** CDc
Gjoia Haven **31** Fb
Gjøvik **4** Bc
Gjuhës, Kep i– **11** Cc
Glace Bay **32** Fa
Gladstone **29** Ic
Gláma (mt.) **4** map no.1
Glåma (riv.) **4** Bcd
Glasgow [U.K.] **7** DEd
Glasgow [U.S.] **33** Cb
Glauchau **5** Dc
Glazov **13** Ed
Glendale **33** Bc
Glendive **33** Cb
Glenelg River **29** Gf
Glen Innes **29** Id
Glen More (phys. reg.) **7** Dc
Glens Falls **32** Da
Glenwood Springs **33** Cbc
Glina **10** EFb
Glittertind (mt.) **4** Bc
Gliwice (mt.) **5** Gc
Globe **33** BCc
Głogów **5** EFc
Glomfjord **4** Cb
Glommersträsk **4** DEb
Glorieuses, Iles– **26** map no.1
Gloucester **7** EFf
Głuchołazy **5** Fc
Glückstadt **5** Bb
Gluhov **12** Dc
Gmünd **5** Ed
Gmunden **5** DEe
Gniezno **5** Fb
Gnjilane **11** Db
Gnowangerup **29** Be
Goa (State) **20** De
Goalpara **19** Jj
Goba **25** DEd
Gobabis **23** DEh
Gobernador Gregores **40** ABb
Gobi Desert **14** De
Gobijski Altaj **16** ABab
Gobò **17** Dgh
Goce Delčev **11** EFc
Godavari (riv.) **20** Ee
Godhavn / Qeqertarsuaq **30** MNc
Godhra **20** Dd
Godollő **6** Dc
Godoy Cruz **39** Bc
Godthåb / Nuuk **30** MNc
Gö–Gawa (riv.) **17** Cg
Gogland, ostrov– (i.) **4** Fc
Goiana **38** Db
Goiânia **39** CDa
Goiás (State) **38** Cc
Goiás **39** Ca
Gökçeada (i.) **11** Fc
Gökırmak (riv.) **22** Eb
Göksu [Tur.] (riv.) **22** Bb
Göksu [Tur.] (riv.) **22** Dd
Göksu [Tur.] (riv.) **22** EFd
Göksun **22** Fc
Gol **4** Bc
Golburn Islands **29** Ea
Golčiha **13** Hb

Gölcük **22** BCb
Gołdap **5** Ia
Gold Coast (phys. reg.) **24** Bd
Gold Coast **29** IJd
Golden **31** Dc
Goléa, El– **24** Ca
Goleniów **5** Eb
Golfito **35** Bc
Golija (mt.) **11** CDb
Goljam Perelik (mt.) **11** EFc
Golmud **15** Df
Golo (riv.) **8** map no.1
Golpāyegān **21** DEc
Golspie **7** Ebc
Goma **25** Ce
Gomati (riv.) **19** Hj
Gombe **24** Dc
Gomel **13** Cd
Gomera (i.) **24** Ab
Gómez Palacio **34** Bb
Gomo **20** Gb
Gonābād **21** FGc
Gonaïves **35** Cb
Gonâve, Isla de la– (i.) **35** Cb
Gonbad–e–Qabus **21** EFb
Gonda **19** Hj
Gonder **25** Dc
Gondia **20** EFd
Gönen **11** Gc
Gong'an **16** Dde
Gongbo'gyamda **19** Bbc
Gongga Shan (mt.) **16** Be
Gonghe **16** ABc
Good Hope, Cape of– **26** Ae
Goodland **33** Cc
Goomalling **29** Be
Goondiwindi **29** HId
Goose Bay **31** Jc
Gorakhpur **20** FGc
Gördes **11** Hd
Gordonvale **29** Hb
Gore **27** De
Goré [Chad] **25** Bd
Goré [Eth.] **25** Dd
Gorgān **21** EFb
Gorgogna, Isla– (i.) **37** Bb
Gorgora **25** Dc
Gorizia **10** Dab
Gorki **12** Dc
Gorki → Nižni Novgorod **13** Dd
Gorlice **5** Hd
Görlitz **5** Ec
Gorlovka **13** CDe
Gorna Orjahovica **11** FGb
Gornjacki **13** Fc
Gornji Vakuf **6** Ce
Gorno Altajsk **13** Hd
Gornozavodsk **14** GHe
Gorny **17** CDb
Gorodec **12** Fb
Gorodenka **6** Gb
Gorodišče **12** Dd
Gorodnica **6** Ha
Gorodok [Mold.] **6** Hb
Gorodok [Ukr.] **12** Cd
Gorohov **6** Ga
Gorontalo **18** Fd
Goryn (riv.) **12** Cc
Gorzów Wielkopolski **5** Eb
Goshogawara **17** FGd
Goslar **5** Cc
Gospić **6** Bd

Gosport **7** Ff
Gostivar **11** Dc
Gostyń **5** Fc
Gostynin **5** Gb
Göta älv (riv.) **4** Cd
Göta kanal **4** CDd
Götaland **4** Cd
Göteborg **4** BCd
Gotel Mountains **24** Dd
Gotha **5** Cc
Gotland (i.) **4** Dd
Gotö–Rettö **16** Gd
Gotska Sandön (i.) **4** Dd
Göttingen **5** BCc
Gough (i.) **23** ABj
Gouin, Réservoir– (res.) **31** Hd
Goulburn **29** HIef
Goulette, La– **10** Cf
Gouménissa **11** Ec
Goundam **24** Bc
Gourdon **8** De
Gouré **24** Dc
Gouro **25** BCc
Govāter **20** Bc
Gove Peninsula **29** Fa
Goverla, gora– (mt.) **6** Gb
Governador Valadares **39** Da
Goya **39** Cb
Göynük **22** Cb
Gozo (i.) **10** Ef
Gračac **6** BCd
Gracias a Dios, Cabo– **35** Bb
Gradaús **38** Bb
Gradaús, Serra dos– (mts.) **38** Bb
Grafton **29** Id
Grafton, Cape– **29** Hb
Graham Island **31** Bc
Graham Land **42** grid square no.1
Grahamstown **26** Be
Grain Coast **24** ABd
Grajaú **38** Db
Grajewo **5** Ib
Grampian Mountains **7** DEc
Granada [Nic.] **35** Bb
Granada [Sp.] **9** Dd
Gran Arber (mt.) **5** Dd
Granby **31** Hd
Gran Canaria (i.) **24** Ab
Gran Chaco (phys. reg.) **39** BCb
Grand Bahama Island **32** Dc
Grand Ballon **8** Gd
Grand–Bassam **24** Bd
Grand Canal **7** Ce
Grand Canyon (v.) **33** Bc
Grand Canyon **33** Bc
Grand'Cayman (i.) **35** Bb
Grand'Combe, La– **8** EFe
Grande, Rio– [Bol.] (riv.) **39** Ba
Grande, Rio– [Braz.] (riv.) **39** Dab
Grande, Rio– [Braz.] (riv.) **38** Cc
Grande, Río– [N. Amer.] (riv.) **33** CDd
Grande, Río– [Nic.] (riv.) **35** Bb
Grande Comore (i.) **26** Dc

Grande Prairie 31 CDc
Grand Erg Occidental 24 BCab
Grand Erg Oriental (des.) 24 Cab
Gran Deserto (phys. reg.) 34 Aa
Grand Falls 31 Gc
Grand Forks 32 Ba
Grand Island 32 Ba
Grand Junction 33 Cc
Grand–Lahou 24 Bd
Grand–Lieu, Lac de– (l.) 8 BCd
Grand Rapids 32 Ca
Grange, La– 32 Cb
Granite City 32 BCb
Granites, The– 29 Ec
Granja 38 Cb
Granollers 9 Gb
Gran Paradiso (mt.) 10 Ab
Gran Sabana, La– (mts.) 37 Cb
Gran San Bernardo (p.) 10 Ab
Gran Sasso d'Italia (mt.) 10 Dc
Gran Teton (mt.) 33 Bb
Grants 33 Cc
Grants Pass 33 Ab
Granville 8 Cc
Gras, Lac de– (l.) 31 Db
Grasse 8 Gf
Grassy 29 map no.1
Gravina in Puglia 10 Fd
Gray 8 Fd
Grays Peak 33 Cc
Graz 5 Ee
Grazalema 9 Cd
Grdelica 11 DEb
Great Artesian Basin 29 FGd
Great Australian Bight 29 DEe
Great Barrier Reef 29 Glab
Great Basin (phys. reg.) 33 Bbc
Great Bear Lake 31 Db
Great Bend 32 Bb
Great Bitter Lake 25 map no.1
Great Channel 19 BCg
Great Dividing Range 29 GHbc
Greater Antilles (is.) 30 JLgh
Greater Khingan Range 14 EFde
Great Exuma Island 32 Dc
Great Falls 33 Bb
Great Inagua Island 35 Ca
Great Namaland (hist. reg.) 26 Ad
Great Nicobar (i.) 19 BCg
Great Poland (hist. reg.) 5 EGb
Great Ruaha (riv.) 26 Cb
Great Salt Lake 33 Bb
Great Sandy Desert [Austl.] 29 CDc
Great Sandy Desert [U.S.] 33 ABb
Great Sleave Lake 31 CDb
Great Victoria Desert 27 BD wd
Great Yarmouth 7 GHe
Grebenka 12 Dcd
Greco, Akra– 22 Ee
Gredos, Sierra de– (mts.) 9 Cb
Greece (Ind. St.) 3 Fd
Greeley 33 Cb

Greem–Bell, ostrov– 13 FGa
Green Bay 32 Ca
Greenland (co.) 30 Nbc
Greenland Sea 41 grid square no.1
Greenock 7 Dd
Green River 33 BCbc
Greensboro 32 CDb
Greenville [Lbr.] 24 ABd
Greenville [Ms.–U.S.] 32 Bb
Greenville [S.C.–U.S.] 32 Cb
Greenville [Tx.–U.S.] 32 Bb
Greenwich 7 FGf
Greenwood 32 BCb
Gregory, Lake– [Austl.] 29 Fd
Gregory, Lake– [Austl.] 29 BCd
Gregory Lake 29 Dc
Gregory Range 29 Gb
Greifswald 5 Da
Grein 5 Ed
Greiz 5 CDc
Gremiha 13 CDc
Gremjačinsk 12 Ib
Grenå 4 Bd
Grenada (Ind. St.) 30 Lh
Grenadine Islands 35 Db
Grenen (cap.) 4 Bd
Grenoble 8 FGe
Grenevná 11 Dc
Grey Range 29 Gd
Gribanovski 12 Fc
Griffith 29 He
Grigoriopol 6 Ic
Grijalva (riv.) 34 Cc
Grimsby 7 Fe
Grimstad 4 Bd
Grintavec (mt.) 6 Bc
Gris–Nez, Cap– 8 Db
Grjazi 12 EFc
Grodno 13 Bd
Groix, Ile de– 8 Bd
Grombalia 10 Cf
Grong 4 Cb
Groningen [Neth.] 8 Ga
Groningen [Sur.] 37 Db
Groote Eylandt 29 Fa
Grootfontein 23 DDgd
Groot Karasberge (mt.) 26 ABd
Grosa, Punta– (cap.) 9 FGc
Grosser Beerberg (mt.) 5 Cc
Grosseto 10 Cc
Großglockner (mt.) 5 De
Grozny 13 De
Grudovo 11 Gb
Grudziądz 5 Gb
Gryfice 5 Eb
Gryfino 5 Eb
Grytviken 40 Ec
Guaçuí 39 Db
Guadalajara [Mex.] 30 Hg
Guadalajara [Sp.] 9 Db
Guadalaviar (Turia) (riv.) 9 Edc
Guadalcanal Island 27 CDc
Guadalquivir (riv.) 9 Cd
Guadalupe 9 Cc
Guadalupe, Isla de– (i.) 30 FGg
Guadarrama, Sierra de– (mts.) 9 CDb
Guadeloupe (i.) 36 DEb
Guadiana (riv.) 9 Bc
Guadix 9 Dd

Guafo, Isla– (i.) 40 Ab
Guainía (riv.) 37 Cb
Guaíra 39 Cb
Guaira, La– 37 Ca
Guajará–Mirim 37 Cd
Guajira, Península de la– (pen.) 37 Ba
Gualeguaychú 39 BCc
Guam (i.) 27 map no.1
Guamá 38 Cb
Guamapi, Sierra de– 37 Cb
Guamúchil 34 Bb
Guanabacoa 35 Ba
Guanajuato 34 BCb
Guanare 37 Cb
Guane 35 Ba
Guangdong (prov.) 16 DEf
Guanghua 16 Db
Guangyuan 15 Df
Guangzhou → Canton 16 Df
Guantánamo 35 Ca
Guantánamo Bay Naval Station 35 Cab
Guanxian 16 Bd
Guapí 37 Bb
Guaporé (riv.) 39 Ba
Guaqui 39 Ba
Guarabira 38 Db
Guarapuava 39 Cb
Guaratinguetá 39 Db
Guarda 9 Bb
Guardafui, Cape– 25 Fc
Guasave 34 Bb
Guastalla 10 Cb
Guatemala (Ind. St.) 30 Ih
Guatemala 30 Ih
Guaviare, Río– (riv.) 37 BCb
Guaxupé 39 Db
Guayama 35 Db
Guayaneco, Archipiélago– (is.) 40 Ab
Guayaquil 36 BCd
Guayaquil, Golfo de– 37 Ac
Guayaramerín 37 Cd
Guaymas 34 Ab
Gubaha 12 Ib
Guban (phys. reg.) 25 Ecd
Gubbio 10 Dc
Guben 5 Ebc
Gubin 5 Ec
Gubkin 12 Ec
Gudbrandsdalen (v.) 4 Bc
Gudivada 20 Fe
Gudiyattam 20 EFf
Gudur 20 EFf
Gudvangen 4 Ac
Guebwiller 8 Gcd
Guelma 24 Ca
Guéret 8 Dd
Guernsey (i.) 8 Bc
Guiana Highlands 37 CDb
Guider 24 Dcd
Guiding 16 Ce
Guijá 26 Cd
Gui Jiang (riv.) 16 Df
Guildford 7 Ff
Guilin 16 De
Guimarães 9 ABb
Guimaras (i.) 18 Fb
Guinea (Ind. St.) 23 ABd
Guinea, Gulf of– 23 BCef
Guinea–Bissau (Ind. St.) 23 Ad
Güines 35 Ba

Guingamp 8 Bc
Guiping 16 Df
Guiratinga 39 Ca
Güiria 37 Ca
Guixian 16 Cf
Guiyang 16 Ce
Guizhou (prov.) 16 Ce
Gujarat (State) 20 Dd
Gujranwala 20 Db
Gujrat 20 Db
Gukovo 12 Fd
Gulbarga 20 Ee
Gulbene 4 Fd
Gulen 4 Ac
Gulfport 32 Cb
Güllük 11 Ge
Gülnar 22 Dd
Gulu 25 Dd
Guna 20 Ed
Gunnbjørns Fjeld (mt.) 41 grid square no.1
Gunnedah 29 HIe
Guntakal 20 Eef
Guntur 20 EFe
Gunungsitoli 18 Ad
Gura Humorului 6 GHc
Gurguéia (riv.) 38 Cb
Gurjev → Aterau 13 DEe
Gurk 10 Ea
Gurkha 19 Ii
Gürün 22 Fc
Gurupá 38 Bb
Gurupi (riv.) 38 Cb
Gurupi 38 Cc
Guru Sikhar (mt.) 20 Dcd
Gusau 24 Cc
Gusev 5 Ia
Gushan 16 Fbc
Gushi 16 Ed
Gus–Hrustalny 12 Fb
Güstrow 5 Db
Güterslof 5 Bc
Guyana (Ind. St.) 36 Ec
Guyenne (hist. reg.) 8 CEef
Guymon 33 Cc
Gwädar 21 Gde
Gwalior 20 Ec
Gwda (riv.) 5 Fb
Gweru 23 Eg
Gyala Shankou 12 Dde
Gyangzê 19 Ac
Gya Pass 19 Ii
Gyda 13 GHb
Gydanski Poluostrov 13 GHbc
Gyirong 19 Ii
Gympie 29 Id
Gyöngyös 6 DEc
Győr 6 Cc
Gypsumville 31 Fc
Gyula 6 Ec

H

Ha'apai Group 28 Acd
Haapajärvi 4 Fc
Haapsalu 4 EFd
Haarlem 8 EFa
Haasts Bluff 29 Ec
Habarovsk 14 Ge
Habarüt 21 Ef

Habban 21 Dg
Haboro 17 Gb
Habost 7 Cb
Hachijō–Jima (i.) 16 IJd
Hachinohe 16 Jb
Hachiōji 17 Fg
Ḥadāribah, Ra's al– 25 Db
Hadd, Al– 21 FGe
Ḥadd, Ra's al– 21 FGe
Haddington 7 Ecd
Hadejia 24 CDc
Hadera 22 Ef
Haderslev 5 Ba
Hadîboh 21 Eg
Haditha 21 Cc
Hadiyah 21 Bd
Ḥaḍramawt (phys. reg.) 21 Dfg
Hadseløya (i.) 4 Ca
Haeju 16 FGc
Hafar al Batin 21 CDd
Hafnarfjörður 4 map no.1
Hafun 23 Hd
Hafun, Ras– 25 Ec
Hagen 5 Ab
Hagerstown 32 Db
Hagfors 4 Cc
Hagi 17 Bg
Ha Giang 19 DEd
Hague, Cap de la– (cap.) 8 BCc
Haguenau 8 Gc
Hahajima–Rettō (i.) 27 Ca
Haicheng 16 Fb
Haifa 22 Ef
Haig 29 De
Haikou 15 Dgh
Ḥā'il 21 Cd
Hailar 16 EFa
Hailar He (riv.) 14 EFe
Hailin 17 Ab
Hailong 16 Gb
Hailun 16 Ga
Hailuoto (i.) 4 EFb
Haimen [China] 16 Fe
Haimen [China] 16 Fd
Hainan (prov.) 15 Dh
Haines 31 Bc
Haines Junction 31 Bb
Hai Phong 15 Dg
Haiti (Ind. St.) 30 Kh
Haiti → Hispaniola (i.) 35 Cb
Haizhou 16 EFd
Hajdúböszörmény 6 Ec
Hajdúnánás 6 EFc
Hajipur 20 Gc
Hajnówka 5 IJb
Hakken–Zan (mt.) 17 Dgh
Hakodate 16 IJb
Ḥalā'ib 25 Db
Halawa 28 map no.1
Halberstadt 5 Cc
Halcon, Mount– 18 Fb
Halden 4 BCd
Haleakala Crater (mt.) 28 map no.1
Hali 21 Cf
Halicarnassus (r.) 22 ABd
Halifax [Can.] 31 Id
Halifax [U.K.] 7 EFe
Halifax Bay 29 Hb
Hālil (riv.) 21 Fd
Halland (hist. reg.) 4 Cd

Ḥallat 'Ammār 22 EFh
Hall Beach 31 GHb
Halle / Saale 5 CDc
Hallein 5 De
Halley Bay 42 grid square no.1
Hall in Tirol 5 Ce
Hall Islands 27 Cb
Hall Peninsula 31 Ib
Halls Creek 29 Db
Halmahera (i.) 18 Gd
Halmahera, Laut– 18 GHe
Halmer–Ju 13 Fc
Halmstad 4 Cd
Haltiatunturi (mt.) 4 Ea
Halturin 12 Gb
Hamada 17 BCg
Hamadān 21 Dbc
Hamāh 21 Bbc
Hamamatsu 16 Id
Hamar 4 Bc
Hamburg 5 Cb
Ḥamd, Wādī al– 21 Bd
Hämeenlinna 4 EFc
Hameln 5 Bb
Hamersley Range 29 Bc
Hamhŭng 14 FGe
Hami 15 De
Hamilton [Austl.] 29 Gf
Hamilton [Can.] 31 GHd
Hamilton [N.Z.] 27 Dd
Hamilton [U.K.] 7 DEd
Hamilton [U.S.] 32 Cb
Hamilton Inlet 31 Jc
Hamina 4 FGc
Hamirpur 19 GHj
Hamm 5 ABc
Ḥammāmāt 10 Cf
Ḥammān, Al– 22 Bg
Ḥammār, Hawr al– 21 Dc
Hammerfest 4 Ea
Hammond 32 Ca
Hampshire (co.) 7 Ff
Ḥamrā', Al Ḥamādah– (des.) 24 Dab
Hāmūn–e Hîrmand, Daryācheh– ye– (sw.) 21 Gc
Hāmun–e–Jāz–Muryān (sw.) 21 FGd
Hāmūn–e Sāberi (l.) 21 Gc
Hamun–i–Mashkel (sw.) 21 Gd
Hana 28 map no.1
Hanak 21 Bd
Hancock 32 BCa
Handa 17 Eg
Handan 16 Dc
Handyga 14 Gc
Hānegev (phys. reg.) 22 Eg
Hanford 33 ABc
Hangaj, Hrebet– 14 CDe
Hanggin Houqi 16 Cb
Hanggin Qi 16 Cbc
Hangö 4 Ed
Hangu 16 Ec
Hangzhou 15 DEf
Hanka, ozero– 16 Hab
Hanmon–Kaikyō 17 ABg
Hann, Mount– 29 CDb
Hanna 31 DEc
Hannamaki 16 Jc
Hannover 5 BCb

Hanöbukten 4 Ce
Hanoi 15 Dg
Hanover, Isla– (i.) 40 Ac
Han Shui (riv.) 16 Dd
Hanty–Mansijsk 13 Fc
Hanyuan 16 Be
Hanzhong 16 Cd
Hao Atoll 28 BCc
Häora 20 Gd
Haparanda 4 EFb
Hapčeranga 14 Ede
Hapur 20 Ec
Haql 21 ABd
Ḥaraḍ 21 DEe
Harare (Salisbury) 26 Cc
Harbin 16 Ga
Harboi Hill (mt.) 20 Cc
Hardangerfjord 4 Ac
Hardangeriøkulen 4 Ac
Hardangervidda (mts.) 4 Acd
Hardoi 19 GHj
Hardwar 20 Ebc
Harer 25 Ed
Harfleur 8 CDc
Hargeysa 25 Ed
Harghita, Munţi– 6 Gc
Har Hu (l.) 16 Ac
Harib 21 CDfg
Hariq, Al– 21 De
Hari Rud 20 Bb
Harjavalta 4 Ec
Harkendi (Stepanakert) 21 Dab
Harkov 13 Cde
Harlingen [Neth.] 8 Fa
Harlingen [U.S.] 32 Bc
Harmanli 11 FGc
Härnösand 4 Dc
Haro 9 Da
Harovsk 12 Fab
Harper 24 Bd
Harrach 9 Gd
Harrach–Algeri, El– 9 Gd
Harrah 21 Efg
Harricanaw (riv.) 32 Da
Harris (phys. reg.) 7 Cc
Harrisburg 32 Dab
Harrismith 26 BCd
Harrogate 7 Fde
Harstad 4 Da
Hartford 32 Da
Hartlepool 7 Fd
Harut rud (riv.) 20 Bb
Harwich 7 Gf
Haryana (State) 20 DEc
Harz (mts.) 5 Cc
Ḥasā, Al– 22 EFg
Hasa, Al– (phys. reg.) 21 DEde
Hasan dağı (mt.) 22 Ec
Hasavjurt 12 Ge
Haskovo 11 Fc
Hassan 20 Ef
Hasselt 8 Fb
Hässleholm 4 Cd
Hastings [U.K.] 7 Gf
Hastings [U.S.] 32 Ba
Haşuri 12 Fe
Ḥasy al Qaṭṭār 22 Ag
Hatanga 14 Dc
Hatanga (riv.) 14 Db
Hatangskij zaliv 14 DEb
Hatches Creek 29 EFc

Hateg 6 Fd
Hatgal 14 CDd
Hathras 20 Ec
Hatia Islands 19 Jk
Ḥaṭibah, Ra's– 21 Be
Ha Tien 19 Dfg
Ha Tinh 19 Ee
Hatteras, Cape– 32 Db
Hattiesburg 32 Cb
Hatvan 6 DEc
Hat Yai 19 CDg
Hatyrka 14 Kc
Haugesund 4 Ad
Haukipudas 4 Fb
Haukivesi 4 FGc
Hausruck (mt.) 5 Dd
Hautmont 8 EFb
Hauts Plateaux 24 BCb
Haut–Zaïre (reg.) 26 Ba
Havana 35 Ba
Havast 13 Fe
Havel (riv.) 5 Db
Haverfordwest 7 Df
Havířov 5 FGd
Havlíčkův Brod 5 Ed
Havre 33 BCb
Havre, Le– 8 CDc
Havza 22 Eb
Hawaii (i.) 28 map no.1
Hawaiian Islands 28 map no.1
Ḥawātah, Al– 25 Dc
Hawd (phys. reg.) 25 Ed
Hawi 28 map no.1
Hawick 7 Ed
Hawkes, Mount– 42 grid square no.1
Hay (riv.) 31 Dbc
Hay 29 GHe
Haynin 21 Df
Hay River 30 Ec
Hay River (riv.) 29 Fc
Hays 32 Bb
Hayy, Al– 21 Dc
Hayyā 25 Dc
Hazārān, Kūh– e– 21 Fd
Hazaribagh 19 IJk
Hazelton 31 Cc
Hearst 31 Gcd
Hebei (prov.) 16 DEc
Hebrides 7 Cbc
Hebrides, Sea of the– 7 Cc
Hebron [Can.] 31 Ic
Hebron [Jor.] 22 Eg
Hecate Strait 31 Bc
Hechuan 16 Cde
Hede 4 Cc
Hedemora 4 Cc
Heerenveen 8 FGa
Heerlen–Kerkrade 8 FGb
Hefei 16 Ed
Hegang 16 GHa
Hegura–Jima (i.) 17 Ef
Heide 5 Ba
Heidelberg [Ger.] 5 Bd
Heidelberg [S. Afr.] 26 Be
Heidenheim an der Brenz 5 Cd
Heilbronn 5 Bd
Heilong Jiang (riv.) 14 Fd
Heilongjiang (prov.) 16 FHa
Heinola 4 Fc
Hekimhan 22 FGc

Hekla (mt.) **4** map no.1
Hel **5** Ga
Helagsfjället (gl.) **4** BCc
Helan Shan (mts.) **16** Cc
Helena [Ar.–U.S.] **32** BCb
Helena [Mt.–U.S.] **33** Bb
Helen Reef (i.) **27** Bb
Helgeland (phys. reg.) **4** Cb
Helgoland (i.) **5** Aa
Hellin **9** Ec
Hell Ville **23** GHg
Helmand (riv.) **20** Bb
Helmsdale **7** Eb
Helmstedt **5** Cb
Helsingborg **4** BCde
Helsingfors / Helsinki **4** Fcd
Helsingør **5** CDa
Helsinki / Helsingfors **4** Fcd
Henan (prov.) **16** Dd
Henares (riv.) **9** Db
Henbury **29** Ec
Henderson **33** Bc
Henderson Island **28** Cd
Hengchun **16** EFf
Hengelo **8** Ga
Hengxian **16** Cf
Hengyang **15** Dg
Hénin–Liétard **8** Eb
Hennebont **8** Bd
Henzada **19** BCe
Hepu **16** Cf
Heras, Colonia de– **36** CDh
Herāt **15** Cf
Hercegnovi **11** Cb
Heredia **35** Bbc
Hereford **7** Ee
Hereheretule Atoll **28** Bc
Hereke **22** BCb
Herford **5** Bb
Herma Ness (cap.) **7** Fa
Hermanus **26** Ae
Hermön (mt.) **22** Ef
Hermosillo **34** Ab
Hernandarias **39** Cb
Herning **4** Bd
Herrera del Duque **9** Cc
Herson **13** Ce
Hertford **7** FGf
Hertogenbosch, 's– **8** FGb
Hervás **9** BCb
Hervey Bay **29** Icd
Hervey Bay (g.) **29** Icd
Herzegovina (phys. reg.) **11** BCb
Hessen (State) **5** Bc
Heta (riv.) **14** Cb
Heves **6** Ec
Hexian **16** Df
Heyuan **16** Df
Hibbing **32** Ba
Hida (mts.) **17** Efg
Hidaka–Sanmyaku (mts.) **17** Hc
Hidalgo del Parral **34** Bb
Hierro (i.) **24** Ab
Higashine **17** FGe
High River **31** Dc
Highs Atlas (mts.) **24** Ba
Hiiumaa (i.) **4** Ed
Hijar **9** Eb
Hijāz, Al– (hist. reg.) **21** BCde
Hikone **17** DEg
Hildesheim **5** BCb

Hilla, El– **25** Cc
Ḥillah, Al– **21** CDc
Hillsboro **32** Bb
Hilo **28** map no.1
Hilok (riv.) **16** Da
Hilok **14** Ed
Hilversum **8** Fa
Himachal Pradesh (State) **20** Eb
Himalayas (mts.) **20** EHbc
Himara **11** CDc
Himeji **16** Hcd
Himi **17** Ef
Himki **12** Eb
Ḥinākīyah, Al– **21** Ce
Hinche **35** Cb
Hinchinbrook Island **29** Hb
Hindukush (mts.) **20** CDa
Hindustan (phys. reg.) **20** DGc
Hingol (riv.) **20** Cc
Hinnøya (i.) **4** CDa
Hınzır Burun **22** Ed
Hiou (i.) **28** map no.4
Hirado **17** Ah
Hīrākud **16** Cf
Hiratsuka **17** Fg
Hirfanlı Barajı **22** DEc
Hirgis–Nur (l.) **14** Ce
Hiroo **17** Hc
Hirosaki **16** Jb
Hiroshima **16** Hd
Hirson **8** Fc
Hîrşova **6** HId
Hisär **20** DEc
Hispaniola (Haiti) (i.) **35** CDb
Hita **17** Bh
Hitachi **16** Jc
Hitiaa **28** map no.2
Hitoyoshi **17** Bh
Hitra (i.) **4** ABc
Hiva **13** Fe
Hiva Oa, Île– (i.) **28** Cc
Hjälmaren (l.) **4** CDd
Hjørring **4** Bd
Hkakabo Razi (mt.) **19** Cc
Hmelnicki **6** Hb
Hmelnik **6** HIb
Ho **24** Cd
Hoa Binh **19** DEd
Hobart **29** map no.1
Hobbs **33** Cc
Hobbs Coast **42** grid square no.3
Hobyo **25** Ed
Hochgolling (mt.) **5** DEe
Ho Chi Minh **15** Dhi
Hodaka–Dake (mt.) **17** Ef
Hodh (phys. reg.) **24** Bc
Hódmezővásárhely **6** Ec
Hodonín **5** Fd
Hodorov **6** Gb
Hodžejä **13** Ee
Hodžent (Leninabad) **13** Fe
Hoek van Holland, Rotterdam– **8** EFb
Hof **5** CDc
Höfn **4** map no.1
Hofrat en Nahas **25** Cd
Hofsjökull (gl.) **4** map no.1
Hōfu **17** Bgh
Hohe Tavern (mts.) **5** De
Hohhot **16** Db

Hoi An **19** Ee
Hojniki **12** CDc
Hokitika **27** De
Hokkaidō (i.) **16** JKb
Holbæk **5** Ca
Holguín **35** Ca
Hollywood, Los Angeles– **33** ABc
Holm **12** Db
Holman Island **31** CDa
Holmsk **14** He
Holmsund **4** Ec
Holon **22** Efg
Holstebro **4** ABd
Holsteinsborg / Sisimiut **31** Jb
Holyhead **7** De
Homalin **19** BCcd
Hombori **24** Bc
Home Bay **31** Ib
Home Hill **29** Hbc
Homestead **32** Cc
Homoljske planina (mts.) **6** EFd
Homs **21** Bc
Honaz dağı **22** Bd
Honbetsu **17** Hc
Hondo (riv.) **34** Dc
Honduras (Ind. St.) **30** Jh
Honduras, Golfo de– **34** Dc
Honghu **16** De
Hong Kong **15** Dg
Hongshui He **16** Cef
Honguedo, Détroit d'– **32** Ea
Hongze Hu (l.) **16** Ed
Honiara **27** CDc
Honjō **17** FGe
Honningsvag **4** EFa
Honokaa **28** map no.1
Honolulu **28** map no.1
Honshū (i.) **16** HIbc
Honuu **14** Hc
Hood, Mount– **33** Ab
Hoogeveen **8** Ga
Hooker, Bir– **22** BCg
Hoolehua **28** map no.1
Hoover Dam (dam) **33** Bc
Hopedale **31** IJc
Hopen (i.) **13** Bb
Hopër (riv.) **12** Fc
Hopetoun **29** Ce
Hopkins, Lake– **29** Dc
Hor (riv.) **16** Ia
Hor **14** Ge
Horlick Mountains **42** grid square no.3
Hormigas **34** Bb
Hormuz, Strait of– **21** Fd
Horn (cap.) **4** map no.1
Horn **5** Ed
Horn, Cabo– **40** Bc
Horn, Cape– **36** Di
Horn Islands **27** DEc
Horog **13** Gf
Horqin Youyi Qianqi **16** EFa
Horqueta **39** Cb
Horsens **4** Bde
Horsham **29** Gf
Horten **4** Bd
Hospet **20** Fe
Hospitalet de Llobregat **9** Gb
Hoste, Isla– (i.) **40** ABc
Hotan **20** EFa

Hotin **6** Hb
Hot Springs [Ar.–U.S.] **32** Bb
Hot Springs [S.D.–U.S.] **33** Cb
Houaïlou **28** map no.4
Houei Sai **19** Dd
Houlton **32** Ea
Houma **32** Bc
Houston **32** Bc
Houtman Abrolhos (is.) **29** Ad
Hovran Gölü **22** Cc
Howar **25** Cc
Howe, Cape– **29** HIf
Howe, West Cape– (cap.) **29** Bf
Howland Island **28** Ab
Hoy (i.) **7** Eb
Høyanger **4** Ac
Hoyos **9** Bb
Hradec Králové **5** EFc
Hristinovka **6** IJb
Hromtau **12** Ic
Hron (riv.) **5** Gd
Hrubieszów **5** Ic
Ḥsakah **21** BCb
Hsinchu **16** Ff
Huachacalla **39** Ba
Huacho **37** Bd
Huai He (riv.) **16** Ed
Huailai **16** Eb
Huainan **16** Ed
Huallaga (riv.) **37** Bc
Huambo **26** Ac
Huanan **17** Ba
Huancane **39** ABa
Huancavelica **37** Bd
Huancayo **36** Ce
Huang Hai → Yellow Sea **16** Fc
Huang He **16** Ed
Huang He (riv.) **16** DEc
Huangshi **16** DEde
Huangyan **16** Fe
Huangyuan **16** Bc
Huánuco **37** Bc
Huaráz **37** Bc
Huascarán, Nevado– (mt.) **37** Bc
Hubei **16** Dd
Hubli **15** Ch
Hubsugul (l.) **14** Dd
Ḥudaydah, Al– **21** Cfg
Huddersfield **7** Fe
Hudiksvall **4** Dc
Hudson (riv.) **32** Da
Hudson Bay **31** Gbc
Hudson Strait **31** HIb
Hue **15** Dh
Huedin **6** Fc
Huehuetenango **35** Ab
Huelma **9** Dd
Huelva **9** Bd
Huércal–Overa **9** DEd
Huesca **9** Ea
Huéscar **9** Dd
Huete **9** Db
Hufūf, Al– **21** DEd
Hughenden **29** Gc
Huila, Nevado del– (mt.) **37** Bb
Huili **16** Be

Huinan **16** Gb
Huinca Renancó **39** Bc
Huixian **16** Cd
Huize **16** Be
Huizhou **16** DEf
Hukuntsi **26** Bd
Hulan **16** Ga
Hulga (riv.) **12** Ja
Hulin **16** Ha
Hull **31** Hd
Hull (i.) **28** Ac
Hulun Nur (l.) **16** Ea
Ḥulwān **22** Ch
Humacao **35** Db
Humaitá **37** Cc
Humansdorp **26** Be
Humber (riv.) **7** FGe
Humberto de Campos **38** Cb
Humboldt (riv.) **33** Bb
Humenné **5** Hld
Hūn **24** Db
Húnaflói (g.) **4** map no.1
Hunan (prov.) **16** De
Hunchun **17** Bc
Hunedoara **6** Fd
Hungary (Ind. St.) **3** EFc
Hüngnam **16** Gbc
Hungtao Yu → Lan Hsu (is.)
  16 Ff
Hunsrück **5** Ad
Hunter Island **29** map no.1
Huntingdon **7** FGe
Huntington **32** Cb
Huntsville [Al.–U.S.] **32** Cb
Huntsville [Tx.–U.S.] **32** Bb
Hunyuan **16** DEc
Huon, Île– (is.) **27** Dc
Huraymila **21** Dd
Huron **32** Bc
Huron, Lake– **32** Ca
Húsavík **4** map no.1
Huși **6** Ic
Huskvarna **4** Cd
Hust **6** Fb
Husum **5** Ba
Hutchinson **32** Bb
Huzhou → Wuxing **16** EFd
Hvalynsk **12** Gc
Hvammstangi **4** map no.1
Hvannadalshnúkur (mt.) **4**
  map no.1
Hvar (i.) **11** Bb
Hwange **26** Bc
Hyderabad [India] **15** Ch
Hyderabad [Pak.] **15** Cg
Hyères **8** Gf
Hyères, Îles d'– **8** Gf
Hyesan **16** Gb
Hyūga **17** BCh
Hyvinkää **4** EFc

I

Iaco (riv.) **37** BCcd
Iaçu **38** Cc
Ialomița (riv.) **6** Hd
Iași **6** Hc
Iauareté **37** Cb
Ibadan **24** Cd
Ibague **37** Bb
Ibar (riv.) **11** Db

Ibarra **37** Bb
Ibb **21** Cg
Iberia **37** Cd
Ibérico, Sistema– (mts.) **9**
  DEab
Ibi **24** CDd
Ibiá **39** Da
Ibiapaba, Serra da– (mts.) **38**
  Cb
Ibicuy **39** Cc
Ibiza (i.) **9** Fc
Ibiza **9** Fc
Iblei, Monti– **10** Ef
Ibn Hāni', Ra's– **22** Ee
Ibo **26** Dc
Ibra **21** Fe
Ibradi **22** Cd
'Ibri **21** Fe
Ibshawāy **22** Ch
Ibusuki **17** Bi
Ica **37** Bd
Içá (riv.) **37** Cc
Içana **37** Cb
Içana (riv.) **37** Cb
Iceland (Ind. St.) **3** ABa
Ichalkaranji **20** De
Ichinomiya **17** Eg
Ichinoseki **17** Ge
Icó **38** Db
Idah **24** Cd
Idaho (State) **33** Bb
Idaho Falls **33** Bb
Iddan **25** Ed
Idfu **25** Db
Ídhi Óros **11** Ff
Ídhra (i.) **11** Ee
Idlib **22** Fe
Idre **4** Cc
Idrija **6** Bcd
Ieper **8** Eb
Ierápetra **11** FGf
Ierisós **11** EFc
Ifakara **26** Cb
Ife **24** Cd
Iferouâne **24** Cc
Iforas, Adrar des– (mt.) **24**
  Cbc
Igarka **13** Hc
Iğdır **22** Eb
Ighil–Izane **24** Ca
Iglesias **10** Be
Igli **24** Ba
Igloolik **31** GHb
Iğneada **22** ABab
Igoumenítsa **11** Dd
Igra **12** Hb
Igreja, Morro da– (mts.) **39**
  CDb
Iguaçu (riv.) **39** Cb
Igualada **9** Fb
Iguala de la Independencia
  34 BCc
Iguape **39** Db
Iguassu Falls **39** Cb
Iguatu **38** CDb
Iharagna **26** map no.1
Iheya–Jima **16** Ge
Ihosy **26** map no.1
Ihtiman **11** Eb
Ii **4** Fb
Ii (riv.) **4** Fb
Iida **17** Eg

Iisalmi **4** FGc
Iizuka **17** Bh
IJsselmeer **8** Fa
Ijuw **27** map no.2
Ikaría (i.) **11** FGe
Ikeda [Jap.] **17** CDgh
Ikeda [Jap.] **17** Hc
Ikela **26** Bb
Iki (i.) **17** Ah
Ilagan (i.) **18** Fa
Ilan **16** Ff
Iława **5** Gb
Ilebo **23** Ef
Ile–de–France (hist. reg.) **8**
  DEc
Ilek (riv.) **12** Ic
Ilesha **24** Cd
Ilfracombe **7** Df
Ilgaz dağları (mts.) **22** DEb
Ilgın **22** CDc
Ilha Grande **37** Cc
Ilhavo **9** Ab
Ilhéus **38** Dc
Ili (riv.) **13** Ge
Iligan (i.) **18** Fc
Ilinski **14** He
Illampu, Nevado de– **39** Ba
Illapel **39** Ac
Illéla **24** Cc
Iller (riv.) **5** Cd
Illimani, Nevado– (mt.) **39** Ba
Illinois (State) **32** BCab
Illizi **24** Cb
Ilmen, ozero– **12** Db
Ilo **39** Aa
Iloilo **18** Fb
Ilomantsi **4** Gc
Ilorin **24** Cd
Imabari **17** Cg
Imandra, ozero– **4** GHb
Imari **17** ABh
Imatra **4** Gc
Imbābah **22** Cg
Imbituba **39** Db
Imola **10** Cb
Imotski **6** Ce
Imperatriz **38** Cb
Imperia **10** ABc
Impfondo **25** Bd
Imphal **15** Dg
Imrali Adası (i.) **22** Bb
İñapari **37** BCd
Inarajan **27** map no.1
Inari **4** Fa
Inarijärvi **4** FGa
Inca **9** Gc
Ince Burun **22** Ea
Inch'ŏn **16** FGc
Incudine, Monte– **8** map no.1
Indals (riv.) **4** Dc
Independence **32** Bb
Inderagiri (riv.) **18** Be
Inderborski **13** Ee
India (Ind. St.) **15** Cg
Indiana (State) **32** Ca
Indianapolis **32** Cab
Indian Ocean **2**
Indiga **13** DEc
Indigirka (riv.) **14** Hbc
Indonesia (Ind. St.) **15** DEj
Indore **20** DEd
Indramayu **18** Cf

Indravati (riv.) **20** Fe
Indre (riv.) **8** Dd
Indus (riv.) **20** CDc
Indus, Mouths of the– **20** Cd
Inebolu **22** DEb
Inegöl **22** Bb
Ineu, Vîrful– (mt.) **6** Gc
Infiernillo, Presa del– (l.) **34**
  Bc
Inga **26** Ab
I–n–Gall **24** Cc
Ingeniero Guillermo Nuño
  Juárez **39** Bb
Ingeniero Jacobacci **40** ABb
Ingham (i.) **29** Hb
Ingolstadt **5** CDd
Ingrāj Bāzār **20** Gcd
Ingrid Christensen Kyst **42**
  grid square no.2
Inhambane **23** Fh
Inini (riv.) **38** Ba
Inírida (riv.) **37** Cb
Inja **14** Hd
Injune **29** Hd
Inland Sea **16** Hd
Inn / En (riv.) **5** Dd
Innamincka **29** FGd
Inner Mongolia (Aut. Reg.) **15**
  DEe
Innisfail **29** Hb
Innsbruck **5** Ce
Inongo **26** Ab
Inoucdjouac **31** Hc
Inowrocław **5** FGb
Inquisivi **39** Ba
In–Salah **24** Cb
Inscription, Cape– **29** Ad
Inta **13** EFc
Intanagar **19** Bc
Interlaken **10** ABa
International Falls **32** Ba
Interview (i.) **19** Bf
Invercargill **27** Dc
Inverell **29** Ide
Invergordon **7** Dc
Inverness **7** DEc
Investigator Group **29** Ee
Investigator Strait **29** Ff
Inyanga, Mountains– **26** Cc
Inza **12** Gc
Inžavino **12** Fc
Ioánnina **11** Dd
Iolotan **21** Gb
Ionian Islands **11** CDde
Iony, ostrov– (i.) **14** Hd
Íos (i.) **11** Fe
Iō–Shima (i.) **17** Bi
Iowa (State) **32** Ba
Iowa City **32** Ba
Ipameri **39** Da
Ipiales **37** Bb
Ipiranga **37** Cc
Ípiros (phys. reg.) **11** Dcd
Ipixuna **37** Bc
Ipoh **19** Dh
Iporá **39** Ca
Ipsala **22** Ab
Ipswich [Austl.] **29** Id
Ipswich [U.K.] **7** Ge
Ipu **38** Cb
Iquique **39** ABab
Iquiri → Ituxi (riv.) **37** Cc
Iquitos **36** Cd

Iracoubo 37 Db
Irafshān 21 Gd
Iráklia (i.) 11 Fe
Íráklion 11 Ff
Iran (Ind. St.) 15 Bf
Iran, Penunungan– 18 Dd
Irānshahr 21 Gd
Irapuato 34 Bb
Iraq (Ind. St.) 15 Bf
Irati 39 Cb
Irazú, Volcán– (mt.) 35 Bc
Irbid 22 Ef
Irbit 12 Jb
Ireland (Ind. St.) 3 BCb
Irgiz 13 Fe
Irian Jaya (prov.) 27 Bc
Irian Jaya 27 Bc
Iringa 26 Cb
Iriomote–Jima (i.) 16 Ff
Iriri (riv.) 38 Bb
Irish Sea 7 De
Irkutsk 14 Dd
Iroise (b.) 8 Ac
Iron Gate (p.) 6 Fd
Iron Knob 29 Fe
Iron Mountain 32 BCa
Ironwood 32 BCa
Irpen 6 Ja
'Irqah, Al– 21 Dg
Irrawaddv, Mouths of the– 19 BCe
Irrawaddy (riv.) 19 Ccd
Irtyš (riv.) 13 Gd
Irún 9 DEa
Isabela, Isla– (i.) 36 Ad
Isafjörður 4 map no.1
Isahaya 17 ABh
Isar (riv.) 5 Dd
Ischia (i.) 10 Dd
Ise 17 Eg
Iseo 10 Cb
Iseo, Lago d'– (l.) 10 Cb
Isère (riv.) 8 Fe
Iserlohn 5 Ac
Isernia 10 Ed
Ise–Wan 17 Eg
Iseyin 24 Cd
Isfendiyar → Küre dağları (mts.) 22 DEb
Ishigaki–Jima (i.) 16 FGf
Ishikari–Gawa (riv.) 17 Hc
Ishikari–Wan 17 Gc
Ishinomaki 16 Jc
Ishizuchi–Yama (mt.) 17 Ch
Ishurdi 20 Gd
Işik däg (mt.) 22 Db
Isilkul 13 Gd
Išim (riv.) 13 Fd
Išim 13 Fd
Isimbaj 12 Ic
Isiro 26 Ba
Iskar (riv.) 11 EFb
İskenderun 22 Fd
İskenderun Körfezi 22 EFd
Iskilip 22 DEb
Iskitim 13 Hd
Isla–Cristina 9 Bd
Islâhiye 22 Fd
Islamabad 15 Cf
Island Lagoon 29 Fe
Islay (i.) 7 Cd
Isle (riv.) 8 De
Ismailia 25 Da

Isna 25 Db
Isoka 26 Cc
Isola del Liri 10 Dd
Isparta 22 Cd
Isperih 11 Gb
Israel (Ind. St.) 15 Bf
Issoire 8 Ee
Issoudun 8 DEd
Issyk–Kul (Rybačje) 13 Ge
Issyk–Kul, ozero– (l.) 13 Ge
İstanbul (Constantinople) 22 Bb
Istanbul–Üsküdar 22 Bb
Istiaia 11 Ed
Istmina 37 Bb
Istra 6 ABd
Itabaiana 38 Dc
Itaberaba 38 Cc
Itabira 39 Da
Itabuna 38 Dc
Itacaiúnas (riv.) 38 BCb
Itacoatiara 38 Bb
Itagüí 37 Bb
Itaituba 38 Bb
Itajaí 39 Db
Itajubá 39 Db
Italia, Cerro– 40 Bc
Italy (Ind. St.) 3 Ec
Itambé, Pico de– (mt.) 39 Da
Itaperuna 39 Db
Itapetinga 38 CDc
Itapeva 39 Db
Itapicuru [Braz.] (riv.) 38 Cb
Itapicuru [Braz.] (riv.) 38 Dc
Itapipoca 38 Db
Itaqui 39 Cb
Itararé 39 Db
Itarsi 20 Ed
Itea 11 Ed
Ithaca 32 Da
Ithaca (i.) 11 Dd
Itoigawa 17 Ff
Itseqqortoormit / Scoresbysund 30 PQb
Ituí (riv.) 37 Bc
Itumbiara 39 Da
Iturup, ostrov– / Etorofu Tō (i.) 14 He
Ituxi (Iquiri) (riv.) 37 Cc
Itzehoe 5 Bb
Iultin 14 KLc
Ival (riv.) 39 Cb
Ivalo 4 FGa
Ivalojoki (riv.) 4 Fa
Ivangorod 4 Gd
Ivanhoe 29 GHe
Ivankov 6 Ia
Ivano–Frankovsk 6 Gb
Ivanovo 3 GHb
Ivdel 13 EFc
Ivittuut 31 Kb
Ivory Coast (Ind. St.) 23 Be
Ivory Coast (phys. reg.) 24 Bd
Ivrea 10 Ab
Ivujvik 31 Hb
Iwaki 16 Jc
Iwakuni 17 BCg
Iwamisawa 17 Gc
Iwanai 17 FGc
Iwanuma 17 Gef
Iwate–San (mt.) 17 Gde
Iwo 24 Cd

Ixtlán del Río 34 Bb
Iyadh 21 Dfg
Izamal 34 Db
Izberbaš 21 Da
Iževsk 13 Ed
Izjaslav 6 Ha
Izjum 12 Ed
Izki 21 Fe
Izmail 6 Id
Izmir 22 Ac
Izmir Bay 22 Ac
Izmit 22 BCb
Iznalloz 9 Dd
Iznik 22 BCb
İznik Gölü 22 Bb
Izozog, Bañados del– 39 Ba
Izúcar de Matamoros 34 Cc
Izu–Hantō 17 Fg
Izumo 17 Cg
Izu–Shotō 16 IJd
Izvesti C.I.K., ostrova– 13 GHb

J

Jabal Iweibid 25 map no.1
Jabalón (riv.) 9 Dc
Jabalpur 15 Cg
Jablah 22 Ee
Jablanica (mt.) 11 Dc
Jablanica 10 Fc
Jablonec–nad–Nisou 5 Ec
Jablonicki, pereval– 6 FGb
Jablunkovsky prusmyk 5 Gd
Jaboatão 38 Db
Jabor 28 map no.3
Jaburu 37 Cc
Jaca 9 Ea
Jacarézinho 39 CDb
Jaciparaná 37 Cc
Jackson [Mi.–U.S.] 32 Ca
Jackson [Ms.–U.S.] 32 BCb
Jackson [Tn.–U.S.] 32 Cb
Jacksonville 32 CDb
Jacobabad 20 Cc
Jacobina 38 Cc
Jacques Cartier, Détroit de– (str.) 32 Eab
Jacuí 39 Cbc
Jadida, El– 24 ABa
Jaén [Peru] 37 Bc
Jaén [Sp.] 9 Dd
Jaffna 15 Chi
Jafr, Al– 22 Ef
Jagdalpur 20 Fe
Jaghbūb, Al– 24 Eab
Jaguarão 39 Cc
Jaguariaíva 39 CDb
Jaguaribe (riv.) 38 Db
Jahrom 21 Ed
Jaipur 15 Cg
Jaisalmer 20 Dc
Jajce 6 Cd
Jajva 12 Ib
Jakarta 18 Cf
Jakobstad 4 Ec
Jakutsk 14 Fc
Jakuvlevca (mt.) 17 Cb
Jalalabad 20 CDb
Jalālah al Baḥrīyah, Jabal– (mt.) 22 CDh

Jalālah al Qiblīah, Jabal– (mt.) 22 CDh
Jalandhar 20 Eb
Jalapa Enríquez 34 Cbc
Jalgaon 20 DEd
Jalingo 24 Dd
Jalna 20 Ee
Jalón (riv.) 9 Eb
Jalpaiguri 19 Jj
Jalta 13 Ce
Jālū, Wāḥāt– 24 Eb
Jaluit Atoll 27 Db
Jaluit Atoll (at.) 28 map no.3
Jalutorovsk 13 Fd
Jamaame 25 Ee
Jamaica (Ind. St.) 30 JKh
Jamaica Channel 35 Cb
Jamalpur [Bngl.] 20 GHcd
Jamalpur [India] 19 Ij
Jamantau, gora– (mt.) 13 Ed
Jamanxim (riv.) 38 Bb
Jambol 11 Gb
Jambongan, Pulau– (i.) 18 Ec
James (riv.) 32 Ba
James Bay 30 JKd
James Ross Island 42 grid square no.1
Jamestown [N.D.–U.S.] 33 CDb
Jamestown [N.Y.–U.S.] 32 Da
Jammu 20 DEb
Jammu·e Kashmir (State) 20 DEab
Jamnagar 15 Cg
Jampol [Ukr.] 6 GHb
Jampol [Ukr.] 6 Ib
Jämsä 4 Fc
Jamshedpur 20 FGd
Jamsk 14 Id
Jana (riv.) 14 Gc
Janaúba 39 Da
Janesville 32 Ca
Janghai 19 Hj
Janin 22 Ef
Janisjärvi, ozero– 4 Gc
Jan Mayen (i.) 30 Rbc
Jánoshalma 6 Dc
Janski 14 Gc
Jantra (riv.) 11 FGb
Januária 39 Da
Japan (Ind. St.) 15 Ef
Japan, Sea of– / East Sea 16 Hlbc
Japurá (riv.) 37 Cc
Japurá 37 Cc
Jar 12 Hb
Jarābulus 22 FGd
Jaramillo 40 Bb
Jaransk 12 Gb
Jarcevo [Russia] 14 BCcd
Jarcevo [Russia] 12 Db
Jardines de la Reina (i.) 35 BCa
Jari (riv.) 38 Bab
Jarīd, Shaṭṭ al– (l.) 24 Ca
Jarocin 5 FGbc
Jaroslavl 13 Cd
Jarosław 5 Icd
Järpen 4 Cc
Jarub 21 Ef
Järvenpää 4 Fc
Jarvis Island 28 Abc
Jäsk 21 Fd

Jasło 5 Hd
Jasper 31 Ab
Jastrebac, Veliki– (mt.) 11 Db
Jászberény 6 DEc
Jataí 39 Ca
Játiva 9 Ec
Jauaperí (riv.) 37 Cbc
Jauja 37 Bd
Jaunpur 20 Fc
Java (i.) 18 CDf
Javalambre, Sierra de– 9 Ebc
Javarí (riv.) 37 Bc
Java Sea 18 CDe
Javor (mts.) 6 Dd
Javorníky (mt.) 5 Gd
Javorov 5 Id
Jawf, Al– 21 Bd
Jawor 5 Fc
Jaworzno 5 Gc
Jazirah, Al– [Asia] (phys. reg.) 21 Cbc
Jazirah, Al– [Sud.] (phys. reg.) 25 Dc
Jazirat Zambra 10 Cf
Jebba 24 Cd
Jędrzejów 5 Hc
Jefferson City 32 Bb
Jefremov 12 Ec
Jegorjevsk 12 EFb
Jejsk 13 Ce
Jekaterinburg (Sverdlovsk) 13 EFd
Jekaterinoslav (Dnepropetrovsk) 13 Ce
Jelabuga 12 Hb
Jelan 12 Fc
Jelec 13 Cd
Jelenia Góra 5 EFc
Jelgava 4 Ed
Jelizavety, mys– 14 Hd
Jelnja 12 Dc
Jemaja, Pulau– (i.) 18 BCd
Jena 5 Cc
Jenakijevo 12 Ed
Jenisej (riv.) 14 Bc
Jenisejsk 14 BCd
Jenisejski zaliv 13 GHb
Jequié 38 Dc
Jequitinhonha (riv.) 39 DEa
Jerborgačen 14 Dc
Jérémie 35 Cb
Jerevan 13 De
Jerez de la Frontera 9 BCd
Jerez de los Caballeros 9 Bc
Jergeni (mts.) 12 Fd
Jericho 22 Eg
Jermak 13 Gd
Jermentau 13 Gd
Jerofej Pavlovič 14 Fd
Jeropol 14 Jc
Jersey (i.) 8 BCc
Jersey City 32 Dab
Jeršov 13 Dd
Jerusalem 22 EFg
Jervis Bay 29 If
Jesenice 10 Eb
Jeseník 5 Fc
Jesi 10 Dc
Jesil 13 Fd
Jessej 14 Dc
Jesup 32 Cb
Jesús María 39 Bc

Jevpatorija 12 Dd
Jezercës (mt.) 11 Cb
Jha–Jha 19 Ij
Jhalida 19 Ik
Jhang Maghiana 20 Db
Jhansi 20 Ec
Jhargram 19 Ik
Jhelum 20 Db
Jhelum (riv.) 20 Db
Jiamusi 16 GHa
Ji'an [China] 16 DEe
Ji'an [China] 16 Gb
Jiangjin 16 Ce
Jiangmen 16 Df
Jiangsu (prov.) 16 EFd
Jiangxi (prov.) 16 DEe
Jian'ou 16 Ee
Jianping 16 Eb
Jianshui 16 Bf
Jianyang 16 Ee
Jiaohe 16 Gb
Jiaoxian 16 EFc
Jiawang 16 Ed
Jiaxing 16 Fd
Jiayuguan 16 Ac
Jibou 6 Fc
Jičín 5 Ec
Jiddah 21 Be
Jiddat al Harasis (phys. reg.) 21 Fef
Jido 19 BCc
Jiexiu 16 Dc
Jieyang 16 Ef
Jihlava 5 EFd
Jijel 24 Ca
Jijiga 25 Ecd
Jilib 25 Ede
Jilin (prov.) 16 Gb
Jilin 16 Gb
Jima 25 Dd
Jimbolia 6 Ed
Jiménez 34 Bb
Jinan → Tsinan 16 Ec
Jind 19 Gi
Jindřichův Hradec 5 Ed
Jingdezhen 16 Ee
Jinggu 19 Dd
Jinghang 16 Bf
Jinghe 13 He
Jingpo Hu (l.) 17 Abc
Jingtai 16 Bc
Jinhua 16 EFe
Jining [China] 16 Db
Jining [China] 16 Ec
Jinja 25 Dd
Jinotepe 35 Bb
Jinxian 16 Fc
Jinzhou 16 Fb
Jiparaná (riv.) 37 Ccd
Jipijapa 37 Ac
Jirjā 25 Db
Jisr ash Shugūr 22 Fe
Jiujiang 16 DEe
Jiul (riv.) 6 Fd
Jiuquan 16 Ac
Jiutai 16 Gb
Jiwa', Al– 21 Ee
Jixi 16 Ha
Jizan 21 Cf
Joaçaba 39 Cb
João Câmara 38 Db
João Pessoa 36 Gd
João Pinheiro 39 Da

Joaquín V. Gonzalez 39 Bb
Jódar 9 Dd
Jodhpur 20 Dc
Jodrell Bank (sc. stat.) 7 EFe
Joensuu 4 Gc
Joerg Plateau (plat.) 42 grid square no.1
Joeuf 8 FGc
Johannesburg 23 Eh
Johnson City 32 Cb
Johnston (i.) 28 Ab
Johnston, Lake– 29 BCe
Johnstown 32 Dab
Johor Baharu 18 BCd
Joigny 8 Ecd
Joinville 39 Db
Jokkmokk 4 Db
Jökulsá á Fjöllum (riv.) 4 map no.1
Joliet 32 Ca
Jolo 18 Fc
Jolo Group (i.) 18 Fc
Jonava 12 Bbc
Jonesboro 32 Bb
Jönköping 4 Cd
Jonzac 8 CDe
Joplin 32 Bb
Jordan (riv.) 22 Efg
Jordan (Ind. St.) 15 Bf
Jorhat 19 Bc
Jörn 4 DEb
Jos 24 Ccd
José de San Martín 40 Ab
Joseph Bonaparte Gulf 29 Da
Joškar Ola 13 Dd
Jos Plateau 24 Ccd
Jostedalsbreen (mts.) 4 Ac
Jotunheimen (mts.) 4 ABc
Jovellanos 35 Ba
Jöwhar 25 Ed
Juan de Fuca, Strait of– 31 Cd
Juan de Nova (i.) 26 Dc
Juan Fernandez, Archipiélago– 36 BCg
Juanjuí 37 Bc
Juankoski 4 Gc
Juárez 39 BCc
Juàzeiro 38 CDb
Juàzeiro do Norte 38 CDb
Juba 25 Dd
Juba (riv.) 25 Ed
Jubaland (phys. reg.) 25 Ede
Jubayl 22 Ee
Jubayl, Al– 21 DEd
Juby, Cap– 24 Ab
Júcar (riv.) 9 Dc
Juchitán 34 Cc
Judenburg 5 Ee
Jufrah, Wāḥāt al– 24 Db
Jugo–Kamski 12 Ib
Juiz de Fora 39 Db
Juliaca 39 Aa
Julia Creek 29 Gc
Julian Alps 10 DEa
Juliana Top (mt.) 37 Db
Julianehåb / Qaqortoq 30 MNc
Jumet 8 Fb
Jumilla 9 Ec
Jumla 19 Hi
Junagadh 20 CDd
Junaynah, Al– 25 Cc

Junction City 32 Bb
Jundah 29 Gc
Jundiaí 39 Db
Jundūbah 10 Bf
Juneau 30 Ed
Junee 29 Hef
Junín 39 Bc
Jūniyah 22 Eef
Junta, La– 33 Cc
Jur (riv.) 25 Cd
Jura (i.) 7 CDcd
Jura (mts.) 8 FGd
Jurga 13 Hd
Jūrmala 12 Bb
Juruá (riv.) 37 Cc
Juruena 38 Bc
Juruena (riv.) 38 Bbc
Juškozero 13 BCc
Jutaí (riv.) 37 Cc
Juticalpa 35 Bb
Juventud, Isla de la– 35 Ba
Juxian 16 Ec
Južno–Sahalinsk 14 He
Južno–Uralsk 12 Jc
Južny Bug (riv.) 13 BCe
Juzovka 13 Ce
Jylland (phys. reg.) 4 Bd
Jyväskylä 4 Fc

K

K 2 (Qogir Feng) 20 Ea
Kaala (mt.) 28 map no.1
Kabaena, Pulau– (i.) 18 Ff
Kabala 24 Ad
Kabale 25 CDe
Kabalega Falls 26 Ca
Kabalo 23 Ef
Kabardino– Balkar (Aut. Rep.) 13 De
Kabinda 26 Bb
Kabongo 26 Bb
Kābul 15 Cf
Kaburuang, Pulau– (i.) 18 Gd
Kabwe (Broken Hill) 26 Bc
Kachin (State) 19 Cc
Kachul 6 Id
Kaçkar dağ (mt.) 21 Ca
Kačug 14 Dd
Kadan Kyun (i.) 19 Cf
Kadina 29 Fe
Kadiolo 24 Bc
Kadirli 22 Fd
Kadoma 26 BCc
Kaduna 24 Ccd
Käduqlī 25 CDc
Kaédi 24 Ac
Kaesŏng 16 Gc
Kaf 21 Bc
Kāf, Al– 24 CDa
Kafr ad Dawwār 22 BCg
Kafr el Zaîyat 22 Cg
Kafue 26 Bc
Kafue (riv.) 26 Bc
Kaga 17 Df
Kaga Bandoro 25 BCd
Kagoshima 16 GHd
Kagoshima–Wan 17 Bi
Kahana 28 map no.1
Kahemba 26 Ab

Kahoolawe (i.) **28** map no.1
Kahovka **12** Dd
Kahovskoje vodohranilišče **12** DEd
Kahramanmaras **21** Bb
Kahuku Point **28** map no.1
Kai, Kepulauan– **27** Bc
Kaiama **24** Cd
Kaieteur Falls **37** Db
Kaifeng **16** DEcd
Kaikoura **27** De
Kailua **28** map no.1
Kainji Reservoir **24** Ccd
Kaiserslautern **5** ABd
Kaishantun **17** ABc
Kaiwi Channel **28** map no.1
Kaiyuan [China] **16** Fb
Kaiyuan [China] **16** Bf
Kajaani **4** Fb
Kajabbi **29** FGbc
Kakamas **26** ABd
Kakegawa **17** EFg
Kakinada **20** Fe
Kala, El– **10** Bf
Kalabáka **11** DEd
Kalabo **26** Bc
Kalač **12** Fc
Kalač–na–Donu **12** Fd
Ka Lae (cap.) **28** map no.1
Kalahari Desert **26** Bd
Kalakan **14** Ed
Kalámai **11** DEe
Kalamazoo **32** Ca
Kalamunda **29** ABe
Kalannie **29** Be
Kalao, Pulau– (i.) **18** EFf
Kalaotoa, Pulau– (is.) **18** Ff
Kalapana **28** map no.1
Kalaraš **6** Hlc
Kalat **20** Cc
Kalaus (riv.) **12** Fd
Kalavarda **22** ABd
Kalávrita **11** Ed
Kale [Tur.] **22** BCd
Kale [Tur.] **22** Bd
Kalecik **22** Db
Kalemie **26** Bb
Kalevala **4** Gb
Kalewa **19** BCd
Kalgoorlie **29** Ce
Kaliakra, Nos– **11** Hb
Kalibo **18** Fb
Kalimantan → Borneo (i.) **18** DEd
Kálimnos (i.) **11** Ge
Kalimpong **19** Jj
Kalinin → Tver **13** Cd
Kaliningrad **13** ABd
Kalininsk **12** FGc
Kalinkoviči **3** FGb
Kalinovka **6** Ib
Kalispell **33** Bb
Kalisz **5** Gc
Kalixälven (riv.) **4** Eb
Kaljazin **12** Eb
Kalkfontein **26** Bd
Kallavesi (l.) **4** Fc
Kallsjön (l.) **4** Cc
Kalmar **4** CDd
Kalmyk (Aut. Rep.) **13** De
Kalmykovo **12** Hd
Kalocsa **6** Dc
Kalpa **20** Eb

Kalpeni Island **20** Dfg
Kalpi **20** EFc
Kaluga **13** Cd
Kalumburu **29** Da
Kalundborg **5** Ca
Kaluš **6** Gb
Kalvarija **5** Ia
Kalyan **20** De
Kama (riv.) **12** Hb
Kamaishi **17** GHe
Kamarän **21** Cf
Kambalda **29** Ce
Kambarka **12** Hlb
Kambove **26** Bc
Kamčatka (riv.) **14** Id
Kamchatka Peninsula **14** Id
Kamčija (riv.) **6** He
Kamenec–Podolski **6** Hb
Kamenjak, Rt– **6** Ad
Kamenka [Russia] **17** DEb
Kamenka [Russia] **12** Fc
Kamenka–Bugskaja **6** Ga
Kamen Kaširski **12** BCc
Kamen–na–Obi **13** GHd
Kamen–Rybolov **17** BCb
Kamenskoje **14** Jc
Kamenskoje (Dneprodzeržinsk) **12** Dd
Kamenskoje vodohranilišče **12** Ib
Kamensk–Šahtinski **12** Fd
Kamensk–Uralski **13** Fd
Kamenz **5** Ec
Kamień Pomorski **5** Eab
Kamina **23** Ef
Kamino–Shima (i.) **17** Ag
Kamloops **33** Aa
Kampala **25** Dde
Kampar (riv.) **18** Bde
Kampar **19** Dh
Kampen **8** Fa
Kâmpóng Chhnăng **19** Df
Kâmpóng Saôm **19** Df
Kampot **19** Df
Kamyšin **13** Dde
Kananga **26** Bb
Kanaš **12** Gb
Kanazawa **16** Ic
Kanchanaburi **19** Cf
Kanchenjunga (mt.) **19** IJj
Kânchipuram **20** EFf
Kandalakša **13** BCc
Kandangan **18** Ee
Kandavu Island **27** Dc
Kandavu Passage (str.) **28** map no.6
Kandi **24** Cc
Kandıra **22** Cb
Kandla **20** CDd
Kandy **20** EFg
Kanem (phys. reg.) **25** Bc
Kaneohe **28** map no.1
Kang **20** Bb
Kangaatsiaq / Kangåtsiaq **31** Jb
Kangaba **24** Bc
Kangåmiut **31** Jb
Kangān **21** Ed
Kangar **19** Dg
Kangaroo Island **29** Ff
Kangaruma **37** Db
Kangåtsiq / Kangaatsiaq **31** Jb

Kangding **16** Bde
Kangean, Kepulauan– **18** Ef
Kangean, Pulau– (i.) **18** Ef
Kanggye **16** Gb
Kangmar **19** Ji
Kangnüng **16** Gc
Kangto (mt.) **19** Bc
Kaniama **26** Bb
Kanin, Poluostrov– **13** Dc
Kanin Nos, mys– **13** Dc
Kanjiža **6** Ec
Kankan **24** Bc
Kankossa **24** ABc
Kannauj **19** GHj
Kano **24** Cc
Kanoya **17** Bi
Kanpur **15** Cg
Kansas (riv.) **32** Bb
Kansas (State) **32** Bb
Kansas City **32** Bb
Kansk **14** Cd
Känthi **19** Ik
Kantō–Heiya (phys. reg.) **17** FGf
Kanton Atoll **28** Ac
Kanye **26** Bd
Kaohsiung **16** EFf
Kaolack **24** Ac
Kaoma **26** Bc
Kapaa **28** map no.1
Kapanga **26** Bb
Kapčagaj **13** Ge
Kapela (mt.) **6** Bd
Kapfenberg **5** Ee
Kapidaği, Yarimadasi– **11** GHc
Kapingamarangi, Atoll– **27** CDb
Kapisigdlit / Kapisillit **31** JKb
Kapisillit / Kapisigdlit **31** JKb
Kapit **18** Dd
Kaposvár **6** Cc
Kapsukas → Marijampolė **5** Ia
Kapuas (riv.) **18** Def
Kapuas Hulu, Pegunungan– **18** Dd
Kapuskasing **31** GHd
Kapuvár **6** Cc
Kara **24** BCd
Karaağaç **11** Gc
Karababa daği (riv.) **22** EFc
Karabaš **12** IJb
Karabiga **11** Gc
Kara–Bogaz–Gol, zaliv– (b.) **13** Ee
Karabük **22** Db
Karacabey **22** Bb
Karacaköy **11** Hc
Karačev **12** Cc
Karachi **15** Cg
Kara Daği (mt.) **22** Dd
Karagajly **13** Ge
Karaganda **13** Ge
Karaginski, ostrov– (i.) **14** Jd
Karagöl daği (mt.) **22** Gb
Karaisalı **22** Ed
Karaj **21** Eb
Karak, Al– **22** Eg
Kara–Kolpak (Aut. Rep.) **13** Ee
Karakoram (mts.) **20** Eab
Karakoram Pass **20** Ea

Karaköse–Ağri **21** Cab
Karakumski Kanal **13** EFf
Karakumy (phys. reg.) **13** EFef
Karaman **22** Dd
Karamay **15** Ce
Karamiran Shankou **20** Ga
Karapınar **22** Dd
Karasburg **26** Ad
Kara Sea **41** grid square no.3
Karasjok **4** Fa
Kara Strait **41** grid square no.3
Karasu **22** Cb
Karasuk **13** Gd
Karatas **22** Ed
Karatau, Hrebet– (mts.) **13** FGe
Karatsu **17** ABh
Karaul **13** Hb
Karauli **19** Gj
Karáva (mt.) **11** Dd
Karažal **13** FGe
Karbalá' **21** Cc
Karcag **6** Ec
Kardhítsa **11** DEd
Kärdla **4** Ed
Kärdžali **11** Fc
Karekelong, Pulau– (i.) **18** Gd
Karelia (phys. reg.) **13** Cc
Karelia (Aut. Rep.) **13** Cc
Karen (State) **19** Ce
Kargopol **12** Ea
Karhula **4** Fc
Kariai **11** EFc
Kariba **26** Bc
Kariba, Lake– **26** Bc
Karibib **26** Ad
Karimata Islands **18** Ce
Karimata Strait **18** Ce
Karimnagar **20** EFe
Karimunjawa Islands **18** CDf
Karin **25** Ec
Karis **4** Ec
Karisimbi (mt.) **26** Bb
Karkheh (riv.) **21** Dc
Karkinitski zaliv **12** Dd
Karlobag **6** Bd
Karlovac **6** Bd
Karlovo **11** Fb
Karlovy Vary **5** Dc
Karlshamn **4** Cd
Karlskoga **4** Cd
Karlskrona **4** CDd
Karlsruhe **5** ABd
Karlstad **4** Cd
Karmah **25** Dc
Karnali (riv.) **20** Fc
Karnataka (State) **20** DEf
Karnobat **11** Gb
Karonga **26** Cbc
Karoo (phys. reg.) **26** Be
Karora **25** Dc
Káros (i.) **11** Fe
Kárpathos (i.) **11** Gf
Kárpathos **11** Gf
Karpaty (mts.) **7** grid square
Karpenision **11** DEd
Karpinsk **12** IJab
Karpuzlu **22** Bd
Kars **21** Ca
Karsakpaj **13** Fe
Karši **13** Ff

Kartal 22 Bb
Kartaly 13 Fd
Karumba 29 Gb
Kärun (riv.) 21 Dc
Karviná 5 Gd
Karwar 20 Df.
Karymskoje 14 Ed
Kaş 22 Bd
Kasai (riv.) 26 ABb
Kasai Occidental (reg.) 26 Bb
Kasai Oriental (reg.) 26 Bb
Kasama 26 Cbc
Kasane 26 Bc
Kasba Lake 31 Eb
Kasempa 26 Bc
Kasenga 26 Bc
Kasese 25 CDde
Kasganj 19 Gj
Käshän 21 Ec
Kashi 15 Cf
Kashipur 19 Gi
Kashiwazaki 17 EFt
Käshmar 21 Fb
Kashmir 20 Eb
Kasimov 12 Fc
Kašira 12 Ec
Kasiruta, Pulau– (i.) 18 Ge
Kaskö 4 Ec
Káson, Stenón– 11 Gf
Kasongo 26 Bb
Kásos (i.) 11 Gf
Kaspijski 12 Gd
Kasr, Ra's– 25 Dc
Kassala 25 Dc
Kassándra (pen.) 11 Ecd
Kassándra, Gulf of– 11 Ecd
Kassel 5 Bc
Kasserine 24 Ca
Kassubia (hist. reg.) 5 FGab
Kastamonu 22 DEb
Kastéllion 11 Ef
Kastoría 11 Dc
Kastornoje 12 Ec
Kasur 20 Db
Katanga (hist. reg.) 26 Bb
Katangli 14 Hd
Katanning 29 Be
Katarnian Ghat 19 Hi
Katav–Ivanovsk 12 Ic
Katchall (i.) 19 Bg
Kateríni 11 Ec
Katha 19 Cd
Katherine 29 Ea
Kathgodam 19 Gi
Kathiawar (phys. reg.) 20 CDd
Kathmandu 15 Cg
Katihar 19 Ij
Katingan (riv.) 18 De
Katiola 24 Bd
Káto Akhaïa 11 Dde
Katoomba 29 Ie
Katowice 5 Gc
Kätrïnä, Jabal– (mt.) 25 Db
Katrineholm 4 CDd
Katsina 24 Cc
Kattakurgan 13 Ff
Kattegat (str.) 4 BCd
Katun (riv.) 13 Hd
Kau 18 Gd
Kauai (i.) 28 Ba
Kauai Channel 28 map no.1
Kaufbeuren 5 Ce

Kauhajoki 4 Ec
Kaula (i.) 28 map no.1
Kaulakahi Channel 28 map no.1
Kauliranta 4 EFb
Kaunas 4 EFe
Kaura Namoda 24 Cc
Kautokeino 4 EFa
Kavacık 22 Bc
Kavaja 11 Cc
Kavála 11 Fc
Kavalerovo 17 Db
Kavaratti (i.) 20 Df
Kavarna 11 Hb
Kawagoe 17 Ffg
Kawaguchi 17 FGfg
Kawaikini (mt.) 28 map no.1
Kawasaki 16 IJc
Kawio, Kepulauan– 18 FGd
Kawm 25 Db
Kawthaung 19 Cfg
Kaya 24 Bc
Kayah (State) 19 Ce
Kayan (riv.) 18 Ed
Kayes 24 Ac
Kayoa, Pulau– (i.) 18 Gde
Kayseri (Cesarea Mazaca) 22 EFc
Kazačje 14 Gb
Kazakhstan (Ind. St.) 13 EGe
Kazalinsk 13 EFe
Kazan 13 Dd
Kazan (riv.) 31 Eb
Kazanlâk 11 Fb
Kazatin 6 Ib
Kaz daği (mt.) 22 Ac
Käzerun 21 Ed
Kažim 12 Ha
Käжimïyah, Al– 21 Cc
Kazincbarcika 6 Eb
Kéa (i.) 11 Fe
Kearney 33 CDb
Kebir (riv.) 22 Fe
Kebnekaise (mt.) 4 Dab
Kecskemét 6 Dc
Kédainiai 4 Ee
Kediri 18 Df
Kédougou 24 Ac
Keele Peak 31 Bb
Keelung 16 Fef
Keetmanshoop 23 DEh
Keewatin, District of– 31 Fb
Kefa (phys. reg.) 25 Cd
Keflavík 4 map no.1
Kehl 5 ABd
Keitele (l.) 4 Fc
Keith 29 Gf
Kelang 18 Bd
Kelang, Pulau– (i.) 18 Ge
Kelasa, Selat– 18 Ce
Kelkit (riv.) 22 Fb
Kéllé 26 Ab
Kelloselkä 4 FGb
Kelowna 31 Dcd
Keltepe (mt.) 22 Db
Keluang 18 Bd
Kem 13 Cc
Kemerovo 13 Hd
Kemi 4 Fb
Kemijärvi (l.) 4 Fb
Kemijärvi 4 Fb
Kemijoki (riv.) 4 Gb
Kempsey 29 Ie

Kempten im Allgäu 5 Ce
Ken (riv.) 20 Ed
Kendal 7 Ed
Kendari 18 Fe
Kenema 24 Ad
Kenge 26 Ab
Kengtung 19 Cd
Kenhardt 26 Bd
Kéniéba 24 ABc
Kénitra 24 Ba
Kenmare 7 Bf
Kenmare River 7 ABf
Kennedy, Cape– →
  Canaveral, Cape– 32 CDc
Keno Hill 31 Bb
Kenora 31 Fd
Kent (co.) 7 Gf
Kent 24 Ad
Kentau 13 FGe
Kent Peninsula 31 Eb
Kentucky (State) 32 Cb
Kenya (Ind. St.) 23 Fe
Kenya (mt.) 25 De
Keokuk 32 Ba
Keonjhargarh 20 Gd
Kerala (State) 20 Efg
Kerama–Rettö 16 Ge
Kerč 13 Ce
Kerčensky Poluostrov 12 Ed
Kerempe Burun 22 Da
Keren 25 Dc
Kerguelen, Îles– (is.) 2
Kerinci, Gunung– (mt.) 18 Be
Kerkennah Islands 24 Da
Kerki 13 Ff
Kerkíras, Stenón– (str.) 11 CDd
Kermadec Islands 27 Ed
Kermän 21 Fc
Kermänshäh 21 Dc
Kerme Körfezi 11 GHe
Kérouané 24 ABd
Kerulen (riv.) 14 Ee
Keşan 11 Gc
Keşap 22 Gb
Kesennuma 17 GHe
Keshan 16 FGa
Kestenga 4 Gb
Kestep 22 Bd
Keszthely 6 Cc
Kéta 24 Cd
Ketapang 18 CDe
Ketchikan 31 BCc
Ketoj, ostrov– (i.) 14 Ie
Ketrzyn 5 Ha
Kettering 7 Fe
Keuruu 4 Fc
Keweenaw Peninsula 32 Ca
Key West 32 Cc
Kezel Owzan (riv.) 21 Db
Kežma 14 CDd
Khäbüra, Al– 21 Fe
Khairpur 20 Cc
Khalïg el Tina (g.) 25 map no.1
Khálki (i.) 11 Ge
Khalkís 11 EFd
Khalüf 21 Fe
Khamasin, Al– 21 CDe
Khambhät 20 Dd
Khambhät, Gulf of– 20 Dd
Khamir 21 Cf
Khamis Mushayt 21 Cf

Khamsa 25 map no.1
Khanabad 20 CDa
Khanaqin 21 CDc
Khandaq, Al– (str.) 25 CDc
Khandwa 20 Ed
Khanewal 20 Db
Khanh Hung 19 Eg
Khánia 11 EFf
Khanion, Kólpos– 11 EFf
Khanpur 20 Dc
Khän Yünus 22 DEg
Kharagpur 15 Cg
Kharga Oasis 25 CDb
Khárijah, Al– 25 CDb
Khärk, Jazireh– ye– (i.) 21 DEd
Khartoum 25 Dc
Khartoum North 25 Dc
Khâsh 21 Gd
Khashm al Qirbah 25 Dc
Khasi–Jaintia Hill 16 Ee
Khawr al Fakkän 21 Fd
Khaybar 21 BCd
Khíos 22 Ac
Kholm 20 Ca
Khong 19 Ef
Khong Sedon 19 Ee
Khon Kaen 19 De
Khoräsän (phys. reg.) 21 Fbc
Khóra Sfakíon 11 Ff
Khorat → Nakhon
  Ratchasima 19 Def
Khorixas 26 Ad
Khorramäbäd 21 Dc
Khorramshahr 21 DEc
Khouribga 24 Ba
Khrisí (i.) 11 Ff
Khufrah, Al– 24 Eb
Khulna 20 GHd
Khums, Al– 24 Da
Khurïyä Murïya, Jazä'ir– 21 Ff
Khurmah, Al– 21 Ce
Khuzdar 20 Cc
Khvoy 21 CDb
Khyber Pass 20 Db
Kiantajärvi 4 Gb
Kibombo 26 Bb
Kibondo 26 Cb
Kičevo 11 Dc
Kidal 24 Cc
Kidderminster 7 Ee
Kidira 24 Ac
Kiel 4 Be
Kiel Canal 5 Bab
Kielce 5 Hc
Kieler Bucht 5 Ca
Kieta 27 Cc
Kiev 13 Cd
Kiffa 24 Ac
Kifísiá 11 EFd
Kigali 26 BCb
Kigoma 23 EFf
Kii–Hantö 17 Eh
Kii–Suidö 17 Dh
Kijevskoje vodohranilišče 12 CDc
Kikai–Jima (i.) 16 GHe
Kikinda 6 Ed
Kikonai 17 FGd
Kikori 27 Cc
Kikwit 26 Ab
Kil 4 Cd

Kilambé, Cerro– (mt.) 35 Bb
Kilauea 28 map no.1
Kilchu 16 GHb
Kilcoy 29 Id
Kildonan 26 Cc
Kilifi 26 CDb
Kilija 6 Id
Kilimane 23 FGg
Kilimanjaro (mt.) 26 Cb
Kilis 22 Fd
Kilkenny 7 Ce
Kilkís 11 Ec
Killarney 7 Be
Killeen 32 Bb
Killini 11 De
Killini (mt.) 11 Ee
Kilmarnock 7 DEd
Kilmez 12 Hb
Kilombero (riv.) 26 Cb
Kilosa 26 Cb
Kilpsjärvi 4 Ea
Kilrush 7 ABe
Kiltän Island 20 Df
Kilwa Kisiwani 26 CDb
Kilwa Kivinje 26 CDb
Kimba 29 Fe
Kimberley (phys. reg.) 29 Db
Kimberley [Can.] 33 Bb
Kimberley [S. Afr.] 26 Bd
Kimberley Plateau 29 Db
Kimch'aek 16 GHb
Kimi 11 Fd
Kímolos (i.) 11 Fe
Kimovsk 12 Ec
Kimry 12 Eb
Kinabalo, Gunong– (mt.) 18 Ec
Kínaros (i.) 11 Ge
Kindersley 33 BCa
Kindia 24 Acd
Kindu 26 Bb
Kinel 12 Hc
Kineshma 12 Fb
Kingaroy 29 Id
King Christian IX Land 41 grid
   square no.1
King Christian X Land 41 grid
   square no.1
King Edward River 29 Dab
King Frederik VIII Land 41
   grid square no.1
King George Island 42 grid
   square no.1
King George Sound 29 BCf
King Island 29 map no.1
Kingissepp → Kuressaare 4
   Ed
King Leopold Ranges 29 CDb
Kingman 33 Bc
Kingman Reef 28 Ab
Kingoonya 29 Fe
Kingscote 29 Ff
King's Lynn 7 Ge
Kingsmill Islands 27 Dc
King Sound 29 Cb
Kingsport 32 Cb
Kings River 33 Bc
Kingston [Can.] 31 Hd
Kingston [Jam.] 30 Kh
Kingston South East 29 FGf
Kingston–upon–Hull 7 FGe
Kingstown 35 Db
Kingsville 32 Bc
Kingussie 7 DEc

King William Island 31 Fb
King William's Town 26 BCe
Kinnairds Head 7 EFc
Kino 34 Ab
Kinsale 7 Bf
Kinshasa 26 Ab
Kintampo 24 Bd
Kintyre (pen.) 7 Dd
Kinyeti (mt.) 25 Dd
Kiparíssia 11 De
Kiparissia, Gulf of– 11 De
Kipengere Range 26 Cb
Kipili 26 Cb
Kirakira 27 Dc
Kirensk 14 Dd
Kiribati (Ind. St.) 28 ABc
Kırıkkale 22 DEc
Kirillov 12 Eb
Kirishima–Yama (mt.) 17 Bhi
Kiritimati (Christmas) 28 map
   no.1
Kırkağaç 22 ABc
Kirkcaldy 7 Ec
Kirkcudbright 7 DEd
Kirkenes 4 Ga
Kirkland Lake 31 GHd
Kırklareli 22 Ab
Kirkpatrick, Mount– 42 grid
   square no.4
Kirksville 32 Ba
Kirkuk 21 Cb
Kirkwall 7 Eb
Kırlangıç Burun 22 Cd
Kirmir (riv.) 22 Db
Kirov 12 Dc
Kirov (riv.) 12 Hb
Kirov → Vjatka 13 Dd
Kirovabad → Giandža 13 De
Kirovgrad 12 IJb
Kirovo–Cepeck 12 Hb
Kirovograd 13 Ce
Kirovsk 13 Cc
Kirovski [Russia] 12 Gd
Kirovski [Russia] 14 Id
Kirowski 17 Cb
Kırşehir 22 Ec
Kirthar Range 20 Cc
Kiruna 4 Eb
Kiryü 17 Ff
Kisangani 26 Ba
Kisar, Pulau– (i.) 18 Gf
Kiselevsk 13 Hd
Kishanganj 19 IJj
Kishiwada 17 DEg
Kishorganj 19 Jj
Kisii 26 Cb
Kišinev → Chişinău 13 BCe
Kiskörös 6 Dc
Kiskunfélegyháza 6 Dc
Kiskunhalas 6 Dc
Kislovodsk 21 Ca
Kismaayo 25 Ee
Kissidougou 24 ABd
Kisumu 25 Dde
Kisvárda 6 EFb
Kita 24 Bc
Kitab 13 Ff
Kita–Daitō–Jima (i.) 16 He
Kitaibaraki 17 Gf
Kita–Iō–Jima (i.) 27 BCa
Kitakami (riv.) 17 Ge
Kitakami–Sanchi (mts.) 17
   Gde

Kitakata 17 FGf
Kitakyūshū 16 GHd
Kitale 25 Dd
Kitami 17 Hc
Kitami–Sanchi 17 Hbc
Kitchener 32 Ca
Kithíron Dhiékplous (str.) 11
   Eef
Kithnos (i.) 11 Fe
Kitimat 31 Cc
Kitinen (riv.) 4 Fb
Kittilä 4 Fb
Kitwe–Nkana 26 Bc
Kitzbühel 5 De
Kiuruvesi 4 Fc
Kivercy 6 Ga
Kıvıköy 22 Bb
Kivu (reg.) 26 Bb
Kivu, Lake– 26 Bb
Kizel 13 Ed
Kizema 12 Fa
Kızıl dağ (mt.) 22 Dd
Kızılın 22 FGd
Kızılırmak (riv.) 22 Eb
Kizljar 13 De
Kizyl–Arvat 13 Ef
Kjahta 14 Dd
Kjusjur 14 FGb
Kjustendil 11 Eb
Klabat, Gunung– (mt.) 18 Gd
Kladno 5 DEc
Kladovo 6 Fd
Klagenfurt 5 Ee
Klaipėda 13 ABd
Klamath Falls 33 ABb
Klamath Mountains 33 Ab
Klamono 18 He
Klarälven (riv.) 4 Cc
Klatovy 5 Dc
Klin 12 Eb
Klincy 12 Dc
Klinovec (mt.) 5 Dc
Kljazma (riv.) 12 Fb
Ključ 6 Cd
Ključevskaja Sopka, vulkan–
   (mt.) 14 Jd
Kłobuck 5 Gc
Kłodzko 5 Fc
Klondike (riv.) 31 Bb
Klosterneuburg 5 Fd
Kluczbork 5 Gc
Kneža 11 Fb
Knin 6 BCd
Knivskjelodden (cap.) 4 Fa
Knjaževac 6 EFe
Knoxville 32 Cc
Knysna 26 Be
Kobdo 14 Ce
Kōbe 16 HId
Koblenz 5 Ac
Koboža 12 DEb
Kobrin 12 Bc
Kočani 11 Ec
Koçarlı 11 Ge
Kocasu (riv.) 22 Bc
Kočevje 6 Bd
Koch Bihar 19 Jj
Kōchi 16 Hd
Köçke 22 Fd
Kodiak Island 30 Cd
Kodok (Fashoda) 25 Dcd
Koel (riv.) 19 HIj
Kofiau, Pulau– (i.) 18 GHe

Köflach 5 Ee
Kōfu 16 Ic
Køge 5 Da
Kohat 20 Db
Kohima 19 Bc
Koh–i–Qaisar (mt.) 20 Bb
Kohtla–Järve 4 Fd
Koitere (l.) 4 Gc
Kóje–Do (i.) 17 Ag
Ko–Jima (i.) 17 Fh
Kokand 13 Gef
Kokčetav 13 FGd
Kok–Jangak 13 Ge
Kokkola 4 EFc
Koko Head (cap.) 28 map
   no.1
Kokstad 26 BCe
Kola 4 Ha
Kolaka 18 Fe
Kola Peninsula 13 Cc
Kolar Gold Fields 20 Ef
Kolari 4 EFb
Kolbuszowa 5 HIc
Kolda 24 Ac
Kolding 5 Ba
Kolgujev, ostrov– (i.) 42 grid
   square no.3
Kolhapur 20 De
Kolín 5 Ecd
Kolkasrags (cap.) 4 Ed
Köln 5 Ac
Kolno 5 HIb
Koloa 28 map no.1
Kołobrzeg 5 Ea
Kolokani 24 Bc
Kolomna 13 CDd
Kolomyja 6 Gd
Kolpino 12 Db
Kolumadulu Atoll 20 Dh
Kolva (riv.) 12 Ia
Kolwezi 23 Eg
Kolyma (riv.) 14 Ic
Kolymskoje Nagorje 14 IJc
Kom (mt.) 6 Fe
Komadugu (riv.) 24 Dc
Komandorski Islands 14 Jd
Komárno 6 Dc
Komárom 6 CDc
Komatsu 16 Ic
Komi (Aut. Rep.) 13 Ec
Komló 6 Dc
Komodo, Pulau– (i.) 18 EFf
Komotiní 11 Fc
Komovi (mt.) 11 Cb
Kompasberg (mt.) 26 Bd
Kompong Cham 19 Ef
Kompong Thom 19 DEf
Komrat 6 Ic
Komsomolec, ostrov– 41 grid
   square no.4
Komsomolsk–na–Amure 14
   Gd
Konar (riv.) 20 Dab
Konarak (r.) 20 Gde
Kondinin 29 Be
Kondoa 26 Cb
Kondopoga 12 DEa
Kondrovo 12 DEc
Kong (riv.) 19 Eef
Kōng, Kaôh– (i.) 19 Df
Kong Frederik VI Kyst 31 Kb

Kongolo 26 Bb
Kongor 25 Dd
Kongsberg 4 Bcd
Kongsvinger 4 BCc
Kongur Shan (mt.) 13 Gf
Konin 5 Gb
Konjic 6 CDe
Konoša 13 CDc
Konotop 13 Cd
Końskie 5 GHc
Konstantinovka 12 Ed
Konstanz 5 Be
Kontagora 24 Cc
Kontiomäki 4 Gb
Kontum (Cong Tum) 19 Ef
Konya 22 Dd
Konžakovski Kamen, gora–
   (mt.) 12 IJb
Kootenay (riv.) 33 Bb
Kopaonik (mts.) 11 Db
Kópavogur 4 map no.1
Kopejsk 13 Fd
Kopervik 4 Ad
Kopetdag, Hrebet– (mts.) 21
   Fb
Köping 4 CDd
Koprivnica 6 Cc
Köprü (riv.) 22 Cd
Korab (mt.) 11 Dc
Koraput 20 Fe
Korba 20 Fd
Korça 11 Dc
Korčula (i.) 11 Bb
Korea Strait 16 Gd
Korec 6 Ha
Korf 14 Jc
Korhogo 24 Bd
Kórinthos 11 Ee
Köriyama 16 Jc
Korjakskaja Sopka, vulkan–
   (mt.) 14 IJd
Korkino 3 Jb
Korkuteli 22 BCd
Kornati 6 Be
Köroğlu dağları (mts.) 22 CDb
Köroğlu tepe (mt.) 22 CDb
Korogwe 26 Cb
Koro Island 28 map no.6
Koror 27 Bb
Körös (riv.) 6 Ec
Korosten 13 Bd
Korostyšev 6 Ia
Korsakov 14 He
Korsør 5 Ca
Kortrijk 8 Eb
Kos 11 Ge
Kos (i.) 11 Ge
Kosa Arabatskaja Strelko
   (pen.) 12 DEd
Koščagyl 12 Hd
Kościan 5 Fb
Kościerzyna 5 FGa
Kosciusko, Mount– 29 Hf
Kösedağ (mt.) 22 FGbc
Koshiki–Rettō 17 Ai
Kosi (riv.) 20 Gc
Košice 5 Hd
Kosmet 11 Db
Kosöng 16 Gc
Kosovo polje (phys. reg.) 11
   Db
Kosovska Mitrovica 11 Db
Kosrae (i.) 27 Db

Kostajnica 6 BCd
Kostopol 6 Ha
Kostroma 13 Dd
Kostrzyn 5 Eb
Koszalin 5 Fa
Kőszeg 6 Cc
Kota 20 Ecd
Kotaagung 18 Bf
Kota Baharu 19 Dg
Kotabaru 18 Ee
Kota Kinabalu 18 Ec
Kotel 11 Gb
Kotelnič 13 DEd
Kotelnikovo 12 Fd
Kotelny, ostrov– (i.) 14 Gb
Kotka 4 Fc
Kotlas 13 Dc
Kotor 11 Cb
Kotorska, Boka– 11 BCb
Kotor Varoš 6 Cd
Kotovsk [Mold.] 6 Ic
Kotovsk [Russia] 12 Fc
Kotovsk [Ukr.] 6 IJc
Kotri 20 Cc
Kottagudem 20 EFe
Kotto (riv.) 25 Cd
Kotuj (str.) 14 Dc
Kotzebue 30 BCc
Koudougou 24 Bc
Koufonísion 11 Gf
Koulamoutou 26 Ab
Koulikoro 24 Bc
Koumac 28 map no.4
Kourou 37 Db
Kouroussa 24 Bc
Koury 24 Bc
Koutiala 24 Bc
Kouvola 4 Fc
Kovdor 4 Gb
Kovel 12 Bc
Kovrov 13 Dd
Kovylkino 12 Fc
Kowloon 16 DEf
Kowŏn 16 Gc
Köyceğiz Gölü 22 Bd
Kozan 22 EFd
Kozáni 11 Dc
Kozle 5 Gc
Kozloduj 11 Eb
Kozmodemjansk 12 Gb
Kōzu–Shima (i.) 17 Fg
Kra, Isthmus of– 19 CDf
Kra Buri 19 Cf
Kragerø 4 Bd
Kragujevac 6 Ede
Krakóv 5 GHc
Kraljevo 6 Ee
Král Sněžnik (mt.) 5 Fc
Kramatorsk 13 Ce
Kramfors 4 Dc
Kranídhion 11 Ee
Kranj 6 Bc
Krapina 6 BCc
Krasavino 12 Ga
Krasino 13 Eb
Kraskino 14 FGe
Kraśnik 5 Ic
Kraśnik Fabryczny 5 HIc
Krasnodar 13 Ce
Krasnograd 12 Ed
Krasnogvardejskoje 12 Fd
Krasnojarsk 14 Cd
Krasnokamsk 13 Ed

Krasnoperekopsk 12 Dd
Krasnorečenski 17 Db
Krasnoselkup 13 Hc
Krasnoslobodsk 12 FGd
Krasnoturinsk 13 EFcd
Krasnoufimsk 12 Ib
Krasnouralsk 12 IJb
Krasnovišersk 13 Ec
Krasnovodsk 21 Ea
Krasnozatonski 12 Ha
Krasnoznamensk 13 Fd
Krasny Barrikady 12 Gd
Krasny Jar 12 Gd
Krasny Kut 12 Gc
Krasny Liman 12 Ed
Krasny Luč 12 Ed
Krasnystaw 5 Ic
Kratié 19 Ef
Krefeld 5 Ac
Kremenčug 12 Dd
Kremenčugskoje
   vodohranilišče 12 Dd
Kremenec 6 Ga
Krems an der Donau 5 Ed
Kretinga 12 Bb
Kribi 24 CDd
Kričev 12 Dc
Krilon, mys– 16 Ja
Kriós, Ákra– 11 Ef
Krishna (riv.) 20 Ee
Krishnanagar 19 Jk
Kristiansand 4 ABd
Kristianstad 4 Cde
Kristiansund 4 Ac
Kristinehamn 4 Cd
Kristinestad 4 Ec
Kriva Palanka 11 DEb
Krivoj Rog 3 Gc
Križevci 10 Fab
Krk (i.) 6 Bd
Krkonoše 5 EFc
Krnov 5 Fc
Kronoki 14 Jd
Kronprinsesse Martha Kyst
   42 grid square no.1
Kronprins Olav Kyst 42 grid
   square no.2
Kronštadt 4 Gcd
Kroonstad 23 Eh
Kropotkin 13 De
Krosno 5 Hd
Krosno Odrzańskie 5 Eb
Krotoszyn 5 Fc
Krugersdorp 26 Bd
Krui 18 Bef
Kruja 11 Cc
Krung Thep → Bangkok 19
   Df
Kruševac 6 Ee
Krymskije Gory 12 De
Krzyż 5 EFb
Ksar–el–Boukhari 24 Ca
Ksar–el–Kébir 24 Ba
Kstovo 12 FGb
Kuala Dungun 19 Dgh
Kuala Krai 19 Dg
Kuala Lipis 19 Dh
Kuala Lumpur 19 Di
Kuala Terengganu 19 DEg
Kuantan 19 Dh
Kuban (riv.) 13 Ce
Kučevo 6 EFd
Kuching 15 Di

Kuchinoerabu–Shima (i.) 17
   ABi
Kuchi–no–Shima (i.) 17 ABi
Kuçova 11 Dc
Kudat 18 Ec
Kudus 18 Df
Kudymkar 13 Ed
Kufra Oasis 24 Eb
Kufstein 5 De
Kuhak 21 Gd
Küh–e Bäbä (mts.) 20 Cb
Kuhestak 21 Fd
Kuhmo 4 Gbc
Kuito 26 Ac
Kuivaniemi 4 EFb
Kujawy (phys. reg.) 5 Gb
Kujbyšev → Samara 13 Ed
Kuji 17 GHd
Kujto, ozero– 4 Gb
Kujü–San (mt.) 17 Bh
Kukēsi 11 Dbc
Kukmor 12 Hb
Kula [Bul.] 11 Eb
Kula [Yugo.] 6 Dd
Kuldiga 12 Bb
Kulebaki 12 Fb
Kulgera 29 Ed
Kuljab 13 FGf
Kulsary 13 Ee
Kulti 19 Ik
Kulu 22 Dc
Kulunda 13 GHd
Kuma (riv.) 12 Gde
Kumai 18 De
Kumamoto 16 GHd
Kumanovo 11 Db
Kumasi 24 Bd
Kumayri (Leninakan) 13 De
Kumbakonam 20 EFf
Kumbo 24 CDd
Kum–Dag 13 Ef
Kume–Jima (i.) 16 Ge
Kumertau 12 Hb
Kumo–Manyčski kanal (riv.)
   12 FGd
Kunasir, ostrov– / Kunashiri–
   Tō (i.) 17 Ibc
Kunda 4 Fd
Kund Rasmussen Land 31
   ILab
Kunene (riv.) 26 Ac
Kungälv 4 Bd
Kungrad 13 Ee
Kungur 13 Ed
Kunlong 19 Cd
Kunlun Shan 20 FGab
Kunming 15 Dg
Kunsan 16 Gc
Kuntilla, El– 22 Eg
Kununurra 29 Db
Kuopio 4 FGc
Kupa (riv.) 6 Bd
Kupang 18 Ffg
Kupino 13 Gd
Kupjansk 12 Ed
Kuqa 13 He
Kura (riv.) 13 DEf
Kurashiki 17 Cg
Kuraymah 25 Dc
Kurayoshi 17 CDg
Kurdistan (phys. reg.) 21 CDf
Kurdufän (State) 25 CDc
Kure 16 Hd

ŭre dağları (İsfendiyar) (mts.) **22** DEb
ŭre Island (Ocean) **27** DEa
ŭrejka (riv.) **14** Cc
ŭressaare (Kingissepp) **4** Ed
ŭurgan **13** Fd
ŭuri Bay **29** Cb
ŭuril Islands **14** Hle
ŭurilsk **14** He
ŭurnool **20** Ee
ŭuro–Shima (i.) **17** Ai
ŭuršenai **4** Ede
ŭursk **13** Cd
ŭurski Zaliv (I.) **4** Ee
ŭuršumlija **11** Db
ŭuru (riv.) **25** Cd
ŭuruman **26** Bd
ŭurume **16** Hd
ŭurunegala **20** Fg
ŭuşada Körfezi **22** Acd
ŭuşadası **11** Ge
ŭusagaki–Guntō **17** Ai
ŭuş Gölü **22** Ab
ŭushima **17** Bi
ŭushiro **16** Jb
ŭushtia **19** Jk
ŭuška **15** Cf
ŭussaro–Ko **17** Hlc
ŭustanaj **13** Fd
ŭüstí **25** Dc
ŭušva **13** EFd
ŭüt, Al– **21** Dc
ŭut, Ko– (i.) **19** Df
ŭütahya **22** Bc
ŭutaisi **21** Ca
ŭutch (phys. reg.) **20** CDd
ŭutch, Gulf of– **20** Cd
ŭutch, Rann of– **20** CDd
ŭutina **6** Cd
ŭutno **5** Gb
ŭutu **26** Ab
ŭutum **25** Cc
ŭuusamo **4** Gb
ŭuusankoski **4** Fc
ŭuvandyk **12** Ic
ŭuwait (Ind. St.) **15** Bfg
ŭuzneck **12** Gc
ŭvaløy (i.) **4** Da
ŭvarner (g.) **6** ABd
ŭvarnerić (g.) **6** Bd
ŭvikkjokk **4** Db
ŭvitøya **13** Ca
ŭwa (riv.) **26** Ab
ŭwajalein Atoll **27** Db
ŭwando (riv.) **26** Bc
ŭwangju **16** Gcd
ŭwango (riv.) **26** Ab
ŭwangsi **15** Dg
ŭwekwe **26** Bc
ŭwenge (riv.) **26** Ab
ŭwidzyn **5** Gb
ŭwilu (riv.) **26** Ab
ŭyangin **19** BCe
ŭyaukpadaung **19** BCd
ŭyaukpyu **19** Be
ŭyaukse **19** Cd
ŭynuna **29** Gc
ŭyoga, Lake– **25** Dd
ŭyöga–Misaki **17** Dg
ŭyöngju **17** ABg
ŭyöngsöng **17** ABd
ŭyöto **16** Icd

Kyrēnia **22** De
Kyrgyzstan (Ind. St.) **13** Ge
Kyštym **12** Jb
Kyūshū (i.) **16** Hd
Kyushū–Sanchi **17** Bh
Kyzyl **14** Cd
Kyzylkum (phys. reg.) **13** Fe
Kzyl–Orda **13** Fe

L

Labé **24** Ac
Labouheyre **8** Ce
Laboulaye **39** Bc
Labrador **31** Hlc
Labrador, Coast of– **31** IJc
Labrador City **31** Ic
Labrador Sea **31** Jc
Lábrea **37** Cc
Labuan, Pulau– **18** Dc
Labuha **18** Ge
Labytnangi **13** Fc
Lacaune, Monts de– (mts.) **8** Ef
Laccadive Islands **20** Df
Lacepede Islands **29** Cb
Lachlan River **29** GHe
Lac la Biche **31** DEc
Laconia, Gulf of– **11** Ee
Lacq **8** Cf
Ladakh Range **20** EFb
Ladoga, Lake– **13** BCc
Ladysmith **26** BCd
Lae **27** Cc
Lærdalsøyri **4** Ac
Læsø (i.) **4** Bd
Lafayette **32** Bbc
Lafia **24** Cd
Laghouat **24** Ca
Lagos [Nig.] **24** Cd
Lagos [Port.] **9** Ad
Lagos de Moreno **34** Bb
Lagrange **29** Cb
Laguna **39** Db
Lahad Datu **18** Ecd
Lahaina **28** map no.1
Lahat **18** Be
Lahǐj **21** CDg
Lāhijān **21** Eb
Lahn **5** Bc
Lahn (riv.) **5** ABc
Laholm **4** Cd
Lahore **15** Cf
Lahti **4** Fc
Laï **25** Bd
Lai Chau **19** Dd
Laingsburg **26** ABe
Lainioälven (riv.) **4** Ea
Lairg **7** Dbc
Laixi (Shuiji) **16** Fc
Lajas, Las– **39** ABc
Lajes **39** CDb
Lajkovac **6** DEd
Lake Charles **32** Bb
Lake City **32** Cbc
Lake Constance **5** BCe
Lake Harbour **31** Ib
Lakeland **32** Cc
Lakemba (i.) **28** map no.6
Lake Nash **29** Fc
Lakewood **32** Ca

Lakhimpur **19** Hj
Lak Sao **19** DEe
Laksefjord (b.) **4** Fa
Lakselv **4** Fa
Lakshadweep **20** Dfg
Lalapaşa **22** Ab
Lalín **9** ABa
Lalitpur **19** Gj
Lamar **33** Cc
Lambaréné **24** De
Lambasa **28** map no.6
Lambert Glacier **42** grid square no.2
Lamego **9** Bb
Lamezia Terme **10** Fe
Lamia **11** Ed
Lamon Bay **18** Fb
Lampang **19** Ce
Lampedusa (i.) **10** Dg
Lamphun **19** CDe
Lamu **26** Db
Lanai (i.) **28** map no.1
Lanbi Kyun (i.) **19** Cf
Lancang Jiang (riv.) **19** CDd
Lancaster [Can.] **31** Id
Lancaster [Ca.–U.S.] **33** Bc
Lancaster [Pa.–U.S.] **9** Hd
Lancaster [U.K.] **7** Ed
Lancelin **29** ABe
Lanciano **10** Ec
Lańcut **5** Ic
Landeck **5** Ce
Landenpohja **4** Gc
Landerneau **8** Ac
Lander River **29** Ec
Landes (phys. reg.) **8** Cef
Land's End (cap.) **7** CDf
Landshut **5** Dd
Landskrona **4** Cde
Langeland (i.) **5** Cc
Langjökull (gl.) **4** map no.1
Langkawi, Pulau– (i.) **19** Cg
Langon **8** Ce
Langoya (i.) **4** Ca
Langreo **9** Ca
Langres **8** Fd
Langres, Plateau de– (plat.) **8** Fd
Langsa **18** Ad
Lang Son **19** Ed
Languedoc (phys. reg.) **8** EFef
Lan Hsu (Hungtao Yu) (is.) **16** Ff
Lannion **8** Bc
Lansing **32** Ca
Lanusei **10** Be
Lanzarote (i.) **24** Ab
Lanzhou **16** BCc
Laoag **15** DEh
Laoang **18** FGb
Lao Cai **19** Dd
Laodicea → Latakia **22** Ee
Laoha He (riv.) **16** EFb
Laon **8** Ec
Laos (Ind. St.) **15** Dh
Lapalisse **8** Ed
La Pérouse Strait **16** Ja
Lapland (phys. reg.) **4** EGab
Lappeenranta **4** FGc
Lâpseki **11** Gc
Laptev Sea **41** grid square no.4

Lapua **4** Ec
Łapy **5** Ib
Lär **21** EFd
Larache **24** Ba
Laramie **33** Cb
Larantuka **18** Ff
Larche, Col de– →
Maddalena, Colle della– **10** Ab
Laredo [Sp.] **9** Da
Laredo [U.S.] **32** Bc
Lärestän (phys. reg.) **21** EFd
Larino **10** Ed
Lárisa **11** Ed
Larkana **20** Cc
Lárnaca **22** DEe
Larne **7** Dd
Larrimah **29** Eb
Larsen Ice Shelf **42** grid square no.1
Larvik **4** Bd
Lascaux (c.) **8** De
Lashio **15** Dg
Laskargah **20** BCb
Lastovo (i.) **11** Bb
Latacunga **37** Bc
Latakia (Laodicea) **22** Ee
Late Island **28** Ac
Latina **10** Dd
Latvia (Ind. St.) **4** EFd
Lauca, Río– (riv.) **39** Ba
Lauenburg an der Elbe **5** Cb
Lau Group **27** Ec
Launceston **29** map no.1
Laura **29** Gb
Laurel [Ms.–U.S.] **32** BCb
Laurel [Mt.–U.S.] **33** BCb
Lauria **10** Ed
Lausanne **10** Aa
Lausitz (hist. reg.) **5** DEc
Laut, Pulau– (i.) **19** Eh
Lautoka **28** map no.6
Laval **8** Cc
Lavaur **8** Df
Laverton **29** Cd
Lavras **39** Db
Lávrion **11** EFe
Lavumisa **26** Cd
Lawdar **21** Dg
Lawrence **32** Bb
Lawton **32** Bb
Lawz, Jabal al– (mt.) **21** Bd
Laylá **21** De
Laysan Island **28** Aa
Lazio (reg.) **10** CDcd
Leaf (riv.) **31** Hc
Learmouth **29** Ac
Łeba **5** Fa
Lebanon (mts.) **22** EFef
Lebanon (Ind. St.) **15** Bf
Lebedin **12** DEc
Lęborek **5** Fa
Lebrija **9** Bd
Łebsko, Jezioro– **5** Fa
Lebu **39** Ac
Lecce **10** Gd
Lecco **10** Bb
Lech (riv.) **5** Cd
Lectoure **8** Df
Leczyca **5** Gb
Ledesma **9** BCb
Ledjanaja, gora– (mt.) **14** Kc

Leeds 7 Fe
Leer in Ostfriesland 5 Ab
Leeuwarden 8 FGa
Leeuwin, Cape– 29 ABe
Leeward Islands 28 Bc
Lefke 22 De
Legazpi 18 Fb
Legges Tor (mt.) 29 map no.1
Legionowo 5 Hb
Legnago 10 Cb
Legnica 5 Fc
Leh 20 Eb
Lehua (i.) 28 map no.1
Leibnitz 5 Ee
Leibo 16 Be
Leicester 7 Fe
Leichhardt River 29 Fb
Leiden 8 Fa
Leie (riv.) 8 Eb
Leigh Creek 29 Fe
Leine (riv.) 5 Bbc
Leinster (prov.) 7 Ce
Leipzig 5 Dc
Leiria 9 Ac
Leirvik 4 Ad
Leitha (riv.) 5 Fe
Leiyang 16 De
Leizhou Bandao 16 Cf
Leman, Lac– → Geneva,
 Lake– 10 Aa
Lemdiyya 24 Ca
Lempa, Río– (riv.) 35 Bb
Lena (riv.) 14 Fc
Lendery 4 Gc
Lenina, pik– 13 Gf
Leninabad → Hodžent 13 Fe
Leningrad → Saint
 Petersburg 13 Cd
Leningradskaja 42 grid
 square no.4
Leninkan → Kumayri 13 De
Leninogorsk [Kaz.] 13 Hd
Leninogorsk [Russia] 12 Hc
Leninsk Kuznecki 13 Hld
Leninskoje 12 Gb
Lenkoran 13 DEf
Lennox, Isla– 40 Bc
Lens 8 Eb
Lensk 14 Ec
Lentini 10 Ef
Léo 24 Bc
Leoben 5 Ee
León (mt.) 34 Cc
León [Mex.] 34 Bb
León [Sp.] 9 Ca
Leonídhion 11 Ee
Leonora 29 Cd
Leopold and Astrid Coast 42
 grid square no.2
Lepel 12 Cc
Leping 16 Ee
Lepontine Alps 10 Ba
Leppävirta 4 FGc
Lepsy 13 GHe
Leptis Magna (r.) 24 Da
Lérida 9 Fb
Lerma 9 Dab
Léros (i.) 11 Ge
Lerwick 7 Fa
Lesbos (i.) 11 FGd
Leshan 16 Be
Leskovac 11 DEb
Lesnoj 13 Ecd

Lesotho (Ind. St.) 23 Ehi
Lesozavodsk 14 Ge
Lesparre–Médoc 8 Ce
Lesser Antilles (is.) 36 Db
Lesser Kingan Range 14 Fde
Lesser Slave Lake 31 Dc
Leszno 5 Fc
Letha Range 19 Bd
Lethbridge 33 Bb
Lethem 37 CDb
Letícia 36 Dd
Leti Island 18 Gf
Letterkenny 7 BCd
Leucas 11 Dd
Leucas (i.) 11 Dd
Leuna 5 CDc
Leuser, Gunong– (mt.) 18 Ad
Leuven 8 Fb
Levádhia 11 Ed
Levanger 4 BCc
Lévanzo (i.) 10 Def
Lévêque, Cape– 29 Cb
Leverkusen 5 Ac
Levice 5 Gd
Lévis 32 Da
Lévitha (i.) 11 Ge
Levká Óri (mts.) 11 EFf
Levski 11 Fb
Lewis, Butt of– (cap.) 7 Cb
Lewis, Isle of– 7 Cbc
Lewiston [Id.–U.S.] 33 Bb
Lewiston [Me.–U.S.] 32 DEa
Lewistown 33 Cb
Lexington 32 Cb
Leyre (riv.) 8 Ce
Leyte (i.) 18 FGb
Leżajsk 5 Ic
Lezha 11 Cc
Lgov 12 DEc
Lhasa 15 CDfg
Lhazê 20 Gc
Lhokseumawe 18 Acd
Lianxian 16 Def
Lianyungang 16 EFcd
Lianyungang (Xinpu) 16 EFd
Liaodong Bandao (pen.) 16
 Fbc
Liao He (riv.) 16 Fb
Liaoning (prov.) 16 Fb
Liaoyang 16 Fb
Liaoyuan 16 FGb
Liard (riv.) 31 Cbc
Libenge 25 Bd
Liberal 33 CDc
Liberec 5 Ec
Liberia (Ind. St.) 23 ABe
Liberia 35 Bb
Libertad, La– 35 ABb
Libertador General San
 Martín 39 Bb
Libertador General San
 Martin, Cumbre del– (mt.)
 39 Bb
Libourne 8 CDe
Libreville 24 CDde
Libya (Ind. St.) 23 DEc
Libyan Desert 24 Eb
Licata 10 Df
Lichinga 26 Cc
Lida 12 Cc
Lidköping 4 Cd
Lido di Ostia 10 Dd
Lidzbark Warminski 5 Ha

Liechtenstein (Ind. St.) 5 Be
Liège 8 Fb
Lieksa 4 Gc
Lielupe (riv.) 4 EFd
Lienz 5 De
Liepāja 4 Ed
Lier 8 Fb
Liestal 5 Ae
Liévin 8 Eb
Liezen 5 Ee
Lifford 7 Cd
Lifou, Île– (i.) 27 Dd
Liguria (reg.) 10 ABbc
Ligurian Sea 10 Bc
Lihou Reefs and Cays (is.) 29
 Ib
Lihue 28 map no.1
Liimaa 4 Ec
Lijiang 16 Be
Lika (mts.) 6 Bd
Likasi 26 Bc
Likiep Atoll 27 Db
Lille 8 Eb
Lille Bælt (str.) 4 Be
Lillehammer 4 BCc
Lillesand 4 Bd
Lilongwe 26 Cc
Lim (riv.) 11 Cb
Lima (riv.) 9 Ab
Lima [Mt.–U.S.] 33 Bb
Lima [Oh.–U.S.] 32 Ca
Lima [Peru] 36 Ce
Limasol 22 De
Limay (riv.) 39 Bcd
Limay Mahuida 39 Bc
Limbe 24 Cd
Limburg an der Lahn 5 Bc
Limeira 39 Db
Limerick 7 BCe
Limfjorden (b.) 4 ABd
Límni 11 Ed
Límnos (i.) 11 Fcd
Limoges 8 De
Limon 33 Cc
Limón 35 Bbc
Limón, El– 35 map no.1
Limón Bay 35 map no.1
Limousin (hist. reg.) 8 Dde
Limousin, Plateaux du– 8 De
Limoux 8 Ef
Limpopo 26 Cd
Linapacan (i.) 18 EFb
Linares [Chile] 39 Ac
Linares [Sp.] 9 Dc
Linares [Ven.] 34 Cb
Lincang 19 CDd
Lincoln [Arg.] 39 Bc
Lincoln [U.K.] 7 Fe
Lincoln [U.S.] 32 Ba
Lindau (Bodensee) 5 BCe
Linden 37 Db
Lindesnes (cap.) 4 Ad
Lindhos 11 Hef
Lindi 26 CDbc
Línea, La– 9 Cd
Line Islands 28 ABbc
Linfen 16 Dc
Lingayen 18 EFa
Lingayen Gulf 18 EFa
Lingen an der Ems 5 Ab
Lingga, Kepulauan– 18 BCe
Lingga, Pulau– (i.) 18 BCde
Lingling 16 De

Linguère 24 Ac
Linhai 16 Fe
Linhares 39 DEa
Linjiang 16 Gb
Linköping 4 CDd
Linkou 16 GHa
Linosa (i.) 10 Dg
Linqing 16 DEc
Linru 16 Dd
Lins 39 Db
Lintao 16 Bc
Linxi 16 Eb
Linxia 16 Bc
Linyi 16 Ecd
Linz 5 Ed
Lion, Golfe du– 8 EFf
Lipari (i.) 10 Ee
Lipari, Isole– → Eolie, Isole–
 10 Ee
Lipeck 13 CDd
Lipno 5 Gb
Lipova 6 EFcd
Lipovcy 17 Bb
Lipovec 6 Ib
Lippe (riv.) 5 Ac
Lira 25 Dd
Liria 9 Ec
Lisala 25 Cd
Lisbon 9 Ac
Lisburn 7 CDd
Lisburne, Cape– 41 grid
 square no.2
Lishi 16 Dc
Lishui 16 EFe
Lisianski Island 28 Aa
Lisičansk 12 Ed
Lisieux 8 Dc
Lismore 29 Id
Listowel 7 Be
Litang [China] 16 Bde
Litang [China] 16 Cf
Litani [Leb.] (riv.) 22 Ef
Litani [S. Amer.] (riv.) 38 Ba
Lith, Al– 21 BCef
Lithgow 29 Hle
Lithinon, Ákra– 11 Ff
Lithuania (Ind. St.) 4 EFe
Litín 6 Ib
Litókhoron 11 Ecd
Litoměřice 5 Ec
Litovko 14 Ge
Little Aden 21 CDg
Little Andaman (i.) 19 Bf
Little Bitter Lake 25 map no.1
Little Cayman (i.) 35 BCab
Little Colorado (riv.) 33 BCc
Little Falls 32 Ba
Little Inagua Island 35 Ca
Little Missouri (riv.) 33 Cb
Little Nicobar (i.) 19 BCg
Little Poland (hist. reg.) 5
 GHc
Little Rock 32 Bb
Liuzhou 16 Cf
Livermore, Mount– 33 Cc
Liverpool [Can.] 32 Ea
Liverpool [U.K.] 7 Ee
Liverpool Bay 7 Ee
Livingston 35 BCb
Livingstone → Maramba 26
 Bc
Livingstone Falls 26 Ab
Livno 6 Ce

vny 12 Ec
vonia (phys. reg.) 4 Fd
vorno 10 Cc
xian 16 De
zard Point 7 Dg
ubar 6 Hb
ubercy 12 Eb
ubljana 6 Bc
uboml 5 IJc
ubotin 12 DEcd
udinovo 12 DEc
ungan (riv.) 4 CDc
ungby 4 Cd
usdal 4 Dc
usnan (riv.) 4 Cc
andrindod Wells 7 Ee
anelli 7 DEf
anes 9 Ca
ano Estacado (plat.) 33 Cc
anos (phys. reg.) 37 BCb
anquihue, Lago– 40 Ab
obregat (riv.) 9 Fab
uchmayor 9 Gc
ullaillaco, Volcán– (mt.) 39 Bb
oa (riv.) 39 ABb
oange (riv.) 26 Bb
obatse 26 Bd
obería 9 Dc
obito 23 Dg
obos 39 Cc
obos, Islas– 37 Ac
obva 12 Jb
ochboisdale 7 BCc
oches 8 Dd
ochgilphead 7 CDc
oc Ninh 19 Ef
ocri 10 Fe
od 22 Efg
odejnoje–Pole 13 Cc
odève 8 Ef
odi [It.] 10 Bb
odi [U.S.] 33 Ac
odja 26 Bb
odwar 25 Dd
ódž 5 Gc
oei 19 De
ofoten (is.) 4 Cab
ogan 33 Bb
ogan, Mount– 31 ABb
ogone (riv.) 24 Dcd
ogroño 9 Da
ogrosán 9 Cc
ohardaga 19 Hlk
oikaw 19 Ce
oir (riv.) 8 Dd
oire (riv.) 8 Cd
oja [Ec.] 37 Bc
oja [Sp.] 9 Cd
okeren 8 Eb
okoja 24 Cd
okomo 24 Dd
ol (riv.) 25 Cd
olland (i.) 4 Be
om (riv.) 11 FGb
om 11 Eb
omami (riv.) 26 Bb
oma Mountains 24 ABd
ombardia (reg.) 10 BCab
omblen, Pulau– (i.) 15 Ff
ombok, Pulau– (i.) 15 Djk
omé 24 Cd
omela 26 Bb

Lomela (riv.) 26 Bb
Lomié 24 Dd
Lomitas, Las– 39 BCb
Lomonosov 4 Gcd
Łomża 5 Hlb
London [Can.] 31 GHd
London [U.K.] 7 FGf
Londonderry 7 Cd
Londonderry, Cape– 29 Da
Londonderry, Isla– (i.) 40 Ac
Londrina 39 Cb
Long Beach 33 Bc
Longford 7 Ce
Long Island [Bah.] 35 Ca
Long Island [U.S.] 32 Da
Longjiang 16 Fa
Longkou 16 EFc
Longreach 29 Gc
Longview [Tx.–U.S.] 32 Bb
Longview [Wa.–U.S.] 33 Ab
Longwy 8 Fc
Longxi 16 BCcd
Long Xuyen 15 Dhi
Longyan 16 Fef
Longyearbyen 13 ABb
Lonja (riv.) 6 Cd
Lons–le–Saunier 8 Fd
Loop Head 7 ABe
Lopatka, mys– 14 Id
Lop Buri 19 Def
Lopez, Cap– 24 Ce
Lop Nur (l.) 15 Def
Lopori (riv.) 25 Cd
Lopphavet (str.) 4 Ea
Lora del Río 9 Cd
Lorain 32 Ca
Lorca 9 Ed
Lord Howe Island 27 CDd
Lordsburg 33 BCc
Lorestän 21 Dc
Loreto [Bol.] 39 Ba
Loreto [Mex.] 34 Ab
Loreto [Par.] 39 Cb
Lorica 37 Bb
Lorient 8 Bd
Lorne, Firth of– (str.) 7 CDc
Lörrach 5 ABe
Lorraine (hist. reg.) 8 FGc
Lošinj (i.) 6 Bd
Los Islands 24 Ad
Lot (riv.) 8 De
Lota 39 Ac
Lotofaga 28 map no.5
Lotta (riv.) 4 Ga
Loubomo 26 Ab
Loudéac 8 Bc
Loudima 26 Ab
Louga 24 Ac
Louisiade Archipelago 27 Cc
Louisiana (State) 32 Bbc
Louis Trichardt 26 BCd
Louisville 32 Cb
Louis XIV, Point– 31 GHc
Louny 5 DEc
Lourdes 8 Cf
Lourenço Marques →
  Maputo 26 Cd
Louth [Austl.] 29 He
Louth [U.K.] 7 FGe
Louviers 8 Dc
Lovat (riv.) 12 Db
Loveč 11 Fb
Lovisa 4 Fc

Lowell 32 DEa
Lower Lough Erne 7 BCd
Lower Tunguska (riv.) 14
  CDc
Lowestoft 7 GHe
Łowicz 5 Gb
Loxton 29 FGe
Loyalty Islands 27 Dcd
Lozère (mt.) 8 Ee
Loznica 6 Dd
Lozovaja 12 Ed
Lozva (riv.) 12 Ja
Lualaba (Zaïre) (riv.) 26 Bb
Luama (riv.) 26 Bb
Lu'an 16 Ed
Luanda 26 Ab
Luanda (prov.) 26 Ab
Luang Prabang 15 Dgh
Luangwa 26 Cc
Luangwa (riv.) 26 Cc
Luan He (riv.) 16 Eb
Luanshya 23 Eg
Luapula (riv.) 26 Bbc
Luarca 9 Ba
Luau 26 Bc
Lubań 5 Ec
Lubango 26 Ac
Lubbock 33 Cc
Lübeck 5 Cb
Lübecker Bucht 5 Ca
Lubefu 26 Bb
Lubin 5 Fc
Lublin 5 Ic
Lubliniec 5 Gc
Lubny 12 Dc
Luboń 5 Fb
Lubuklinggau 18 Be
Lubumbashi 26 Bc
Lubutu 25 Ce
Lucca 10 Cc
Lucena [Phil.] 18 Fb
Lucena [Sp.] 9 Cd
Lučenec 5 Gd
Lucera 10 Ed
Luciara 38 Bc
Lucipara, Kepulauan– 18 Gf
Luck 13 Bd
Luckeesarai 19 Ij
Luckenwalde 5 Db
Lucknow 15 Cg
Luçon 8 Cd
Lüderitz 23 Dh
Ludhiana 20 Eb
Ludogorije (mts.) 11 Gb
Luduş 6 Gc
Ludvika 4 Ccd
Ludwigsburg 5 BCd
Ludwigshafen am Rhein 5
  ABd
Ludwigslust 5 Cb
Ludza 4 FGd
Luebo 26 Bb
Luena 26 ABc
Lüeyang 16 BCd
Lufeng 16 Ef
Lufkin 32 Bb
Luga 13 BCd
Luga (riv.) 4 Gd
Lugano 10 Ba
Lugansk (Vorošilovgrad) 13
  CDe
Lugenda (riv.) 26 Cc
Lugnaquillia Mountain 7 Ce

Lugo [It.] 10 Cb
Lugo [Sp.] 9 Ba
Lugoj 6 EFd
Lugovoj 13 Ge
Luhayyah, Al– 21 Cf
Luiana 26 Bc
Luiro (riv.) 4 Fb
Luishia 26 Bc
Luitpold Coast 42 grid square
  no.1
Lukenie (riv.) 26 Bb
Lukojanov 12 FGb
Luków 5 Ic
Lukuga (riv.) 26 Bb
Luleå 4 Eb
Luleälven (riv.) 4 Eb
Lüleburgaz 11 Gc
Lulonga (riv.) 26 Aa
Lulua (riv.) 26 Bb
Lumajang 18 Df
Lumbala 26 Bc
Lumbo 26 CDc
Lumding 19 Bc
Lumphät 19 Ef
Lund [Nor.] 4 Ad
Lund [Swe.] 4 Ce
Lunda 26 ABb
Lundy (i.) 7 Df
Lüneburg 5 BCb
Lüneburger Heide 5 Cb
Lunenburg 32 Ea
Lunéville 8 Gc
Lungué–Bungo (riv.) 26 ABc
Luni (riv.) 20 Dcd
Luo He (riv.) 16 Cc
Luohe 16 Dd
Luoyang 16 Dd
Lupeni 6 Fd
Lure 8 Gd
Lúrio 26 Dc
Lúrio (riv.) 26 Cc
Lusaka 23 Eg
Lusambo 26 Bb
Lushnja 11 Cc
Lushoto 26 Cb
Luton 7 Fef
Lutong 18 Dd
Lützow–Holm Bay 42 grid
  square no.2
Luuq 25 Ed
Luvua (riv.) 26 Bb
Luwegu (riv.) 26 Cb
Luwuk 18 Fe
Luxembourg (Ind. St.) 3 Dbc
Luxembourg 5 CDd
Luxor 25 Db
Luza 12 Ga
Luzern 5 ABe
Luzhou 16 BCe
Luzilândia 38 Cb
Luzon (i.) 18 Fa
Luzon Strait 16 Ffg
Lvov 13 Bde
Lyakhov Islands 14 Hlb
Lycksele 4 Db
Lyme Bay 7 Ef
Łyna (riv.) 5 Ha
Lynchburg 32 CDb
Lyngen (b.) 4 Ea
Lynn Lake 30 Hld
Lyon 8 Fe
Lys (riv.) 8 Eb
Lysva 12 Ib

M

Ma (riv.) **19** Ed
Maalaea **28** map no.1
Ma'än **22** Eg
Maanselkä (mts.) **4** FGab
Ma'arrat an Nu'män **22** Fe
Maas (riv.) **5** Ac
Maastricht **8** Fb
Mabaruma **37** CDb
Mabote **26** Cd
Macaé **39** Db
McAlester **32** Bb
McAllen **32** Bc
Macao **15** Dg
Macapá **36** Ec
Macas **37** Bc
Macau **38** Db
Macauley Island **27** DEd
McCall **33** Bb
McClintock Channel **31** Ea
McCook **33** CDbc
Macdonald, Lake– **29** Dc
Macdonnell Ranges **29** EFc
Macedonia (phys. reg.) **11** De
Macedonia (Ind. St.) **11** DEc
Macedonia (reg.) **11** DFc
Maceió **36** Gd
Mcensk **12** Ec
Macenta **24** Bd
Macerata **10** Dc
Machala **37** ABc
Machaneng **26** Bd
Machilipatnam **20** Fe
Machiques **37** Bab
Machupicchu (r.) **37** Bd
Mäcin **6** Id
Macina (phys. reg.) **24** Bc
Macintyre River **29** Hld
Mackay [Austl.] **29** Hlc
Mackay [U.S.] **33** Bb
Mackay, Lake– **29** Dc
Mckean Atoll **28** Ac
Mackenzie (riv.) **30** EFc
Mackenzie, District of– **31** CEb
Mackenzie Bay **31** ABab
Mackenzie Mountains **31** BCb
Mackenzie River **29** Hc
Mackinaw City **32** Ca
McKinley, Mount– **41** grid square no.2
Maclear **26** BCe
McLennan **31** Dc
McLeod, Lake– **29** Ac
McMurdo **42** grid square no.4
McMurdo Sound **42** grid square no.4
McMurray **30** GHd
Macon **32** Cb
Mâcon **8** Fd
Macquarie (i.) **2**
Macquarie River **29** He
Mac Robertson Land **42** grid square no.2
Macumba, The– (riv.) **29** Fd
Madagascar (Ind. St.) **23** Ggh
Madama **24** Db
Madan **11** Fc
Madang **27** Cc
Madaniyin **24** CDa
Madaripur **19** Jk

Maddalena, Colle della– (Larche, Col de–) (p.) **10** Ab
Maddalena, La– (i.) **10** Bd
Madden Dam **35** map no.1
Madden Lake **35** map no.1
Madeira (i.) **24** Aa
Madeira (riv.) **38** Ab
Madeira Islands **24** Aa
Madeleine, Île de la– (i.) **32** Ea
Madhubani **19** Ij
Madhya Pradesh (State) **20** EFd
Madina do Boé **24** Ac
Madinat ash Sha'b **21** Cg
Madingo–Kayes **26** Ab
Madingou **26** Ab
Madison **32** BCa
Madisonville **32** Cb
Madiun **18** Df
Madonie, Le– (mts.) **10** DEf
Madra dağ (mt.) **11** Gd
Madran dağ (mt.) **22** Bd
Madras **15** Ch
Madre, Laguna– **34** Cb
Madre, Sierra– [Mex.] (mts.) **34** Cc
Madre, Sierra– [Phil.] (mts.) **18** Fa
Madre de Dios, Isla– **40** Abc
Madre de Dios, Río– (riv.) **37** BCd
Madre del Sud, Sierra– (mts.) **34** BCc
Madre Occidental, Sierra– (mts.) **34** Bb
Madre Oriental, Sierra– (mts.) **34** BCb
Madrid **9** CDb
Madrid–Villaverde **9** Db
Madura, Pulau– (i.) **18** Df
Madurai **15** Chi
Madyan (phys. reg.) **21** Bd
Maebashi **16** Ic
Mae Hong Son **19** Ce
Mae Sai **19** Cd
Maestra, Sierra– (mts.) **35** Cab
Maevatanana **26** map no.1
Maéwo, Île– (i.) **28** map no.4
Mafia Island **26** CDb
Mafikeng **26** Bd
Mafra **39** CDb
Mafraq, Al– **22** Ff
Magadan **14** Id
Magadi **25** De
Magangué **37** Bb
Magdagači **14** Fd
Magdalena (riv.) **37** Bb
Magdalena [Bol.] **39** Ba
Magdalena [Mex.] **34** ABa
Magdalena, Isla– **40** Ab
Magdeburg **5** CDb
Magelang **18** CDf
Magellan, Strait of– **36** BCi
Magellan, Strait of– / Magellanes, Estrecho de– **40** ABc
Magellanes, Estrecho de– / Magellan, Strait of– **40** ABc
Magerøya (i.) **4** EFa
Maggiore, Lago– (Verbano) (l.) **10** Bab

Maglić (mt.) **11** Cb
Maglie **10** Gd
Magna, Fossa– **17** EFfg
Magnitogorsk **13** EFd
Magua **27** map no.1
Magude **26** Cd
Magwe **19** BCd
Mahäbäd **21** CDb
Mahabharat Range **19** Hli
Mahačkala **13** DEe
Mahajanga **23** Gg
Mahakam (riv.) **18** Ede
Mahalapye **26** Bd
Maḥallah al Kubrä, Al– **25** Da
Mahambet **12** Hd
Mähän **21** Fc
Mahanadi (riv.) **20** Fd
Mahanoro **26** map no.1
Maharashtra (State) **20** DEe
Mahdiyah, Al– **24** Da
Mahé (i.) **15** Bj
Mahe **20** DEf
Mahenge **26** Cb
Mahesäna **20** Dd
Mahoba **19** GHj
Mahón **9** GHc
Mahrah, Al– (phys. reg.) **21** DEf
Maiana Atoll **27** Db
Maicuru (riv.) **38** Bab
Maidstone **7** FGf
Maiduguri **24** Dc
Maiella, La– (mt.) **10** Ec
Maigualida, Sierra– (mts.) **37** Cb
Maihar **19** Hj
Maijdi **19** Jk
Main (riv.) **5** Bcd
Maï–Ndombe, Lake– **26** ABb
Maine (State) **32** DEa
Maine (hist. reg.) **8** CDc
Maingkwan **19** BCc
Mainland (i.) **7** Fa
Mainland (Pomona) (i.) **7** DEb
Mainpuri **19** Gj
Maintirano **26** map no.1
Mainz **5** Bcd
Maipo, Volcán– (mt.) **39** ABc
Maipú **39** Cc
Maiquetía **37** Cc
Maitland **29** Ie
Maíz, Islas del– **35** Bb
Maizuru **16** Hlc
Maja (riv.) **14** Gd
Majabat el Kubra (phys. reg.) **24** Bbc
Majardah, Wadi– (riv.) **10** Bf
Majene **18** Ee
Majevica (mts.) **6** Dd
Maji **25** Dd
Majja **14** Gc
Majkop **13** CDe
Majma'ah **21** Dd
Majorca (i.) **9** Gc
Majuro Atoll **27** Db
Makabana **26** Ab
Makalehi, Pulau– (i.) **18** FGd
Makarjev **12** FGb
Makarov **14** He
Makarska **11** Bb
Makasar → Ujung Pandang **18** Eef
Makassar Strait **15** Dij

Makat **12** Hd
Makatea, Île– (i.) **28** Bc
Makejevka **13** CDe
Makemo Atoll **28** Bc
Makeni **24** Ad
Makgadikgadi Pans **26** Bd
Makhfar al Ḥamman **21** Bb
Makian, Pulau– (i.) **18** Gd
Makinsk **13** Gd
Makó **6** Ec
Makokou **24** Dd
Makoua **24** Dde
Makrän (phys. reg.) **21** FGd
Makrónisos (i.) **11** Fe
Maksimovka **17** EFab
Makurazaki **17** ABi
Makurdi **24** Cd
Malabar Coast **20** DEfg
Malabo **24** Cd
Malacca **15** Di
Malacca → Melaka **18** Bd
Malacca, Strait of– **15** Di
Málaga **9** Cd
Malaita Island **27** Dc
Malaja Višera **12** Db
Malakal **25** Dd
Malang **18** Df
Malanje **23** Fg
Malanville **24** Cc
Mälaren (l.) **4** Dd
Malargüe **39** Bc
Malaspina Glacier **31** ABbc
Malatya **22** FGc
Malawi (Ind. St.) **23** Fg
Malawi, Lake– (Nyasa, Lake) **26** Cc
Malaybalay **18** Gc
Maläyer **21** DEc
Malaysia (Ind. St.) **15** Di
Malbork **5** Gb
Malden Island **28** Bc
Malditos, Montes– **9** Fa
Maldives (Ind. St.) **15** Ci
Maldonado **39** Cc
Male **20** Dh
Malea, Cape– **11** Ee
Male Atoll **20** Dh
Malebo, Pool– **26** Ab
Malegaon **20** DEd
Malé Karpaty (mts.) **5** Fd
Malékoula, Île– (i.) **28** map no.4
Mali (Ind. St.) **23** Bd
Malik, Wädï al– (riv.) **25** CDe
Malili **18** Fe
Malin **6** Ia
Malindi **26** CDb
Malin Head **7** Cd
Malino, Bukit– (mt.) **18** Fd
Malinovka (riv.) **17** Db
Malipo **16** BCf
Malita **18** Gc
Malkara **11** Gc
Malko Tärnovo **11** GHbc
Mallaig **7** CDc
Mallawï **25** CDb
Mallow **7** Be
Malmberget **4** Eb
Malmédy **8** FGb
Malmesbury **26** Ae
Malmö **4** Cc
Malo (i.) **28** map no.4
Maloelap Atoll **27** Db

Malolos 27 map no.1
Malosmadulu Atoll 20 Dg
Måløy 4 Ac
Malpelo, Isla de– (i.) 37 Ab
Malta (Ind. St.) 10 Efg
Malta (i.) 10 Efg
Maltahöhe 26 Ad
Malung 4 Cc
Malůţ 25 Dc
Maly Anjuj (riv.) 14 Jc
Maly Jenisej (riv.) 14 Cd
Maly Ljahovski, ostrov– (i.) 14 GHb
Maly Tajmyr, ostrov– 14 DEb
Maly Uzen (riv.) 12 Gd
Mamaia 6 Id
Mamatlar 22 BCd
Mambasa 26 Ba
Mamfe 24 Cd
Mammola 10 Fe
Mamonovo 5 Ha
Mamoré (riv.) 37 Cd
Mamou 24 Acd
Mampong 24 BCd
Mamry, Jezioro– 5 Ha
Mamuju 18 Ee
Mamuno 26 ABd
Man 24 Bd
Man, Isle of– 7 Dd
Mana [Fr. Gui.] 37 Db
Mana [Hi.–U.S.] 28 map no.1
Manacapuru 37 CDc
Manacor 9 Gc
Manado 18 Fd
Managua 30 Jh
Managua, Lago de– 34 Bc
Manakara 23 GHh
Manāmah, Al– 21 Ed
Mananara 26 map no.1
Mananjary 26 map no.1
Manantiales 40 ABc
Manas (riv.) 19 Jj
Manaus 36 DEd
Manavgat 22 CDd
Mancha, La– (phys. reg.) 9 Dc
Manchester [U.K.] 7 EFe
Manchester [U.S.] 32 DEa
Manciuria (hist. reg.) 16 FGa
Mand (riv.) 21 Ed
Manda 26 Cc
Mandal 4 ABd
Mandalay 15 Dg
Mandal–Gobi 14 De
Mandalya Körfezi 22 Ad
Mandan 33 Cb
Mandasor 20 DEd
Mandera 26 Da
Mandla 20 Fd
Mandurah 29 ABe
Manduria 10 Fd
Mandya 20 Ef
Manfredonia 10 Ed
Manfredonia, Golfo di– 10 EFd
Manga (phys. reg.) 24 Dc
Mangabeiras, Chapada del– (plat.) 38 Cbc
Mangaia Island 28 ABd
Mangalia 6 Ie
Mangalore 15 Ch
Mangareva, Île– (i.) 28 Cd

Mangoche 26 Cc
Mangoky (riv.) 26 map no.1
Mangole, Pulau– (i.) 18 FGe
Manhattan 32 Bb
Manica 26 Cc
Manicoré 37 Cc
Manicouagan, Réservoir– 31 Ic
Manihiki Atoll 28 ABc
Maniitsoq / Sukkertoppen 31 Jb
Manikpur 20 Fc
Manila 15 DEh
Manila Bay 18 EFb
Maningrida 29 Ea
Manipur (State) 19 Bcd
Manisa 22 Ac
Manitoba (prov.) 31 EFc
Manitoba, Lake– 31 Fc
Manitoulin (i.) 32 Ca
Manitowoc 32 Ca
Manizales 36 Cc
Manja 26 map no.1
Manjacaze 26 Cd
Manjra (riv.) 20 Ee
Mankato 32 Ba
Manna 18 Be
Mannahill 29 FGe
Mannar 20 EFg
Mannar, Gulf of– 20 Eg
Mannheim 5 Bd
Manokwari 27 Bbc
Manono 26 Bb
Manosque 8 FGf
Manresa 9 FGb
Mans, Le– 8 Dd
Mansa 26 BCc
Mansel Island 31 GHb
Mansfield [U.K.] 7 Fe
Mansfield [U.S.] 32 Ca
Manşūrah, Al– 25 Da
Manta 37 Ac
Mantalingajan, Mount– 18 Ec
Mantaro (riv.) 37 Bd
Mantes–la–Jolie 8 Dc
Mantova 10 Cb
Mänttä 4 Fc
Manturovo 12 FGb
Manu 39 Aa
Manuae Atoll [Cook] 28 ABcd
Manuae Atoll [Fr. Poly.] 28 Bc
Manua Islands 28 map no.5
Manui, Pulau– (i.) 18 Fe
Manuk, Pulau– (i.) 18 GHf
Manus Island 27 Cc
Manyč (riv.) 13 De
Manyč–Gudilo, ozero– 12 Fd
Manzanares 9 Dc
Manzaneda, Cabeza de– (mt.) 9 Ba
Manzanillo [Cuba] 35 Ca
Manzanillo [Mex.] 30 Hh
Manzhouli 14 Ee
Manzilah, Al– 22 CDg
Manzilah, Buḩayrat al– 25 map no.1
Manzil Bū Ruqaybah 10 Bf
Manzil Tamin 10 Cf
Mao 25 Bc
Maoke, Pegunungan– 27 BCc
Maoming 16 Df
Mapai 26 Cd

Mapi 27 BCc
Mapire 37 Cb
Mapuera (riv.) 38 Bb
Maputo (Lourenço Marques) 26 Cd
Maputo, Baía de– 26 Cd
Maquan He → Brahmaputra (riv.) 20 FGc
Maquela do Zombo 26 Ab
Maquinchao 40 Bb
Mar, Serra do– 39 CDb
Maraã 37 Cc
Marabá 38 Cb
Maracá, Ilha de– (i.) 38 BCa
Maracaibo 36 Cb
Maracaibo, Lago de– 37 Bab
Maracaju, Serra de– (mts.) 39 Cab
Maracay 36 Dbc
Marādah 24 Db
Maradi 24 Cc
Marāgheh 21 Db
Marahuaca, Cerro– (mt.) 37 Cb
Maraió, Ilha de– 38 BCb
Marajó, Baia de– (b.) 38 Cab
Maralal 26 Ca
Maramba (Livingstone) 26 Bc
Marana, La– 10 Bc
Maranhão (State) 38 Cb
Maranhão (riv.) 38 Cc
Marañón (riv.) 37 Bc
Marão 26 Cd
Marari 37 Cc
Mărăşeşti 6 Hd
Marathón 11 EFd
Maratua, Pulau– (i.) 18 Ed
Maraú 38 Dc
Marawi 25 Dc
Marbella 9 Cd
Marble Bar 29 BCc
Marburg an der Lahn 5 Bc
Marca 25 Ed
Marcaria 10 Cb
Marche (reg.) 10 Dc
Marche (hist. reg.) 8 DEde
Marchena 9 Cd
Marchinbar Island 29 Fa
Mar Chiquita, Laguna– 39 Bc
Marcus Island 27 Ca
Mardan 20 Db
Mar del Plata 39 Cc
Mardin 21 Cb
Maré, Île– (i.) 27 Dd
Mareeba 29 GHb
Marettimo (i.) 10 Df
Marganec 12 Dd
Margaret River 29 Db
Margarita, Isla de– (i.) 35 Db
Margate 7 Gf
Margerie, Monts de la– (mts.) 8 Ee
Marghita 6 Fc
Marha (riv.) 14 Ec
Mari (Ant. Rep.) 13 Dd
Maria Atoll 28 Bd
Maria Island 29 Fab
Mariano 35 Ba
Mariánské Lázně 5 Dd
Marías, Islas– 34 Bb
Maria Theresa Reef 28 Bd
Ma'rib 21 Df
Maribo 5 Ca

Maribor 6 BCc
Maricourt 31 Hb
Maridi 25 CDd
Marie Byrd Land 42 grid square no.3
Marie–Galante (i.) 35 DEb
Marienhamn 4 DEc
Mariental 26 Ad
Mariestad 4 Cd
Marignane 8 Ff
Mariinsk 13 Hld
Marijampolė (Kapsukas) 5 Ia
Marília 39 CDb
Marinduque (i.) 18 Fb
Marinette 32 Ca
Maringa (riv.) 25 Cde
Maringá 39 Cb
Marinha Grande 9 Ac
Marion Reefs (i.) 29 Ib
Mariscal Estigarribia 39 BCb
Marismas, Las– (phys. reg.) 9 BCd
Mariupol (Ždanov) 13 Ce
Marj, Al– (Barce) 24 DEa
Markovo 14 JKc
Marktredwitz 5 CDcd
Marlborough 29 Hlc
Marmande 8 De
Marmara, Sea of– 22 ABb
Marmara Adası (i.) 22 ABb
Marmara ereğlisi 22 ABb
Marmara Gölü 11 GHd
Marmaris 22 ABd
Marmelos 37 Cc
Marmolada (mt.) 10 Ca
Marne (riv.) 8 Fc
Marne au Rhin, Canal de la– 8 Gc
Maro (riv.) 25 Bc
Maroa 37 Cb
Maroantsetra 26 map no.1
Maroni (riv.) 37 Db
Maroua 24 Dc
Marovoay 26 map no.1
Marowijne (riv.) 37 Db
Marqab, Qal'at al– 22 Ee
Marquesas Islands 28 BCc
Marquette 32 Ca
Marrah, Jabal– (mt.) 25 Cc
Marrakech 24 Ba
Marrawah 29 map no.1
Marree 29 Fd
Marromeu 26 Cc
Marrupa 26 Cc
Marsá al Burayqah 24 DEab
Marsabit 25 Dd
Marsala 10 Df
Marseille 8 FGf
Marshall 32 Bb
Marshall Islands (Ind. St.) 27 Db
Martaban 19 Ce
Martaban, Gulf of– 19 Ce
Martapura 18 De
Martigny 10 Aab
Martigues 8 Ff
Martim Vaz, Ilhas– 36 Hef
Martin 5 Gd
Martina Franca 10 Fd
Martinique (i.) 35 DEb
Martos 9 CDd
Martre, Lac la– (l.) 31 CDb
Marutea Atoll 28 Cd

Marvdasht 21 Ed
Marx 12 Gc
Mary 13 Ff
Maryborough 29 Id
Maryland (State) 32 Db
Masaka 25 De
Masan 16 Gcd
Masasi 23 Fg
Masaya 35 Bb
Masbate 18 Fb
Masbate (i.) 18 Fb
Mascara 24 Ca
Mascarene Islands 23 map no.1
Masela (i.) 17 Hlg
Maseru 23 Eh
Mashhad 21 FGb
Mashike 17 Gc
Mashkel (riv.) 20 Bc
Mashra'ar Raqq 25 CDd
Masīlah, Wādī al– 21 DEf
Masindi 25 Dd
Maşīrah, Jazīrat– (i.) 21 FGe
Maşīrah, Khalīj– 21 Fef
Masjed–Soleymān 21 DEc
Mask, Lake– 7 Be
Masoala, Cap– 26 map no.1
Mason City 32 Ba
Massa 10 Cbc
Massachusetts (State) 32 Da
Massa Marittima 10 Cc
Massangena 26 Cd
Massapê 38 CDb
Massat 8 Df
Massawa 25 DEc
Massena 32 Da
Massénya 25 Bc
Masset 31 Bc
Massif Central (mts.) 8 EFe
Massinga 26 Cd
Mastouta 10 Bf
Masuda 17 BCg
Masuku 26 Ab
Masvingo 26 Ccd
Maşyāf 22 Fe
Matadi 26 Ab
Matagalpa 35 Bb
Matagorda Bay 32 Bc
Mataiea 28 map no.2
Matak, Pulau– (i.) 18 Cd
Matala 26 Ac
Matam 24 Ac
Matamoros 30 Ig
Matanzas 35 Ba
Matão, Serra do– (mts.) 38 Bbc
Matapán, Cape– 11 Ee
Mataporquera → Valdeolea 9 CDa
Matara 20 EFg
Mataram 18 Ef
Mataranka 29 Eab
Matariya, El– 25 map no.1
Mataró 9 Gb
Matehuala 34 BCb
Matera 10 Fd
Matese (mts.) 10 Ed
Mátészalka 6 Fc
Mathura 20 Ec
Mati 18 Gc
Mätir 10 Bf
Matočkin Šar 13 EFb
Matočkin Šar, proliv– 13 EFb

Mato Grosso (State) 38 Bc
Mato Grosso 39 BCa
Mato Grosso, Plateau of– 38 Bc
Mato Grosso do Sul (State) 39 Cab
Matopo Hills 26 Bcd
Matosinhos 9 Ab
Mátra 6 DEc
Matrah 21 Fe
Maţrūh 25 Ca
Matsue 16 Hc
Matsu Liehtao 16 Fe
Matsumae 17 FGd
Matsumoto 16 Ic
Matsusaka 17 Egh
Matsuyama 16 Hd
Matua, ostrov– (i.) 14 Ie
Matuku Island 28 map no.6
Maturin 37 Cb
Mau 19 Hj
Maubeuge 8 EFb
Maui 28 Ba
Maumere 18 Ff
Maun 26 Bc
Mauna Kea (mt.) 28 map no.1
Mauna Loa (mt.) 28 map no.1
Maungdaw 19 Bd
Mau Ranipur 19 Gj
Mauriac 8 Ee
Mauritania (Ind. St.) 23 ABcd
Mauritius (Ind. St.) 23 map no.1
Mawchi 19 Ce
Mawlaik 19 BCd
Mawson 42 grid square no.2
Mayaguana Island 32 Dc
Mayagüez 35 Db
Maydh 25 Ec
Maydi 21 Cf
Mayenne 8 Cc
Mayenne (riv.) 8 Cd
Maynas (phys. reg.) 37 Bc
Mayo 31 Bb
Mayor, Puig– (mt.) 9 Gc
Mayotte (i.) 23 Gg
May Pen 35 Cb
Mayumba 26 Ab
Mayum La (p.) 20 Fb
Mazabuka 26 Bc
Mazagão 38 Bb
Mazamet 8 Ef
Mazara del Vallo 10 Df
Mazār–e Sharīf 15 Cf
Mazarrón 9 Ed
Mazaruni (riv.) 37 CDb
Mazatlán 30 Hg
Mažeikiai 12 Bb
Mazirbe 12 Bb
Mazovia (phys. reg.) 5 GHb
Mbabane 26 Cd
Mbaïki 25 Bd
Mbala (Abercorn) 26 Cb
Mbale 26 Ca
Mbalmayo 24 Dd
Mbandaka 26 Aab
M'banza Congo 26 Ab
Mbanza–Ngungu 26 Ab
Mbeya 23 Ff
Mbinda 26 Ab
Mbini (phys. reg.) 24 CDd
Mbomou (riv.) 26 Ba

Mbout 24 Ac
M'Bridge (riv.) 26 Ab
Mbuji–Mayi 26 Bb
Mbulu 26 Cb
Mburucuya 39 Cb
Mead, Lake– 33 Bc
Meadow Lake 31 DEc
Mealháda 9 ABb
Mearim (riv.) 38 Cb
Meaux 8 Ec
Mecca 21 BCe
Mechelen 8 Fb
Mecklenburg (hist. reg.) 5 CDb
Mecklenburger Bucht 5 Ca
Mecsek (mt.) 6 Dc
Medan 15 Di
Medellín 36 Cc
Mederdra 24 Ac
Medford 33 Ab
Medgidia 6 Id
Media Agua 39 Bc
Mediaş 6 Gc
Medicine Hat 33 BCab
Medina 21 BCe
Medinaceli 9 Db
Medina del Campo 9 Cb
Medina del Rioseco 9 Cb
Medina–Sidonia 9 Cd
Medinipur 20 Gd
Mediterranean Sea 23 CEb
Medjerda, Montes de la– 10 ABf
Medjez el–Bab 10 Bf
Mednogorsk 12 Ic
Médoc (phys. reg.) 8 Ce
Medvedica (riv.) 12 Fc
Medveži, ostrova– 14 Jb
Medvežjegorsk 13 Cc
Medyado Atoll 28 map no.3
Medyai Atoll 28 map no.3
Medžibož 6 Hb
Meekatharra 29 Bd
Meerut 20 Ec
Mega 25 Dd
Mega, Pulau– (i.) 18 Be
Megara 11 Ede
Meghalaya (State) 19 Bc
Meghna (riv.) 19 Jjk
Meia Ponte (riv.) 39 Da
Meiganga 24 Dd
Meiktila 19 Cd
Meiningen 5 Cc
Meissen 5 Dc
Meixian 16 Ef
Mejillones 39 Ab
Mékambo 24 Dd
Mekele 25 DEc
Meknès 24 Ba
Mekong (riv.) 19 Eef
Mekong Delta 19 Efg
Mekongga, Gunung– (mt.) 18 Fe
Melaka (Malacca) 18 Bd
Melalap 18 Ec
Melanesia (is.) 27 BDbc
Melawi (riv.) 18 Dde
Melbourne 29 GHf
Melchor Ocampo 34 Bc
Melenki 12 Fb
Meleuz 12 Hlc
Melfi [Chad] 25 Bc

Melfi [It.] 10 Ed
Melilla 24 Ba
Mélito di Porto Salvo 10 Ef
Melitopol 12 DEd
Mělník 5 Ec
Melo 39 Cc
Melrhir, Chott– (l.) 24 Ca
Melun 8 Ec
Melville 33 Ca
Melville, Cape– 29 GHa
Melville Bay 29 Fa
Melville Island [Austl.] 29 Ea
Melville Island [Can.] 41 grid square no.2
Melville Peninsula 31 Gb
Memmingen 5 Cde
Mempawah 18 Cd
Memphis 32 Cb
Menai Strait 7 De
Ménaka 24 Cc
Mende 8 Ee
Mendocino, Cape– 33 Ab
Mendoza 39 Bc
Menemen 22 Ac
Meneng Point 27 map no.2
Mengdingjie 19 CDd
Menggala 18 Ce
Menglian 19 CDd
Mengzi 16 Bf
Menindee 29 Ga
Meningie 29 Ff
Menongue 26 Ac
Menphis (r.) 22 Ch
Mentakab 18 Bd
Mentawai, Selat– 18 ABde
Mentawai Islands 18 Ae
Mentok 18 BCe
Menzies 29 Cde
Menzies, Mount– 42 grid square no.2
Meppel 8 FGa
Meppen 5 Ab
Mequinenza, Embalse de– (l.) 9 EFb
Merabéllou, Kólpos– 11 FGf
Merak 18 Cf
Méralab (i.) 28 map no.4
Merano 10 Ca
Meratus, Pegunungan– 18 Ee
Merauke 27 BCc
Merced 33 ABc
Mercedes [Arg.] 39 Cc
Mercedes [Arg.] 39 Cb
Mercedes [Arg.] 39 Bc
Mercedes [Ur.] 39 Cc
Merceg 25 Ed
Merefa 12 Ed
Mergenevo 12 Hd
Mergui 19 Cf
Mergui Archipelago 19 Cf
Meriç (riv.) 11 Gc
Mérida [Mex.] 30 IJg
Mérida [Sp.] 9 Bc
Mérida [Ven.] 37 Bc
Mérida, Cordillera de– (mts.) 37 BCb
Meridian 32 Cb
Mérignac 8 Ce
Merir (i.) 27 Bb
Merksen 5 Cc
Merredin 29 Be
Merrick (mt.) 7 Dd

Merritt 31 CDc
Merriwa 29 Ie
Mersa Fatma 21 Cg
Merseburg 5 CDc
Mersey (riv.) 7 Ee
Mersin 22 Ed
Merta Road 20 Dc
Merthyr Tydfil 7 Ef
Merzifon 22 Eb
Mesa 33 Bc
Mesagne 10 Fd
Mesola 10 Db
Mesolóngion 11 Dd
Mesopotamia [Arg.] (phys. reg.) 39 Cbc
Mesopotamia [Iraq] (phys. reg.) 21 CDbc
Messalo (riv.) 26 Cc
Messaoud, Hassi– 24 Ca
Messina [It.] 10 Ee
Messina [S. Afr.] 23 EFh
Messina, Gulf of– 11 Ee
Messina, Stretto di– 10 Ee
Messini 11 DEe
Mesta (Néstos) (riv.) 11 Fc
Mestghanem 24 BCa
Meta (riv.) 37 Bb
Meta, La– (mt.) 10 DEd
Metán 39 Bb
Metauro (riv.) 10 Dc
Metković 11 BCb
Metrz Glacier 42 grid square no.4
Métsovon 11 Dd
Metz 8 Gc
Meulaboh 18 ABd
Meurthe (riv.) 8 Gc
Meuse (riv.) 8 Fc
Mexiana, Ilha– 38 Cab
Mexicali 34 Aa
Mexico (Ind. St.) 30 HIgh
Mexico, Gulf of– 34 CDb
Mexico City 30 Igh
Meyísti (i.) 22 Bd
Meymaneh 20 BCa
Mezdra 11 EFb
Mezen (riv.) 13 Dc
Mezen 13 Dc
Mézenc, Mont– (mt.) 8 Fe
Mezőkövesd 6 Ec
Mezőtúr 6 Ec
Mhow 20 Ed
Miami 32 Cc
Miandrívazo 26 map no.1
Miäneh 21 Db
Miangas, Pulau– (is.) 18 Gc
Mianwali 20 Db
Mianyang 16 BCd
Miaodao Qundao 16 EFc
Miarinarivo 26 map no.1
Miass 13 EFd
Miastko 5 Fab
Micenae (r.) 11 Ee
Michalovce 5 HId
Michigan (State) 32 Ca
Michigan, Lake– 32 Ca
Michigan City 32 Ca
Michipicoten 31 Gd
Micronésia (is.) 27 BDbc
Mičurin 11 GHb
Mičurinsk 12 Fc
Midar 24 Ba
Middelburg [S. Afr.] 26 BCd

Middelburg [S. Afr.] 26 Be
Middelfart 5 BCa
Middle Andaman (i.) 19 BCf
Middle Atlas (mts.) 24 Ba
Middlesbrough 7 FGd
Midi, Canal du– 8 DEf
Midi d'Ossau, Pic du– (mt.) 8 Cf
Midland 33 Ca
Midway Islands 28 Aa
Midžor (mt.) 11 Fe
Miechów 5 GHc
Międzyrzec Podlaski 5 Ibc
Międzyrzecz 5 EFb
Mielec 5 Hc
Miercurea Ciuc 6 GHc
Mieres 9 BCa
Miguel Alves 38 Cb
Mihajlovgrad 11 Fe
Mihajlovka 13 Dd
Mikkeli 4 FGc
MíKonos (i.) 11 Fe
Mikun 13 DEc
Mikuni–Sanmyaku (mts.) 17 Ff
Mikura–Jima (i.) 17 FGh
Miladummadulu Atoll 20 DEg
Milagro, El– 39 Bc
Milan 10 Bb
Milâs 22 ABd
Milazzo 10 Ee
Mildura 29 Ge
Miles 29 HId
Miles City 33 Cb
Miletus (r.) 22 Ad
Milford Haven 7 Df
Miliana 9 FGd
Milikapiti 29 Ea
Miling 29 Bde
Milk (riv.) 33 Cb
Millau 8 Ee
Millerovo 12 Fd
Millevaches, Plateau de– (plat.) 8 Ee
Millicent 29 FGf
Mílos (i.) 11 Fe
Milparinka 29 Gde
Milwaukee 32 Ca
Milwaukee Depth 35 Dab
Mimizan 8 Ce
Mimmaya 17 FGd
Mïnä' al 'Aḥmadï 21 Dd
Minahassa 18 Fd
Minamata 17 ABh
Minami–Daitô–Jima (i.) 16 He
Minami–lô–Jima 27 BCa
Minas 39 Cc
Minas–cué 39 Cb
Minas de Ríotinto 9 BCd
Minas de São Domingos 9 ABd
Minas Gerais (State) 39 Da
Minatitlán 34 Cc
Minbu 19 Bde
Minbya 19 Bd
Minchinmávida, Volcán– (mt.) 40 Ab
Mindanao (i.) 15 Ei
Minden 5 Bb
Mindoro (i.) 15 DEh
Mindoro Strait 18 EFb
Mineiros 39 Ca
Mineralnyje Vody 12 Fe

Minervino Murge 10 Fd
Minfeng 20 Fa
Mingan 31 Ic
Minhe 16 Bc
Minho (riv.) 9 Aab
Minho (hist. reg.) 9 Ab
Minicoy Island 20 Dg
Minigwal, Lake– 29 Cd
Minilya 29 Ac
Minjar 12 Ib
Min Jiang (riv.) 16 Ee
Minna 24 Cd
Minneapolis 32 Ba
Minnesota (State) 32 Ba
Minnipa 29 EFe
Miño (riv.) 9 Ba
Minorca (i.) 9 GHc
Minot 33 Cb
Minqin 16 Bc
Min Shan (mts.) 16 Bd
Minsk 13 Bd
Mińsk Mazowiecki 5 HIb
Minto, Lac– 31 Hc
Minusinsk 14 Cd
Minxian 16 Bd
Minyä, Al– 25 CDb
Miquelon (i.) 31 Jd
Mira (riv.) 9 Ad
Miracema do Tocantins 38 Cbc
Miraflores 37 Bb
Miraflores Locks 35 map no.1
Miraj 20 DEe
Miramar 39 Cc
Miranda 39 Cb
Miranda de Ebro 9 Da
Miranda do Douro 9 Bb
Mirande 8 CDf
Mirandela 9 Bb
Mirandola 10 Cb
Mirbat 21 EFf
Mirecourt 8 FGc
Mirgorod 12 Dd
Miri 18 Dd
Mirim, Lagoa– (lag.) 39 Cc
Mirina 11 Fd
Mirny [Ant.] 42 grid square no.4
Mirny [Russia] 14 Ec
Mirpur Khas 20 CDc
Miryang 17 Ag
Mirzapur 20 Fcd
Mishan 16 Ha
Mi–Shima (i.) 17 Bg
Misiones, Sierra de– (mts.) 39 Cb
Miskitos, Cayos– (is.) 35 Bb
Miskolc 6 Eb
Mismär 21 Bf
Mismïyah, Al– 22 Ff
Misool, Pulau– (i.) 18 He
Mississauga 31 GHd
Mississippi (riv.) 32 Bb
Mississippi (State) 32 BCb
Missoula 33 Bb
Missouri (State) 32 Bb
Missouri (riv.) 32 Bb
Mistassini, Lac– 31 Eb
Mistelbach an der Zaya 5 Fd
Misti, Volcán– (volc.) 39 Aa
Misurata 24 Da
Mitchell [Austl.] 29 Hd
Mitchell [U.S.] 32 Ba

Mitchell, Mount– 32 Cb
Mitchell River 29 Gb
Mitchell River (riv.) 29 Gb
Mit Ghamr 22 Cg
Mithimna 11 FGd
Mitiaro Island 28 Bc
Mitilíni 22 Ac
Mitilinis, Stenón– 11 Gd
Mitla Pass 25 map no.2
Mito 17 Gf
Mittellandkanal (can.) 5 ABb
Mitú 37 BCb
Mitumba, Monts– 26 Bbc
Mitwaba 26 Bb
Mitzic 24 Dd
Miyake–Jima (i.) 17 FGg
Miyako 16 Jc
Miyako–Jima (i.) 16 Gef
Miyakonojô 16 Hd
Miyanoura–Dake (mt.) 17 Bi
Miyazaki 16 Hd
Miyun 16 Eb
Mizdah 24 Da
Mizen Head 7 ABf
Mizil 6 Hd
Mizoč 6 GHa
Mizoram (State) 19 Bd
Mizuho 42 grid square no.2
Mizusawa 17 Ge
Mjölby 4 Cd
Mjøsa (l.) 4 Bc
Mkuze 26 Cd
Mladá Boleslav 5 Ec
Mladenovac 6 Ed
Mława 5 GHb
Mljet (i.) 11 Bb
Mo 4 Cb
Moa (riv.) 24 Ad
Moa, Pulau– (i.) 18 Gf
Moala (i.) 28 map no.6
Moanda 26 Ab
Moba 26 Bb
Mobaye 26 Ba
Mobayi–Mbongo 26 Ba
Mobile 32 Cb
Mobridge 33 Cb
Moçambique 23 FGg
Mocha, Isla– (i.) 39 Ac
Mochis, Los– 34 ABb
Mochudi 26 Bd
Mocímboa da Praia 26 Dc
Môco, Serra– (mts.) 26 Ac
Mocoa 37 Bb
Mocuba 23 Fg
Modane 8 Ge
Módena 10 Cb
Modica 10 Ef
Modřany 5 Ecd
Moe 29 Hf
Mogadishu 25 Ed
Mogaung 19 Cc
Mogi das Cruzes 39 Db
Mogilev 13 Cd
Mogilev–Podolski 6 Hb
Mogoča 14 EFd
Mogok 19 Cd
Mogrein 24 ABb
Moguer 9 Bd
Mohács 6 Dd
Mohanganj 19 Jj
Mohenjo Daro (r.) 20 Cc
Moineşti 6 Hc
Moissac 8 De

Moj - Mug

Mojave 33 Bc
Mojave Desert 33 Bc
Mojynty 13 Ge
Mokolo 24 Dc
Mokp'o 14 Ff
Mola di Bari 10 Fd
Moldav (riv.) 5 Ed
Moldavia (phys. reg.) 6 Hcd
Molde 4 Ac
Moldefjorden (b.) 4 Ac
Moldova (Ind. St.) 6 Ic
Moldova Nouă 6 Ed
Moldoveanu, Vîrful– (mt.) 6 Gd
Molepolole 26 Bd
Molfetta 10 Fd
Molise (reg.) 10 Ed
Mollendo 39 Aa
Mölndal 4 BCd
Molodečno 12 Cb
Molodežnaja 42 grid square no.2
Mologa (riv.) 12 Eb
Molokai (i.) 28 Ba
Molopo (w.) 26 Bd
Moluccas (is.) 18 GHde
Molucca Sea 18 Gef
Moma 26 CDc
Mombasa 23 FGf
Mombetsu 16 Jb
Momboyo (riv.) 25 BCe
Momčilgrad 11 Fc
Møn (i.) 5 Da
Mona, Isla– (i.) 35 Db
Monaco (Ind. St.) 10 Ac
Monaghan 7 Cd
Mona Passage (str.) 35 Db
Moncayo, Sierra del– (mts.) 9 DEb
Mončegorsk 13 Cc
Mönchengladbach 5 CDc
Monclova 34 Bb
Moncton 31 Id
Mondego (riv.) 9 ABb
Mondego, Cape– 9 Ab
Mondello 10 De
Mondovì 10 Ab
Monemvasía 11 Ee
Moneron, ostrov– (i.) 17 Ga
Monfalcone 10 Db
Monforte de Lemos 9 Ba
Monga 26 Ba
Mongalla 25 Dd
Mong Cai 19 Ed
Monger, Lake– 29 Bd
Monghpayak 19 CDd
Mongnai 16 Af
Mongo 25 BCc
Mongolia (Ind. St.) 15 De
Mongolski Altaj (mts.) 14 Ce
Mongororo 25 Cc
Mongu 26 Bc
Monkoto 25 BCe
Monmouth 7 Ef
Monopoli 10 Fd
Monor 6 Gc
Monreale 10 De
Monroe 32 Bb
Monrovia 24 Ad
Mons 8 EFb
Monselice 10 Db
Montagne Noire (mt.) 8 Ef
Montalbán 9 Eb
Montana (State) 33 BCb

Montaña, La– (phys. reg.) 37 Bcd
Montánchez 9 Bc
Montargis 8 Ed
Montauban 8 DEef
Montbard 8 Fd
Montbéliard 8 Gd
Montceau–les–Mines 8 EFd
Mont–de–Marsan 8 CDef
Montdidier 8 Ec
Mont Dore 8 Ee
Monteagudo 39 Ba
Monte Albán (r.) 34 Cc
Monte Alegre 38 Bb
Monte Azul 39 Da
Monte Bello Islands 29 ABc
Monte Caseros 39 Cbc
Montecatini Terme 10 Cc
Monte Comán 39 Bc
Montecristo (i.) 10 Cc
Montefiascone 10 Dc
Montego Bay 35 Cb
Monteiro 38 Db
Montélimar 8 Fe
Monte Lindo (riv.) 39 BCb
Monte Lirio 35 map no.1
Montemorelos 34 Cb
Montenegro 11 Cb
Montepuez 26 Cc
Montepulciano 10 Cc
Montereau–Faut–Yonne 8 Ec
Monterey 33 Ac
Montería 37 Bb
Monterós 39 Bb
Monterrey 34 BCb
Monte Sant'Angelo 10 Ed
Montes Claros 39 Da
Montevideo 39 Cc
Montgenèvre (p.) 10 Ab
Montgomery [U.K.] 7 Ee
Montgomery [U.S.] 32 Cb
Montigny–lès–Metz 8 Gc
Montijo [Port.] 9 Ac
Montijo [Sp.] 9 Bc
Montilla 9 Cd
Mont–Joli 32 Ea
Mont–Laurier 32 Da
Montluçon 8 Ed
Montmagny 31 Hd
Montmorillon 8 Dd
Monto 29 Icd
Montoro 9 Ccd
Montpelier 32 Da
Montpellier 8 EFf
Montréal 31 Hd
Montreux 10 Aa
Montrose [U.K.] 7 EFc
Montrose [U.S.] 33 Cc
Mont–Saint–Michel, Le– 8 Cc
Montserrat (i.) 35 Db
Monywa 19 BCd
Monza 10 Bb
Monzón 9 Fb
Moonie 29 Id
Moonta 29 Fe
Moora 29 Be
Moore, Lake– 29 Bde
Moorea (i.) 28 map no.2
Moorhead 32 Ba
Moose (riv.) 32 Ca
Moose Jaw 33 Cab
Moosonee 31 Db
Mopti 24 Bc

Moquegua 39 ABa
Mora [Port.] 9 Ac
Mora [Sp.] 9 CDc
Mora [Swe.] 4 Cc
Moradabad 15 Cg
Mora de Rubielos 9 Eb
Moratalla 9 DEc
Morava 5 Fd
Morava, Južna– 11 DEb
Moravia (phys. reg.) 5 Fd
Morawa 29 Bd
Morawhanna 37 Db
Moray Firth (b.) 7 Ec
Morcenx 8 Cef
Mordvinia (Aut. Rep.) 13 Dd
Morecambe Bay 7 Ede
Moree 29 Hld
Morelia 34 Bc
Morella 9 EFb
Morena 19 Gj
Morena, Sierra– (mts.) 9 BDc
Morenci 33 Cc
Moresby Island 31 Bc
Moreton 29 Ga
Moreton Bay 29 Id
Moreton Island 29 Id
Mórfou 22 De
Morgan 29 FGe
Mori 17 Gc
Morioka 16 Jc
Morlaix 8 ABc
Mornington Island 29 FGb
Morocco (Ind. St.) 23 Bbc
Morogoro 23 Ff
Moro Gulf 18 Fc
Morombe 26 map no.1
Morón 35 Ca
Morondava 23 Gh
Morón de la Frontera 9 Cd
Moroni 26 Dc
Morotai, Pulau– 18 Gd
Morotai, Selat– 18 Gd
Moroto 26 Ca
Morozovsk 12 Fd
Morphou Bay 22 De
Morris Jesup, Kap– 41 grid square no.1
Morrumbene 26 Cd
Moršansk 12 Fc
Mortara 10 Bb
Mortes, Rio das– (riv.) 38 Bc
Mortlock Islands 27 Cb
Morvan, Monts du– 8 EFd
Morven (mt.) 7 Eb
Morven 29 Hd
Morvi 20 Dd
Morwell 29 Hf
Moscow 13 Cd
Mosel (riv.) 5 Acd
Moselle (riv.) 5 Acd
Moshi 26 Cb
Mosjøen 4 Cb
Moskenesøya (i.) 4 BCb
Moskva (riv.) 12 Eb
Mosonmagyaróvár 5 Fc
Mosqueiro 38 Bc
Mosquitia (phys. reg.) 35 Bb
Mosquitos, Costa de– 35 Bbc
Mosquitos, Golfo de los– 35 Bbc
Moss 4 Bd
Mossaka 24 De
Mosselbaai 23 Ei

Mossendjo 26 Ab
Mossman 29 Hb
Mossoró 38 Db
Moss Vale 29 Hle
Most 5 Dc
Mostar 11 BCb
Mostiska 5 Id
Mosty 12 Bc
Mosul 21 Cb
Motagua (riv.) 35 ABb
Motala 4 Cd
Motherwell 7 Ed
Motihari 20 FGc
Motril 9 Dd
Motu One Atoll 28 Bc
Moudjéria 24 Ac
Moúdros 11 Fd
Mouila 26 Ab
Mould Bay 41 grid square no.2
Moulins 8 Ed
Moulmein 15 Dh
Moulouya (riv.) 24 Ba
Moultrie 32 Cb
Moundou 25 Bd
Mountain Nile (riv.) 25 Dd
Mount Barker 29 Bef
Mount Douglas 29 Hc
Mount Gambier 29 FGf
Mount Garnet 29 GHb
Mount Isa 29 Fc
Mount Magnet 29 Bd
Mount Morgan 29 Hlc
Mount Vernon 32 Cb
Moura [Austl.] 29 Hc
Moura [Braz.] 37 Cc
Moura [Port.] 9 Bc
Mourne Mountains 7 CDd
Mouscron 8 Eb
Moussoro 25 Bc
Moyale 25 Dc
Moyo, Pulau– (i.) 18 Ef
Moyobamba 37 Bc
Mozambique (Ind. St.) 23 Fgh
Mozambique Channel 26 CDcd
Možga 12 Hb
Mozyr 12 Cc
Mpanda 26 Cb
Mpika 26 Cc
Mragowo 5 Hb
Mreïti, El– 24 Bb
Mreyyé, El– (phys. reg.) 24 Bc
Mtwara 23 FGfg
Muang Pakxan 19 De
Muang Sing 19 Dd
Muang Xaignabouri 19 De
Muang Xépôn 19 Ee
Muar 18 Bd
Muarasiberut 18 Ae
Muaratebo 18 Be
Muaratewe 18 De
Mubarraz, Al– 21 CDd
Mubi 24 Dc
Muchinga Mountains 26 Cc
Mudan Jiang (riv.) 17 Ab
Mudanjiang 16 GHb
Mudanya 22 Bb
Mudawwarah, Al– 22 Fh
Mueda 26 Cc
Muende 26 Cc
Mufulira 26 Bc
Mugi 17 Dh

Muğla 22 Bd
Muglad, Al– 25 Cc
Mugodžary (mts.) 13 Ee
Muḩammad Qawl 25 Db
Mühldorf am Inn 5 CDd
Mühlhausen 5 Cc
Mühlig–Hofmann Gebirge 42 grid square no.1
Muhu (i.) 4 Ed
Muisne 37 ABb
Mujnak 13 Ee
Mukačevo 5 Id
Mukalla, Al– 21 Dg
Mukhā, Al– 21 Cg
Mukinbudin 29 Be
Mula 9 Ec
Mulhacén (mt.) 9 Dd
Mulhouse 8 Gd
Muling 17 Bb
Muling He (riv.) 17 Bbc
Mull, Island of– 7 CDc
Mullewa 29 Bd
Mullingar 7 Ce
Mulobezi 26 Bc
Mulock Glacier 42 grid square no.4
Multan 15 Cfg
Mumbwa 26 Bc
Mun (riv.) 19 De
Muna, Pulau– (i.) 18 Fef
Münden 5 Bc
Mundiwindi 29 BCc
Mundo Novo 38 Cc
Mundubbera 29 Hld
Mungbere 25 Cd
Munger 20 Gcd
Mungindi 29 Hd
Munich 5 CDd
Munku–Sardyk, gora– (mt.) 14 CDd
Muñoz Gamero, Península– 40 Ac
Munster (prov.) 7 BCe
Münster 5 ABbc
Muntele Mare, Vîrful– (mt.) 6 Fc
Muntenia (phys. reg.) 6 GHd
Muong Sen 19 DEe
Muonio 4 EFb
Muonioälven (riv.) 4 Ea
Mur (riv.) 5 Ee
Mura (riv.) 6 Cc
Murakami 17 Fe
Murallón, Cerro– (mt.) 40 Ab
Muraši 13 Dd
Murat (riv.) 21 Cb
Murat daği (mt.) 22 Bc
Muratlı 22 Ab
Murchison River 29 Bd
Murcia 9 Ed
Murcia (phys. reg.) 9 Ec
Muren 14 CDe
Mureş (riv.) 6 FGc
Muret 8 Df
Murgab 16 Ac
Murge, Le– (mts.) 10 Fd
Murghab (riv.) 20 BCa
Murgon 29 Id
Müritz (l.) 5 Db
Murmansk 13 Cc
Murmaši 4 GHa
Muro Lucano 10 Ed
Murom 12 Fb

Muroran 16 Jb
Muros 9 Aa
Muroto 17 Dh
Muroto–Zaki 17 Dh
Murray Bridge 29 FGf
Murray River 29 Hf
Murrumbidgee River 29 GHe
Murud, Gunong– (mt.) 18 Ed
Mururoa Atoll 28 BCd
Murwara 20 Fd
Murwillumbah 29 IJd
Murzuq 24 Db
Mürzzuschlag 5 EFe
Muş 21 Cb
Musala (mt.) 11 Eb
Musan 16 Gb
Muscat (phys. reg.) 21 Fe
Muscat 21 Fe
Musgrave 29 Ga
Musgrave Ranges 29 Ed
Mus–Haja, gora– (mt.) 14 Hc
Mushie 26 Ab
Musi (riv.) 18 Be
Muskegon 32 Ca
Muskogee 32 Bb
Musoma 25 De
Mussende 26 Ac
Mustafa–Kemalpaşa 22 Bbc
Mustang 19 Hli
Mustvee 4 Fd
Muswellbrook 29 Hle
Mut 25 Cb
Mutarara 26 Cc
Mutare 26 Cc
Mutatá 37 Bb
Mutsu 16 Jb
Mutsu–Wan 17 Gd
Muwayh, Al– 21 Ce
Muxima 26 Ab
Muyinga 26 BCb
Muzaffarpur 20 Gc
Muztag (mt.) 20 Fa
Mvolo 25 Cd
Mwali (i.) 26 Dc
Mwanza 26 Cb
Mweelrea (mt.) 7 Be
Mwene Ditu 26 Bb
Mweru, Lake– 26 Bb
Mwinilunga 26 Bc
Myanmar (Burma) (Ind. St.) 15 Dg
Myaungmya 19 Be
Myingyan 19 Cd
Myitkyina 15 Dg
Mymensingh 20 Hd
Myoshi 17 Cg
Mýrdalsjökl (gl.) 4 map no.1
Mysore 15 Ch
Mys Šmidta 14 KLc
My Tho 19 Efg
Mytišči 12 Eb
Mzimba 26 Cc
Mzuzu 26 Cc

N

Naab (riv.) 5 Dd
Naalehu 28 map no.1
Naantali 4 Ec
Naas 7 Ce
Nabadwip 19 Jk

Naberežnyje Čelny 13 DEd
Nabesna 31 Ab
Nabire 27 Bc
Nabk, An– 22 Fef
Nablus 22 Ef
Nābul 10 Cf
Nacala 26 Dc
Nacala–a–Velha 26 CDc
Nacaome 35 Bb
Nachingwea 26 Cbc
Náchod 5 EFc
Nacozari de García 34 Bab
Nadiad 20 Dd
Nádusa 11 DEc
Nadvornaja 6 Gb
Næstved 4 BCe
Nafidah, An– 10 Cf
Nafūd, Al– (phys. reg.) 21 BCd
Naga 18 Fb
Nagaland (State) 19 Bc
Nagano 16 Ic
Nagaoka 16 Ic
Nagappattinam 20 EFf
Nagasaki 16 Gd
Nagato 17 Bg
Nagda 20 Ed
Nagercoil 20 Eg
Nagorny 14 Fd
Nagoya 16 Ic
Nagpur 15 Cg
Nagqu 19 Bb
Nagyatád 6 Cc
Nagykanizsa 6 Cc
Nagykörös 6 DEc
Naha 16 Ge
Nahodka 14 Ge
Nahuel Huapi, Lago– 40 Ab
Nain 31 Ic
Nā'īn 21 Ec
Nairn 7 Ec
Nairobi 25 De
Naivasha 26 Cb
Najafābād 21 Ec
Najd (hist. reg.) 21 CDe
Najin 16 Hb
Najran 21 CDf
Nakadōri–Jima (i.) 17 Ah
Naka–Iō–Jima (i.) 27 BCa
Nakaminato 17 Gf
Naka–no–Shima (i.) 17 ABj
Nakashibetsu 17 Ic
Nakatsu 17 Bh
Nakhichevan (Aut. Rep.) 13 De
Nakhl, An– 22 DEh
Nakhon Pathom 19 CDf
Nakhon Phanom 19 De
Nakhon Ratchasima (Khorat) 19 Def
Nakhon Sawan 19 CDe
Nakhon Si Thammarat 19 CDg
Nakina 31 Gc
Nakło nad Noteć 5 Fb
Nakonde 26 Cb
Nakskov 5 Ca
Naktong–gang (riv.) 17 Ag
Nakuru 25 De
Nal (riv.) 20 Cc
Nalčik 13 De
Nalut 24 Da
Namak, Daryācheh– ye– 21 Ec

Naberežnyje Čelny 13 DEd
Namakzār (l.) 20 Bb
Namakzar–e–Shandäd 21 Fcd
Namangan 13 Ge
Namapa 26 CDc
Nambour 29 Id
Nambucca Heads 29 IJe
Namcha Barwa (mt.) 19 BCc
Namche Bazar 19 Ij
Nam Co (l.) 19 Bb
Namdalen (phys. reg.) 4 Cb
Nam Dinh 19 Ed
Namib Desert 26 Acd
Namibe 23 CDg
Namibia (Ind. St.) 23 Dh
Naminga 14 EFd
Namlea 18 Ge
Namoi River 29 HIe
Namonuito Atoll 27 Cb
Namorik Atoll 27 Db
Nampa 33 Bb
Nampala 24 Bc
Namp'o 16 FGc
Nampula 26 CDc
Namsos 4 Bb
Nam Tha 19 Dd
Namtu 19 Cd
Namur 8 Fb
Namuruputh 26 Ca
Namwala 26 Bc
Nan (riv.) 19 De
Nan 19 De
Nanaimo 33 Ab
Nanao 17 Ef
Nanatsu–Shima 17 Ef
Nancha 16 Ga
Nanchang 15 DEg
Nancheng 16 Ee
Nanchong 16 Cd
Nancy 8 Gc
Nanda Devi (mt.) 20 EFb
Nänded 20 Ee
Nandi [Fiji] 28 map no.6
Nandi [Zimb.] 26 Cd
Nanga Parbat (mt.) 20 Dab
Nangapinoh 18 De
Nangatayap 18 De
Nanjing (Nanking) 16 Ed
Nanking → Nanjing 16 Ed
Nan Ling (mts.) 16 Def
Nanning 15 Dg
Nanortalik 31 Kbc
Nanping 16 Ee
Nansei–Shotō → Ryukyu Islands 16 FGef
Nanshan Islands 18 Dcd
Nanterre 8 DEc
Nantes 8 Cd
Nantes–Brest, Canal– 8 Bcd
Nantong 16 Fd
Nanumea Atoll 27 Dc
Nanuque 39 DEa
Nanusa, Pulau– Pulau– 18 Gd
Nanxiong 16 DEef
Nanyang 16 Dd
Nanyuki 25 Dde
Nanzhang 16 Dd
Näo, Cabo de la– (cap.) 9 Fc
Napier 27 Id
Napier Mountains 42 grid square no.2
Naples 10 Ed

Naples, Gulf of– 10 Ed
Napo (riv.) 37 Bc
Napuka, Île– (is.) 28 BCc
Nara [Jap.] 17 DEg
Nara [Mali] 24 Bc
Naracoorte 29 FGf
Narayanganj 20 GHd
Narbonne 8 Ef
Nardò 10 Gd
Nares Strait 41 grid square no.1
Narew (riv.) 5 Hb
Narjan–Mar 13 Ec
Narlı 22 Fd
Narmada (riv.) 20 Ed
Narnaul 19 Gij
Narodnaja, gora– (mt.) 13 EFc
Naro–Fominsk 12 DEb
Narrabri 29 HIe
Narrandera 29 Hef
Narrogin 29 Be
Narsaq / Narssaq 31 Kb
Narsimhapur 20 EFd
Narssaq / Narsaq 31 Kb
Narva 4 Gd
Narva (riv.) 4 Fd
Narvik 4 Da
Naryn 13 Ge
Naryn (riv.) 16 ABb
Năsăud 6 FGc
Nashville 32 Cb
Našice 6 Dd
Näsijärvi (l.) 4 EFc
Näsik 20 Dde
Nassau 32 Dc
Nassau Island 28 Ac
Nasser, Lake– 25 Db
Nässjö 4 Cd
Nata 26 Bcd
Natal (prov.) 26 Cd
Natal [Braz.] 36 Gd
Natal [Indon.] 18 Ad
Natchez 32 Bb
Natividade 38 Cc
Natuna Islands 18 Cd
Naturaliste, Cape– 29 Ae
Naturaliste Channel 29 Acd
Nauâdhibou, Dakhlet– 24 Abc
Nauâdhibou 24 Ab
Náuplion 11 Ee
Nauru (Ind. St.) 27 Dc
Nautanwa 19 HIj
Nautla 34 Cb
Navan / An Uaimh 7 CDe
Navarin, mys– 14 KLc
Navarino, Isla– (i.) 40 Bc
Navarra (phys. reg.) 9 DEa
Navassa Island 35 Cb
Navaya Sibir, ostrov– (i.) 41 grid square no.4
Navoi 13 Fe
Navojoa 34 ABb
Návpaktos 11 DEd
Navsari 20 Dd
Nawabganj [Bngl.] 19 Jj
Nawabganj [India] 19 Hj
Nawabshah 20 CDc
Nawakot 19 Iij
Náxos (i.) 11 Fe
Náxos 11 Fe
Nāyband 21 Ed

Nayoro 16 Jb
Nazaré [Braz.] 38 Dc
Nazaré [Port.] 9 Ac
Nazareth 22 Ef
Nazarovo 13 Hld
Nazca 39 Aa
Naze 16 Ge
Nazilli 22 Bcd
Nazwa 21 Fe
Nazyvajevsk 13 Gd
Ndalatando 26 Ab
Ndélé 25 Cd
N'djamena 25 Bc
Ndjolé 24 CDde
Ndola 23 EFg
Neagh, Lake– 7 Cd
Neale, Lake– 29 DEc
Neales, The– (riv.) 29 EFd
Neápolis [Grc.] 11 Dc
Neápolis [Grc.] 11 Ee
Nebit–Dag 13 Ef
Neblina, Pico da– (mt.) 37 Cb
Nebraska (State) 33 CDb
Nebrodi (mts.) 10 Ef
Neckar (riv.) 5 Bd
Necker Island 28 Aa
Necochea 39 Cc
Nêdong 19 Bc
Needles 33 Bc
Neftekamsk 12 HIb
Negelli 25 DEd
Negola 26 Ac
Negombo 20 Eg
Negonego Atoll 28 Bc
Negotin 6 Fd
Negra, Cordillera– (mts.) 37 Bc
Negreşti 6 Hc
Negro, Río– (riv.) 39 Bcd
Negro, Rio– [Braz.] (riv.) 37 Cbc
Negro, Rio– [Ur.] (riv.) 40 Bab
Negros (i.) 18 Fbc
Negru Vodă 6 Ie
Nehbandán 21 FGc
Neijiang 14 Fe
Neisse (riv.) 5 Ec
Neiva 37 Bb
Neja 12 Fb
Nekemt 25 Dd
Nekso 5 Ea
Nelidovo 12 Db
Nelkan 14 Gd
Nellore 20 EFf
Nelma 14 Ge
Nelson (riv.) 31 Fc
Nelson [Can.] 33 Bb
Nelson [N.Z.] 27 De
Nelspruit 26 Cd
Néma 24 Bc
Neman 4 Ee
Nemira, Vîrful– (mt.) 6 GHc
Nemirov 6 Ib
Nemuna, Bjeshkët e– 11 CDb
Nemunas / Neman (riv.) 13 Bd
Nemuro 16 Ic
Nemuro–Kaikyō 17 Ib
Nenagh 7 BCe
Nendo Island 27 Dc
Nene (riv.) 7 Ge
Nen Jiang (Nun Kiang) (riv.) 16 Fa

Nepal (Ind. St.) 15 Cg
Nepalganj 19 Hij
Nephin (mt.) 7 Bde
Nérac 8 CDe
Nerčinsk 14 Ed
Nerehta 12 Fb
Neretva (riv.) 6 De
Neringa 4 Ee
Neriquinha 26 ABc
Neris (riv.) 4 Fe
Nerva 9 Bd
Nesebăr 11 GHb
Neskaupstadur 4 map no.1
Ness, Loch– (l.) 7 Dc
Nesterov [Russia] 5 Ia
Nesterov [Ukr.] 5 Ic
Néstos → Mesta (riv.) 11 Fc
Netanya 22 Ef
Netherdale 29 Hc
Netherlands (Ind. St.) 3 Db
Neubrandenburg 5 Db
Neuchâtel 5 Ae
Neuchâtel, Lac de– 10 Aa
Neufchâteau [Bel.] 8 Fc
Neufchâteau [Fr.] 8 Fc
Neumünster 5 BCa
Neunkirchen [Aus.] 5 EFe
Neunkirchen [Ger.] 5 Ad
Neuquén 39 Bc
Neuquén (riv.) 39 ABc
Neusiedler See 5 Fe
Neustrelitz 5 Db
Neu Ulm 5 BCd
Neuwied 5 Ac
Neva (riv.) 12 Db
Nevada (State) 33 Bc
Nevada, Sierra– [Sp.] (mts.) 9 Dd
Nevada, Sierra– [U.S.] (mts.) 33 ABbc
Nevada del Cocuy, Sierra– (mt.) 37 Bb
Nevada de Santa Marta, Sierra– (mts.) 37 Ba
Nevel 12 CDb
Nevelsk 17 Ga
Never 14 Fd
Nevers 8 Ed
Nevis (i.) 35 Db
Nevjansk 12 Jb
Nevşehir 22 Ec
New Albany 32 Cb
New Amsterdam 38 Ba
Newark 32 Da
Newark–on–Trent 7 FGe
New Bedford 32 DEa
New Bern 32 Db
New Britain 27 Cc
New Byrd 42 grid square no.3
New Caledonia (i.) 27 Dd
Newcastle [Austl.] 29 Ie
Newcastle [Can.] 32 Ea
Newcastle [S. Afr.] 26 BCd
Newcastle [U.S.] 33 Cb
Newcastle upon Tyne 7 EFd
Newcastle Waters 29 Eb
Newdegate 29 BCe
New Delhi 19 Gi
New England Range 29 Ide
Newfoundland (prov.) 31 IJcd
Newfoundland (i.) 30 Me
New Georgia Island 27 CDc
New Glasgow 32 Ea

New Guinea (i.) 27 BCc
New Hampshire (State) 32 Da
New Hanover Island 27 Cc
Newhaven 7 FGf
New Haven 32 Da
New Hebrides (is.) 27 Dc
New Iberia 32 Bbc
New Ireland Island 27 Cc
New Jersey (State) 32 Da
New Liskeard 31 Hd
New London 32 Da
Newman 29 BCc
New Mexico (State) 33 Cc
New Norfolk 29 map no.1
New Orleans 32 BCc
New Plymouth 27 Dd
Newport [Eng.–U.K.] 7 Ff
Newport [Wales–U.K.] 7 Ef
Newport News 32 Db
New Providence 32 Dc
New Ross 7 Ce
Newry 7 Cd
New Schwabenland 42 grid square no.1
New Siberian Island 41 grid square no.4
New South Wales (State) 29 GHe
Newton 32 Bb
Newtownabbey 7 Dd
New Westminster 33 Ab
New York (State) 32 Da
New York 32 Dab
New Zealand (Ind. St.) 27 DEe
Neyriz 21 Ed
Neyshābūr 21 Fb
Nežin 13 Cd
Ngain Atoll 28 map no.3
Ngaliema, Chutes– (Stanley Falls) 26 Ba
Ngami, Lake– 26 Bd
Ngangla Ringco (l.) 20 Fb
Nganglong Kangri (mt.) 16 Cc
Ngaoundéré 24 Dd
Ngau Island 28 map no.6
Ngoc Linh (mt.) 19 Eef
Ngoring Hu (l.) 16 Dcd
Ngourti 24 Dc
Nguigmi 24 Dc
Ngulu Atoll 27 BCb
Nguru 24 CDc
Nhamundá (riv.) 38 Bb
Nha Trang 19 EFf
Nhill 29 Gf
Nhulunbuy 29 Fa
Niagara Falls (wf.) 32 Da
Niagara Falls [Can.] 32 CDa
Niagara Falls [U.S.] 32 Da
Niamey 24 Cc
Niangara 25 Cd
Nias, Pulau– (i.) 15 Di
Nicaragua (Ind. St.) 30 Jh
Nicaragua, Lago de– 35 Ba
Nice 8 Gf
Nichinan 17 BCi
Nicholson River 29 Fb
Nicobar Islands 19 Bg
Nicosia [Cyp.] 22 De
Nicosia [It.] 10 Ef
Nicoya, Golfo de– 35 Bc
Nicoya, Peninsula de– (pen.) 35 Bbc

ida (riv.) **5** Hc
iedere Tavern (mts.) **5** DEe
ieder–Österreich (phys.
reg.) **5** DFd
iedersachsen **5** ACb
ienburg an der Weser **5** Bb
ieuw Amsterdam **37** Db
ieuw Nickerie **38** Ba
iğde **22** Ecd
iger (Ind. St.) **23** CDd
iger (riv.) **24** Cd
iger Delta **24** Cd
igeria (Ind. St.) **23** CDe
igrita **11** Ec
ihoa (i.) **28** ABa
iigata **16** Ic
iihama **17** Cgh
iihau (i.) **28** Aa
ii–Jima (i.) **17** Fg
iimi **17** Cg
iitsu **17** Ff
ijar **9** DEd
ljmegen **8** Fb
ikel **13** BCc
ikki **24** Ccd
kkö **17** Ff
ikolajev **13** Ce
ikolajevsk **12** Gd
ikolajevsk–na–Amure **14**
GHd
ikólaos, Áyios– **11** FGf
ikolsk [Russia] **12** Gb
kolsk [Russia] **12** Gc
ikopol [Bul.] **11** Fb
ikopol [Ukr.] **12** Dd
iksar **22** Fb
ikshahr **21** Gd
ikšić **11** Cb
ikumaroro (i.) **28** Ac
ila, Pulau– (i.) **18** Gf
ilande Atoll **20** Dh
ile (riv.) **25** Db
lphamari **19** Jj
mba Mountains **24** Bd
lmes **8** EFf
mrod Glacier **42** grid
square no.4
mule **25** Dd
ne Degree Channel **20** Dg
neveh (r.) **21** Cb
ng'an **16** Gb
ngbo **15** Eg
ngde **16** EFe
ngdu **16** Ee
ngsia **15** Df
ngwu **16** Dc
nigo Group **27** Cc
nnis Glacier **42** grid square
no.4
obrara (riv.) **33** CDd
oro du Sahel **24** Bc
ort **8** Cd
pigon **31** Gd
pigon, Lake– **31** Gcd
pissing, Lake– **31** GHd
quelândia **38** Cc
š **11** DEb
sa **9** Bc
sab **21** Dg
šava (riv.) **11** Eb
scemi **10** Ef
shinoomote **17** Bi
shino–Shima (i.) **27** BCa

Nísiros (i.) **11** Ge
Niterói **39** Db
Nith (riv.) **7** DEd
Nitra **5** Gd
Nittilling Lake **31** HIb
Niuafo'ou Island **28** Ac
Niue (i.) **28** Ac
Niu'erhe **14** Fd
Niulakita Island **27** DEc
Nivernais (phys. reg.) **8** Ed
Nivski **4** GHb
Nizamabad **20** Ee
Nizina Podlaska (hist. reg.) **5**
Ib
Nizip **22** Fd
Nízke Tatry (mts.) **5** Gd
Nižneangarsk **14** DEd
Nižnejansk **14** GHb
Nižnekamsk **12** GHb
Nižne–Leninskoje **14** Ge
Nižneudinsk **14** CDd
Nižnevartovsk **13** GHc
Nižnij Novgorod (Gorki) **13**
Dd
Nižnij Novgorod
vodohranilišče **12** Fb
Nižni Lomov **12** Fc
Nižni Tagil **13** EFd
Nižnjaja Pojma **14** CDd
Nižnjaja Tura **12** IJb
Nizzana (r.) **22** Eg
Njandoma **12** Fa
Njazepetrovsk **12** Ib
Njombe **26** Cb
Njurba **14** Ec
Njurunda **4** Dc
Nkhata Bay **26** Cc
Nkhota–Kota **26** Cc
Nkongsamba **24** CDd
Nobeoka **16** Hd
Nogales **33** Bc
Nogent–le–Rotrou **8** Dc
Noginsk **12** Eb
Noheji **17** Gd
Noires, Montagnes– (mts.) **8**
Bc
Noirmoutier, Ile de– (i.) **8** Bd
Noirmoutier–en–l'Ile **8** Bd
Nojima–Kaki **17** FGg
Nokia **4** Ec
Nok Kundi **20** Bc
Nolinsk **12** GHb
Nome **30** Bc
Nong'an **16** FGb
Nong Khai **15** Dh
Nonouti Atoll **27** Dc
Nontron **8** De
Noqui **26** Ab
Noranda **32** Da
Nord **30** Qa
Nordaustlandet **41** grid
square no.3
Norden **5** Ab
Nordenham **5** Bb
Nordenskjolda, ostrova– **14**
BCb
Nordfjord (b.) **4** Ac
Nordhausen **5** Cc
Nordkinn (cap.) **4** FGa
Nordmaling **4** Dc
Nordvik **14** Eb
Nore (riv.) **7** Ce
Norfolk (co.) **7** Ge

Norfolk [Nb.–U.S.] **32** Ba
Norfolk [Va.–U.S.] **32** Db
Norfolk Island **27** Dd
Norilsk **14** BCc
Normandie, Collines de–
(mts.) **8** Cc
Normandy (phys. reg.) **8**
CDc
Norman River **29** Gb
Normanton **29** Gb
Norman Wells **31** BCb
Nørresundby **4** Bd
Norrköping **4** Dd
Norrland (phys. reg.) **4** CDb
Norrtälje **4** Dd
Norseman **29** Ce
Norte, Cabo– **38** Ca
Norte, Submeseta– (phys.
reg.) **9** Cab
Northallerton **7** EFd
Northam **29** Be
Northampton [Austl.] **29** ABd
Northampton [U.K.] **7** FGe
North Andaman (i.) **19** BCf
North Battleford **31** Ec
North Bay **31** Hd
North Cape [Nor.] **4** Fa
North Cape [N.Z.] **27** Dd
North Carolina (State) **32**
CDb
North Channel **7** CDd
North Dakota (State) **33** CDb
Northeast Pass (str.) **28** map
no.3
Northeim **5** BCc
Northern Dvina (riv.) **13** Dc
Northern Ireland (reg.) **7** Cd
Northern Mariana Islands **27**
Cb
Northern Territory (State) **29**
EFbc
North Foreland **7** GHf
North Frisian Islands **5** ABa
North Island **27** Dd
North Korea (Ind. St.) **15** Eef
North Lakhimpur **19** Bc
North Little Rock **32** Bb
North Magnetic Pole (1980)
41 grid square no.2
North Minch (str.) **7** CBb
North Ossetia (Aut. Rep.) **13**
De
North Platte **33** CDb
North Platte (riv.) **33** Cb
North Pole **41** grid square
no.1
North Rona (i.) **7** Db
North Saskatchewan (riv.) **31**
Ab
North Sea **7** Gc
North Uist (i.) **7** BCc
Northumberland Islands **29** Ic
North West Cape **29** Ac
North West Highlands (mts.)
7 Dbc
North West River **31** IJc
Northwest Territories **31**
CHb
Norway (Ind. St.) **3** DEa
Norway, Kapp– **42** grid
square no.1
Norway House **31** Cb
Norwegian Sea **4** ABb

Noshiro **16** IJb
Nossob (riv.) **26** Bd
Nosy–Bé (i.) **26** map no.1
Nosy Boraha (i.) **26** map no.1
Nota (riv.) **4** Ga
Noteć (riv.) **5** Eb
Nótios Evvoïkós, Kólpos– **11**
EFd
Noto **10** Ef
Notodden **4** Bd
Noto–Hantō **17** DEf
Nottingham **7** Fe
Nottingham Island **31** GHb
Nouakchott **24** Ac
Nouméa **28** map no.4
Nova Cruz **38** Db
Nova Friburgo **39** Db
Nova Gaia **26** Ac
Nova Gorica **6** Acd
Nova Gradiška **6** Cd
Nova Iguaçu **39** Db
Novaja Kahovka **12** Dd
Novaja Ljalja **12** Jb
Novaja Zemlja (i.) **13** DEb
Nova Mambone **26** Cd
Novara **10** Bb
Nova Scotia (prov.) **31** Id
Nova Varoš **11** CDb
Nova Zagora **11** FGb
Nové Zámky **5** Gd
Novgorod **13** Cd
Novi Bečej **6** Ed
Novi Ligure **10** Bb
Novi Pazar [Bul.] **11** Gb
Novi Pazar [Yugo.] **11** Db
Novi Sad **6** DEd
Novi Vinodolski **6** Bd
Novoaltajsk **13** Hd
Novoanninski **12** Fc
Nôvo Aripuanã **37** CDc
Novočerkassk **12** Fd
Novograd–Volynski **6** Ha
Nôvo Hamburgo **39** CDb
Novokazalinsk **13** Fe
Novokujbyševsk **13** Ed
Novokuzneck **13** Hd
Novolazarevskaja **42** grid
square no.2
Novo Mesto **6** Bd
Novopokrovka **17** Db
Novopolock **12** Cb
Novorossijsk **13** Ce
Novošahtinsk **12** Ed
Novosergijevka **12** HIc
Novosibirsk **13** GHd
Novosibirsk–Akademgorodok
13 GHd
Novoskovsk → Bobriki **13**
CDd
Novotroick **13** Ed
Novoukrainka **12** Dd
Novouzensk **12** Gc
Novovjatsk **12** GHb
Novovolynsk **6** Ga
Novozybkov **12** Dc
Novska **6** Cd
Novy Port **13** FGc
Novy Uzen **13** Ee
Nowa Huta **5** Hcd
Nowa Sól **5** Ec
Nowe **5** Gb
Nowgong **19** Bc
Nowra **29** Ief

Nowshera 20 Db
Nowy Dwór Mazowiecki 5 Hb
Nowy Sącz 5 Hd
Nowy Targ 5 Hd
Noya 9 Aa
Nsanje 26 Cc
Nsukka 24 Cd
Nuayriyah, An– 21 Dd
Nubian Desert (phys. reg.) 25 Dbc
Nueltin Lake 31 Fbc
Nueva Casas Grandes 34 Ba
Nueva Gerona 35 Ba
Nueva Rosita 34 Bb
Nueve de Julio 39 Bc
Nuevitas 35 Ca
Nuevo, Golfo– 40 Bb
Nuevo Arraiján 35 map no.1
Nuevo Chagres 35 map no.1
Nuevo Laredo 34 BCb
Nuevo Rocafuerte 37 Bc
Nuhüd, An– 25 Cc
Nui Atoll 27 Dc
Nukhayb 21 Cc
Nuku'alofa 28 Ad
Nukufetau Atoll 27 DEc
Nuku Hiva, Île– (i.) 28 BCc
Nukunonu Atoll 28 Ac
Nukuoro Atoll 27 Cb
Nukus 13 EFe
Nules 9 EFc
Nullagine 29 BCc
Nullarbor Plain 29 DEe
Numancia (r.) 9 Db
Numata 17 Ff
Numazu 17 Fg
Nunivak Island 41 grid square no.2
Nunkun (mt.) 20 Eb
Nuoro 10 Bd
Nurmes 4 Gc
Nürnberg 5 Cd
Nuruhak dağ (mt.) 22 Fcd
Nutak 31 IJc
Nutrias, Ciudad de– 37 Cb
Nuuk / Godthåb 30 MNc
Nuwaybi' al Muzayyinah 22 Eh
Nuyts Archipelago 29 Ee
Nyainqêntanglha Shan 20 GHbc
Nyala 25 Cc
Nyasa, Lake– → Malawi, Lake– 26 Cc
Nyborg 5 Ca
Nybro 4 CDd
Nyda 13 Gc
Nyingchi 19 Bc
Nyíregyháza 6 EFbc
Nykarleby 4 Ec
Nykøbing 4 Be
Nyköping 4 CDd
Nymburk 5 Ec
Nynäshamn 4 Dd
Nyngan 29 He
Nyong (riv.) 24 CDd
Nysa 5 Fc
Nysa (riv.) 5 Ec
Nytva 12 Hlb
Nzega 26 Cb
Nzérékoré 24 Bd
Nzeto 26 Ab
Nzwani (i.) 26 Dc

O

Oahe, Lake– 33 CDd
Oahu (i.) 28 Ba
Oakham 7 Fe
Oakland 33 Ac
Oak Ridge 32 Cb
Oamaru 27 De
Oaxaca de Juarez 34 Cc
Ob (riv.) 13 Gc
Oba 31 Gd
Obama 17 Dg
Oban 7 Dc
Oberá 39 Cb
Oberhausen 5 Ac
Ober–Österreich (phys. reg.) 5 DFd
Ob Gulf 13 Gc
Obi, Pulau– (i.) 18 Ge
Óbidos 38 Bb
Obihiro 16 Jb
Oblačnaja (mt.) 17 Dc
Oblučje 14 Ge
Obninsk 12 Ebc
Obo 26 Ba
Obojan 12 Ec
Obozerski 13 Dc
Obrenovac 6 DEd
Obšči Syrt (mts.) 12 Hc
Ocakbaşı 12 EFf
Ocala 32 Cc
Ocaña 37 Bb
Ocean → Kure Island 27 DEa
Ocean Falls 31 Cc
Ocean Island 27 Dc
Öda 17 Cg
Oda, Jabal– (mt.) 25 Dbc
Odate 17 Gd
Odawara 16 IJcd
Odda 4 Ac
Odemira 9 Ad
Ödemiş 22 ABc
Odense 4 Be
Odenwald (mt.) 5 Bd
Oder (riv.) 5 Eb
Odessa [Ukr.] 13 Ce
Odessa [U.S.] 33 Cc
Odienné 24 Bcd
Odorheiu Secuiesc 6 Gc
Odra (riv.) 5 Eb
Oeiras 38 Cb
Oeno Island 28 Cd
Offenbach am Main 5 Bcd
Offenburg 5 ABd
Ofotfjord (g.) 4 CDa
Ofu (i.) 28 map no.5
Ofunato 17 GHe
Oga 17 Fe
Ogaden (phys. reg.) 25 Ed
Oga–Hantō 17 Fde
Ōgaki 17 EFg
Ogallala 33 Cb
Ogbomosho 24 Cd
Ogden 33 Bd
Oglio (riv.) 10 Cb
Ogooué (riv.) 26 Ab
Ogre 4 Fd
Ogulin 6 Bd
Oha 14 Hd
Ohanet 24 CDb
Ohansk 12 Hlb

Ōhata 17 Gd
Ohio (riv.) 32 Cb
Ohio (State) 32 Cab
Ohotsk 14 Hd
Ohře (riv.) 5 DEc
Ohrid 11 Dc
Ohrid, Lake– 11 Dc
Oi (riv.) 17 Fg
Oiapoque (riv.) 38 Ba
Oiapoque 38 Ba
Oil City 32 Da
Oise (riv.) 8 Ec
Ōita 16 Hd
Ojinaga 34 Bb
Ojmjakon 14 Hc
Ojos del Salado, Nevado– (mt.) 39 Bb
Oka [Russia] (riv.) 14 Dd
Oka [Russia] (riv.) 13 Cd
Okahandja 26 Ad
Okara 20 Db
Okavango (riv.) 26 ABc
Okavango Swamp 26 Bc
Okaya 17 EFfg
Okayama 16 Hcd
Okazaki 17 Eg
Okeechobee, Lake– 32 Cc
Okha 15 Cg
Okhaldhunga 19 Ij
Okhostk, Sea of– 41 grid square no.4
Oki–Daitō–Jima (i.) 16 Hef
Okinawa–Jima (i.) 16 Ge
Okinoerabu–Jima (i.) 16 Ge
Okino–Shima 17 Cn
Okino–Tori–Shima (i.) 27 BCab
Oki–Shotō 17 Cf
Oklahoma (State) 32 Bb
Oklahoma City 32 Bb
Oknica 6 Hb
Øksfjord 4 Ea
Okstindane (mt.) 4 Cb
Oktjabrsk 13 Ee
Oktjabrski [Bela.] 12 Cc
Oktjabrski [Russia] 12 Hc
Oktjabrski [Russia] 14 Id
Oktjabrskoje 13 Fc
Oktjabrskoj Revoljuci, ostrov– 41 grid square no.4
Okulovka 12 Db
Okushiri–Tō (i.) 16 Ib
Okusi 18 Ff
Olafsfjördur 4 map no.1
Olanchito 35 Bb
Öland (i.) 4 Dd
Olanga 4 Gb
Olavarría 39 Bc
Oława 5 Fc
Olbia 10 Bd
Old Crow 31 ABb
Olden 4 Ac
Oldenburg in Holstein 5 Ca
Oldenburg in Oldenburg 5 ABb
Oldham 7 EFe
Oldman (riv.) 33 Bab
Olëkma (riv.) 14 Fd
Olëkminsk 14 EFc
Olenegorsk 4 GHa
Olenëk 14 Ec
Olenëk (riv.) 14 Fb
Oleni, ostrov– 13 Gb

Oléron, Ile d'– (i.) 8 BCe
Oleśnica 5 Fc
Olevsk 6 Ha
Olga 14 Ge
Olhão 9 Bd
Olib 10 Eb
Olimarao Atoll 27 Cb
Olimbía (r.) 11 De
Ólimbos 11 Gf
Olinda 38 Db
Olivenza 9 Bc
Oljutorski 14 Kc
Oljutorski, mys– 14 Kd
Olkusz 5 Gc
Ollagüe 39 Bb
Olmedo 9 Cb
Olomouc 5 Fd
Olonec 12 Da
Olongapo 18 Fb
Oloron–Sainte–Marie 8 Cf
Olot 9 Ga
Olovjannaja 14 Ed
Olsztyn 5 Hb
Olt (riv.) 6 Gcd
Olten 5 ABe
Oltenia (phys. reg.) 6 FGd
Oltenita 6 Hd
Oltetul 6 FGd
Oluanpi (cap.) 16 Ff
Olvera 9 Cd
Olympia 33 Ab
Olympus → Troödos, Mount– 22 De
Olympus, Mount– [Grc.] 11 Ec
Olympus, Mount– [U.S.] 33 Ab
Omagh 7 Cd
Omaha 32 Ba
Ōma–Kaki 17 Gd
'Oman (phys. reg.) 21 Fe
'Oman (Ind. St.) 21 EFef
Oman, Gulf of– 21 FGe
Omaruru 26 Ad
Omboué 24 Ce
Ombrone (riv.) 10 Cc
Ombu 20 Gb
Omdurman 25 Dc
Omiš 10 Fc
Omo (riv.) 25 Dd
Omolon (riv.) 14 Jc
Omsk 13 Gd
Ōmu 17 Hb
Omu, Vírful– (mt.) 6 Gd
Ōmuta 17 Bh
Omutninsk 12 Hb
Ondangwa 26 Ac
Ondjiva 26 Ac
Ondo 24 Cd
Onega 13 Cc
Onega (riv.) 13 Cc
Onega, Lake– 13 Cc
Onekotan (i.) 14 Ie
Ongjin 16 FGc
Ongole 20 EFe
Onitsha 24 Cd
Ōno 17 Efg
Ono–i–Lau Islands 27 DEd
Onomichi 17 Cg
Onon (riv.) 14 Ed
Onslow 29 Bc
Ontario (prov.) 31 FGcd
Ontario 33 Bb

Ontario, Lake– 32 Da
Onteniente 9 Ec
Ontong Java Atoll 27 CDc
Ooa Atoll 28 map no.3
Oodnadatta 29 EFd
Ooldea 29 Ee
Oostende 8 Eb
Opala 25 Ce
Oparino 12 Gb
Opava 5 Fd
Opelika 32 Cb
Opobo 24 Cd
Opočka 12 Cb
Opole 5 FGc
Opuwo 26 Ac
Or (riv.) 12 Id
Oradea 6 EFc
Oraefajökull (gl.) 4 map no.1
Orai 19 Gj
Oran 24 BCa
Orange (prov.) 26 Bd
Orange [Austl.] 29 Hle
Orange [Fr.] 8 Fe
Orange [U.S.] 32 Bbc
Orange, Cabo– 38 Ba
Oranienburg 5 Db
Oranje (riv.) 26 Be
Oranjemund 26 Ad
Oranžerej 12 Gd
Orbetello 10 Cc
Orbost 29 Hf
Orcadas 42 grid square no.1
Orcera 9 Dc
Orchej 6 Ic
Orchila, Isla la– (i.) 35 Db
Ord, Mount– 29 Db
Ordos (phys. reg.) 16 Cc
Ord River (riv.) 29 Db
Ord River 29 Db
Ordu 22 FGb
Ordžonikidze 12 Dd
Ordžonikidze → Vladikavkaz 13 De
Örebro 4 CDd
Oregon (State) 33 ABb
Öregrund 4 Dc
Orehovo–Zujevo 13 CDd
Orel 13 Cd
Orem 33 Bb
Ore Mountains 5 Dc
Ören 11 GHe
Orenburg 13 Ed
Orense 9 Ba
Orestiás 11 Gc
Öresund 5 Dab
Orhangazi 11 Hc
Orhei (Orgejev) 6 Ic
Orhon (riv.) 14 De
Orihuela 9 Ec
Orinoco (riv.) 37 Cb
Orinoco, Mouths of the– 37 CDb
Orissa (State) 20 FGd
Oristano 10 Be
Oristano, Golfo di– 10 Be
Orivesi (l.) 4 Gc
Orizaba 34 Cc
Orjahovo 11 EFb
Orjen (mt.) 11 Cb
Orjiva 9 Dd
Orkanger 4 Bc
Orkney Islands 7 EFb
Orlando 32 Cc

Orléanais (hist. reg.) 8 DEcd
Orléans 8 DEd
Ormara 20 BCc
Ormoc 18 Fb
Orne (riv.) 8 Cc
Örnsköldsvik 4 DEc
Orohena (mt.) 28 map no.2
Oroluk Atoll 27 Cb
Oroqen Zizhiqi 14 Fd
Orosei, Golfo di– 10 Bd
Orosháza 6 Ec
Oroya, La– 37 Bd
Orsa 4 Cc
Orša 13 BCd
Orsk 13 EFd
Orşova 6 EFd
Ortegal, Cabo– 9 ABa
Orthez 8 Cf
Ortigueira 9 ABa
Ortles (mt.) 10 Ca
Orümiyeh 21 CDb
Oruro 39 Ba
Orust (i.) 4 Bd
Orvieto 10 Dc
Oš 13 Ge
Os 4 Ac
Osa 12 Ib
Osa, Península de– 35 Bc
Ōsaka 16 Id
Osakov, ostrov– (i.) 13 GHa
Osām (riv.) 11 Fb
Oshawa 31 Hd
Oshika–Hantō 17 GHe
Ō–Shima 17 Fd
Ō–Shima (i.) 17 Fg
Oshima–Hantō 17 FGcd
Oshkosh 32 BCa
Oshogbo 24 Cd
Oshwe 26 ABb
Osijek 6 Dd
Osinniki 13 Hd
Osipovići 12 Cc
Oskarshamn 4 Dd
Oslo 4 Bd
Oslofjorden (b.) 4 Bd
Osmaniye 22 Fd
Osnabrück 5 Bb
Osogovske planina 11 Eb
Osorno [Chile] 40 Ab
Osorno [Sp.] 9 Ca
Osprey Reef (i.) 29 Ha
Óssa (mt.) 11 Ed
Ossa, Mount– 29 map no.1
Ossora 14 Jd
Ostaškov 12 Db
Østerdalen (v.) 4 Bc
Östersund 4 Cc
Östhammar 4 Dc
Ostia (r.) 10 Dd
Ostrava 5 Fd
Ostróda 5 GHb
Ostrog 6 Ha
Ostrogožsk 12 Ec
Ostrołeka 5 Hb
Ostrov [Czech Rep.] 5 Dc
Ostrov [Russia] 4 FGd
Ostrowiec Świętokrzyski 5 Hc
Ostrów Mazowiecka 5 Hlb
Ostrów Wielkopolski 5 Fc
Ostuni 10 Fd
Ōsumi–Hantō 17 Bi
Ōsumi–Kaikyō 16 Hd
Ōsumi–Shotō 16 GHd

Osuna 9 Cd
Oświęcim 5 Gcd
Ota–Porto 8 map no.1
Otaru 16 Jb
Otavalo 37 Bb
Otavi 26 Ac
Ōtawara 17 FGf
Othonoi (i.) 11 Cd
Óthrys (mt.) 11 Ed
Otish, Monts– 31 EFb
Otjiwarongo 26 Ad
Otočac 6 Bd
Otoineppu 17 Hb
Otra (riv.) 4 Ad
Otradny 12 Hc
Otranto, Capo d'– 10 Gd
Otranto, Strait of– 11 Ccd
Ōtsu 17 DEg
Ottawa 32 Bb
Ottawa (riv.) 32 Da
Ottawa [Can.] 31 Hd
Ottumwa 32 Ba
Otway, Cape– 29 Gf
Otwock 5 Hb
Ou (riv.) 19 Dd
Ouachita Mountains 32 Bb
Ouadane 24 Ab
Ouadda 25 Cd
Ouaddaï (phys. reg.) 25 BCc
Ouagadougou 24 Bc
Ouahigouya 24 Bc
Oualata 24 Bc
Ouanda–Djallé 25 Cd
Ouargla 24 Cb
Oubangui (riv.) 25 ABd
Oudtshoorn 26 Be
Oued, El– 24 Ca
Oued ben Tili 24 Bb
Oued–Zem 24 Ba
Ouessant, Ile d'– (i.) 8 Ac
Ouesso 24 Dd
Oujda 24 Ba
Oulainen 4 Fb
Oullins 8 Fe
Oulu 4 Fb
Oulujärvi 4 Fb
Oulujoki (riv.) 4 Fb
Oum Chalouba 25 Cc
Oum er–Rbia (riv.) 24 Ba
Ounasjoki (riv.) 4 Fb
Ou Neua 19 Dd
Ounianga Kébir 25 Cc
Ourinhos 39 CDb
Ourique 9 ABd
Ouro Prêto 39 Bb
Òu–Sanmyaku (mts.) 17 Gde
Ouse [Eng.–U.K.] (riv.) 7 Fe
Ouse [Eng.–U.K.] (riv.) 7 Fe
Oust (riv.) 8 Bd
Outjo 26 Acd
Outokumpu 4 Gc
Ouvéa, Ile– (i.) 27 Dcd
Ouyen 29 Gf
Ovalle 39 Ab
Ovamboland (hist. reg.) 26 Ac
Ovar 9 Ab
Övertorneå 4 Eb
Ovidiopol 6 Jc
Oviedo 9 Ca
Øvre Årdal 4 ABc
Ovruč 12 Cc
Owando 24 De

Owase 17 Eg
Owensboro 32 Cb
Owen Sound 32 Ca
Owerri 24 Cd
Oxapampa 37 Bd
Oxelösund 4 Dd
Oxford 7 Ff
Oxnard 33 ABc
Oyama 17 FGf
Oyapock (riv.) 38 Ba
Oyem 24 Dd
Oyo 24 Cd
Oyonnax 8 Fd
Øy Peter Island 42 grid square no.3
Ozamis 18 Fc
Ozark Plateau 32 Bb
Ózd 6 DEb
Ozernovski 14 Id
Ozersk 5 Ia
Ozerski 17 Ha
Ozery 12 Ec
Ozieri 10 Bd
Ozinki 12 GHc
Ozorków 5 Gbc

P

Paamiut / Frederikshåb 31 JKb
Paarl 26 Ae
Paauilo 28 map no.1
Pabianice 5 GHc
Pabna 19 Jjk
Pab Range 20 Cc
Pacaás Novos, Serra dos– (mts.) 37 Cd
Pacajá (riv.) 38 Bb
Pacaraima, Sierra– (mts.) 37 Cb
Pacasmayo 37 ABc
Pachino 10 Ef
Pachitea (riv.) 37 Bc
Pachuca de Soto 34 Cbc
Pacific Ocean 2
Pacitan 18 Df
Padang 15 Dj
Paderborn 5 Bc
Padre Island 32 Bc
Padua 10 Cb
Paducah 32 Cb
Paéa 28 map no.2
Paestum (r.) 10 Ed
Páfos 22 De
Pag (i.) 6 Bd
Pagadian 18 Fc
Pagai, Kepulauan– 18 Ae
Pagai Selantan (i.) 18 ABe
Pagai Utara (i.) 18 ABe
Pagan Island 27 Cb
Pagasitikós Kólpos 11 Ed
Page 33 Bc
Paget, Mount– 40 Ec
Pagoda Point 19 Be
Pago Pago 28 Ac
Pahkaing Bum 19 Cc
Pahoa 28 map no.1
Paia 28 map no.1
Paide 4 Fd
Paijänne (l.) 4 Fc
Pailolo Channel 28 map no.1

Paisley **7** Dd
Paistunturit (mt.) **4** FGa
Paita **37** Ac
Pajala **4** Eb
Pajaros, Farallon de– (i.) **27** Ca
Pakanbaru **18** Bd
Pakistan (Ind. St.) **15** Cg
Pakokku **19** Bd
Pak Phanang **19** Dg
Paks **6** Dc
Pakxé **19** Ee
Pala **25** Bd
Palagruža **11** Bb
Palana **14** IJd
Palangkaraya **18** De
Palanpur **20** Dd
Palapye **26** Bd
Palau **10** Bd
Palau Islands **27** Bb
Palauli **28** map no.5
Palaw **19** Cf
Palawan (i.) **15** Dhi
Palayankottai **20** Eg
Paldiski **4** EFd
Paleleh **18** Fd
Palembang **15** Dj
Palencia **9** CDab
Palermo **10** De
Palestina **39** ABb
Palestine (phys. reg.) **22** Efg
Paletwa **19** Bd
Palghat **20** Ef
Pali **20** Dc
Palikir **27** Cb
Palinuro, Capo– **10** Ed
Palk Strait **20** EFfg
Pallasovka **12** Gc
Pallastunturi (mt.) **4** EFa
Palles, Bisthi i– **11** Cc
Palma **9** Gc
Palma, La– **35** Cc
Palma, La– (i.) **24** Ab
Palmas, Cape– **24** Bd
Palmas, Las– **24** Ab
Palma Soriano **35** Cab
Palmeira dos Indios **38** Db
Palmer Land **42** grid square no.1
Palmer Station (sc. stat.) **42** grid square no.1
Palmerston Atoll **28** Ac
Palmi **10** Ee
Palmira **37** Bb
Palm Springs **33** Bc
Palmyra **21** Bc
Palmyra Atoll **28** Ab
Paloma, La– **39** Cc
Palomani, Nevado– (mt.) **39** Ba
Palomar Mountain (mt.) **33** Bc
Palopo **18** EFe
Palos, Cabo de– (cap.) **9** Ed
Palu **18** EFe
Pamekasan **18** Df
Pamiers **8** DEf
Pamir (plat.) **13** Gf
Pamlico Sound **32** Db
Pampa **33** CDc
Pampas (phys. reg.) **39** Bc
Pamplona [Col.] **37** Bb
Pamplona [Sp.] **9** DEa
Panagjurište **11** Fb

Panaitan, Pulau– (i.) **18** BCf
Panaji (Nova Goa) **20** De
Panamá (Ind. St.) **30** JKi
Panamá **36** Cbc
Panama, Gulf of– **35** Cc
Panama City **32** Cbc
Panaro (riv.) **10** Cb
Panay (i.) **15** Eh
Pančevo **6** Ed
Panciu **6** Hd
Panevėžys **4** Fe
Panfilov **13** GHe
Pangaion Óros (mts.) **11** EFc
Pangi **26** Bb
Pangkalanberandan **18** Ad
Pangkalpinang **18** Ce
Pangnirtung **31** Ib
Pangutaran Group **18** EFc
Panié, Mont– (mt.) **28** map no.4
Panjgur **20** Bc
Panna **19** Hj
Pannawonica **29** Bc
Panorama **39** Cb
Pantanal (sw.) **39** Ca
Pantar, Pulau– (i.) **18** Ff
Pantelleria (i.) **10** CDf
Pánuco (riv.) **34** Cb
Pao, El– **37** Cb
Pão de Açúcar **38** Db
Paola **10** Fe
Papa **28** map no.3
Pápa **6** Cc
Papaikou **28** map no.1
Papeete **28** map no.2
Papenoo **28** map no.2
Papetoai **28** map no.2
Papua, Gulf of– **27** Cc
Papua New Guinea (Ind. St.) **27** Cc
Papuk (mts.) **6** Cd
Papun **19** Ce
Pará (State) **38** Bb
Pará (riv.) **38** BCb
Paraburdoo **29** Bc
Paracatu (riv.) **39** Da
Paracatu **39** Da
Paracel Islands **15** Dh
Paraguá (riv.) **39** Ba
Paragua (riv.) **37** Cb
Paragua, La– **37** Cb
Paraguai (riv.) **38** Bc
Paraguaipoa **37** Ba
Paraguaná, Peninsula de– (pen.) **37** Ca
Paraguay (riv.) **39** Cb
Paraguay (Ind. St.) **36** DEf
Paraíba (State) **38** Db
Paraíba do Sul (riv.) **39** Db
Paraíso **35** map no.1
Parakou **24** Cd
Paramaribo **36** Ec
Paramonga **37** Bd
Paramušir, ostrov– (i.) **14** Id
Paraná **39** BCc
Paranã **38** Cc
Paranã (riv.) **38** Cc
Paraná (riv.) **39** Cb
Paraná (State) **39** Cb
Paranaguá **39** Db
Paranaíba **39** Cab
Paranaíba (riv.) **39** Da
Paranapanema (riv.) **39** Cb

Paranapiacaba, Serra do– (mts.) **39** CDb
Paranavaí **39** Cb
Parapetí (riv.) **39** Bab
Paray–le–Monial **8** Fd
Parbati (riv.) **20** Ed
Parbhani **20** Ee
Parchim **5** Cb
Parczew **5** Ic
Pardo [Braz.] (riv.) **38** CDc
Pardo [Braz.] (riv.) **39** Db
Pardubice **5** EFcd
Parecis, Chapada dos– (mts.) **38** ABc
Parepare **18** Ee
Párga **11** Dd
Paria, Golfo de– **37** Ca
Pariaman **18** ABe
Parika **37** Db
Parima, Sierra– (mts.) **37** Cb
Pariñas, Punta– (cap.) **37** Ac
Paríngul Mare, Vírful– (mt.) **6** FGd
Parintins **38** Bb
Paris [Fr.] **8** Ec
Paris [U.S.] **32** Bb
Parkersburg **32** CDb
Parkes **29** He
Park Range **33** Cbc
Parma **10** Cb
Parnaguá **38** Cbc
Parnaíba **36** FGd
Parnaíba (riv.) **38** Cb
Parnassós Óros (mt.) **11** Ed
Párnon Óros (mts.) **11** Ee
Pärnu **13** Bd
Paroo Channel (riv.) **29** Gde
Paroo River **29** GHd
Paropamisus (mts.) **20** BCab
Páros (i.) **11** Fe
Parral **39** Ac
Parras **34** Bb
Parry, Cape– **31** Cab
Parry Islands **41** grid square no.2
Parry Sound **31** GHd
Parṣeta (riv.) **5** Fb
Parsons **32** Bb
Parthenay **8** CDd
Partinico **10** De
Partizansk **14** Ge
Paru (riv.) **38** Ba
Párvomaj **11** Fb
Pas, The– **31** Bb
Pasadena [Ca.–U.S.] **33** Bc
Pasadena [Tx.–U.S.] **32** Bc
Pa Sak (riv.) **19** Def
Paşcani **6** Hc
Pasco **33** Bb
Pascoal, Monte– **38** CDc
Pasewalk **5** DEb
Pasir Mas **19** Dg
Pasni **20** Bc
Paso, El– **33** Cc
Paso de Indios **40** Bb
Paso de los Libres **39** Cb
Paso de los Toros **39** Cc
Passau **5** Dd
Passero, Capo– **10** Ef
Passo Fundo **39** Cb
Passos **39** Db
Pastaza (riv.) **37** Bc
Pasto **36** Cc

Pastos Bons **38** Cb
Pasvik (riv.) **4** Ga
Patagonia (phys. reg.) **40** ABbc
Patagonica, Cordillera– (mts.) **40** Aab
Patan [India] **20** Dd
Patan [Nep.] **20** Gc
Paternò **10** Ef
Paterson **32** Da
Pathankot **20** Eb
Pati **18** Df
Patía **37** Bb
Patía (riv.) **37** Bb
Patiala **20** Ebc
Pátmos (i.) **11** Ge
Patna **15** Cg
Patomskoje Negorje **14** Ed
Patos **38** Db
Patos, Lagoa dos– (lag.) **39** Cc
Patos de Minas **39** Da
Patquía **39** Bbc
Pátrai **11** DEd
Patraïkós Kólpos **11** Dd
Patrocinio **39** Da
Pattani **19** Dg
Patti **10** Ee
Patuakhali **19** Jk
Patuca (riv.) **35** Bb
Patuca, Punta– (cap.) **35** Bb
Pau **8** Cf
Pau d'Arco **38** Cb
Pau dos Ferros **38** Db
Pauillac **8** Ce
Pauini **37** Cc
Pauini (riv.) **37** Cc
Paulatuk **31** Cb
Paulista **38** Db
Paulistana **38** Cb
Paulo Alfonso, Cachoeira de– **38** Db
Pavia **10** Bb
Pavlodar **13** Gd
Pavlovo **12** Fb
Pavlovsk **12** EFc
Pavlovskaja **12** EFd
Paxoí (i.) **11** Dd
Payne Bay → Bellin **31** Hlbc
Payne's Find **29** Bd
Paysandú **39** Cc
Pays de Caux (phys. reg.) **8** Dc
Paz, La– [Arg.] **39** Cc
Paz, La– [Arg.] **39** Bc
Paz, La– [Bol.] **39** Ba
Paz, La– [Mex.] **34** Ab
Pazardžik **11** EFb
Peace River (riv.) **31** Dc
Peace River **31** Dc
Peak Hill **29** Bd
Pearl Harbor **28** map no.1
Peary Land **41** grid square no.1
Pebane **26** Cc
Pebas **37** Bc
Peć **11** Db
Peçanha **39** Da
Pečenga **13** Cbc
Pečora (riv.) **13** Ec
Pečora **13** Ec
Pecoraro, Monte– **10** Fe
Pečory **4** Fd

Pecos (riv.) 33 Cc
Pecos 33 Cc
Pécs 6 CDc
Pedra Azul 39 Da
Pedreiras 38 Cb
Pedrera, La– 37 BCc
Pedro Afonso 38 Cb
Pedro Cays (is.) 35 Cb
Pedro de Valdivia 39 ABb
Pedro II, Ilha– 37 Cb
Pedro Juan Caballero 39 Cb
Pedro Miguel 35 map no.1
Pedro Miguel Locks 35 map no.1
Peebles 7 Ed
Pee Dee (riv.) 32 CDb
Peel Sound 31 Fa
Peene (riv.) 5 Db
Pegai 11 Dd
Pegu 19 Ce
Pegu Yoma 19 Cde
Pehuajó 39 Bc
Peipus, Lake– 13 Bd
Peixe 38 Cc
Pekalongan 18 CDf
Peking → Beijing 16 Ebc
Pelagie, Isole– 10 Dg
Pélagos (i.) 11 EFd
Pelat, Mont– (mt.) 8 Ge
Peleaga, Virful– (mt.) 6 Fd
Pelechuco 39 Ba
Peleduj 14 Ed
Peleng, Pulau– (i.) 18 Fe
Pelješac (pen.) 11 Bb
Pello 4 EFb
Pelly (riv.) 31 Bb
Pelly Bay 31 FGb
Pelopónnisos (phys. reg.) 11 DEe
Peloritani (mts.) 10 Eef
Peloro o Punta del Faro, Capo– (cap.) 10 Ee
Pelotas 39 Cc
Pelotas, Rio– (riv.) 39 Cb
Pelusium (r.) 25 map no.1
Pelvoux, Massif du– (mt.) 8 Ge
Pelym (riv.) 12 Ja
Pematangsiantar 18 ABd
Pemba 26 Dc
Pemba (i.) 26 CDb
Pemberton 29 Be
Pembroke [Can.] 32 Da
Pembroke [U.K.] 7 Df
Pembuang (riv.) 18 De
Penafiel 9 ABb
Peñafiel 9 CDb
Peñalara (mt.) 9 CDb
Penambo Range 18 Ed
Peña Nevada, Cerro– (mt.) 34 BCb
Peña Prieta (mt.) 9 Ca
Peñaranda de Bracamonte 9 Cb
Peñarroya–Pueblonuevo 9 Cc
Peñas, Cabo de– (cap.) 9 Ca
Penas, Golfo de– (b.) 40 Ab
Peña Ubiña (mt.) 9 BCa
Pendembu 24 ABd
Pendleton 33 ABb
Peneda (mt.) 9 Ab
Penedo 38 Dc
Penganga (riv.) 20 Ede

Peniche 9 Ac
Peñíscola 9 Fb
Penitente, Serra do– (mts.) 38 Cb
Penju, Kepulauan– 18 Gf
Penne 10 Dc
Penner (riv.) 20 Ef
Pennine Alps 10 Aab
Pennines 7 EFde
Pennsylvania (State) 32 Da
Peno 12 Db
Penong 29 Ee
Penonomé 35 Bc
Penrhyn Atoll 28 ABc
Penrith 29 Ie
Pensacola 32 Cb
Pentecôte, Île– (i.) 28 map no.4
Penticton 33 ABb
Pentland Firth 7 Eb
Penza 13 Dd
Penzance 7 CDf
Penžina (riv.) 14 Jc
Penžinskaja guba 14 Jc
Peoria 32 Ca
Pequiri (riv.) 39 Ca
Perabumulih 18 BCe
Perche, Col de la– (p.) 8 Ef
Perche, Collines du– (mts.) 8 Dc
Percival Lakes 29 CDc
Perdido, Monte– 9 EFa
Perečin 5 Id
Pereira 37 Bb
Pereslavl–Zalesski 12 Eb
Pergamino 39 BCc
Pergamum → Bergama 22 Ac
Peribonca (riv.) 32 Da
Périgord (phys. reg.) 8 De
Périgueux 8 De
Perija, Sierra de– (mts.) 37 Bab
Peristéri (mt.) 11 Dd
Perito Moreno 40 Ab
Perlas, Archipiélago de las– (is.) 35 Cc
Perm 13 Ed
Përmeti 11 Dc
Pernambuco (State) 38 Db
Pernik 11 Eb
Péronne 8 Ebc
Pérouse Pinnacle, La– (i.) 28 Aa
Perpignan 8 Ef
Perry Island 31 Eb
Persepolis (r.) 21 Ecd
Persian Gulf 21 DEd
Perth [Austl.] 29 ABe
Perth [U.K.] 7 Ec
Perthus, Col de– 9 Ga
Pertusato, Capo– 8 map no.1
Perú (Ind. St.) 36 Cde
Peru, Altiplano del– 37 Bd
Perugia 10 Dc
Peruibe 39 Db
Pervomajsk [Russia] 12 Fc
Pervomajsk [Ukr.] 12 CDd
Pervouralsk 13 EFd
Pesaro 10 Dc
Pescadores (is.) 16 EFf
Pescara 10 Ec
Peschici 10 Fd

Peshāwar 15 Cf
Peshkopia 11 Dc
Peskovka [Russia] 12 Hb
Peskovka [Ukr.] 6 IJa
Pesqueira 38 Db
Pessac 8 Ce
Peštera 11 Fbc
Pestovo 12 Eb
Petah Tiqwa 22 Ef
Petalioi, Gulf of– 11 Fde
Petauke 26 Cc
Peterborough [Austl.] 29 FGe
Peterborough [Can.] 32 Da
Peterborough [U.K.] 7 Fge
Peterhead 7 Fc
Petermann Ranges 29 DEcd
Petersburg [Ak.–U.S.] 31 Bc
Petersburg [Va.–U.S.] 32 Db
Peter's Mine 37 CDb
Peter the Great Bay 16 Hb
Peto 34 Dbc
Petrel 42 grid square no.1
Petrič 11 Ec
Petrila 6 Fd
Petrolândia 38 Db
Petrolina 38 Cb
Petropavlovsk 13 FGd
Petropavlovsk Kamčatski 14 IJd
Petrópolis 39 Db
Petroşani 6 Fd
Petrovsk 12 Gc
Petrovsk–Zabaikalski 14 Dd
Petrozavodsk 13 BCc
Petuhovo 13 Fd
Peureulak 18 Ad
Pevek 14 Kc
Pforzheim 5 Bd
Phalodi 20 Dc
Phangan, Ko– (i.) 19 CDg
Phang–nga 19 Cg
Phan Rang 18 CDb
Phan Thiet 19 Ef
Phatthalung 19 CDg
Phet Buri 19 CDf
Phetchabun 19 De
Philadelphia 32 Dab
Philippines (Ind. St.) 15 GHi
Philippine Sea 27 Bb
Phitsanulok 19 De
Phnum Pénh 15 Dh
Phoenix (i.) 28 Ac
Phoenix 33 Bc
Phoenix Islands 28 Ac
Phôngsali 19 Dd
Phrae 19 De
Phu Bia (mt.) 19 De
Phuket 19 Cg
Phu Miang (mt.) 19 De
Phu Qui 19 Ee
Phu Quoc, Dao– (i.) 19 Df
Piacenza 10 Bb
Pianosa (i.) 10 Cc
Piaozero, ozero– 4 Gb
Piaseczno 5 Hbc
Piatra Neamţ 6 Hc
Piauí (riv.) 38 Cb
Piauí (State) 38 Cb
Piave (riv.) 10 Da
Piazza Armerina 10 Ef
Pibor Post 25 Dd
Picardy (hist. reg.) 8 DEbc
Pichilemu 39 Ac

Pickle Crow 31 FGc
Pico, El– 39 Ba
Picos 38 Cb
Pico Truncado 40 Bb
Picton, Isla– 40 Bc
Pidurutalagala (mt.) 20 Fg
Piedras, Río de las– (riv.) 37 BCd
Piedras Negras 34 Bb
Pieksämäki 4 Fc
Pielavesi 4 Fc
Pielinen (l.) 4 Gc
Piemonte (reg.) 10 Ab
Pierre 33 Cb
Piešťany 5 Fd
Pietermaritzburg 26 Cd
Pietersburg 26 BCd
Pietrasanta 10 Cc
Pietrosu, Virful– (mt.) 6 Gc
Pigs, Bay of– 35 Ba
Pikalevo 12 DEb
Pikelot Island 27 Cb
Piła 5 Fb
Pilar 39 Cb
Pilcomayo (riv.) 39 Bb
Pilibhit 20 EFc
Pilica (riv.) 5 Hc
Pilion Óros (mt.) 11 Ed
Pilos 11 De
Pimenta Bueno 37 Cd
Piña 35 map no.1
Pinang (i.) 19 CDg
Pınarbaşı 22 Fc
Pinar del Río 35 Ba
Pincota 6 EFc
Pindus Mountains 11 Dd
Pine Bluff 32 Bb
Pine Creek 29 Ea
Pine Island Bay 42 grid square no.3
Pine Point 31 Db
Pinerolo 10 Ab
Ping (riv.) 19 Ce
Pingdingshan 16 Dd
Pingelap Atoll 27 Cb
Pinglap Atoll 28 map no.3
Pingle 16 CDf
Pingliang 16 Dd
Pingtung 16 Ff
Pingwu 16 Bd
Pingxiang [China] 16 DEe
Pingxiang [China] 16 Cf
Pingyao 16 Dc
Pinheiro 38 Cb
Pini, Pulau– (i.) 18 Ad
Pinios (riv.) 11 DEd
Pinjarra 29 Be
Pinnaroo 29 Gef
Pinotepa Nacional 34 Cc
Pins, Îles des– 27 Cd
Pinsk 13 Bd
Pintados 39 ABb
Pinto 39 Bb
Piombino 10 Cc
Pioner, ostrov– 14 BCab
Pionki 5 Hc
Piotrków Trybunalski 5 Gc
Pipanaco, Salar de– (s. m.) 39 Bb
Piperi (i.) 11 Fd
Piqua 32 Ca
Piracambu, Serra do– (mts.) 38 Cb

Piracanjuba **39** Da
Piracicaba **39** Db
Piraeus **11** Ee
Piramide, Cerro– (mt.) **40** Ab
Pirapora **39** Da
Pirdop **11** EFb
Pires do Rio **39** Da
Pírgos **11** De
Piriápolis **39** Cc
Pirin (mts.) **11** Ec
Pirineus, Serra dos– (mts.) **38** Cc
Piripiri **38** Cb
Pirmasens **5** ABd
Pirna **5** DEc
Pirot **11** Eb
Piru **18** Ge
Pisa **10** Cc
Pisagua **39** Aa
Pisco **37** Bd
Pisek **5** Ed
Pisticci **10** Fd
Pistoia **10** Cc
Pisuerga (riv.) **9** Ca
Pital **34** Cc
Pitcairn Island **28** Cd
Pitcairn Islands **28** Cd
Pite (riv.) **4** Db
Piteå **4** Eb
Piteşti **6** Gd
Pithiviers **8** DEc
Piti **27** map no.1
Pitkjaranta **12** Da
Pitt Island **28** Ae
Pittsburg **32** Bb
Pittsburgh **32** CDa
Piuí **39** Db
Piura **37** Ac
Piva (riv.) **11** Cb
Pivan **14** Gd
Pivka **10** Eb
Pjandž (riv.) **13** FGf
Pjandž **13** Ff
Pjasina (riv.) **14** BCb
Pjatigorsk **13** De
Pjórsá (riv.) **4** map no.1
Placetas **35** Ca
Plainview **33** Cc
Planeta Rica **37** Bb
Planet Depth **18** CDg
Plasencia **9** BCbc
Plast **12** Jc
Plastun **17** Eb
Plata, La– [Arg.] **39** Cc
Plata, La– [Col.] **37** Bb
Plata, Río de la– (riv.) **39** Cc
Plato **37** Bb
Platte (riv.) **33** CDb
Platte (i.) **15** Bj
Plauen **5** CDc
Plaviņas **5** JKa
Plavsk **12** Ec
Pleiku (Po–Lay Cu) **19** Ef
Plenty, Bay of– **27** Dd
Pleseck **13** Dc
Pleszew **5** Fc
Pleven **11** Fb
Plitvice **10** Eb
Pljevlja **11** Cb
Ploče **11** Bb
Płock **5** GHb
Plöckenstein (mt.) **5** Dd
Ploёrmel **8** BCd

Ploieşti **6** GHd
Plombières–les–Bains **8** FGcd
Płońsk **5** Hb
Plovdiv **11** Fb
Plumas, Las– **40** Bb
Plunge **12** Bb
Plymouth **7** DEf
Plzeň **5** Dd
Pô **24** Bc
Po (riv.) **10** Db
Pobé **24** Cd
Pobeda, gora– **14** Hc
Pobeda Ice Island **42** grid square no.4
Pobedino **14** Hde
Pobedy, Pik– (mt.) **13** GHe
Pobla de Lillet, La– **9** FGa
Pobla de Segur **9** Fa
Pocatello **33** Bb
Počep **12** Dc
Poções **38** CDc
Poços de Caldas **39** Db
Podgorica (Titograd) **11** Cb
Podkova **11** Fc
Podolsk **13** Cd
Podolskaja vozvyšennost (phys. reg.) **6** Glb
Podor **24** Ac
Podporožje **12** DEa
Podravina (phys. reg.) **6** CDcd
Podravska Slatina **6** CDd
Podvoločisk **6** Hb
Poel (i.) **5** Ca
Pogibi **14** Hd
Pograničny **17** BCb
Pogrebišče **6** Ib
Poh **18** Fe
P'ohang **16** GHc
Pohorje (mt.) **6** Bc
Poiana Mare **6** Fe
Poinsett, Cape– **42** grid square no.4
Pointe–à–Pitre **35** DEb
Pointe Noire **26** Ab
Poipet **19** Df
Poitiers **8** Dd
Poitou **8** CDd
Pojarkovo **14** Fe
Pojezierze Mazurskie (phys. reg.) **5** Hlab
Pokaran **20** Dc
Pokhara **20** Fc
Pokrovsk **14** Fc
Pola de Lena **9** BCa
Pola de Siero **9** Ca
Poland (Ind. St.) **3** EFb
Polatli **22** Dc
Po–Lay Cu → Pleiku **19** Ef
Polcura **39** Ac
Pol–e Khomrī **20** Ca
Polock **13** Bd
Polonnoje **6** Hla

Polos **22** Ab
Poltava **13** Ce
Polunočnoje **12** IJa
Poluostrov Rybači **4** Ha
Polýgyros **11** Ec
Polynesia (is.) **28** ABbc
Pombal [Braz.] **38** Db
Pombal [Port.] **9** Ac
Pomerania (hist. reg.) **5** DEab
Pomeranian Bay **5** Ea
Pomona → Mainland (i.) **7** DEb
Pomorije **11** GHb
Pompei (r.) **10** Ed
Ponca City **32** Bb
Ponce **35** Db
Pondicherry **20** EFf
Pond Inlet **31** Ha
Ponferrada **9** Ba
Pongo Mansériche (v.) **37** Bc
Pong Qu (riv.) **19** Ii
Ponoj **13** CDc
Ponta Delgada **40** ABc
Ponta Grossa **39** Cb
Pont–à–Mousson **8** FGc
Ponta Porã **39** Cb
Pontarlier **8** FGd
Pontchartrain, Lake– **32** BCbc
Pontevedra **9** ABa
Pontianak **15** Dij
Pontivy **8** Bcd
Ponto (mts.) **22** FGb
Pontremoli **10** Bb
Ponza (i.) **10** Dd
Ponziane, Isole– **10** Dd
Poole **7** Ef
Poona → Pune **20** De
Poopó, Lago de– **39** Ba
Popayán **37** Bb
Poplar Bluff **32** Bb
Popocatépetl, Volcán– (mt.) **34** Cc
Popovo **11** FGb
Poprad **5** Hd
Porbandar **20** Cd
Porcupine (riv.) **31** Ab
Pordenone **10** Db
Poreč **6** Ad
Porhov **12** Cb
Pori **4** Ec
Porirua **27** De
Porjus **4** Db
Pornic **8** Bd
Poronajsk **14** He
Póros (i.) **11** Ee
Poroshiri–Dake (mt.) **17** Hc
Porpoise Bay **42** grid square no.4
Porriño **9** Aa
Porsangen (b.) **4** Fa
Porsgrunn **4** Bd
Porsuk (riv.) **22** Cc
Portadown **7** Cd
Portage la Prairie **31** Fcd
Portalegre **9** Ac
Port–Alfred **32** Da
Port Alfred **26** Be
Port Angeles **33** Ab
Port Antonio **35** Cb
Port Arthur **32** Bc
Port Augusta **29** Fe
Port–au–Prince **30** Kh

Port Blair **15** Dh
Portbou **9** Ga
Port Burwell **31** Ib
Port–Cartier **31** Icd
Port–de–Bouc **8** Ff
Port–de–Paix **35** Cab
Port Douglas **29** Hb
Portel **38** Bb
Port Elizabeth **23** EFi
Port–Gentil **24** Ce
Port Harcourt **24** Cd
Port Hawkesbury **32** EFa
Port Hedland **29** Bbc
Porticcio **10** Bd
Portimão **9** Ad
Port Keats **29** Da
Portland [Austl.] **29** Gf
Portland [Me.–U.S.] **32** DEa
Portland [Or.–U.S.] **33** Ab
Port–la–Nouvelle **8** Ef
Portlaoise **7** Ce
Port Lincoln **29** EFef
Port Loko **24** Ad
Port Louis **23** map no.1
Port Macquarie **29** IJe
Port–Menier **31** Icd
Port Moresby **27** Cc
Port Nolloth **26** Ad
Port Nouveau–Québec **31** Ic
Porto **9** Ab
Pôrto Alegre [Braz.] **39** CDc
Pôrto Alegre [Braz.] **38** Bb
Porto Amboim **26** Ac
Porto Azzurro **10** Cc
Porto Cervo **10** Bd
Pôrto de Moz **38** Bb
Porto Empedocle **10** Df
Pôrto Esperança **39** Cab
Pôrto Esperidião **39** Ca
Portoferraio **10** Cc
Port–of–Spain **36** DEb
Pôrto Grande **38** BCa
Portogruaro **10** Db
Pôrto Murtinho **39** Cb
Pôrto Nacional **38** Cc
Porto Novo **24** Cd
Pôrto Santana **38** Bb
Porto Santo (i.) **24** Aa
Pôrto Seguro **39** Ea
Porto Torres **10** Bd
Porto–Vecchio **8** map no.1
Pôrto Velho **37** Cc
Portoviejo **37** Ac
Pôrto Walter **37** Bc
Port Phillip Bay **29** GHf
Port Pirie **29** Fe
Portree **7** Cc
Port Said **25** Da
Port Saint Johns **26** BCe
Port Shepstone **26** Ce
Portsmouth [N.H.–U.S.] **32** DEa
Portsmouth [U.K.] **7** Ff
Portsmouth [Va.–U.S.] **32** Db
Port Sudan **25** Dbc
Port Talbot **7** DEf
Portugal (Ind. St.) **3** Ccd
Port Vila **27** Dc
Posadas **39** Cb
Posavina (phys. reg.) **6** CDd
Posio **4** FGb
Positano **10** Ed
Poso **18** Fe

Postavy **12** Cbc
Poste–de–la–Baleine **31** Hc
Poste–Maurice–Cortier (Bidon 5) **24** Cb
Poste–Weygand **24** Cb
Postmasburg **26** Bd
Potchefstroom **26** Bd
Potenza **10** Ed
Potgietersrus **26** BCd
Poti **13** De
Potiskum **24** Dc
Potomac (riv.) **32** Db
Potosí **39** Bab
Potrerillos **39** Bb
Potsdam **5** Db
Póvoa de Varzim **9** Ab
Povorino **12** Fc
Povorotny, mys– **17** Cc
Povungnituk **31** GHbc
Powder (riv.) **33** Cb
Powell, Lake– **33** BCc
Powell River **31** Ccd
Poyang Hu (l.) **16** Ee
Požarevac **6** Ed
Poza Rica de Hidalgo **34** Cb
Pozarskoje **17** Da
Poznań **5** Fb
Pozoblanco **9** Cc
Pozzallo **10** Ef
Pozzuoli **10** Ed
Prachuap Khiri Khan **19** CDf
Praděd (mt.) **5** Fc
Prades **8** Ef
Præstø **5** CDa
Prague **5** Ec
Prahovo **6** Fd
Pranhita (riv.) **20** EFe
Prasonísion **11** Gf
Prato **10** Cc
Predeal, Pasul– **6** Gd
Pregolja (riv.) **5** Ha
Preili **4** Fd
Prenzlau **5** Db
Preobraženije **17** CDc
Preparis Island **19** Bf
Přerov **5** Fd
Prescott **33** Bc
Presidencia Roque Sáenz Peña **39** BCb
Presidente Dutra **38** Cb
Presidente Epitácio **39** Cb
Presidente Frei **42** grid square no.1
Presidente Prudente **39** Cb
Prešov **5** Hd
Prespa, Lake– **11** Dc
Presque Isle **32** Eb
Preston **7** Ee
Pretoria **23** Eh
Préveza **11** Dd
Priargunsk **14** EFd
Pribilof Islands **30** Bd
Priboj **6** De
Příbram **5** DEd
Prichard **32** Cb
Priekulė **12** Bb
Prieska **26** Bde
Prievidza **5** Gd
Prijedor **6** Cd
Prilep **11** Dc
Priluki **12** Dc
Primorsk **4** Gc
Primorski **17** Bc

Primorsko–Ahtarsk **12** Ed
Prince Albert **31** Bb
Prince Albert Peninsula **31** Da
Prince Albert Sound **31** Da
Prince Charles Island **31** Hb
Prince Charles Mountains **42** grid square no.2
Prince Edward Island (prov.) **31** Id
Prince Edward Islands **2**
Prince George **30** Fd
Prince of Wale, Cape– **41** grid square no.2
Prince of Wales Island [Ak.–U.S.] **31** Bc
Prince of Wales Island [Austl.] **29** Ga
Prince of Wales Island [Can.] **31** EFa
Prince Patrick Island **41** grid square no.2
Prince Regent Inlet **31** FGa
Prince Rupert **30** Fd
Princess Charlotte Bay **29** Ga
Príncipe (i.) **24** Cd
Principe da Beira **39** Ba
Prinsesse Astrid Kyst **42** grid square no.2
Prinsesse Ragnhild Kyst **42** grid square no.2
Prinzapolca **35** Bb
Priozersk **4** Gc
Pripjat (riv.) **13** Bd
Priština **11** Db
Pritzwalk **5** CDb
Privas **8** Fe
Priverno **10** Dd
Privolžski **12** Gc
Prizren **11** Db
Probolinggo **18** Df
Proddatur **20** Eef
Progreso **34** Db
Prokopievsk **13** Hd
Prokuplje **11** Db
Proletarsk **12** Fd
Prome **19** Ce
Propriá **38** Dc
Proserpine **29** Hlc
Prosna (riv.) **5** Gc
Prostějov **5** Fd
Provadija **11** Gb
Provence (phys. reg.) **8** FGef
Providence **32** DEa
Providence (i.) **23** Hf
Providencia, Isla de–(i.) **35** BCb
Providenija **14** Lc
Provo **33** Bbc
Pruszków **5** Hb
Prut (riv.) **12** Cd
Przemyśl **5** Fd
Prževalsk **13** Ge
Psará (i.) **11** Fd
Psël (riv.) **12** Dc
Pskov **13** BCd
Pskov, Lake– **4** FGd
Pszczyna **5** Gd
Ptič (riv.) **12** Cc
Ptolemaïs **11** Dc
Ptuj **6** BCc
Pucallpa **36** Cd
Puca Urco **37** Bc
Pucheng **16** Ee
Pucioasa **6** Gd

Pudož **12** Ea
Pudukkotai **20** Ef
Puebla, La– **9** Gc
Puebla de Guzmán **9** Bd
Puebla de Sanabria **9** Bab
Puebla de Zaragoza **30** Hlh
Pueblo **33** Cc
Pueblo Hundido **39** ABb
Puente–Genil **9** Cd
Pu'er **16** Bf
Puerto Acosta **38** Ac
Puerto Aisén **40** Ab
Puerto Ángel **34** Cc
Puerto Armuelles **35** Bc
Puerto Asís **37** Bb
Puerto Ayacucho **37** Cb
Puerto Barrios **30** Jh
Puerto Berrio **37** Bb
Puerto Cabello **37** Ca
Puerto Cabezas **35** Bb
Puerto Carreño **37** Cb
Puerto Casado **39** Cb
Puerto Chicama **37** ABc
Puerto Cortés [C.R.] **35** Bb
Puerto Cortés [Hond.] **35** Bc
Puerto Cumarebo **37** Ca
Puerto de Santa María, El– **9** Bd
Puerto Deseado **36** Dh
Puerto Huasco **39** Ab
Puerto Huitoto **37** Bb
Puerto Jesus **35** Bbc
Puerto Juárez **34** Db
Puerto La Cruz **37** Ca
Puerto Leguízamo **37** Bbc
Puertollano **9** CDc
Puerto Madryn **40** Bb
Puerto Maldonado **39** Ba
Puerto México → Coatzacoalcos **34** Cc
Puerto Montt **36** Ch
Puerto Morelos **34** Db
Puerto Natales **40** Ac
Puerto Páez **37** Cb
Puerto Peñasco **34** Aa
Puerto Pilón **35** map no.1
Puerto Pinasco **39** Cb
Puerto Princesa **18** Ebc
Puerto Rico (i.) **35** Db
Puerto Rico (Dep.) **30** Lgh
Puerto Rondón **37** Bb
Puerto Santa Cruz **40** Bbc
Puerto Siles **39** Ba
Puerto Suárez **39** Ca
Puerto Vallarta **34** Bb
Puerto Varas **40** Ab
Puerto Villazón **39** Ba
Puerto Wilches **37** Bb
Pugačev **12** Gc
Puget–Théniers **8** Gf
Puglia (reg.) **10** EFde
Pukapuka Atoll [Cook] **28** Ac
Pukapuka Atoll [Fr. Poly.] **28** Cc
Pula **6** Bd
Pulacayo **39** Bb
Pulap Atoll **27** Cb
Pulawy **5** Hlc
Pullman **33** Bb
Pulog, Mount– **18** Gb
Pułtusk **5** Hb
Puná, Isla– **37** ABc
Punaauia **28** map no.2

Punakha **20** GHc
Puncak Jaya (mt.) **27** Bc
Pune (Poona) **20** De
Punia **26** Bb
Punjab (phys. reg.) **20** DEb
Punjab (State) **20** DEb
Puno **39** ABa
Punta Alta **39** Bc
Punta Arenas **36** Ci
Punta del Este **39** Cc
Puntarenas **35** Bbc
Punto Fijo **37** Ba
Puquio **39** Aa
Pur (riv.) **13** Gc
Purchena **9** Dd
Puri **20** Gde
Purnia **19** Ij
Pursat **19** Df
Purukcahu **18** De
Puruliya **20** Gd
Purús (riv.) **37** Cc
Purús, Alto– (riv.) **37** Bcd
Purworkerto **18** Cf
Pusan **14** FGf
Puškin **4** Gd
Püspökladány **6** Ec
Putao **19** Cc
Putian **16** Ee
Puting, Tanjung– **18** De
Putjatin **16** Hb
Putorana, Plato– **14** Cc
Puttalam **20** Eg
Puttgarden **4** BCe
Putumayo (riv.) **37** Bc
Puulavesi (l.) **4** Fc
Puuwai **28** map no.1
Puy, Le– **8** EFe
Puy de Dôme (mt.) **8** Ee
Puyo **37** Bc
Pweto **26** Bb
Pwllheli **7** De
Pyapon **19** Ce
Pyhäjoki (riv.) **4** Fb
Pyinmana **19** Cde
P'yŏngyang **14** Ff
Pyrenees (mts.) **9** EFa
Pytalovo **4** FGd

Q

Qaanaaq / Thule **30** LMb
Qäbis **24** CDa
Qaḍārif, Al– **25** Dc
Qaḍīmah, Al– **21** Be
Qafşah **24** Ca
Qala–i–Panja **20** Da
Qal'at Bishah **21** Cef
Qal'eh–ye Now **20** Bab
Qallābāt **25** Dc
Qamar, Ghubbat al– **21** Ef
Qamdo **15** Df
Qāmishlī, Al– **21** Cb
Qandahār **15** Cd
Qanţarah, Al– **25** map no.1
Qaqortoq / Julianehåb **30** MNc
Qardho **25** Ed
Qarnayt, Jabal– (mt.) **21** BCe
Qarqan He (riv.) **16** Dc
Qārūn, Birkat– (l.) **22** Ch
Qaryat al'Ulya **21** Dd

Qaryatayn, Al– 22 Fe
Qaṣr, Al– 25 Cb
Qaṣr Farāfirah 25 Cb
Qasr Ḥamān 21 De
Qaṭanā 22 EFf
Qatar (Ind. St.) 21 Ed
Qatif, Al– 21 Dd
Qaṭrānī, Al– 22 Fg
Qaṭrūn, Al– 24 Db
Qattara Depression 25 Cab
Qayrawān, Al– 24 CDa
Qaysūmah, Al– 21 Dd
Qazvin 21 DEb
Qeqertarsuaq / Godhavn 30 MNc
Qeshm (i.) 21 Fd
Qiansuo 16 Be
Qiemo 15 Cf
Qilian Shan (mts.) 16 ABc
Qimantag (mts.) 16 DEc
Qinā 25 Db
Qingdao → Tsingtao 16 Fc
Qinghai (prov.) 16 EFc
Qinghai Hu (l.) 16 ABc
Qingjiang 16 Ed
Qingyang 16 Cc
Qinhuangdao 16 EFbc
Qin Ling (mts.) 16 CDd
Qinyang 16 Dcd
Qiongzhou Haixia 16 CDfg
Qiqihar 16 FGa
Qishn 21 Ef
Qixian 16 Dc
Qogir Feng → K 2 (mt.) 20 Ea
Qohrūd, Kūhhā– ye– 21 EFc
Qom 21 Ebc
Qomolangma Feng → Everest (mt.) 20 Gc
Qomsheh 21 Ec
Qondūz 20 CDa
Qornet es Saouda (mt.) 22 EFe
Qualāt 20 Cb
Quang Ngai 19 EFef
Quang Tri 19 Ee
Quan Long 19 DEg
Quanzhou 16 Eef
Quarai 39 Cc
Quartu Sant'Elena 10 Be
Quchān 21 Fb
Québec 31 Hld
Québec (prov.) 31 Hlc
Quedlinburg 5 Cc
Queen Charlotte Islands 31 Bc
Queen Charlotte Strait 31 BCc
Queen Elizabeth Islands 41 grid square no.2
Queen Mary Land 42 grid square no.4
Queen Maud Gulf 31 Eb
Queen Maud Land 42 grid square no.1
Queen Maud Range 42 grid square no.3
Queensland (State) 29 GHc
Queenstown [Austl.] 29 map no.1
Queenstown [S. Afr.] 26 Be
Queimadas 38 CDc
Quellón 40 Ab

Querétaro 34 BCb
Quetta 15 Cf
Quetzaltenango 35 Ab
Quezon City 15 Eh
Quiaca, La– 39 Bb
Quibala 26 Ac
Quibdó 37 Bb
Quiberon 8 Bd
Quillan 8 DEf
Quilon 20 Eg
Quilpie 29 GHd
Quimili 39 Bb
Quimper 8 Ad
Quimperlé 8 Bd
Quines 39 Bc
Qui Nhon 19 EFf
Quintanar de la Orden 9 DEc
Quito 36 BCcd
Quixadá 38 Db
Qujing 16 Be
Qulaybīyah 10 Cf
Qulbān an Nabk al Gharbī 22 Fg
Qunayṭirah, Al– 21 Bc
Qunfudhah, Al– 21 BCf
Qûs 25 Db
Quṣaymah, Al– 22 DEg
Quṣayr, Al– 25 Db
Quthing 26 Be
Quxian 16 Ee
Qyteti Stalin → Kuçovë 11 Dc

R

Raahe 4 Fb
Rab (i.) 10 Eb
Rába (riv.) 6 Cc
Raba 18 Ef
Rabat 24 Ba
Rabaul 27 Cc
Rabigh 21 Be
Rabyānah, Ramlat– (phys. reg.) 24 DEb
Race, Cape– 31 Jd
Rach Gia 19 DEfg
Racibórz 5 FGc
Racine 32 Ca
Rādăuţi 6 Gc
Radehov 6 Ga
Radom 5 Hc
Radomsko 5 Gc
Radomyśl 6 la
Raḍwā, Jabal– (mt.) 21 Be
Rae 31 Db
Rae Bareli 19 Hj
Rae Istmus 31 Gb
Raevavae, Île– (i.) 28 Bd
Rafaela 39 Bc
Rafha 21 Cd
Rafsanjān 21 EFc
Raga 25 Cd
Ragged Island Range 35 Ca
Ragusa 10 Ef
Raha 18 Fe
Rahad, Ar– 25 CDc
Rahov 6 FGbc
Raichur 20 Ee
Raiganj 19 IJj
Raigarh 20 Fd
Raijuva, Pulau– (i.) 18 Fg

Rainbow 29 Gf
Rainbow City 35 map no.1
Rainier, Mount– 33 Ab
Raippaluoto (i.) 4 DEc
Raipur 20 Fd
Raja, Bukit– (mt.) 18 Df
Rajahmundry 20 Fe
Rajang (riv.) 18 Dd
Rajasthan (State) 20 DEc
Rajgarh 19 Gi
Rajkot 20 Dd
Rājshāhi 19 Jj
Rakahanga Atoll 28 ABc
Rakata, Pulau– (is.) 18 BCf
Rakovník 5 Dc
Rakvere 4 Fd
Raleigh 30 Kf
Ralik Chain 27 Db
Rama 35 Bb
Ramapo Deep 27 Ca
Ramat Gan 22 Ef
Rambouillet 8 Dc
Ramganga (riv.) 19 Gj
Ramgarh 19 Ik
Rāmhormoz 21 DEc
Ramm, Jabal– (mt.) 22 EFh
Rampur 20 EFc
Ramree (i.) 19 Be
Ramsele 4 Dc
Ramsgate 7 Gf
Rancagua 39 ABc
Rance (riv.) 8 BCc
Ranchi 20 FGd
Ranco, Lago– 39 Acd
Randazzo 10 Ef
Randers 4 Bd
Randolph, Fort– 35 map no.1
Randon (mt.) 8 Ee
Rangia 19 Kj
Rangiroa Atoll 28 Bc
Rangoon 19 BCe
Rangpur 20 Gc
Raniganj 19 IJj
Rankin Inlet 31 FGb
Ranong 19 Cg
Rantauprapat 18 ABd
Rantekombola, Bulu– (mt.) 18 EFe
Ranua 4 Fb
Raohe 16 Ha
Raoul Island 27 DEd
Rapa, Île– (i.) 28 Bd
Rapallo 10 Bb
Rapid City 33 Cb
Rapla 4 Fd
Rapti (riv.) 19 Hj
Raqqah, Ar– 21 Bb
Rāqūbah, Ar– 24 Db
Raroïa Atoll 28 BCc
Rarotonga Atoll 28 ABd
Ra's ad Daqm 21 Ff
Ras al Khaymah 21 EFd
Ra's an Naqb 22 EFgh
Ra's as Saffānīyah 21 DEd
Ra's as Sidr 22 Dh
Ra's at Tannūrah 21 Ed
Ras Dashen Terara (mt.) 25 Dc
Ras el Ish 25 map no.1
Rashīd 22 BCg
Rasht 21 DEb
Raška 11 Db
Raskoh (mt.) 20 BCc

Ra's Lānūf 24 Da
Rason Lake 29 CDd
Rasskazovo 12 Fc
Rasšva, ostrov– (i.) 14 le
Rastatt 5 ABd
Rasu, Monte– 10 Bd
Ratak Chain 27 Db
Ratangarh 20 Dc
Rathenow 5 Db
Ratlam 20 DEd
Ratnagiri 20 De
Raton 33 Cc
Rättvik 4 Cc
Ratzeburg 5 Cb
Rauch 39 Cc
Raul Leoni, Represa– 37 Cb
Rauma 4 Ec
Rauma (riv.) 4 Bc
Raurkela 20 FGd
Ravānsar 21 Dbc
Rava–Russkaja 5 IJc
Ravenna 10 Db
Ravensburg 5 BCe
Ravenshoe 29 GHb
Ravensthorpe 29 BCe
Ravi (riv.) 20 Db
Rawalpindi 20 DEb
Rawicz 5 Fc
Rawlinna 29 CDe
Rawlins 33 Cc
Rawson 36 Dh
Raxaul 20 FGc
Raysut 21 Ef
Razdelnaja 6 IJc
Razdolnoje 17 BCc
Razgrad 11 Gb
Razlog 11 Ec
Ré, Ile de– (i.) 8 BCd
Reading [Pa.–U.S.] 32 Da
Reading [U.K.] 7 Ff
Read Island 31 Db
Real, Cordillera– (mts.) 37 Bc
Realicó 39 Bc
Reao Atoll 28 Cc
Reaside, Lake– 29 Cd
Rebecca, Lake– 29 Ce
Reboly 4 Gc
Rebun–Tō (i.) 16 Ja
Recherche, Archipelago of the– 29 Ce
Rečica 12 CDc
Recife 36 Gd
Recife, Cape– 26 Be
Reconquista 39 BCb
Red Bluff 33 Abc
Red Deer (riv.) 33 Ba
Red Deer 31 Dc
Redding 33 Ab
Red Lake (l.) 32 Ba
Red Lake 31 Fc
Redon 8 Bd
Redondela 9 Aa
Red River [Asia] 19 Dd
Red River [N.D.–U.S.] 32 Ba
Red River [N.M.–U.S.] 32 Bb
Redruth 7 Df
Red Sea 25 EFbc
Ree, Lake– 7 BCe
Regensburg 5 CDd
Reggane 24 BCb
Reggio di Calabria 10 Ee
Reggio nell'Emilia 10 Cb
Reghin 6 Gc

Regina [Can.] **31** Ec
Regina [Fr. Gui.] **38** Ba
Registan (phys. reg.) **20** BCb
Regnitz (riv.) **5** Cd
Reguengos de Monsaraz **9** Bc
Rehoboth **26** Ad
Rehovot **22** Eg
Reigate **7** Ff
Reims **8** Fc
Reina Adelaida, Archipiélago– (is.) **40** Ac
Reindeer Depot **31** Bb
Reindeer Lake **31** Ec
Reinosa **9** Ca
Remanso **38** Cb
Rembang **18** Df
Remiremont **8** Gc
Remscheid **5** Ac
Rendsburg **5** BCa
Rengat **18** Be
Reni **6** Id
Renmark **29** Ge
Rennell Island **27** CDc
Rennes **8** Fc
Rennick Glacier **42** grid square no.4
Reno (riv.) **10** Cb
Reno **33** ABbc
Réole, La– **8** CDe
Republican River **32** Bab
Repulse Bay **30** IJc
Requena [Peru] **37** Bc
Requena [Sp.] **9** Ec
Reşadiye Yarimadasi **11** Ge
Resia, Passo di– **10** Ca
Resistencia **39** BCb
Reşiţa (mts.) **6** Ed
Resolute **31** Fa
Resolution Island **31** Ib
Rethel **8** Fc
Réthimnon **11** Ff
Reunion (i.) **23** map no.1
Reus **9** Fb
Reuss (riv.) **5** Be
Reutlingen **5** Bd
Revda **12** IJb
Revelstoke **33** Ba
Revermont (mt.) **8** Fd
Revillagigedo, Islas– **30** GHh
Rewa **20** Fd
Rewari **19** Gij
Rex, Mount– **42** grid square no.1
Rey **21** Eb
Reykjanes (cap.) **4** map no.1
Reykjavik **4** map no.1
Reynosa **34** Cb
Rež **12** Jb
Rezé **8** Cd
Rēzekne **4** Fd
Rezina **6** Ic
Rhein (riv.) **5** Be
Rheine **5** Ab
Rheinland–Pfalz (phys. reg.) **5** Acd
Rhir, Cap– **24** ABa
Rhode Island (State) **32** Da
Rhodes **22** Bd
Rhodes (i.) **22** Bde
Rhodope Mountains **11** EFbc
Rhön (mt.) **5** BCc
Rhône (riv.) **10** Aa

Rhum (i.) **7** Cc
Riaño **9** Ca
Riau, Kepulauan– **18** Bd
Ribadeo **9** Ba
Ribas do Rio Pardo **39** Cb
Ribatejo (phys. reg.) **9** Ac
Ribáuè **26** Cc
Ribe **5** Ba
Ribeira (riv.) **39** Db
Ribeira → Santa Eugenia **9** Aa
Ribeirão Prêto **39** Db
Ribérac **8** CDe
Riberalta **37** Cd
Riccione **10** Dc
Richard's Bay **26** Cd
Richardson Mountains **31** Bb
Richard Toll **24** Ac
Richfield **33** Bc
Richland **33** Bb
Richmond [Austl.] **29** Gc
Richmond [In.–U.S.] **32** Cb
Richmond [Ky.–U.S.] **32** Cb
Richmond [Va.–U.S.] **32** Db
Ried im Innkreis **5** Dd
Riesa **5** Dc
Riesco, Isla– (i.) **40** Ac
Riesi **10** Ef
Rieti **10** Dc
Rif (mts.) **24** Ba
Rifstangi (cap.) **4** map no.1
Rift Valley **26** Cab
Riga **4** Fd
Riga, Gulf of– **4** EFd
Rihand (riv.) **20** Fd
Rihand Sägar **20** Fd
Riihimäki **4** EFc
Riiser–Larsen Halvøya **42** grid square no.2
Rijeka **6** Bd
Riksgränsen **4** Da
Rila (mts.) **11** Eb
Rimal, Ar– → Rub' al Khali **21** DEef
Rimatara, Île– (i.) **28** Bd
Rimavská Sobota **5** GHd
Rimini **10** Db
Rîmnicu Sărat **6** Hd
Rîmnicu Vîlcea **6** Gd
Ringebu **4** Bc
Ringerike **4** Bc
Ringsted **5** CDa
Ringus **19** Gj
Ringvassøy (i.) **4** Da
Rinjani, Gunung– (mt.) **18** Ef
Riobamba **37** Bc
Rio Branco **37** Ccd
Rio Brilhante **39** Cb
Rio Claro **39** Db
Rio Colorado **39** Bc
Rio Cuarto **39** Bc
Rio de Janeiro (State) **39** Db
Rio de Janeiro **39** Db
Rio Gallegos **36** Di
Rio Grande **39** Cc
Rio Grande **40** Bc
Rio Grande do Norte (State) **38** Db
Rio Grande do Sul (State) **39** Cbc
Riohacha **37** Ba
Rioja, La– **39** Bb
Rioja, La– (phys. reg.) **26** DEa

Rio Largo **38** Db
Riom **8** Ee
Rio Mayo **40** ABb
Río Mulatos **39** Ba
Rio Negro **39** CDb
Río Negro, Embalse del– (l.) **39** Cc
Rio Tercero **39** Bc
Rio Tinto **38** Db
Rio Verde **39** Ca
Rio Verde de Mato Grosso **39** Ca
Rishiri–Tō (i.) **16** Jab
Risle (riv.) **8** Dc
Risør **4** Bd
Ritchie's Archipelago **19** Bf
Ritter, Mount– **33** Bc
Riva → Cayağzi **22** Bb
Rivadavia [Arg.] **39** Bb
Rivadavia [Chile] **39** Ab
Riva del Garda **10** Cb
Rivas **35** Bb
Rive–de–Gier **8** Fe
Rivera [Arg.] **39** Bc
Rivera [Ur.] **39** Cc
River Cess **24** ABd
Riverside **33** Bc
Rivière–du–Loup **32** Ea
Rivoli **10** Ab
Riyadh **21** De
Rize **21** Ca
Rizzuto, Capo– **10** Fe
Rjazan **13** CDd
Rjažsk **12** Fc
Rjukan **4** ABd
Roa **9** CDb
Roanne **8** Fd
Roanoke **32** CDb
Roanoke (riv.) **32** Db
Roatán **35** Bb
Robert English Coast **42** grid square no.1
Robertsport **24** Ad
Robeson Channel **41** grid square no.1
Robinvale **29** Ge
Robla, La– **9** BCa
Roboré **39** BCa
Robson, Mount– **31** CDc
Roca, Cabo da– (cap.) **9** Ac
Roca Partida, Isla– (i.) **34** Ac
Rocas, Atol das– (i.) **38** Db
Rocha **39** Cc
Rochechouart **8** De
Rochefort **8** Ce
Rochelle, La– **8** Cd
Rochester [Mn.–U.S.] **32** Ba
Rochester [N.Y.–U.S.] **32** Da
Roche–sur–Yon, La– **8** Cd
Rockefeller Plateau (plat.) **42** grid square no.3
Rockford **32** Ca
Rockhampton **29** Ic
Rockingham **29** ABe
Rock Island **32** Ba
Rockland **32** Ea
Rock Springs **33** BCb
Rocky Mount **32** Db
Rocky Mountains **31** CDcd
Roda, La– **9** DEc
Rødberg **4** ABc
Rødbyhavn **5** Ca
Rodez **8** Ee
Rodrigues (i.) **23** map no.1

Roebourne **29** Bc
Roebuck Bay **29** Cb
Roermond **8** FGb
Roeselare **8** Eb
Roes Welcome Sound **31** Gb
Rogaguado, Lago– **39** Ba
Rognan **4** Cb
Rohtak **20** Ec
Roi Et **19** De
Roja, La– **36** Dfg
Rojo, Cabo– **34** Cb
Rokan (riv.) **18** Bd
Rolla **32** Bb
Roma **29** Hd
Roman **6** Hc
Romana, La– **35** Db
Romang, Pulau– (i.) **18** Gf
Români **25** map no.1
Romania (Ind. St.) **3** Fc
Romanovka **14** DEd
Romans–sur–Isère **8** Fe
Rome [Ga.–U.S.] **32** Cb
Rome [It.] **10** Dd
Romilly–sur–Seine **8** EFc
Romny **12** Dc
Rømø (i.) **5** Ba
Romorantin–Lanthenay **8** DEd
Ronas Hill **7** Fa
Ronave **27** map no.2
Roncador, Cayos de– (is.) **35** BCb
Roncador, Serra do– (mts.) **38** Bc
Roncesvalles **9** Ea
Ronda **9** Cd
Rondane (mt.) **4** Bc
Rondônia **37** Cd
Rondônia (State) **37** Cd
Rondonópolis **39** Ca
Rong, Kaôh– (i.) **19** Df
Ronge, La– **31** Bb
Rongelap Atoll **27** Db
Rønne **4** Ce
Rooniu (mt.) **28** map no.2
Roosendaal **8** Fb
Roosevelt, Rio– (riv.) **38** Ab
Roosevelt Island **42** grid square no.3
Roosevelt Lake **33** Bb
Roper River **29** Ea
Roper Valley **29** EFa
Roques, Islas los– (is.) **35** Db
Roquetas de Mar **9** Dd
Roraima (State) **37** Cb
Roraima, Monte– **37** CDb
Røros **4** BCc
Rørvik **4** BCb
Ros (riv.) **6** Ib
Rosa, Monte– **10** Ab
Rosário **38** Cb
Rosario [Arg.] **39** Bc
Rosario [Mex.] **34** Bb
Rosario [Mex.] **34** Aab
Rosario de la Frontera **39** Bb
Rosário do Sul **39** Cc
Rosário Oeste **39** Ca
Roseau **35** Db
Rosebery **29** map no.1
Rosebud **29** GHf
Roseburg **33** Ab
Rosenheim **5** CDe
Rosetown **31** Ec

Rosignano Marittimo **10** Cc
Roşiori de Vede **6** Gd
Roskilde **5** Da
Roslavl **13** Cd
Rossano **10** Fe
Ross Ice Shelf (gl.) **42** grid square no.3
Ross Island **42** grid square no.4
Rosslare **7** CDe
Rosso **24** Ac
Rossoš **12** Ec
Ross River **31** Bb
Ross Sea **42** grid square no.3
Røssvatnet (l.) **4** Cb
Røst (i.) **4** Bb
Rostock **5** Da
Rostock–Warnemünde **5** CDa
Rostov **12** Eb
Rostov–na–Donu **13** CDe
Roswell **33** Cc
Rota Island **27** Cb
Rothaar–Gebirge (mts.) **5** Bc
Rothera (i.) **42** grid square no.1
Rothesay **7** Dd
Roti, Pulau– (i.) **18** Fg
Rotidian Point **27** map no.1
Roto **29** GHe
Rotondo, Monte– **8** map no.1
Rotterdam **8** EFb
Rotterdam–Hoek van Holland **8** EFb
Rottweil **5** Bd
Rotuma Island **27** Dc
Roúbaix **8** Eb
Rouen **8** Dc
Round Mountain, The– (mt.) **29** le
Rousay (i.) **7** Eb
Roussillon (phys. reg.) **8** Ef
Rouyn **31** Hd
Rov (riv.) **6** Hb
Rovaniemi **4** Fb
Rovereto **10** Cb
Rovigo **10** Cb
Rovno **13** Bd
Rovuma (riv.) **26** Cc
Rowley Shoals (is.) **29** Bb
Roxas **18** Fb
Royal Canal **7** Ce
Royale, Isle– **32** Ca
Royal Tunbridge Wells **7** Gf
Royan **8** Ce
Roy Hill **29** BCc
Rozewie, Przylądek– (cap.) **4** De
Rožňava **5** Hd
Roztocze (mts.) **5** Icd
Rtanj (mt.) **6** EFe
Rtišćevo **13** Dd
Ruafa, El– **22** Eg
Ruapehu, Mount– **27** Dd
Rub'al Khali **21** DEef
Rub'al Khali (Ar Rimal) **21** DEef
Rubcovsk **13** Hd
Rubežnoje **12** Ed
Rubinéia **39** CDab
Rubio **37** Bb
Ruda Śląska **5** Gc
Rüdbär **20** Bbc
Rudkøbing **5** Ca
Rudnaja–Pristan **14** Ge
Rudnica **6** Ib

Rudničny **12** Hb
Rudny [Kaz.] **13** Fd
Rudny [Russia] **17** Db
Rudolf, Lake– **25** Dd
Rueil–Malmaison **8** DEc
Rufiji (riv.) **26** Cb
Rufino **39** Bc
Rufisque **24** Ac
Rugby **7** Fe
Rügen (i.) **4** Ce
Rügen → Bergen **5** Da
Ruhea **19** Jj
Ruhr (riv.) **5** Bc
Rui'an **16** Fe
Ruijin **16** Ee
Rujen (mt.) **11** Eb
Ruki (riv.) **26** Aab
Rukwa, Lake– **26** Cb
Ruma **6** Bd
Rumbek **25** Cd
Rum Cay (i.) **32** Dc
Rumia **5** Ga
Rum Jungle **29** DEa
Rummah, Wādī ar– **21** Cd
Rumoi **17** Gbc
Rungwa (riv.) **26** Cb
Rungwa **26** Cb
Ruo Shui (riv.) **16** Bb
Rupununi (riv.) **37** Db
Rurrenabaque **39** Ba
Rurutu, Île– (i.) **28** Bd
Ruşayris, Ar– **25** Dc
Ruse **11** FGb
Russas **38** Db
Russia (Ind. St.) **15** BDc
Russki, Ostrov– **17** BCc
Rustavi **13** De
Ruţbah, Ar– **21** Cc
Ruteng **18** Ff
Ruthenia (phys. reg.) **6** FGb
Rutland **32** Da
Rutland (i.) **19** Bf
Rutog **15** Cf
Ruvuma (riv.) **26** Cc
Ruwenzori (mt.) **25** CDde
Ruzajevka **12** Fc
Ružomberok **5** Gd
Rwanda (Ind. St.) **26** BCb
Rybačje → Issyk–Kul **13** Ge
Rybinsk **13** CDd
Rybinskoje vodohranilišče **13** Cd
Rybnica **6** Ic
Rybnik **5** Gc
Rylsk **12** DEc
Ryōtsu **17** EFef
Ryukyu Islands (Nansei–Shotō) **16** FGef
Rzeszów **5** HIc
Ržev **13** Cd

S

Saale (riv.) **5** Cc
Saalfeld **5** Cc
Saar (riv.) **5** Ad
Saarbrücken **5** Ad
Saaremaa (i.) **4** Ed
Saarlouis **5** Ad
Šabac **6** Bd
Sabadell **9** FGb

Sabah (State) **15** Di
Sabalān, Kūhhā– ye– (mt.) **21** Db
Sabanalarga **37** Ba
Sab'Bi' Ār **22** Ff
Sabhā **24** Db
Šabia, Nos– **11** Hb
Sabinas **34** Bb
Sabinas Hidalgo **34** BCb
Sabine (riv.) **32** Bb
Sabini, Monti– **10** Dc
Sable, Cape– [Can.] **31** Id
Sable, Cape– [U.S.] **32** Cc
Sable Island **30** LMe
Sables–d'Olonne, Les– **8** BCd
Sabor (riv.) **9** Bb
Şabrätah **24** Da
Sabrina Coast **42** grid square no.4
Sabya **21** Cf
Sabzevār **21** Fb
Sabzevārān **21** Fd
Sacajawea Peak **33** Bb
Sacedón **9** Db
Sachs Harbour **31** Ca
Šack **12** Fc
Sacramento (riv.) **33** Ac
Sacramento **33** ABc
Sacramento, Pampas del– (phys. reg.) **37** Bc
Sádaba **9** Ea
Sa' dah **21** Cf
Saddle Island **28** map no.4
Sadiya **15** Dg
Sado (riv.) **9** Ac
Sado–Shima (i.) **16** Ic
Şadrinsk **13** Fd
Şafāqis **24** CDa
Säffle **4** Cd
Safi **24** ABa
Şāfī, Aş– **22** Eg
Safid (riv.) **21** Db
Safonovo **12** Db
Saga [Chͥna] **19** Jj
Saga [Jap.] **16** GHd
Sagaing **19** BCd
Sagar **20** Ed
Sagauli **19** Ij
Saginaw **32** Ca
Sagiz (riv.) **12** Hd
Sagiz **12** HId
Sagra, La– (mt.) **9** Dd
Sagres **9** Ad
Sagua La Grande **35** BCa
Sagunto **9** EFc
Sahagún **9** Ca
Sahara (des.) **24** CDb
Saharan Atlas (mts.) **24** BCa
Saharanpur **20** Dc
Saharsa **19** Ij
Sahibganj **19** IJj
Sahiwal **20** Db
Šahty **13** De
Šahunja **12** Gb
Sai (riv.) **19** Hj
Sa'īdābād **21** EFd
Saidpur [Bngl.] **19** Jj
Saidpur [India] **19** Hj
Saiki **17** BCh
Saimaa **4** FGc
Saimaan Canal **4** FGc
Saint Affrique **8** Ef

Saint Albans **7** Ff
Saint Amand–Mont–Rond **8** Ed
Saint André, Cap– (cap.) **26** map no.1
Saint Andrews **7** Ec
Saint Anthony **31** Jc
Saint Augustine **32** CDbc
Saint Austell **7** Df
Saint Bernard Paß (p.) **10** Ba
Saint Boniface **31** Fcd
Saint Brieuc **8** Bc
Saint Catharines **32** CDa
Saint Céré **8** DEe
Saint Chamond **8** EFe
Saint Charles **32** Bb
Saint Christopher / Saint Kitts **35** Db
Saint–Claude **8** FGd
Saint Cloud **32** Ba
Saint Croix (i.) **35** Db
Saint David's Head (cap.) **7** Df
Saint Denis [Fr.] **8** Ec
Saint Denis [Reu.] **23** map no.1
Saint Dié **8** Gc
Saint Dizier **8** Fc
Saint Elias, Mount– **31** ABbc
Saint Elias Mountains **31** ABbc
Saint Elie **37** Db
Sainte Marie, Cap– (cap.) **26** map no.1
Saintes **8** Ce
Sainte Savine **8** EFc
Saint Étienne **8** Ee
Saint Étienne–du–Rouvray **8** Dc
Saint Florent, Golfe de– **8** map no.1
Saint Flour **8** Ee
Saint Gaudens **8** Df
Saint George [Austl.] **29** Hd
Saint George [U.S.] **33** Bc
Saint Georges (i.) **35** Db
Saint George's **37** Ca
Saint Georges **38** Ba
Saint George's Channel **7** CDef
Saint Girons **8** Df
Saint Helena (i.) **23** Bg
Saint Helena Bay **26** Ae
Saint Helens **7** Ee
Saint Helier **8** Bc
Saint Hyacinthe **31** Hd
Saint Jean, Lac– (l.) **31** Hd
Saint Jean–d'Angély **8** Cde
Saint Jean–de–Luz **8** Cf
Saint Jean–Pied–de–Port **8** Cf
Saint John **31** Id
Saint John (riv.) **32** Ea
Saint John's [Atg.] **35** Db
Saint John's [Can.] **31** JKd
Saint Joseph **32** Bab
Saint Jurien **8** De
Saint Kilda (i.) **7** Bc
Saint Kitts / Saint Christopher (i.) **35** Db
Saint Kitts–Nevis (Ind. St.) **30** Lh
Saint Laurent **37** Db

Saint Lawrence (riv.) 31 Id
Saint Lawrence 29 Hc
Saint Lawrence, Gulf of– 31 Id
Saint Lawrence Island 15 Gcd
Saint Lô 8 Cc
Saint Louis 32 BCb
Saint–Louis 24 Ac
Saint Lucia (Ind. St.) 30 Lh
Saint Magnus Bay 7 EFa
Saint Maixent–l'École 8 CDd
Saint Malo 8 BCc
Saint–Malo, Golfe de– 8 BCc
Saint Marc 35 Cb
Saint Martin / Sint Maarten (i.) 35 Db
Saint Mary Peak 29 FGe
Saint Marys 29 map no.1
Saint Mathew Island 30 Ac
Saint–Mathieu, Pointe de– (cap.) 8 Ac
Saint Matthias Group 27 Cc
Saint Maur–des–Fossés 8 Ec
Saint Nazaire 8 Bd
Saint–Omer 8 DEb
Saintonge (phys. reg.) 8 Ce
Saint Paul 32 Ba
Saint Paul, Île– (i.) 2
Saint Petersburg 32 Cc
Saint Petersburg (Leningrad) 13 Cd
Saint Pierre (i.) 31 Jd
Saint Pierre and Miquelon 31 Jd
Saint–Quentin 8 Ec
Saint Raphaël 8 Gf
Saint Sever 8 Cf
Saint Tropez 8 Gf
Saint Vincent, Gulf– 29 Fef
Saint Vincent and the Grenadines (Ind. St.) 36 DEb
Saipan Island 27 Cb
Saito 17 Bh
Sajak 13 Ge
Sajama, Nevado de– (mt.) 39 Ba
Sajn–Šand 14 Ee
Sakai 16 Id
Sakaiminato 17 CDg
Sakakah 21 Ccd
Sakakawea, Lake– 33 Cb
Sakania 26 BCc
Sakarya (riv.) 22 Cb
Sakata 16 IJc
Sakhalin (i.) 14 Hd
Sakishima–Shotō 16 FGf
Sakmara (riv.) 12 Ic
Sakon Nakhon 19 De
Sakrivier 26 ABe
Sala 4 Dcd
Sala Consilina 10 Ed
Saladillo 39 Cc
Salado, Ojos del– 39 Bb
Salado, Río– [Arg.] (riv.) 39 Bc
Salado, Río– [Arg.] (riv.) 39 Bb
Salado, Río– [Mex.] (riv.) 34 Bb
Šalakuša 12 Fa
Salalah 21 Ef

Salamanca [Mex.] 34 Bb
Salamanca [Sp.] 9 Cb
Salamat, Bahr– (riv.) 25 BCcd
Salamís (i.) 11 Ee
Salamīyah, As– 22 Fe
Salamiyah, As– 21 De
Salavat 13 Ed
Salawati, Pulau– (i.) 18 GHe
Sala y Gomes (i.) 2
Salcantay (mt.) 37 Bd
Saldanha 23 Di
Sale 29 Hf
Salehard 13 FGc
Salem [India] 20 Ef
Salem [U.S.] 33 Ab
Salemi 10 Df
Sälen 4 Cc
Salerno 10 Ed
Salerno, Golfo di– 10 Ed
Salgótarján 6 Db
Sálhīya, El– 22 CDg
Salihli 22 Bc
Salima 26 Cc
Salīmah, Wāḥāt– 25 Cb
Salina 31 Ab
Salina (i.) 10 Ee
Salina Cruz 34 Cc
Salinas [Braz.] 39 Da
Salinas [Ec.] 37 Ac
Salinas [U.S.] 33 Ac
Salinas de Hidalgo 34 Bb
Salinas Grandes (s. m.) 39 Bbc
Salinas Grandes 39 Bb
Salinas Victoria 34 Bb
Salinópolis 38 Cb
Salins–les–Bains 8 FGd
Salisbury [U.K.] 7 EFf
Salisbury [U.S.] 32 Db
Salisbury [Zimb.] 23 Fg
Salisbury → Harare 26 Cc
Salisbury Island 31 Hb
Šalkar, ozero– 12 Hc
Salla 4 Gb
Sallūm, As– 25 Ca
Sallyana 20 Fc
Salmon 33 Bb
Salmon River 33 Bb
Salo 4 Ec
Salon–de–Provence 8 Ff
Salonga (riv.) 26 Bb
Salonika 11 Ec
Salonika, Gulf of– 11 Ecd
Salonta 6 EFc
Salpausselkä (mts.) 4 FGc
Salsk 12 Fd
Salso (riv.) 10 Df
Salsomaggiore Terme 10 Bb
Salṭ, As– 22 Efg
Salta 39 Bb
Salten (phys. reg.) 4 CDb
Saltfjord (g.) 4 Cb
Saltillo 34 Bb
Salt Lake City 33 Bbc
Salto 36 Eg
Salto, El– 34 Bb
Salton Sea 33 Bc
Salt Range 20 Db
Salt River 33 Bc
Salur 20 Ef
Saluzzo 10 Ab
Salvador 38 Dc
Salvaleón de Higüey 35 Db

Salween (riv.) 19 Cde
Salzach (riv.) 5 De
Salzburg 5 De
Salzgitter 5 Cb
Salzwedel 5 Cb
Samalaeulu 28 map no.5
Samales Group 18 Fc
Samana Cay (is.) 35 Ca
Samandaği 22 Ede
San Carlos de Bolivar 39 Bc
Samar (i.) 15 Eh
Samara (riv.) 12 Hc
Samara (Kujbyšev) 13 Ed
Samarai 27 Cc
Samariapo 37 Cb
Samarinda 18 Ee
Samarkand 13 FGf
Samarra 21 Cc
Samar Sea 18 Fb
Samarskoje vodohranilišče 12 GHc
Samastipur 19 Ij
Samaúma 37 CDc
Samāwash, As– 21 Dc
Sambalpur 20 Fd
Sambas 18 Cd
Sambava 26 map no.1
Sambhal 19 Gj
Sambhar 20 DEc
Sombor 6 Fb
Sambre (riv.) 8 Eb
Samch'ŏk 17 Af
Samoa Islands 28 Ac
Samokov 11 Eb
Sámos 22 Ad
Sámos (i.) 22 Ad
Samothrace (i.) 11 Fc
Sampit 18 De
Samsun 22 Fb
Samui, Ko– (i.) 19 CDg
Samut Prakan 19 Df
San 24 Bc
San (riv.) 5 Ic
Sana 19 Cd
San'a 21 CDf
Sanae 42 grid square no.1
Sanaga (riv.) 24 Dd
San Agustín 37 Bb
San Ambrosio (i.) 36 Cf
Sanana 18 Ge
Sanana, Pulau– (i.) 18 Ge
Sanandaj 21 Db
Sanandita 39 Bb
San Andrés, Isla– 35 Bb
San Andrés Tuxtla 34 Cc
San Angelo 33 Cc
San Antonio [Chile] 39 Ac
San Antonio [Chile] 39 ABb
San Antonio [U.S.] 32 Bc
San Antonio, Cabo– [Arg.] 39 Cc
San Antonio, Cabo– [C.R.] 35 Ba
San Antonio de Lipez 39 Bb
San Antonio de los Cobres 39 Bb
San Antonio Oeste 40 Bb
San Benedetto del Tronto 10 Dc
San Benedicto, Isla– (i.) 34 ABc
San Bernardino 33 Bc
San Bernardo 39 Ac
San Blas 34 Bb

San Borja 39 Ba
San Carlos [Chile] 39 Ac
San Carlos [Nic.] 35 Bb
San Carlos [Phil.] 18 EFa
San Carlos [Phil.] 18 Fb
San Carlos [Ven.] 37 Cb
San Carlos de Bariloche 40 ABb
San Carlos de Bolivar 39 Bc
San Carlos de la Rapita 9 Fb
San Carlos de Río Negro 37 Cb
San Carlos de Zulia 37 Bb
Sánchez 35 Db
Sanchi (mts.) 17 Gf
San Cristóbal [Arg.] 39 Bc
San Cristóbal [Ven.] 37 Bb
San Cristóbal de las Casas 34 Cc
San Cristóbal Island 27 Dc
Sancti Spíritus 35 BCa
Sančursk 12 Gb
Sandakan 15 DEi
Sandanski 11 Ec
Sanday (i.) 7 EFb
San Diego 33 Bc
San Diego, Cabo– 40 Bc
Sandıklı 22 Cc
Sandila 19 Hj
Sanding, Pulau– (i.) 18 ABe
Sandnes 4 Ad
Sandnessjøen 4 BCb
Sandoa 26 Bb
Sandomierz 5 Hc
San Donà di Piave 10 Db
Sandover River 29 Fc
Sandowaj 19 Be
Sandpoint 33 Bb
Sandras dağ (mt.) 22 Bd
Sandspit 31 Bc
Sandstone 29 BCd
Sandur 4 map no.1
Sandusky 32 Ca
Sandvig–Allinge 5 Ea
Sandviken 4 CDc
Sandwip (i.) 19 Jk
Sandy Cape 29 Ic
Sandy Lake 31 Fc
Sandžak (phys. reg.) 11 CDb
San Felipe [Chile] 39 Ac
San Felipe [Col.] 37 Cb
San Felipe [Mex.] 34 Aa
San Felipe [Ven.] 37 Ca
San Felipe de Puerto Plata 35 CDab
San Félix (i.) 36 Bf
San Fernando [Chile] 39 Ac
San Fernando [Mex.] 34 Cb
San Fernando [Phil.] 18 EFa
San Fernando [Phil.] 18 EFa
San Fernando [Sp.] 9 Bd
San Fernando [Trin.] 37 CDab
San Fernando de Apure 37 Cb
San Fernando de Atabapo 37 Cb
Sanford 32 Cc
San Francisco [Arg.] 39 Bc
San Francisco [U.S.] 33 Ac
San Francisco, Paso– (p.) 39 Bb
San Francisco de Macorís 35 CDb

San Francisco Javier **9** Fc
San Gallan, Isla– **37** Bd
Sangar **14** FGc
Sangeang, Pulau– (i.) **18** Ef
Sanggau **18** CDde
Sangha (riv.) **24** Dd
Sangihe, Pulau– (i.) **18** FGd
Sangi Islands **18** Gd
San Gil **37** Bb
San Giovanni in Fiore **10** Fe
Sangkulirang **18** Ed
Sangli **20** DEe
San Gottardo (p.) **10** Ba
Sangre de Cristo Mounts **33** Cc
Sangue, Rio do– (riv.) **38** Bc
San Ignacio **39** Ba
San Javier **39** Ba
Sanjö **17** Ff
San Joaquin (riv.) **33** Ac
San Jorge, Golfo– **40** Bb
San José [Bol.] **39** Ba
San José [C.R.] **35** Bc
San José [Guat.] **35** Ab
San Jose [Phil.] **18** Fa
San Jose [Phil.] **18** Fb
San José [U.S.] **33** Ac
San Jose de Buenavista **18** Fb
San José de Jáchal **39** Bbc
San José del Cabo **34** Bb
San José del Guaviare **37** Bb
San José de Mayo **39** Cc
San José de Ocune **37** BCb
San Juan (i.) **30** Lh
San Juan (riv.) **33** BCc
San Juan [Arg.] **39** ABc
San Juan [Peru] **39** Aa
San Juan, Río– **35** Bb
San Juan Bautista **39** Cb
San Juan de la Maguana **35** Cb
San Juan del Norte **35** Bb
San Juan de los Cayos **37** Ca
San Juan de los Morros **37** Cb
San Julián **36** Dh
San Justo **39** BCc
Sankh (riv.) **19** Ik
Sankosh (riv.) **15** Pj
Sankt Gallen **5** Be
Sankt Moritz **10** Ba
Sankt Pölten **5** Ed
Sankt Veit an der Glan **5** DEe
Sankuru (riv.) **26** Bb
San Lázaro, Cabo– **34** Ab
San Lorenzo **37** Bb
San Lorenzo de El Escorial **9** CDb
Sanlúcar de Barrameda **9** Bd
San Luis [Arg.] **39** Bc
San Luis [Mex.] **33** Cd
San Luis Obispo **33** Ac
San Luis Potosí **30** HIg
San Marco, Capo– **10** Be
San Marcos **32** Bbc
San Marino **10** Dbc
San Marino (Ind. St.) **10** Dbc
San Martín (sc. stat.) **42** grid square no.1
San Martín **37** Bb
San Martin (riv.) **39** Ba
San Martin, Lago– **40** Ab

San Martín de los Andes **40** ABab
San Martín de Valdeiglesias **9** Cb
San Mateo **33** Ac
San Matías **39** Ca
San Matías, Golfo– **40** Bb
San Miguel (riv.) **39** Ba
San Miguel **35** Bb
San Miguel de Tucumán **39** Bb
San Miguel Islands **18** Ec
San Miguel Islands **18** Ec
Sanmyaku (mts.) **17** EFg
Sannär **25** Dc
Sannicandro Garganico **10** Ed
San Nicolás de los Arroyos **39** Bc
Sanok **5** HId
San Pablo **18** Fb
San Pedro [Arg.] **39** Bb
San Pedro [I.C.] **24** Bd
San Pedro [Par.] **39** Cb
San Pedro de Arimena **37** Bb
San Pedro de las Bocas **37** Cb
San Pedro de las Colonias **34** Bb
San Pedro Sula **35** Bb
San Pietro **10** Be
Sanquhar **7** DEd
San Quintín **34** Aa
San Rafael [Arg.] **39** Bc
San Rafael [Ven.] **37** Ba
San Ramón de la Nueva Orán **39** Bb
San Remo **10** Ac
San Roque **9** Cd
San Salvador **35** Bb
San Salvador (i.) **32** Dc
San Salvador de Jujuy **39** Bb
Sansanné–Mango **24** Cc
San Sebastián **9** DEa
San Severo **10** Ed
Santa, Río– (riv.) **37** Bc
Santa Ana [Bol.] **39** Ba
Santa Ana [El Sal.] **35** ABb
Santa Ana [U.S.] **33** Bc
Santa Bárbara **34** Bb
Santa Barbara **33** ABc
Santa Catarina (State) **39** CDb
Santa Clara **35** BCa
Santa Coloma de Gramanet **9** Gb
Santa Cruz (riv.) **40** ABc
Santa Cruz [Phil.] **18** Fb
Santa Cruz [U.S.] **33** Ac
Santa Cruz de la Sierra **39** Ba
Santa Cruz del Sur **35** Ca
Santa Cruz de Moya **9** Ec
Santa Cruz de Tenerife **24** Ab
Santa Cruz do Sul **39** Cb
Santa Cruz Islands **27** Dc
Santa Elena de Uairén **37** CDb
Santa Eugenia (Ribeira) **9** Aa
Santa Eulália del Río **9** FGc
Santafé **9** Dd
Santa Fe **30** Hf
Santa Fe **36** DEg
Santa Fe de Bogotá **36** Cc
Santa Genoveva (mt.) **34** Ab

Santahar **19** Jj
Santa Inés, Isla– (i.) **40** Ac
Santa Isabel [Arg.] **39** Bc
Santa Isabel [Braz.] **39** Ba
Santa Isabel Island **27** CDc
Santa Maria [Braz.] **39** Cb
Santa Maria [U.S.] **33** Ac
Santa Maria da Vitória **38** Cc
Santa Maria di Leuca, Capo– **10** Ge
Santa María Island **28** map no.4
Santa Marta **37** Ba
Santa Maura → Leucade (i.) **11** Dd
Santa Monica **33** ABc
Santana do Livramento **39** Cc
Santander **9** Da
Sant'Antioco (i.) **10** Be
Santañy **9** Gc
Santarém [Braz.] **36** Ed
Santarém [Port.] **9** Ac
Santa Rosa [Arg.] **39** Bc
Santa Rosa [Braz.] **39** Cb
Santa Rosa [Ca.–U.S.] **33** Ac
Santa Rosa [Hond.] **35** Bb
Santa Rosa [N.M.–U.S.] **33** Cc
Santa Rosalía **34** Ab
Santa Vitória do Palmar **39** Cc
Sant'Eufemia, Golfo di– **10** Fe
Sant Felíu de Guíxols **9** Gb
Santiago (riv.) **37** Bc
Santiago [Chile] **39** ABc
Santiago [Pan.] **35** Bc
Santiago [Sp.] **9** Aa
Santiago, Río Grande de– (riv.) **34** Bb
Santiago de Cuba **35** Cab
Santiago de la Ribera **9** EFd
Santiago del Estero **39** Bb
Santiago Papasquiaro **34** Bb
Santo Amaro **38** Dc
Santo André **39** Db
Santo Antonio Abad **9** Fc
Santo Antônio de Jesus **38** CDc
Santo Antônio do Içá **37** Cc
Santo Antônio do Leverger **39** Ca
Santo Domingo [Dom. Rep.] **30** KLh
Santo Domingo [Mex.] **34** Bb
Santo Domingo del Pacífico **34** Ab
Santoña **9** Da
Santos **39** Db
Santo Tomé **39** Cb
San Valentín, Cerro– (mt.) **40** Ab
San Vicente **35** Bb
San Vicente de Cañete **37** Bd
San Vicente de la Barquera **9** CDa
San Vito, Capo– **10** De
São Borja **39** Cb
São Félix **38** Bc
São Félix do Xingu **38** Bb
São Francisco (riv.) **38** Cc
São Francisco do Sul **39** Db

São João del Rei **39** Db
São José do Rio Prêto **39** CDb
São Leopoldo **39** CDb
São Lourenço (riv.) **39** Ca
São Luís **38** Cb
São Luís Gonzaga **39** Cb
São Marcos, Baía de– (b.) **38** Cb
São Mateus **39** Ea
Saône (riv.) **8** Fd
São Paulo (State) **39** CDb
São Paulo **39** Db
São Paulo de Olivença **37** Cc
São Pedro e São Paulo, Penedos de– (is.) **36** GHc
São Raimundo Nonato **38** Cb
São Roque, Cabo– **38** Db
São Sebastião, Ilha de– (i.) **39** Db
São Sebastião, Ponta– (cap.) **26** Cd
São Simão **39** CDa
São Tomé (i.) **24** Cde
Sao Tome and Principe (Ind. St.) **23** Ce
Saoura (riv.) **24** Bb
São Vicente, Cabo de– (cap.) **9** Ad
Sapiénta (i.) **11** De
Sapporo **16** Jb
Sapudi, Pulau– (i.) **18** Df
Saqqez **21** Db
Saraburi **19** Df
Saragossa **9** Eb
Sarajevo **6** DEe
Saraji Mine **29** Hc
Sarakhs **21** Gb
Saraktaš **12** Ic
Saramati (mt.) **19** BCc
Saran **13** Ge
Saranda **11** CDd
Sarangani Islands **18** Gc
Saransk **13** Dd
Sarapul **13** Ed
Sarasota **32** Cc
Saratov **13** Dd
Saratovskoje vodohranilišče **12** Gc
Saravan **19** Ee
Sarawak (State) **15** Di
Säräyä **22** Ee
Sarbisheh **21** FGc
Sardinia (reg.) **10** Bde
Sarektjåkkå (mt.) **4** Db
Sargodha **20** Db
Šargorod **6** HIb
Sarh **25** BCd
Sârî **21** Eb
Saría (i.) **11** Gf
Sarikei **18** Cd
Sarina **29** HIc
Sariñena **9** Eb
Sarïr **24** Eb
Sariwon **16** Gc
Šarja **13** Dd
Sark (i.) **8** Bc
Şarkişla **22** Fc
Şarköy **22** Ab
Sarlat–la–Canéda **8** De
Sarmiento **40** Bb
Särna **4** Cc
Sarnen **5** ABe

Sarnia 31 Gd
Sarny 13 Bd
Saroako 18 Fe
Saroma–Ko 17 Hlb
Saronikos Kólpos 11 Ee
Saros, Gulf of– 22 Ab
Sárospatak 6 Eb
Šar planina (mts.) 11 Dbc
Sarpsborg 4 BCd
Sarrebourg 8 Gc
Sarreguemines 8 Gc
Sarria 9 Ba
Sars, As– 10 Bf
Sartène 8 map no.1
Sarthe (riv.) 8 Cd
Sárvár 6 Cc
Saryč, mys– 12 De
Sary–Šagan 13 Ge
Sarysu (riv.) 13 Fe
Sary–Taš 13 Gef
Saryžaz 13 GHe
Sasebo 16 Gd
Saskatchewan (prov.) 31 Ec
Saskatchewan (riv.) 31 Bb
Saskatoon 33 Ca
Saskylah 14 Eb
Sasovo 12 Fc
Sassandra (riv.) 24 Bd
Sassandra 24 Bd
Sassari 10 Bd
Sassnitz 4 Ce
Sata–Misaki 17 Bi
Satara 20 De
Satawal Island 27 Cb
Säter 4 CDc
Satka 12 Ibc
Satna 20 Fcd
Sátoraljaújhely 6 Eb
Sätpura Range 20 Ed
Satsuma–Hantō 17 ABi
Sattahip 19 CDf
Satu Mare 6 Fc
Satun 19 Cg
Sauda 4 Ad
Saudárkrókur 4 map no.1
Saudi Arabia (Ind. St.) 15 Bgh
Sauldre (riv.) 8 Ed
Sault Sainte Marie [Can.] 31 Gd
Sault Sainte Marie [U.S.] 32 Ca
Saumur 8 Cd
Saurimo 26 Bbc
Sava (riv.) 6 Dd
Savai'i Island 28 Ac
Savannah (riv.) 32 Cb
Savannah 32 CDb
Savannakhet 19 DEe
Savanna–la–Mar 35 Cb
Savaştepe 22 ABc
Savé 24 Cd
Save [Fr.] (riv.) 8 Df
Save [Moz.] (riv.) 26 Cd
Saveh 21 DEb
Savigliano 10 Ab
Savona 10 Bb
Savoy (hist. reg.) 8 Gde
Savran 6 IJb
Savusavu 28 map no.6
Savu Sea 18 Ffg

Sawahlunto 18 Be
Sawai Madhopur 20 Ec
Sawäkin 25 Dc
Sawhāj 25 Db
Sawqirah 21 Ff
Şawqirah, Ghubbat– 21 Ff
Sawu, Pulau– (i.) 18 Fg
Saxony (phys. reg.) 5 DEc
Say 24 Cc
Sayhut 21 Efg
Sazanit, Ishull i– (i.) 11 Cc
Sázava (riv.) 5 Ed
Scapa Flow (g.) 7 Eb
Scarborough 7 FGd
Scarborough Reef (i.) 18 Ea
Šćekino 12 Ec
Schaffhausen 5 Be
Schefferville 30 Ld
Schelde (riv.) 8 EFb
Schenectady 32 Da
Schleswig 5 Ba
Schleswig–Holstein (State) 5 BCab
Schlüchtern 5 Bc
Schmidta, ostrov– 14 BCa
Schouwen (i.) 8 Eb
Schwaben (phys. reg.) 5 BCde
Schwäbische Alb (mts.) 5 BCd
Schwäbisch Hall 5 BCd
Schwandorf in Bayern 5 Dd
Schwaner, Pegunungan– 18 De
Schwarze Elster (riv.) 5 Dc
Schwedt 5 Eb
Schweinfurt 5 Cc
Schwerin 5 Cb
Sciacca 10 Df
Scicli 10 Ef
Šćigry 12 Ec
Scilly, Isles of– 7 Cg
Scoresby Land 41 grid square no.1
Scoresbysund / Itseqqortoormit 30 PQb
Šćors 12 Dc
Scotland (reg.) 7 DEcd
Scott 42 grid square no.4
Scott, Cape– 31 Cb
Scott, Mount– 33 Ab
Scott Island 42 grid square no.3
Scott Reef (i.) 29 Ca
Scottsbluff 33 Cb
Scottsdale [Austl.] 29 map no.1
Scottsdale [U.S.] 33 Bc
Scranton 32 Da
Šćučinsk 13 Gd
Scunthorpe 7 FGe
Scutari, Lake– 11 Cb
Seabra 38 Cc
Seal, Cape– 26 Be
Seattle 33 Ab
Sebastián Vizcaíno, Bahía– (g.) 34 Ab
Šebekino 12 Ec
Seben 22 Cb
Sebeş 6 Fd
Sebuku, Pulau– (i.) 18 Ee
Secchia (riv.) 10 Cb
Sechura, Bahía de– 37 Ac

Sechura, Desierto de– (des.) 37 ABc
Second Cataract 25 CDb
Sedan 8 Fc
Sederot 22 Eg
Sédhiou 24 Ac
Seeheim 26 Ad
Sefidar, Küh– e– (mt.) 21 Ed
Segeža 13 Cc
Ségou 24 Bc
Segovia 9 Cb
Segré 8 Cd
Segre (riv.) 9 Fb
Seguédine 24 Dbc
Séguéla 24 Bd
Seguin 32 Bc
Segura (riv.) 9 DEc
Segura, Sierra de– (mts.) 9 Dcd
Sehwan 20 Cc
Seinäjoki 4 EFc
Seine (riv.) 8 Dc
Seine, Baie de la– 8 Cc
Sejm (riv.) 12 Dc
Sejmčan 14 Ic
Sekondi–Takoradi 24 Bd
Sekota 25 DEc
Šeksna 12 Eb
Šelagski, mys– 14 Kb
Selajar, Pulau– (i.) 18 EFf
Selajar, Selat– 18 EFf
Selatan, Cape– 18 De
Selçuk 11 Gde
Selemdža (riv.) 14 Gd
Selenga (riv.) 14 De
Sélestat 8 Gc
Sélibabi 24 Ac
Selinunte (r.) 10 Df
Selkirk 7 Ed
Selkirk Mountains 33 Bab
Selma 32 Cb
Selvagens, Ilhas– 24 Aab
Selvas (phys. reg.) 37 CDc
Selwyn 29 Gc
Selwyn Range 29 FGc
Semani (riv.) 11 Cc
Semara 24 ABb
Semarang 15 Dj
Semenovka 12 Dc
Semeru, Gunung– (mt.) 18 Df
Semiluki 12 Ec
Semipalatinsk 13 GHd
Semmering (p.) 5 Ee
Semnān 21 Eb
Šemonaiha 13 GHd
Semur–en–Auxois 8 Fd
Senador Pompeu 38 Db
Sena Madureira 37 Cc
Senanga 26 Bc
Sendai [Jap.] 17 ABhi
Sendai [Jap.] 16 Jc
Senegal (riv.) 24 Ac
Senegal (Ind. St.) 23 Ad
Senftenberg 5 Ec
Sengilej 12 Gc
Senhor do Bonfim 38 CDc
Senigallia 10 Dc
Senj 6 Bd
Senja (i.) 4 Da
Senkaku–Shotō 16 Fd
Šenkursk 12 Fa
Senmonorom 19 Ef
Senneterre 31 Hd

Sens 8 Ec
Senta 6 Ecd
Sento Sé 38 Cbc
Senyavin Islands 27 CDb
Seo de Urgel 9 Fa
Seoni 20 Ed
Seoul (Sŏul) 14 Ff
Sepanjang, Pulau– (i.) 18 Ef
Šepetkovo 14 IJc
Šepetovka 6 Ha
Sept–Iles 31 Ic
Serafimovič 12 Fd
Seraing 8 Fb
Serang 18 Cf
Serbia 6 Ede
Serdobsk 12 FGc
Šereflikochisar 22 Dc
Seremban 18 Bd
Serena, La– 39 Bc
Serengeti Plain 26 Cb
Seret (riv.) 6 Gb
Sergeja Kirova, ostrova– 14 BCb
Sergiev Posad (Zagorsk) 13 Cd
Sergino 13 Fc
Sergipe (State) 38 Dc
Seria 18 Dd
Seribu Kepulauan 18 Cf
Sérifos (i.) 11 Fe
Sernyje Vody 12 Hc
Serov 13 Fd
Serowe 26 Bd
Serpa 9 Bd
Serpentine Lakes 29 DEd
Serpuhov 3 Gb
Sérrai 11 Ec
Serrana, Banco de– (is.) 35 BCb
Serranilla, Banco de– (is.) 35 BCb
Serrat, Cap– 10 Bf
Serra Talhada 38 Db
Serrezuela 39 Bc
Serrinha 38 Dc
Sertão (phys. reg.) 38 CDbc
Serua, Pulau– (i.) 18 Hf
Sesfontein 26 Ac
Sesheke 26 Bc
Sesimbra 9 Ac
Sestao 9 Da
Sestroreck 4 Gc
Setana 17 Fc
Sète 8 Ef
Sete Lagoas 39 Da
Sete Quedas, Saltos das– 39 Cb
Sétif 24 Ca
Settat 24 Ba
Setté Cama 26 Ab
Setúbal 9 Ac
Seul, Lac– 31 Fc
Sevan, Lake– 21 Da
Sevastopol 13 Ce
Ševčenko → Aktau 13 Ee
Severn [Can.] (riv.) 31 FGc
Severn [U.K.] (riv.) 7 Eef
Severnaja Zemlja (i.) 41 grid square no.4
Severnyje Uraly (mts.) 12 GHab

Severodvinsk 13 CDe
Severo–Jenisejski 14 Ccd
Severo Krymski Kanal 12 DEd
Severo–Kurilsk 14 Id
Severomorsk 13 Cc
Severouralsk 13 EFc
Seville 9 Bd
Sevlijevo 11 Fb
Sèvre (riv.) 8 Cd
Seward 30 Dcd
Seychelles (Ind. St.) 15 Bj
Seydişehir 22 Cd
Seyđisfiörður 4 map no.1
Seyhan (riv.) 22 Ed
Seyhan Barajı 22 Ed
Seyitgazi 22 Cc
Seylac 25 Ec
Seymour 29 Hf
Seyne–sur–Mer, La– 8 Ff
Sézanne 8 EFc
Sezze 10 Dd
Sfintu Gheorghe 6 GHd
Sha'ab, Al– 21 Cg
Shaanxi (prov.) 16 Cd
Shaba (reg.) 26 Bb
Shabunda 26 Bb
Shache 15 Cf
Shackleton Coast 42 grid
  square no.4
Shackleton Ice Shelf (gl.) 42
  grid square no.4
Shag Rocks 40 Dc
Shahdol 20 Fd
Shahganj 19 Hj
Shahjahanpur 20 EFc
Shakawe 26 Bc
Shakotan–Misaki 17 FGc
Shali 19 Jj
Sha'm, Ash– 21 Fd
Shām, Jabal ash– (mt.) 21 Fe
Shammar, Jabal– (mts.) 21
  BCd
Shamva 26 Cc
Shan (State) 19 Cd
Shandan 16 Bc
Shandī 25 Dc
Shandong (phys. reg.) 16 Ec
Shandong Bandao (pen.) 16
  Ec
Shanghai 15 Ef
Shangqiu 16 Ed
Shangrao 16 Ee
Shangzhi 16 Gab
Shanhaiguan 16 EFb
Shannon (riv.) 7 Be
Shantar Islands 14 GHd
Shantou 16 Ef
Shanxi (prov.) 16 Dc
Shaoguan 16 DEf
Shaowu 16 Ee
Shaoxing 16 EFde
Shaoyang 16 De
Shaqrā 21 Dg
Shaqrā', Ash– 21 CDd
Shāriqah, Ash– 21 EFd
Shark Bay 29 Acd
Sharm ash Shaykh 21 Ad
Sharqāt, Ash– 21 Cb
Shashe (riv.) 26 Bd
Shashi 16 Dd
Shasta, Mount– 33 Ab
Shatt–al–Arab (riv.) 21 Dcd

Shawinigan 31 Hd
Shay Gap 29 Cc
Shaykh 'Uthman 21 Dg
Sheberghan 20 Ca
Sheboygan 32 Ca
Sheffield 7 Fe
Shelby 33 Bb
Shelikhov Gulf 14 IJcd
Shenyang 16 Fb
Sheopur 19 Gj
Shepparton 29 GHf
Sherbro Island 24 Ad
Sherbrooke 31 HId
Sheridan 33 Cb
Sheringham 7 Ge
Sherman 32 Bb
Sherman, Fort– 35 map no.1
Sherridon 31 Ec
Shetland Isles 7 FGa
Shibam 21 Df
Shibata 17 Fef
Shibecha 17 Ic
Shibetsu 17 GHb
Shibin al Kawm 25 CDa
Shidao 16 Fc
Shihr, Ash– 21 DEfg
Shijiazhuang 15 Df
Shikarpur [India] 19 Ij
Shikarpur [Pak.] 20 CDc
Shikoku (i.) 16 Hd
Shilla (mt.) 20 Eb
Shillong 15 Dg
Shimizu 17 EFg
Shimoga 20 DEf
Shimokita–Hantō 17 GHd
Shimonoseki 16 GHd
Shimono–Shima 17 Ag
Shinano–Gawa (riv.) 17 Ff
Shingū 17 DEh
Shinji–Ko 17 Cd
Shinjō 17 FGe
Shinyanga 26 Cb
Shiōgama 17 Ge
Shio–no–Misaki 17 DEh
Shiquan 16 Cd
Shiquanhe 15 Cf
Shiragami–Misaki 17 FGd
Shirampur 19 IJk
Shirane–San (mt.) 17 Ff
Shiranuka 17 HIc
Shirāz 21 Ecd
Shirbin 22 Cg
Shire (riv.) 26 Cc
Shiretoko–Hantō 17 Ib
Shiretoko–Misaki 17 Ib
Shir–Kuh (mt.) 21 Ec
Shiroishi 17 Gef
Shiwpuri 20 Ec
Shizuishan 16 Cc
Shizukawa 17 GHe
Shizunai 17 GHc
Shizuoka 16 IJcd
Shkodra 11 Cb
Shkumbini (riv.) 11 CDc
Shoshone Mountains 33 Bbc
Shoshong 26 Bd
Shreveport 32 Bb
Shrewsbury 7 Ee
Shuangcheng 16 Gab
Shuangliao 16 Fb
Shuangyashan 16 Ha
Shuiji → Laixi 16 Fc
Shumlul, Ash– 21 Dd

Shuoxian 16 Dc
Shuqayq, Ash– 21 Cf
Shurayk, Ash– 25 Dc
Shushtar 21 Dc
Shwebo 19 Cd
Shweli (riv.) 16 Af
Siahan Range 20 BCc
Sialkot 20 DEb
Siam → Thailand (Ind. St.) 19
  De
Siantan, Pulau– (i.) 18 Cd
Siapa (riv.) 37 Cb
Siargao (i.) 18 Gbc
Šiaškotan, ostrov– (i.) 14 Ie
Siau, Pulau– (i.) 18 Gd
Šiauliai 13 Bd
Siazan 21 DEa
Sibaj 13 Ed
Sibenik 6 BCe
Siberia (phys. reg.) 13 GOc
Siberut, Pulau– (i.) 15 Dj
Sibi 20 Cc
Sibillini, Monti– 10 Dc
Sibirjakova, ostrov– 13 Gb
Sibirtsevo 17 Cb
Sibiu 6 FGd
Sibolga 18 Ad
Sibu 18 Dd
Sibut 25 Bd
Sibutu Islands 18 Ed
Sibuyan (i.) 18 Fb
Sicasica 39 Ba
Sichuan (prov.) 16 BCd
Sicily (reg.) 10 DEef
Sicuani 39 Aa
Sideby 4 Ec
Siđeròkastron 11 Ec
Sideros, Ákra– 11 Gf
Sidhi 19 Hj
Sīdi Barrâni 25 Ca
Sidi–Bel–Abbès 24 BCa
Sidi Ifni 24 Ab
Sidley, Mount– 42 grid square
  no.3
Sidon 22 Ef
Sidra, Gulf of– 24 Da
Sidrah, As– 24 Dab
Siedlce 5 Ib
Sieg (riv.) 5 Ac
Siegburg 5 Ac
Siegen 5 ABc
Siemiatycze 5 Ib
Siĕmréab 18 IJe
Siena 10 Cc
Sieradz 5 Gc
Sierpc 5 GHb
Sierra Blanca 33 Cc
Sierra Blanca Peak 33 Cc
Sierra Colorada 40 Bab
Sierra Leone (Ind. St.) 23 Ae
Sierra Mojada 34 Bb
Sífnos (i.) 11 Fe
Sıgaçık 22 Ac
Sighetul Marmaţiei 6 FGc
Sighişoara 6 Gc
Sigli 18 Ac
Siglufjörður 4 map no.1
Signy Island 42 grid square
  no.1
Sigüenza 9 Db
Siguiri 24 ABc
Sigulda 4 Fd
Sihote–Alin (mts.) 14 Ge

Siirt 21 Cb
Sikar 20 DEc
Sikaram (mt.) 20 CDb
Sikasso 24 Bc
Sikinos (i.) 11 Fe
Sikkim (State) 19 Ac
Siktjah 14 Fb
Sil (riv.) 9 Ba
Sila, la– (mt.) 10 Fe
Silchar 19 Bd
Silesia (phys. reg.) 5 EFc
Silgarhi 19 Hi
Silifke 22 DEd
Siliguri 20 Gc
Siling Co (l.) 19 ABb
Silistra 11 Gab
Silivri 11 GHc
Siljan 4 Cc
Šilka (riv.) 14 Ed
Silkeborg 4 Bd
Sillajhuay, Cordillera de–
  (mts.) 39 Bab
Sillon de Talbert (cap.) 8 Bc
Šilovo 12 Fc
Silvassa 20 Dde
Silver City 33 Cc
Silverton 29 Ge
Silves 9 Ad
Simanggang 18 CDd
Šimanovsk 14 Fd
Simão Dias 38 Dc
Simav 22 Bc
Simbirsk 13 DEd
Simelue, Pulau– (is.) 15 Di
Simeri Crichi 10 Fe
Simferopol 13 Ce
Simhan, Gebel– (mt.) 21 EFf
Simi (i.) 22 Ad
Šimkent (Čimkent) 13 FGe
Simla 20 Eb
Şimleu Silvaniei 6 Fc
Simojärvi 4 Fb
Simonstown 26 Ae
Simplon (p.) 10 Ba
Simpson Desert 29 Fcd
Simrishamn 5 Ea
Simušir (i.) 14 Ie
Sinabang 18 Ad
Sinai Peninsula 25 Db
Sinan 16 Ce
Sincelejo 37 Bb
Sind (riv.) 19 Gj
Sind (phys. reg.) 20 Cc
Sındırgı 11 Hd
Sindri 19 Ik
Sinelnikovo 12 Ed
Sines 9 Ad
Singapore (Ind. St.) 15 Di
Singaraja 18 Ef
Singatoka 28 map no.6
Singen 5 Be
Singida 26 Cb
Singitic Gulf 11 EFcd
Singkang 18 EFe
Singkawang 18 CDd
Singkep, Pulau– (i.) 18 BCe
Sinj 6 Ce
Sinjah 25 Dc
Sinkat 25 Dc
Sinkiang (Aut. Reg.) 15 Cef

nnicolaul Mare 6 Ecd
nnüris 22 Ch
nop 22 Eab
ntana 6 Ec
ntang 18 Dde
nt Maarten / Saint Martin 35
Jb
nt Niklaas 8 EFb
ntra 9 Ac
nüiju 14 Ff
ófok 6 CDc
on 10 Aa
oux City 32 Ba
oux Falls 32 Ba
oux Lookout 31 Fcd
ping 16 Fb
ple, Mount– 42 grid square
no.3
ple Station 42 grid square
no.3
pora, Pulau– (i.) 18 Ae
quijor 18 Fc
racusa 10 Ef
irajganj 20 Gd
ir Edward Pellew Group 29
Fb
iret (riv.) 6 Hc
iret 6 GHc
irḩān, Wādī as– (w.) 21 Bc
irina (i.) 11 Ge
irino, Monte– 10 Ed
iros (i.) 11 Fe
irsa 20 DEc
irtica (phys. reg.) 24 Da
isak 6 Cd
i Sa Khet 19 DEef
isimiut / Holsteinsborg 31 Jb
istan (phys. reg.) 20 Bb
isteron 8 Fe
itapur 20 Fc
ithonia (pen.) 11 Ec
itia 11 Gf
itio da Abadia 39 Da
itka 31 Bc
ittang (riv.) 19 Ce
ittwe (Akyab) 19 Bde
ivaki 14 Fd
ıvas 22 Fc
ivaš, ozero– 12 Dd
iverek 21 Bb
ivrihisar 22 CDc
īwah 25 Cb
iwálik Range 19 Hlij
iwan 19 Ij
iwa Oasis 25 Cb
ixth Cataract 25 Dc
jælland 4 BCe
jöbo 5 Da
kadovsk 12 Dd
kagerrak (str.) 4 ABd
kagway 30 EFd
kåne (phys. reg.) 4 Ce
kanör–Falsterbo 5 Da
kara 4 Cd
kardu 20 Eab
karżysko–Kamienna 5 Hc
kawina 5 GHcd
kegness 7 Ge
kellefteå 4 Eb
kellefteälven (riv.) 4 Db
kelleftehamn 4 Eb
khíza (i.) 11 De
khoinoúsa (i.) 11 Fe

Skíatos (i.) 11 Ed
Skibbereen 7 Bf
Skierı 4 Bd
Skierniewice 5 Hc
Skikda 24 Ca
Skirakawa 17 Gf
Skíro (i.) 11 Fd
Skive 4 Bd
Skjoldungen 31 KLb
Skole 5 Id
Skópelos 11 Ed
Skopin 12 EFc
Skopje 11 Dbc
Škotovo 17 Cc
Skövde 4 Cd
Skovorodino 14 Fd
Skvira 6 Ib
Skye, Island of– 7 Cc
Slagesle 5 Ca
Slamet, Gunung– (mt.) 18 Cf
Slancy 4 Gd
Slatina 6 Gd
Slautnoje 14 JKc
Slave Coast 24 Cd
Slave River 31 Dbc
Slavgorod 13 Gd
Slavjanka 17 Bc
Slavjansk 13 Cd
Slavjansk na–Kubani 12 Ed
Slavonia (phys. reg.) 6 CDd
Slavonska Požega 6 CDd
Slavonski Brod 6 Dd
Slavuta 6 Ha
Sławno 5 Fa
Sleaford 7 Fe
Sliema 10 Efg
Sligo 7 Bd
Slite 4 Dd
Sliven 11 Gb
Slivnica 11 Eb
Sljudjanka 14 Dd
Slobodka 6 Ic
Slobodskoj 12 Hb
Slobodzeja 6 IJc
Slobozia 6 Hd
Słonie 5 Hb
Slonim 12 Cc
Slough 7 Ff
Slovakia (Ind. St.) 3 EFc
Slovakia (phys. reg.) 5 GHd
Slovenia (Ind. St.) 6 Bcd
Slovenské Rudohorie 5 GHd
Słubice 5 Eb
Sluč (riv.) 6 Ha
Sluck 12 Cc
Slunj 6 Bd
Słupsk 5 Fa
Småland (phys. reg.) 4 Cd
Smederevo 6 Ed
Smederevska Palanka 6 Ed
Smela 12 Dd
Smith Strait 41 grid square
no.1
Smithton 29 map no.1
Smøla (i.) 4 Ac
Smolensk 13 Cd
Smólicas (mt.) 11 Dc
Smoljan 11 Fc
Smorgon 4 Fe
Snæfellsjökull (gl.) 4 map
no.1
Snag 31 ABb
Snake River 33 Bb

Snake River Plain 33 Bb
Sneek 8 Fa
Sniardwy, Jezioro– 5 Hlb
Śnieżka (mt.) 5 EFc
Snigirevka 12 Dd
Snøhetta (mt.) 4 Bc
Snowdon (mt.) 7 DEe
Snowdrift 31 DEb
Snowy River 29 Hf
Snyder 33 Cc
Soalala 26 map no.1
Soasiu 18 Gd
Sobat (riv.) 25 Dd
Sobral 38 CDb
Sochaczew 5 GHb
Soči 13 Ce
Society Islands 28 Bc
Socna 24 Db
Socompa, Paso de– (p.) 39
Bb
Socorro [Col.] 37 Bb
Socorro [U.S.] 33 Cc
Socorro, Isla– (i.) 34 ABc
Socotra (i.) 25 Fc
Socuéllamos 9 Dc
Sodankyla 4 Fb
Soddu 25 Dd
Söderala 4 Dc
Söderhamn 4 Dc
Söderköping 4 Dd
Södertälje 4 Dd
Soest 5 Bc
Sofala, Baía de– 26 Cd
Sofia 11 Eb
Sofijsk 14 Gd
Sōfu Gan (i.) 27 BCa
Sogamoso 37 Bb
Soğanlı (riv.) 22 Db
Sognefjorden (b.) 4 Ac
Sögüt Gölü 22 Bd
Soissons 8 Ec
Soitué 39 Bc
Sokal 5 Jc
Söke 22 Ad
Sokodé 24 BCd
Sokol 13 Dd
Sokółka 5 Ib
Sokolo 24 Bc
Sokolov 5 Dc
Sokoto (riv.) 24 Cc
Sokoto 24 Cc
Sol, Costa del– 9 CDd
Solápur 15 Ch
Soledade 37 Cc
Soligalič 12 Fb
Soligorsk 12 Cc
Solikamsk 13 Ecd
Sol–Ileck 13 Ed
Solingen 5 Ac
Sollefteå 4 Dc
Sóller 9 Gc
Solling (mts.) 5 Bc
Solnečnogorsk 12 Eb
Solo → Surakarta 18 Df
Sologne (phys. reg.) 8 DEd
Solomon Islands 27 CDc
Solomon Islands (Ind. St.) 27
Dc
Solomon Sea 27 Cc
Solothurn 5 Ae
Solta (i.) 11 Bb
Soltau 5 Bb
Solvyčegodsk 12 Ga

Solway Firth (b.) 7 DEd
Solwezi 26 Bc
Soma 22 Ac
Somalia (Ind. St.) 23 Ge
Sombor 6 Dd
Sombrerete 34 Bb
Sombrero, El– 37 Cb
Somcuţa Mare 6 FGc
Somerset 29 Ga
Somerset (co.) 7 Ef
Somerset Island 31 Fa
Someş (riv.) 6 Fc
Somme (riv.) 8 Ec
Somport, Puerto de– (p.) 9
Ea
Son (riv.) 20 Fd
Sønderborg 4 Be
Søndre Strømfjord 31 JKb
Sondrio 10 Ba
Songea 26 Cc
Songhua Hu 16 Gb
Songhua Jiang → Sungari 17
Aab
Songjiang 16 Fd
Songkhla 15 Di
Songnim 16 Gc
Songo 26 Cc
Sonhat 19 Hk
Sonid Youqi 16 Db
Son La 19 Dd
Sonneberg 5 Cc
Sonora (riv.) 34 Ab
Sonoyta 34 Aa
Sonsón 37 Bb
Sonsonate 35 ABb
Sonsorol Islands 27 Bb
Son Tay 19 Ed
Sopot 5 Ga
Sopron 6 Cc
Sorbas 9 Dd
Sorel 32 Da
Sorgues 8 Fef
Soria 9 Db
Sorø 5 Ca
Sorocaba 39 Cb
Soročinsk 12 Hc
Soroki 6 Hlb
Sorol Atoll (i.) 18 IJc
Sorong 18 He
Soroti 25 Dd
Sørøya (i.) 4 Ea
Sorraia (riv.) 9 Ac
Sorrento 10 Ed
Sør Rondane 42 grid square
no.2
Sorsatunturi (mt.) 4 Gb
Sorsele 4 Db
Sorsogon 18 FGb
Sort 9 Fa
Sortavala 4 Gc
Sortland 4 Ca
Sosnovka 12 Hb
Sosnowiec 5 Gc
Šostka 12 Dc
Sosva 12 Jb
Sotteville–lès–Rouen 8 Dc
Souanké 26 Aa
Soudan 29 Fbc
Souflíon 11 FGc
Souk–Ahras 10 ABf
Sŏul → Seoul 16 Ff
Soure 38 Cb
Sousel 38 Bb

Sousse 24 Da
Souterraine, La– 8 DEd
South Africa (Ind. St.) 23 Ehi
Southampton 7 EFf
Southampton Island 31 Gb
South Andaman (i.) 19 Bf
South Australia (State) 29 EFde
South Bend 32 Ca
South Carolina (State) 32 CDb
South China Sea 16 DEf
South Dakota (State) 33 CDb
South East Cape 29 Hg
Southeast Pass 28 map no.3
South East Point 29 Hf
Southend–on–Sea 7 Gf
Southern Alps 27 De
Southern Cross 29 BCe
Southern Indian Lake 31 Fc
Southern Uplands (mts.) 7 DEd
Southern Urals (mts.) 12 Ic
South Geomagnetic Pole (1975) 42 grid square no.4
South Georgia (i.) 40 Ec
South Island 27 De
South Korea (Ind. St.) 15 Ef
South Magnetic Pole (1980) 42 grid square no.4
South Orkney Islands 36 Fj
South Platte (riv.) 33 Cb
South Point 28 map no.3
South Pole 42 grid square no.1
Southport 7 Ee
South Ronaldsay (i.) 7 EFb
South Sandwich Islands 36 Hli
South Saskatchewan (riv.) 33 BCa
South Shetland Islands 36 Dj
South Shields 7 Fd
South Uist (i.) 7 BCc
Southwest Cape 27 De
Southwest Pass (str.) 28 map no.3
Southwold 7 GHe
Sovetsk [Russia] 12 Bbc
Sovetsk [Russia] 12 Gb
Sovetskaja Gavan 14 GHe
Sōya–Misaki 17 GHb
Soyo 26 Ab
Sož (riv.) 12 Dc
Sozopol 11 GHib
Spain (Ind. St.) 3 Ccd
Spalding 7 Fe
Spanish Town 35 Cb
Sparks 33 Bc
Sparta 11 Ee
Spartanburg 32 Cb
Spartha, Cape– 11 Ef
Spartivento, Capo– [It.] 10 Be
Spartivento, Capo– [It.] 10 Ff
Spassk–Dalni 14 Ge
Spencer, Cape– 29 Ff
Spencer Bay 31 Fb
Spencer Gulf 29 Fe
Spey (riv.) 7 Ec
Spezia, La– 10 Bb
Spilimbergo 10 Da
Spišská Nová Ves 5 Hd
Spittal an der Drau 5 De

Spitzbergen (i.) 41 grid square no.3
Split 6 Ce
Spokane 33 Bb
Spoleto 10 Dc
Sporades, Northern– (is.) 11 EFd
Spree (riv.) 5 Dbc
Spremberg 5 Ec
Springbok 26 Ade
Springfield [Il.–U.S.] 32 BCb
Springfield [Ma.–U.S.] 32 Da
Springfield [Mo.–U.S.] 32 Bb
Springfield [Or.–U.S.] 33 Ab
Springfontein 23 Ehi
Springlands 37 Db
Springs 26 BCd
Springsure 29 Hc
Spurn Head 7 Ge
Squamish 33 Ab
Squillace, Golfo di– 10 Fe
Sredinny Hrebet (mts.) 14 IJd
Sredna Gora (mts.) 11 Fb
Srednekolymsk 14 Ic
Srednerusskaja vozvyšennost 13 Cd
Sredni Ural (mts.) 12 IJb
Śrem 5 Fb
Sremska Mitrovica 6 Dd
Srepok (riv.) 19 Ef
Sretensk 14 EFd
Srikakulam 20 FGe
Srī Lanka (Ceylon) (Ind. St.) 15 Ci
Srinagar 20 DEb
Srivardhan 20 De
Środa 5 Fb
Stade 5 Bb
Stadlandet (pen.) 4 Ac
Staffa (i.) 7 Cc
Stafford 7 Ee
Stahanov 12 Ed
Stalowa Wola 5 Ic
Standerton 26 BCd
Stanke Dimitrov 11 Eb
Stanley 36 Eh
Stanovoje Nagorje 14 EFd
Stanovoy Range 14 FGd
Stanthorpe 29 Id
Starachowice 5 Hc
Staraja Russa 12 Db
Stara Pazova 6 DEd
Stara Zagora 11 Fb
Starbuck Island 28 Bc
Stargard Szczecinski 5 Eb
Starica 12 DEb
Starnberg 5 Cde
Starnberger See 5 Cde
Starogard Gdański 5 Gb
Starokonstantinov 6 Hb
Starominskaja 12 Ed
Start Point 7 Ef
Stary Oskol 12 Ed
Stassfurt 5 CDbc
Staunton 32 CDb
Staurós 11 Ec
Stavanger 4 Ad
Stavropol 13 De
Stavropol → Togliatti 13 Dd
Stefanie, Lake– 25 Dd
Stefansson Island 31 Ea
Stege 5 Da
Steinkjer 4 BCbc

Stelvio, Passo dello– 10 Ca
Stendal 5 Cb
Stenhouse Bay 29 Ff
Stepanakert → Harkendi 21 Dab
Stephenville 32 Fa
Sterling 33 Cb
Sterlitamak 13 Ed
Stettin 5 Eb
Stettiner Haff (g.) 5 Eb
Stewart 31 BCc
Stewart Island 27 De
Steyr 5 Ede
Stikine (riv.) 31 BCc
Stikine Ranges 31 BCbc
Stilis 11 Ed
Stilo, Punta– (cap.) 10 Fe
Stintu Gheorghe, Bratul– (riv.) 6 Id
Štip 11 Ec
Stirling 7 DEc
Stirling Range 29 Be
Stjørdal 4 Bc
Stockerau 5 EFd
Stockholm 4 Dd
Stockport 7 Ee
Stockton 33 ABc
Stockton on Tees 7 EFd
Stoěng Trêng 19 Ef
Stojba 14 Gd
Stoke–on–Trent 7 Ee
Stokes, Cerro– 40 Ac
Stolac 11 BCb
Stolbovj, ostrov– (i.) 14 Gb
Ston 11 Bb
Stonehaven 7 EFc
Stonehenge (r.) 7 EFf
Stony Tunguska (riv.) 14 Cc
Stora Lulevatten (l.) 4 DEb
Store Bælt (str.) 4 Be
Storfjord (b.) 4 Ac
Storlien 4 Cc
Storm Bay 29 map no.1
Stornoway 7 CDb
Storsjön (l.) 4 Cc
Storuman 4 CDb
Strakonice 5 Dd
Stralsund 5 Da
Strängnäs 4 Dd
Stranraer 7 Dd
Strasbourg 8 Gc
Stratford–upon–Avon 7 Fe
Straubing 5 Dd
Streaky Bay 29 Ee
Strehaia 6 Fd
Stresa 10 Bb
Streževoj 13 GHc
Stříbro 5 Dc
Strimonikós Kólpos 11 EFc
Strofádhes, Nísoi– 11 De
Strómboli (i.) 10 Ee
Strömstad 4 BCd
Strömsund 4 Cc
Stronsay (i.) 7 EFb
Struga 11 Dc
Struma (Strymón) (riv.) 11 Ec
Strumica 11 Ec
Stry 6 FGb
Strymón → Struma (riv.) 11 Ec
Strzelecki Creek 29 FGd
Stubbeköbing 5 Da
Stupino 12 Ebc

Stura (riv.) 10 Ab
Stura di Demonte (riv.) 10 Ab
Sturge Island 42 grid square no.4
Sturt Desert 29 map no.1
Stuttgart 5 BCd
Styria (phys. reg.) 5 Ee
Suao 16 Ff
Šubarkuduk 13 Ee
Subotica 6 Dcd
Suceava 6 Hc
Sucre 39 Ba
Sucunduri (riv.) 37 Dc
Sudak 12 DEe
Sudan (phys. reg.) 24 CDc
Sudan (Ind. St.) 23 EFd
Sudbury 31 GHd
Sudd (phys. reg.) 25 CDd
Suddie 37 Db
Sudety (mts.) 5 EFc
Sueca 9 Ec
Sueco, El– 34 Bab
Suez 25 Dab
Suez, Gulf of– 25 Db
Suez Canal 25 map no.2
Suffolk (co.) 7 Ge
Suffolk 32 Db
Suğla Gölü 22 Dd
Suhar 21 Fe
Suhe–Bator 14 Dde
Suhiniči 12 DEc
Suhl 5 Cc
Suhona (riv.) 13 Dc
Suhumi 13 CDe
Suiá–Missu (riv.) 38 Bc
Suide 16 CDc
Suifenhe 16 Hb
Suihua 16 Ga
Suining 16 BCd
Suir (riv.) 7 Ce
Suita 17 Dg
Šuja 12 Fb
Sujfun (riv.) 17 Bbc
Sukabumi 18 Cf
Sukadana 18 CDe
Şukhayrah, Aş– 24 CDa
Sukhothai 19 CDe
Sukkertoppen / Maniitsoq 31 Jb
Sukkur 15 Cg
Sukumo 17 Ch
Sula, Kepulauan– 18 FGe
Sulaimâniya 21 CDb
Sulaimān Range 20 CDbc
Sula Sgeir (i.) 7 Cb
Sulawesi (Celebes) (is.) 18 EFe
Sulayyil, As– 21 De
Sulina 6 IJd
Sulina, Bratul– (riv.) 6 Id
Sulitjelma 4 CDb
Sulitjelma (mt.) 4 Db
Sullana 37 ABc
Sulmona 10 Dc
Sultan dağları (mts.) 22 Ccd
Sultanpur 19 Hj
Sulu Archipelago 18 EFcd
Sulüq 24 DEa
Sulu Sea 18 EFd
Šumadija (phys. reg.) 6 Ed
Sumatra (i.) 15 Dij
Sumba, Pulau– (i.) 15 DEjk
Sumba Strait 18 EFf

Sumbawa, Pulau– (i.) **15** DEj
Sumbawa Besar **18** Ef
Sumbawanga **26** Cb
Sumbe **26** Ac
Sumburgh Head **7** Fb
Sumen **11** Gb
Sumerlja **12** Gb
Sumgait **13** DEe
Sumisu–Jima (i.) **17** FGi
Summerside **32** Ea
Summit **35** map no.1
Sumperk **5** Fcd
Sumprabum **19** Cc
Sumter **32** CDb
Sumy **13** Cd
Sundarbans (phys. reg.) **20** GHd
Sunda Strait **18** Cf
Sunderland **7** Fd
Sundiken dağı (mt.) **22** Cbc
Sundsvall **4** Dc
Sungai Petani **19** Dg
Sungari (Songhua Jiang) (riv.) **16** Gb
Sungurlu **22** Eb
Sun Kosi (riv.) **19** Ij
Sunndalsöra **4** Bc
Sunne **4** Cd
Suntar **14** Ec
Suntar–Hajata, Hrebet– **14** GHc
Sunyani **24** Bd
Suojarvi **12** Da
Suolahti **4** Fc
Suomenselkä (mts.) **4** EGc
Suomussalmi **4** Gb
Suonenjoki **4** Fc
Superior **32** Ba
Superior, Lake– **32** Ca
Süphan dağ (mt.) **21** Cb
Suqian **16** Ed
Sur **21** Fe
Sur, Submeseta– (phys. reg.) **9** CDbc
Sura (riv.) **12** Gbc
Surabaya **15** Djk
Surakarta (Solo) **18** Df
Surat [Austl.] **29** Hd
Surat [India] **15** Cg
Surat Thani **15** Di
Surgut **13** Gc
Suri **19** Ijk
Surigao **18** Gc
Surin **19** Def
Suriname (Ind. St.) **36** Ec
Suriname (riv.) **37** Db
Surkhab (riv.) **20** Ca
Surprise, Île– (i.) **28** map no.4
Surrey (co.) **7** Ff
Surt **24** Da
Surtsey (i.) **4** map no.1
Suruga–Wan **17** Fg
Surulangun **18** Be
Susa **10** Ab
Susa (r.) **21** Dc
Susaki **17** Ch
Suşehri **22** Gb
Susong **16** Ed
Susques **39** Bb
Sussex (co.) **7** FGf
Susuman **14** Hc
Susurluk **22** ABc
Sutlej (riv.) **20** Eb

Suttor River **29** Hc
Suva **28** map no.6
Suvorovo **6** Id
Suwałki **5** Ia
Suwarrow Atoll **28** Ac
Suwaydā, As– **22** Ff
Suwŏn **16** Gc
Suxian [China] **16** Dd
Suxian [China] **16** Ed
Suzhou **16** Fd
Suzu **17** Ef
Suzu–Misaki **17** Ef
Svålbard **41** grid square no.3
Svartisen (mt.) **4** Cb
Svealand (phys. reg.) **4** CDd
Svedala **5** Da
Sveg **4** Cc
Švenčionėlia **12** Cbc
Svendborg **4** Be
Sverdlovsk → Jekaterinburg **13** EFd
Sverdrup, ostrov– **13** Gb
Sverdrup Islands **41** grid square no.2
Svetlaja **14** Ge
Svetlogorsk **12** Cc
Svetlograd **12** Fd
Svetlovodsk **12** Dd
Svetly **13** Fd
Svetogorsk **4** Gc
Svetozarevo **6** Ede
Svilengrad **11** FGc
Svir (riv.) **12** Da
Svištov **11** Fb
Svitavy **5** Fd
Svobodny **14** FGd
Svolvær **4** Ca
Swain Reefs (is.) **29** Ic
Swains Atoll **28** Ac
Swakop (riv.) **26** Ad
Swakopmund **23** Dh
Swale (riv.) **7** Fd
Swan Hill **29** Gf
Swan River **33** Ca
Swansea **7** DEf
Swarzędz **5** Fb
Swaziland (Ind. St.) **23** Fh
Sweden (Ind. St.) **3** Ea
Sweetwater **33** Cc
Swellendam **26** Be
Świdnica **5** Fc
Świdnik **5** Ic
Świdwin **5** EFb
Świebodzin **5** Eb
Świecie **5** FGb
Swift Current **33** Cab
Swindon **7** Ff
Swinoujście **5** Eab
Switzerland (Ind. St.) **3** Dc
Syčevka **12** Db
Sydney [Austl.] **29** Ie
Sydney [Can.] **31** IJd
Sydprøven / Alluitsup Paa **31** Kb
Syktyvkar **13** Ec
Sylarna (mt.) **4** BCc
Sylhet **20** Hcd
Sylt **5** Ba
Syowa **42** grid square no.2
Syracuse **32** Da
Syrdarja (riv.) **13** Fe
Syria (Ind. St.) **15** Bf
Syriam **19** Ce

Syrian Desert **21** BCc
Sysert **12** Jb
Sysmä **4** Fc
Syvulja (mt.) **5** IJd
Syzran **13** Dd
Szamos (riv.) **5** Ide
Szamotuły **5** Fb
Szczecinek **5** Fb
Szczytno **5** Hb
Szeged **6** DEc
Székesfehérvár **6** Dc
Szekszárd **6** Dc
Szentes **6** Ec
Szolnok **6** Ec
Szombathely **6** Cc

T

Tabajara **37** Cc
Ţabarqah **10** Bf
Ţabas **21** Fc
Tabašino **12** Gb
Tabelbala **24** Bb
Taberg (mt.) **5** DEa
Tabernas **9** DEd
Tablas (i.) **18** Fb
Tablas, Las– **35** BCc
Tábor **5** Ed
Tabor **14** Hlb
Tabora **26** Cb
Tabory **12** Jb
Tabou **24** Bd
Tabrīz **21** Db
Tabuaeran (Fanning) **28** Bb
Tabuk **21** Bd
Tacazzè (riv.) **25** Dc
Tacheng **13** He
Tacloban **18** FGb
Tacna **39** Aa
Tacoma **33** Ab
Tacora (mt.) **39** ABa
Tacuarembó **39** Cc
Tacutu (riv.) **37** CDb
Tademaït, Plateau du– **24** Cb
Taegu **14** FGf
Taeჯŏn **14** Ff
Tafalla **9** Ea
Ţafīlah, Aţ– **22** Eg
Tafí Viejo **39** Bb
Taftān, Kuh– e– (mt.) **21** Gd
Taga **28** map no.5
Taga Dzong **20** GHc
Taganrog **13** CDe
Taganrogski zaliv **12** Ed
Tagatay City **18** EFb
Tagbilaran **18** Fc
Tagula Island **27** Cc
Tahan, Gunong– (mt.) **19** Dgh
Tahat (mt.) **24** Cb
Tahiti, Île– **28** Bc
Tahlab (riv.) **21** Gd
Tahoua **24** Cc
Tahtalı dağ (mt.) **22** Fc
Tahulandang, Pulau– (i.) **18** FGd
Tai'an **16** Ec
Taiarapu, Presqu'île de– **28** map no.2
Taichung **16** Ff
Ta'if, Aţ– **21** BCe
Tai Hu (l.) **16** Fd

Tailai **16** Fa
Tain **7** DEc
Tainan **16** EFf
Taipei **15** Eg
Taiping **19** CDgh
Taisetsu–Zan (mt.) **16** Jb
Taitao, Peninsula de– **40** Ab
Taitao, Peninsula de– **36** Ch
Taitung **16** Ff
Taivalkoski **4** FGb
Taiwan (Formosa) (Ind. St.) **15** Eg
Taiwan Strait **15** DEg
Taíyetos Óros (mts.) **11** Ee
Taiyuan **15** Df
Taizhou **16** EFd
Ta'izz **21** Cg
Tajga **13** Hd
Tajgonos, Poluostrov– **14** Jc
Tajikistan (Ind. St.) **13** FGf
Tajimi **17** Eg
Tajmyr, Ozero– **14** Db
Tajmyr, Poluostrov– **14** CDb
Tajmyra (riv.) **14** Cb
Tajo (riv.) **9** Db
Tajrish **21** Eb
Tajšet **14** Cd
Tajumulco, Volcán– (mt.) **34** Cc
Tajuña (riv.) **9** Db
Tak **19** Ce
Takada **17** Eff
Takahe, Mount– **42** grid square no.3
Takamatsu **16** Hld
Takaoka **17** Ef
Takaroa Atoll **28** Bc
Takasaki **17** Ff
Takayama **17** Ef
Takefu **17** DEfg
Takengon **18** Ad
Take–Shima / Tok–Do (i.) **17** Bf
Takikawa **17** Gc
Tako–Bana **17** Cg
Talak (phys. reg.) **24** Cc
Talara **37** Ac
Talas **13** Ge
Talâta **25** map no.1
Talaud, Kepulauan– **18** Gd
Talavera de la Reina **9** Cbc
Talca **39** Ac
Talcahuano **39** Ac
Talcher **20** Gd
Taldy–Kurgan **13** Ge
Talence **8** Ce
Talgar **16** Bb
Taliabu, Pulau– (i.) **18** FGe
Talica **12** Jb
Tall 'Afar **21** Cb
Tallahassee **32** Cbc
Tallinn **4** Fd
Tall Kalakh **22** Fe
Taloqān **20** CDa
Talsi **4** Ed
Taltal **39** Ab
Tamale **24** BCd
Tamanrasset **24** Cb
Tamar River **29** map no.1
Tamarugal, Pampa del– **39** Bab
Tamazunchale **34** Cb
Tambacounda **24** Ac

Tambao **24** BCc
Tambej **13** FGb
Tambelan Islands **18** Cd
Tambo **29** Hcd
Tambo (riv.) **37** Bd
Tambov **13** Dd
Tambura **25** Cd
Tamchaket **24** ABc
Tamdybulak **13** Fe
Tāmega (riv.) **9** Bb
Tamel Aike **40** Ab
Tamil Nadu (State) **20** Efg
Tamīyah, Jabal– (mt.) **21** Cde
Tampa **32** Cc
Tampere **4** EFc
Tampico **30** Ig
Tamsag–Bulak **14** Ee
Tamsweg **5** De
Tamworth **29** Ie
Tana [Kenya] (riv.) **25** De
Tana [Nor.] (riv.) **4** Fa
Tana, Lake– **25** Dc
Tanabe **17** Dh
Tanacross **31** Ab
Tanafjorden **4** Ga
Tanágra **11** Ed
Tanahbala, Pulau– (i.) **18** Ae
Tanahgrogot **18** Ee
Tanahjampea, Pulau– (i.) **18** Ff
Tanahmasa, Pulau– (i.) **18** Ade
Tanakpur **19** Hi
Tanami **29** DEbc
Tanami Desert **29** Eb
Tanana (riv.) **31** Ab
Tananarive → Antananarivo **23** GHgh
Tanaro (riv.) **10** Bb
Tanch'ŏn **17** Ad
Tanda **19** Hj
Tandag **18** Gc
Tandaltī **25** Dc
Tandil **39** Cc
Tandjungkarang **18** Cef
Tandjungpinang **18** CDd
Tane–ga–Shima (i.) **16** Hd
Tanew (riv.) **5** Ic
Tanezrouft (phys. reg.) **24** BCb
Tanga **23** FGf
Tanganyika, Lake– **26** BCb
Tanggu **16** Ec
Tangier **24** Ba
Tang La (cap.) **20** Gc
Tangra Yumco (l.) **20** Gb
Tangshan **16** EFc
Tanimbar, Kepulauan– **27** Bc
Tanjung **18** Ee
Tanjungbalai **18** ABd
Tanjung Cina **18** Bf
Tanjungkarang **18** BCef
Tanjungpandan **18** Ce
Tanjungredeb **18** Ed
Tanjungselor **18** Ed
Tanna, Île– (i.) **28** map no.4
Tannou–Ola (mts.) **14** Cd
Tanout **24** Cc
Tansing **19** Hij
Ţanţā **25** Da
Tanzania (Ind. St.) **23** Ff
Tao'an **16** Fa
Tao'er He (riv.) **16** EFa

Taongi Atoll **27** Db
Taormina **10** Ef
Taoudenni **24** Bb
Taouz **24** Ba
Tapa **4** Fd
Tapachula **34** Cc
Tapajós (riv.) **38** Bb
Tapaktuan **18** Ad
Tapauá (riv.) **37** Cc
Tapirapeco, Sierra– (mts.) **37** Cb
Tapti (riv.) **20** Dd
Tapul Group **18** EFc
Taquari Novo (riv.) **38** Bc
Tara **13** Gd
Tara (riv.) **11** Cb
Tarakan **18** Ed
Taraklı **22** Cb
Taraklija **6** Id
Tarama–Jima (i.) **16** FGf
Tarancón **9** Dbc
Taranto **10** Fd
Taranto, Gulf of– **10** Fd
Tarapacá **37** BCc
Tarapoto **37** Bc
Tarare **8** Fe
Tarascon **8** Ff
Tarata **39** ABa
Tarauacá **37** Bc
Tarauacá (riv.) **37** Bc
Taravao **28** map no.2
Taravao, Isthmus of– **28** map no.2
Tarazona **9** DEb
Tarbagataj, Hrebet– (mts.) **13** He
Tarbela **20** Db
Tarbert **7** Cc
Tarbes **8** Df
Tarcoola **29** Ee
Taree **29** Ie
Tareja **14** BCb
Tarfaya **24** Ab
Tārgovişte **11** Gb
Tarhankut, mys– **12** Dd
Tarhūnah **24** Da
Tarif **21** Ee
Tarifa **9** Cd
Tarifa, Punta de– (cap.) **9** BCd
Tarija **39** Bb
Tarim (riv.) **22** Ce
Tarim **21** Df
Tarīn Kowt **20** Cb
Tarko–Sale **13** Gc
Tarlac **18** Fa
Tarma **37** Bd
Tarn (riv.) **8** Df
Tärnaby **4** CDb
Tarnobrzeg **5** Hlc
Tarnów **5** Hcd
Taroom **29** Hld
Tarquinia **10** Cc
Tarragona **9** Fb
Tarraleah **29** map no.1
Tarrasa **9** FGb
Tarso Emisu (mt.) **25** BCb
Tarsus **22** Ed
Tartagal **39** Bb
Tartu **4** Fd
Ţarţūs **22** Ee
Tarutau, Ko– (i.) **19** Cg
Tarutung **18** Ad

Tašauz → Dašhovuz **13** Ee
Tasejeva (riv.) **14** Cd
Tasikmalaya **18** Cf
Taškent **13** Fe
Taşköprü **22** DEb
Taşköy **22** EFb
Taš–Kumyr **13** Ge
Tasman (State) **29** map no.1
Tasman Penïnsula **29** map no.1
Tasman Sea **27** CDde
Tāsnad **6** Fc
Tassili–n–Ajjer (mt.) **24** Cb
Tassili Oua–n–Ahaggar (plat.) **24** Cbc
Taštagol **13** Hd
Tata **6** CDc
Tatabánya **6** Dc
Tatakoto Atoll **28** Cc
Tatar Autonomous Republic (Aut. Rep.) **13** DEd
Tatarbunary **6** IJd
Tatarsk **13** Gd
Tatar Strait **16** Jab
Tateyama **17** FGg
Tathlïth **21** Cf
Tatta **20** Cd
Tatuí **39** Db
Tau **28** map no.5
Taubaté **39** Db
Taujsk **14** Hcd
Taukum (phys. reg.) **13** Ge
Taunggyi **19** Cd
Taungup **19** Be
Taunton **7** Ef
Taunus (mt.) **5** ABc
Tauragè **12** Bb
Taurus Mountains **22** CEd
Tautira **28** map no.2
Tavas **22** Bd
Tavda (riv.) **13** Fd
Tavda **13** Fd
Taveuni Island **28** map no.6
Tavira **9** Bd
Tavričanka **17** Bc
Tavşanli **22** Bc
Tavua **28** map no.6
Tawau **18** Ed
Tawitawi Group (is.) **18** EFcd
Ţawkar **25** Dc
Tawzar **24** Ca
Taxila (r.) **20** Db
Tay (riv.) **7** Ec
Taymā **21** Bd
Tay Ninh **19** Ef
Taytay **18** EFb
Taz (riv.) **13** Hc
Taza **24** Ba
Tāzirbū, Wāḩāt al– **24** Eb
Tazovski **13** Gc
Tbilisi **13** De
Tchibanga **26** Ab
Tchien **24** Bd
Tczew **5** Ga
Teano **10** Ed
Tébessa **24** Ca
Tecer dağları (mts.) **22** FGc
Tecuci **6** Hd
Tedžen **13** Ff
Tedžen (riv.) **13** Ff
Tees (riv.) **7** EFd
Tefé **37** Cc
Tefé (riv.) **37** Cc

Tefenni **22** Bd
Tegal **18** Cf
Tegucigalpa **30** Jh
Tehuantepec, Golfo de– **34** Cc
Tehuantepec, Istmo de– **34** Cc
Tehaupoo **28** map no.2
Tehrān **21** DEb
Tehuacán **34** Cc
Tehuantepec **34** Cc
Teifi (riv.) **7** Def
Tejkovo **12** EFb
Tejo (riv.) **9** Bc
Tekeli **13** Ge
Tekirdağ **22** Ab
Tektjur **14** Gc
Tel (riv.) **20** Fd
Tela **35** Bb
Telares, Los– **39** Bb
Telavi **21** Da
Tel Aviv–Yafo **22** DEfg
Telegraph Creek **31** BCc
Telemark (phys. reg.) **4** ABd
Telen (riv.) **18** Ede
Telén **39** Bc
Teleno (mt.) **9** Ba
Teles Pires, Rio– (riv.) **38** Bc
Teles Pires o São Manuel, Rio– (riv.) **38** Bb
Tell Atlas (mts.) **24** BCa
Telok Anson **19** Dh
Telposiz, gora– (mt.) **13** EFc
Telsen **40** Bb
Telšiai **12** Bb
Téma **24** BCd
Tematangi Atoll **28** Bd
Tembilahan **18** Be
Temerloh **19** Dh
Temirtau → Akmol **13** Gd
Temnikov **12** Fc
Tempio Pausania **10** Bd
Temple **32** Bb
Temrjuk **12** Ed
Temuco **39** Ac
Tena **37** Bc
Tenali **20** Fe
Tenasserim (phys. reg.) **19** Cef
Tenasserim (riv.) **19** Cf
Tenda, Col di– (p.) **10** Ab
Ten Degree Channel **19** Bfg
Ténéré (phys. reg.) **24** Dbc
Tenerife (i.) **24** Ab
Ténès **24** Ca
Tengchong **19** Ccd
Tengiz, ozero– **13** Fd
Tengréla **24** Bc
Tengxian **16** Ec
Teniente Matienzo **42** grid square no.1
Tenke **26** Bc
Tenkodogo **24** BCc
Tennant Creek **29** Eb
Tennessee (State) **32** Cb
Tennessee (riv.) **32** Cb
Tenojoki (riv.) **4** Fa
Tenosique **34** Cc
Tenryū **17** EFg
Tenryū–Gawa (riv.) **17** EFg
Tenterfield **29** Id
Teófilo Otoni **39** Da
Teotihuacán **34** Cbc

Tepehuanes **34** Bb
Tepic **34** Bb
Teplice **5** Dc
Teques, Los– **37** Cab
Ter (riv.) **9** Gab
Tera (riv.) **9** Cb
Téra **24** Cc
Teraina (Washington) **28** ABb
Teramo **10** Dc
Terek (riv.) **21** Da
Teresina **36** Fd
Teresinha **36** Ec
Teressa (i.) **19** Bg
Termas, Las– **39** Bb
Termez **13** Ff
Termini Imerese **10** Df
Termoli **10** Ed
Ternate **18** Gd
Ternej **17** Eb
Terni **10** Dc
Ternopol **6** Gb
Terrace **31** Cc
Terracina **10** Dd
Terre Haute **32** Cb
Territorio della Federazione Australiana **29** If
Teruel **9** Eb
Teseney **25** Dc
Teshio **17** Gb
Tessalit **24** BCb
Testa del Gargano (cap.) **10** Fd
Teste, La– **8** Ce
Tete **26** Cc
Tête Jaune Cache **31** CDc
Teterev (riv.) **6** Ia
Tétouan **24** Ba
Tetovo **11** Dbc
Teulada **10** Be
Teulada, Capo– **10** Be
Teun, Pulau– (i.) **18** Gf
Teuri–Tō (i.) **17** Gb
Teutoburgerwald (mts.) **5** ABbc
Tevere (riv.) **10** Dc
Teverya **22** Ef
Texarcana **32** Bb
Texas (State) **33** CDc
Texel (i.) **8** Fa
Tezpur **19** Bc
Thabana Ntlenyana (mt.) **26** BCd
Thabazimbi **26** Bd
Thailand (Siam) (Ind. St.) **15** Dh
Thailand, Gulf of– **19** Dfg
Thai Nguyen **19** Ed
Thakhek **18** DEe
Thamad, Ath– **22** DEh
Thames (riv.) **7** Gf
Thamud **21** DEf
Thana **20** De
Thanh Hoa **19** Ee
Thanjavur **20** EFf
Thar (Great Indian Desert) **20** Dc
Thargomindah **29** Gd
Tharrawaddy **19** Ce
Tharsis **9** Bd
Thásos (i.) **11** Fc
Thásos **11** Fc

Thaton **19** Ce
Thaya (riv.) **5** Ed
Thayawthadangyi Kyun (i.) **19** Cf
Thayetmyo **19** Ce
Thebes **11** Ed
Thebes (r.) **25** Db
The Hague **8** EFa
The Little Minch (str.) **7** Cc
Thelon (riv.) **31** Eb
Theodore **29** Hlcd
Théra → Santorino (i.) **11** Fe
Thermopolis **33** Cb
Thermopylae (p.) **11** Ed
Thessalía (phys. reg.) **11** DEd
Thetford **7** Ge
The Wash (b.) **7** Ge
Thiers **8** Ee
Thiès **24** Ac
Thika **26** Cb
Thikombia (i.) **28** map no.6
Thimphu **15** CDg
Thio **28** map no.4
Thionville **8** FGc
Thíra (i.) **11** Fe
Third Cataract **25** CDc
Thisted **4** ABd
Thithia (i.) **28** map no.6
Thompson **31** Fc
Thompson (riv.) **33** ABa
Thomson River **29** Gcd
Thon Buri **19** CDf
Thonon–les–Bains **5** Ae
Thouars **8** CDd
Thrace (phys. reg.) **11** FGc
Three Springs **29** ABd
Thule / Qaanaaq **30** LMb
Thule Air Base **30** LMb
Thun **10** Aa
Thunder Bay (Fort William) **31** FGd
Thunder Bay (Port Arthur) **31** FGd
Thuringer Wald (mts.) **5** Cc
Thuringia (phys. reg.) **5** Cc
Thursday Island **29** Ga
Thurso **7** Eb
Thurston Island **42** grid square no.3
Tianjin → Tientsin **16** Ec
Tianmen **16** Dd
Tianqiaoling **17** ABc
Tian Shan (mts.) **13** GHe
Tianshui **16** BCd
Tiarei **28** map no.2
Tiaret **24** Ca
Tiavea **28** map no.5
Tibasti, Sarìr– (des.) **24** Db
Tibati **24** Dd
Tiberias, Lake– (Galilee, Sea of–) **22** EFf
Tibesti (mts.) **25** Bbc
Tibet (Aut. Reg.) **15** Cf
Tibetan Plateau **22** FGb
Tibooburra **29** Gd
Tiburón, Isla– (i.) **34** Ab
Tichît **24** Bb
Tichla **24** Ab
Ticino (riv.) **10** Bb
Ticul **34** CDb
Tidjikja **24** Ac
Tidra, Île– **24** Abc
Tieling **16** FGb

Tientsin (Tianjin) **16** Ec
Tierra del Fuego (prov.) **36** DEi
Tierra del Fuego, Isla Grande de– (i.) **40** Bc
Tiétar (riv.) **9** Cb
Tietê (riv.) **39** Db
Tigil **14** IJd
Tigre (riv.) **37** Bc
Tigre, El– **37** Cb
Tigris (riv.) **21** Cb
Tih, Gebel el– (mt.) **22** DEh
Tihamat (phys. reg.) **21** Cf
Tihoreck **13** CDe
Tihvin **12** Db
Tijuana **34** Aa
Tikal (r.) **35** Bb
Tikamgarh **19** Gj
Tikrit **21** Cc
Tiksi **14** FGb
Tiladummati Atoll **20** Dg
Tilburg **8** Fb
Tiliçiki **14** Jc
Tîlos (i.) **11** Ge
Tilpa **29** Ge
Timaševsk **12** Ed
Timbédra **24** Bc
Timfristós (mt.) **11** Dd
Timimoun **24** Cb
Timiris, Cap– **24** Ac
Timiş (riv.) **6** Ed
Timişoara **6** Ed
Timmins **31** Gd
Timok (riv.) **6** Fd
Timor, Pulau– (i.) **15** Ejk
Timor Sea **18** Gg
Timote **39** Bc
Timsah, Bahra al– **25** map no.1
Tina, El– **25** map no.1
Tinaca Point **18** FGc
Tindouf **24** Bb
Tineo **9** Ba
Tingo María **37** Bc
Tingri **19** Ii
Tinogasta **39** Bb
Tinos (i.) **11** Fe
Tinrhert, Hamada de– (des.) **24** CDb
Tinsukia **19** Cc
Tintina **39** Bb
Tioman, Pulau– (i.) **18** BCd
Tioro Selat **18** Fef
Tipperary **7** Be
Tirana **11** Cc
Tiraspol **13** BCe
Tire **22** Acd
Tiree (i.) **7** Cc
Tîrgovişte **6** Gd
Tirgu Jiu **6** Fd
Tîrgu Mureş **6** Gc
Tîrgu Neamţ **6** Hc
Tîrgu Ocna **6** Hc
Tirich Mir (mt.) **20** Da
Tîrnaveni **6** Gc
Tîrnava Mare (riv.) **6** Gc
Tîrnăveni **6** Gc
Tîrnavos **11** Ed
Tiruchchirappalli **15** Ch
Tirunelveli **20** Eg
Tisza (riv.) **6** Fb

Tiszakécske **6** Ec
Tit Ary **14** Fb
Titicaca, Lago– **39** Ba
Titograd → Podgorica **11** Cb
Titovo Užice **6** De
Titov Veles **11** Dc
Titov vrh (mt.) **11** Dc
Titule **25** Cd
Titusville **32** CDc
Tivaouane **24** Ac
Tivoli **10** Dd
Tizimin **34** Db
Tizi–Ouzou **24** Ca
Tiznit **24** Bb
Tjačev **6** Fbc
Tjörn (i.) **4** Bd
Tjulgan **12** Ic
Tjumen **13** Fd
Tjung (riv.) **14** Fc
Tlemcen **24** BCa
Toaca, Vírful– (mt.) **6** Gc
Toamasina **23** GHg
Toba, Danau– **18** Ad
Tobago (i.) **35** Db
Tobarra **9** DEc
Tobermory **7** CDc
Tobi–Shima (i.) **17** Fe
Toblach / Dobbiaco **10** Da
Tobol (riv.) **13** Fd
Tobol **13** Fd
Tobolsk **13** FGd
Tocantinópolis **38** Cb
Tocantins (State) **38** Cc
Tocantins (riv.) **38** Cc
Tocopilla **39** Ab
Tocorpuri, Cerro de– (mt.) **39** Bb
Tocuyo, El– **37** Cb
Todd River **29** EFc
Todi **10** Dc
Tõdi (mt.) **10** Ba
Todo–ga–Saki **17** GHe
Todos os Santos, Baía de– (b.) **38** Dc
Todos Santos **34** Ab
Tofua Island **28** Acd
Togian, Kepulauan– **18** Fde
Togliatti (Stavropol) **13** Dd
Togo (Ind. St.) **23** Ce
Togtoh **16** Db
Tohivea (mt.) **28** map no.2
Tohma (riv.) **22** FGc
Toijala **4** Ec
Tokachi–Gawa (riv.) **17** Hc
Tokaj **6** Eb
Tokara–Rettō **16** Ge
Tokat **22** Fb
Tokelau / Union Islands **28** Ac
Tokmak [Kyrg.] **13** Ge
Tokmak [Ukr.] **12** Ed
Tokunoshima (i.) **16** Ge
Tokushima **16** Hid
Tokuyama **17** BCgh
Tōkyō **16** IJc
Tõlañaro **23** Gh
Tolbuhin → Dobrič **11** GHb
Toledo [Phil.] **18** Fb
Toledo [Sp.] **9** CDc
Toledo [U.S.] **32** Ca
Toledo, Montes de– **9** CDc
Toliara **23** Gh
Tolima, Nevado del– (mt.) **37** Bb

Tol - Tub

Tolitoli **18** EFd
Tolmezzo **10** Da
Tolo, Gulf of– **18** Fe
Tolosa **9** DEa
Tolstoje **6** Gb
Toltén **39** Ac
Tolú **37** Bb
Toluca de Lerdo **34** BCc
Tom (riv.) **13** Hd
Toma, La– **39** Bc
Tomakomai **17** GHc
Tomari **14** He
Tomaševka **5** IJc
Tomašpol **6** Ib
Tomaszów Lubelski **5** IJc
Tomaszów Mazowiecki **5** Hc
Tombador, Serra do– (mts.) **38** Bc
Tomb–e Bozorg **21** EFd
Tombôco **26** Ab
Tombouctou **24** Bc
Tombua **26** Ac
Tomé **39** Ac
Tomelilla **5** Ea
Tomelloso **9** Dc
Tomini **18** Fd
Tomini, Teluk– **18** Fde
Tommot **14** Fd
Tomorit (mt.) **11** Dc
Tom Price **29** Bc
Tomsk **13** Hd
Tomtabacken (mt.) **4** Cd
Tonalá **34** Cc
Tondano **18** FGd
Tønder **5** Ba
Tone (riv.) **17** Gg
Tonekäbon **21** Eb
Tonga Islands (Ind. St.) **28** Acd
Tongatapu Group **28** Ad
Tongchuan **16** CDc
Tonghe **16** Ga
Tonghua **16** FGb
Tongjiang **16** Ha
Tongliao **16** Fb
Tongoa (i.) **28** map no.4
Tongzi **16** Ce
Tónichi **34** Bb
Tonk **20** Ec
Tonkin (phys. reg.) **19** DEd
Tonkin, Gulf of– **19** Ede
Tonle Sap (l.) **19** Df
Tonneins **8** CDe
Tonopah **33** Bc
Tonota **26** Bd
Tons (riv.) **19** Hj
Tønsberg **4** Bd
Toora–Hem **14** Cd
Toowoomba **29** Id
Topakli **22** Ec
Topeka **32** Bb
Topki **13** Hd
Toplița **6** Gc
Topol'čany **5** FGd
Topolovgrad **11** Gbc
Topozero, ozero– **4** Gb
Torat–e–Heydariyeh **21** FGbc
Torbali **11** Gd
Torbay **7** Ef
Toréz **12** Ed
Torgau **5** Dc
Tori–Shima (i.) **17** Gi

Tormes (riv.) **9** Bb
Torneälven (riv.) **4** EFb
Torneträsk (l.) **4** DEa
Torngat Mountains **31** Ic
Tornio **4** Fb
Tornionjoki (riv.) **4** EFb
Toro **9** Cb
Toro, Cerro del– (mt.) **39** ABb
Toro, Punta– (cap.) **35** map no.1
Törökszentmiklós **6** Ec
Toronto **31** GHd
Toropec **12** Db
Tororo **25** Dd
Torre del Greco **10** Ed
Torrelavega **9** CDa
Torremolinos **9** Cd
Torrens, Lake– **29** Fe
Torrens Creek **29** GHc
Torrente **9** Ec
Torreón **30** Hg
Torrés, Îles– **28** map no.4
Torres Strait **27** Cc
Torrijos **9** Cc
Torrington **33** Cb
Torsby **4** Cc
Tortona **10** Bb
Tortosa **9** Fb
Tortosa, Cabo de– (cap.) **9** Fb
Tortue, Ile de la– (i.) **35** Cab
Tortuga, Isla la– (i.) **37** Ca
Toruń **5** Gb
Toržok **12** DEb
Tosashimizu **17** Ch
Tosa–Wan **17** Ch
Toscana (reg.) **10** BCbc
Toscano, Arcipelago– **10** BCc
Tossa **9** Gb
Tostado **39** Bb
Tosya **22** Eb
Totana **9** Ed
Totma **12** Fab
Totness **37** Db
Totoya (i.) **28** map no.6
Tottori **16** Hc
Toubkal, Jebel– (mt.) **24** Ba
Touggourt **24** Ca
Touho **28** map no.4
Toul **8** FGc
Toulon **8** FGf
Toulouse **8** DEf
Toungoo **19** Ce
Touraine (phys. reg.) **8** Dd
Tourcoing **8** Eb
Touriñan, Cabo– (cap.) **9** Aa
Tournon **8** Fe
Tours **8** Dd
Towada **17** Gd
Townshend, Cape– **29** Ic
Townsville **29** Hb
Towuti, Danau– **18** Fe
Toyama **16** Ic
Toyama–Wan **17** Ef
Toyohashi **16** Id
Toyooka **17** Dg
Toyota **17** Eg
Tozanli (riv.) **22** Fb
Trabzon **21** BCa
Trafalgar, Cabo– (cap.) **9** Bd
Trail **33** Bb
Trajan's wall **6** Hld

Tralee **7** ABe
Tranås **4** Cd
Trang **19** Cg
Trani **10** Fd
Transantarctic Mountains **42** grid square no.4
Transcona **33** Da
Transkei (hist. reg.) **26** Be
Transvaal (prov.) **26** BCd
Transylvania (phys. reg.) **6** FGc
Transylvanian Alps (Southern Carpathians) **6** FGd
Trapani **10** Df
Trasimeno, Lago– **10** Dc
Tras–os–Montes (phys. reg.) **9** Bb
Trat **19** Df
Traunstein **5** Dde
Traverse City **32** Ca
Travnik **6** Cd
Trbovlje **6** Bc
Trebbia (riv.) **10** Bb
Trebinje **11** Cb
Trebišov **5** Hd
Trebová **5** Fd
Tree Pagodas Pass **19** Cef
Treinta y Tres **39** Cc
Trélazé **8** Cd
Trelew **40** Bb
Trelleborg **4** Ce
Tremiti, Isole– **10** Ec
Tremp **9** Fa
Trenčín **5** Gd
Trenque Lauquen **39** Bc
Trent (riv.) **7** Fe
Trentino–Alto Adige (reg.) **10** Ca
Trento **10** Ca
Trenton **32** Dab
Tréport, Le– **8** Dbc
Tres Arroyos **39** BCc
Três Casas **37** Cc
Tres Esquinas **37** Bb
Três Lagoas **39** Cb
Tres Lagos **40** ABb
Tres Picos, Cerro– (mt.) **39** Bc
Tres Puntas, Cabo– **40** Bcd
Três Rios **39** Db
Tres Virgenes, Las– (mt.) **34** Ab
Treungen **4** ABd
Treviso **10** Db
Tricase **10** Ge
Trichur **20** Ef
Tridentine Alps **10** Ca
Trier **5** Ad
Trieste **10** Db
Trikala **11** Dd
Trikhonís, Límni– **11** Dd
Trincomalee **15** Ci
Trindade, Ilha da– (i.) **36** Gef
Trinec **5** Gd
Trinidad (i.) **37** CDa
Trinidad [Bol.] **39** Ba
Trinidad [U.S.] **33** Cc
Trinidad, Río– (riv.) **35** map no.1
Trinidad and Tobago (Ind. St.) **36** DEbc

Trinity (riv.) **32** Bb
Tripoli [Leb.] **22** Ee
Tripoli [Lib.] **24** Da
Trípolis **11** Ee
Tripura (State) **19** Bd
Tristan da Cunha (is.) **23** ABi
Trivandrum **15** Ci
Trnava **5** FGd
Trogir **10** Fc
Troglav (mt.) **6** Ce
Troia **10** Ed
Troick **13** Fd
Troicko–Pečorsk **13** EFc
Trois–Rivières **31** Hld
Trojan **11** Fb
Trojansky prohod **11** Fb
Trollhättan **4** BCd
Trollheimen (mt.) **4** Bc
Trombetas (riv.) **38** Ba
Tromelin (i.) **23** map no.1
Tromsø **4** DEa
Tronador (mt.) **40** Ab
Trondheim **4** Bc
Trondheimsfjorden (b.) **4** Bc
Troódos, Mount– (Olympus) **22** De
Trotus (riv.) **6** Hc
Trouville–sur–Mer **8** CDc
Trowbridge **7** EFf
Troy (r.) **22** Ac
Troy [Al.–U.S.] **32** Cb
Troy [N.Y.–U.S.] **32** Da
Troyes **8** Fc
Trucial Coast **21** EFe
Trudovoje [Kaz.] **13** Fd
Trudovoje [Russia] **17** Ch
Trujillo [Hond.] **35** Bb
Trujillo [Peru] **36** BCd
Trujillo [Sp.] **9** BCc
Trujillo [Ven.] **37** BCb
Truk Islands **27** Cc
Truro [Can.] **31** Id
Truro [U.K.] **7** Df
Truskavec **6** FGb
Trutnov **5** Ec
Trysil (riv.) **4** Cc
Trzcianka **5** EFb
Tsaratanana (mt.) **26** map no.1
Tsau **26** Bcd
Tshabong **26** Bd
Tshela **26** Ab
Tshikapa **26** Bb
Tshuapa (riv.) **26** Bb
Tsinan (Jinan) **15** Df
Tsingtao (Qingdao) **16** Fc
Tsu **16** Id
Tsugaro–Kaikyō **16** IJb
Tsumeb **23** Dg
Tsuruga **16** Ic
Tsuruoka **17** Fe
Tsushima **17** Ag
Tsushima (is.) **16** Gd
Tsushima–Kaikyō **17** Agh
Tsuyama **16** Hcd
Tual **18** Hf
Tuamoto Archipelago **28** BCcd
Tuapse **13** Ce
Tuban **18** Df
Tubarão **39** Db
Tübingen **5** Bd
Țubruq **24** Ea

© ISTITUTO GEOGRAFICO DE AGOSTINI - Novara

186

Tubuaï, Île– (i.) **28** Bd
Tubuai Islands **28** Bd
Tucson **33** Bc
Tucumcari **33** Cc
Tucupita **37** Cb
Tucuruí **38** Cb
Tudela **9** Ea
Tufi **27** Cc
Tuguegarao **18** Fa
Tugur **14** Gd
Tujmazy **12** Hc
Tukangbesi, Kepulauan– **18** FGf
Tükrah **24** DEa
Tuktoyaktuk **31** BCb
Tukums **4** Ed
Tula **13** Cd
Tulancingo **34** Cb
Tulcán **37** Bb
Tulcea **6** Id
Tulčin **6** Ib
Tuli **26** BCd
Tullamore **7** Ce
Tulle **5** De
Tully **29** Hb
Tuloma (riv.) **4** GHa
Tulsa **32** Bb
Tuluá **37** Bb
Tulun **14** Dd
Tumaco **37** Bb
Tuman–gang **17** Ac
Tumbes **37** ABc
Tumd Youqi **16** Db
Tumen (riv.) **16** Gb
Tumkur **20** Ef
Tumpat **19** Dg
Tumucumaque, Serra– (mts.) **37** Db
Tumut **29** Hf
Tunduru **26** Cc
Tundža (riv.) **11** Gb
Tungabhadra (riv.) **20** Ee
Tungsten **31** Cb
Tūnis **24** CDa
Tunis, Gulf of– **10** Cf
Tunisia (Ind. St.) **23** CDb
Tunja **37** Bb
Tunuyán **39** Bc
Tunxi **16** Ede
Tupelo **32** Cb
Tupiza **39** Bb
Tuque, La– **31** Hd
Tura (riv.) **12** Jb
Tura [India] **19** Jj
Tura [Russia] **14** Dc
Turabah **21** Ce
Turan **14** Cd
Turayf, At– **21** Bc
Turbah, At– **21** Cg
Turbat **20** Bc
Turbo **37** Bb
Turda **6** Fc
Tureia Atoll **28** Cd
Turek **5** Gbc
Turgaj (riv.) **13** Fe
Turgaj **13** Fe
Turgutlu **22** Ac
Tûri **4** Fd
Turia → Guadalaviar (riv.) **9** Ebc
Turiaçu **38** Cb
Turin **10** Ab
Turinsk **12** Jb

Turi Rog **17** Bb
Turka **5** Id
Turkana, Lake– **25** Dd
Turkestan **13** Fe
Turkey (Ind. St.) **15** ABf
Turkmenistan (Ind. St.) **13** EFf
Turks Islands **32** Dc
Turku **4** Ec
Turneffe Islands **35** Bb
Turnhout **8** Fb
Turnov **5** Ec
Turnu–Măgurele **6** Ge
Turnu Roşu, Pasul– **6** FGd
Turnu–Severin **6** Fd
Turpan **15** Ce
Turuhansk **14** BCc
Tuscaloosa **32** Cb
Tutajev **12** Eb
Tuticorin **20** Eg
Tutóia **38** Cb
Tutrakan **11** Gab
Tuttlingen **5** Bde
Tutuila Island **28** map no.5
Tuva (Aut. Rep.) **14** Cd
Tuvalu Islands (Ind. St.) **27** Dc
Tuwayq, Jabal– **21** Def
Tüxpan **34** Bb
Tuxpan de Rodríguez Cano **34** Cb
Tuxtla Gutiérrez **34** Cc
Tüy **9** Aab
Tuy Hoa **19** Ef
Tuz, Lake– **22** Dc
Tüz Khurmätü **21** Cc
Tuzla **6** Dd
Tvedestrand **4** ABd
Tver (Kalinin) **13** Cd
Tweed (riv.) **7** Ed
Twillingate **31** Jcd
Twin Falls **33** Bb
Tychy **5** Gc
Tyler **32** Bb
Tympákion **11** Ff
Tynda **14** Fd
Tynemouth **7** Fd
Tynset **4** Bc
Tyre **22** Ef
Tyrrhenian Sea **10** De

U

Uaboe **27** map no.2
Ua Huka, Île– (i.) **28** Cc
Ualdia **21** BCg
Uaroo **29** Bc
Uatumã (riv.) **37** Dc
Uaupés **37** Cbc
Uaupés (riv.) **37** Cb
Ubá **39** Db
Ubaitaba **38** Dc
Ubangi (riv.) **26** Aa
'Ubaylah, Al– **21** DEe
Ubayyid, Al– **25** CDc
Ube **17** Bgh
Ubeda **9** Dcd
Uberaba **39** Da
Uberlândia **39** Da
Ubon Ratchathani **15** Dh
Ubsu–Nur (l.) **14** Cd

Ubundu **26** Bab
Učaly **12** Ic
Ucayali (riv.) **37** Bcd
Uchiura–Wan **17** Gc
Učur (riv.) **14** Gd
Uda [Russia] (riv.) **14** Gd
Udaipur **20** Dd
Uddevalla **4** Bd
Uddjaur **4** Db
Udhampur **20** Eb
Udine **10** Da
Udipi **20** Df
Udmurt (Aut. Rep.) **13** Ed
Udon Thani **19** De
Ueda **17** Ff
Uele (riv.) **25** Cd
Uelen **14** Lc
Uelzen **5** Cb
Ufa **13** Ed
Ufa (riv.) **12** Ib
Uganda (Ind. St.) **23** Fef
Uglegorsk **14** He
Uglekamensk **17** CDc
Uglič **12** Eb
Uherské Hradiště **5** Fd
Uhta **13** Ec
Uige **26** Ab
Uil (riv.) **12** Hd
Uil **12** Hd
Uinta Mountains **33** BCb
Üisöng **17** Af
Uitenhage **26** Be
Ujae Atoll **27** Db
Ujelang Atoll **27** CDb
Uji–Guntō (i.) **17** Ai
Ujiji **26** Bb
Ujjain **20** Ed
Ujung Pandang (Makasar) **18** Eef
Ukiah **33** Ac
Ukmergé **4** Fe
Ukraine (Ind. St.) **13** BCe
Uku–Jima (i.) **17** Ah
Ula **11** He
Ula, Al– **21** Bd
Ulahe **17** CDb
Ulan–Bator **14** De
Ulangom **14** Ce
Ulan–Ude **14** DEd
Ulaş **22** Fc
Ulchin **17** Af
Ulcinj **11** Cc
Ulegej **14** BCe
Ulhasnagar **20** De
Ulithi Atoll **27** Cb
Uljanovsk → Simbirsk **13** DEd
Uljasutaj **14** Ce
Ullapool **7** Dc
Ullŭng–Do (i.) **16** Hc
Ulm **5** BCd
Ulsan **16** GHc
Ulster (prov.) **7** BCd
Ulubat Gölü **22** Bb
Uludağ (mt.) **22** Bbc
Ulukişla **22** DEd
Ulungur He (riv.) **14** BCe
Uman **12** CDd
Umanak / Uummannaq **30** MNb
Umatac **27** map no.1
Umbria (reg.) **10** CDc

Umbro–Marchigiano, Appennino– **10** Dc
Umeå **4** Ec
Umeälven (riv.) **4** Db
Umm al Hayt, Wädi– **21** Ef
Umm Lajj **21** Bd
Umm Qaşr, Khawr– **21** Dcd
Umm Ruwäbah **25** Dc
Umtata **26** Be
Una (riv.) **6** Cd
'Unayzah **21** Cd
Under–Han **16** Da
Uneča **12** Dc
Ungava, Péninsula d'– **31** Hb
Ungava Bay **31** Ic
Ungeny **6** HIc
Unggi **17** ABc
União da Vitória **39** Cb
Unimak Island **30** BCd
Unión, La– [Col.] **37** Bb
Unión, La– [El Sal.] **35** Bb
Unión, La– [Sp.] **9** Ed
Uniondale **26** Be
Union Islands / Tokelau **28** Ac
United Arab Emirates (Ind. St.) **21** EFe
United Kingdom (Ind. St.) **3** CDb
United States (Ind. St.) **30** GJef
Unnao **19** Hj
Unst (i.) **7** Fa
Unstrut (riv.) **5** Cc
Unter, Île– **27** Dd
Ünye **22** Fb
Unža (riv.) **12** Fb
Upata **37** Cb
Upernavik **30** MNb
Upi **27** map no.1
Upington **23** DEh
Upolu Island **28** map no.5
Upolu Point **28** map no.5
Upper Lough Erne **7** Cd
Uppsala **4** Dcd
'Uqaylah, Al– **24** DEab
Ur (r.) **21** Dc
Urakawa **17** Hc
Ural (riv.) **13** Ee
Ural Mountains **13** EFcd
Uralsk **13** Ed
Urandangi **29** Fc
Urandí **39** Da
Uranium City **30** Hcd
Uraricoera (riv.) **37** Cb
Uraricoera (riv.) **37** Cb
Urawa **17** FGfg
Urbett Atoll **28** map no.3
Urbino **10** Dc
Urbión, Picos de– (mts.) **9** Dab
Urdoma **12** Ga
Ure (riv.) **7** Fd
Uren **12** Gb
Urfa **21** Bb
Urgenč **13** Fe
Uribia **37** Bb
Urjupinsk **12** Fc
Urla **11** Gd
Urmia, Lake– **21** CDb
Uroševac **11** Db
Uruaçu **38** BCc
Uruapan del Progreso **34** Bc
Urubamba (riv.) **37** Bd

Urubamba 39 Aa
Uruçuí 38 Cb
Uruguaiana 39 Cbc
Uruguay (riv.) 39 Cc
Uruguay (Ind. St.) 36 Eg
Ürümqi 15 Ce
Urup, ostrov– (i.) 14 Hle
Urussu 12 Hc
Urziceni 6 Hd
Uržum 12 Hb
Usa (riv.) 13 Ec
Uşac 22 Bc
Usakos 26 Ad
Usedom (i.) 5 DEab
Ushuaia 36 CDi
Usman 12 EFc
Usolje–Sibirskoje 14 Dd
Ussel 8 Ee
Ussuri (Wusuli Jiang) (riv.) 16 Ha
Ussurijsk 14 Ge
Ust–Barguzin 14 DEd
Ust–Čaun 14 JKc
Ùstica (i.) 10 De
Ust–Ilimsk 14 Dd
Ùstí nad Labem 5 Ec
Ustjurt (phys. reg.) 13 Ee
Ustka 5 Fa
Ust–Kamčatsk 14 Jd
Ust–Kamenogo'rsk 13 GHe
Ust–Katav 12 Ibc
Ust–Kut 14 Dd
Ust–Labinsk 12 Ed
Ust–Maja 14 Gc
Ust–Nera 14 GHc
Uštobe 13 Ge
Ust–Ordynski 14 Dd
Usulután 35 Bb
Usumacinta (riv.) 34 Cc
Utah (State) 33 Bc
Utah Lake 33 Bbc
Utena 12 Cb
Uthai Thani 19 CDe
Utica 32 Da
Utirik Island 27 Db
Utraula 19 Hj
Utrecht 8 Fab
Utrera 9 Cd
Utsjoki 4 Fa
Utsunomiya 16 IJc
Uttaradit 19 CDe
Uttar Pradesh (State) 20 EFc
Uummannaq / Umanak 30 MNb
Uusikaupunki 4 DEc
Uva 12 Hb
Uvalde 33 CDd
Uvarovo 12 Fc
Uvinza 26 Cb
Uvira 26 Bb
Uwajima 16 Hd
Uwayl 25 Cd
'Uwaynāt, Jabal al– (mt.) 25 Cb
'Uwayrid, Ḥarrat Al– 21 Bd
Uyuni 39 Bb
Uyuni, Salar de– (s. m.) 39 Bab
Uzbekistan (Ind. St.) 13 Fef
Uzerche 8 De
Užgorod 6 Fb
Uzlovaja 12 Ec
Užokski, pereval– 5 Id
Uzunköprü 11 Gc
Užur 14 BCd

V

Vaal (riv.) 26 Bd
Vaala 4 Fb
Vaasa 4 Ec
Vác 6 Dc
Vacaria 39 Cb
Vaccares, Étang de– (sw.) 8 EFf
Vadodara 20 Dd
Vadsø 4 Ga
Værøy (i.) 4 BCb
Vaga (riv.) 12 Fa
Váh (riv.) 5 FGd
Vaiaku 27 DEc
Vairaatea Atoll 28 Ccd
Vajgač, ostrov– (i.) 13 Ebc
Valdagno 10 Cb
Valdaj 12 Db
Valdajskaja vozvišennost (mts.) 13 Cd
Valdemarsvik 4 Dd
Valdeolea (Mataporquera) 9 CDa
Valdepeñas 9 Dc
Valderaduey (riv.) 9 Cab
Valdés, Península– 40 Bb
Valdez 31 Ab
Valdivia 39 Ac
Val–d'Or 32 Da
Valdosta 32 Cb
Valença 38 Dc
Valença do Piauí 38 Cb
Valençay 8 Dd
Valence 8 Fe
Valencia (phys. reg.) 9 EFbc
Valencia [Sp.] 9 EFc
Valencia [Ven.] 37 Cab
Valencia, Golfo de– 9 Fc
Valencia de Alcántara 9 Bc
Valenciennes 8 EFb
Vălenii de Munte 6 GHd
Valentin 17 Dc
Valentine 33 CDb
Valenza 10 Bb
Valera 37 Bb
Valga 4 Fd
Valka 4 Fd
Valkeakoski 4 EFc
Valladolid 9 Cb
Valle d'Aosta (reg.) 10 Ab
Valle de la Pascua 37 Cb
Valledupar 37 Bab
Valle Grande 39 Ba
Vallejo 33 Ac
Vallenar 39 Ab
Valletta 10 Eg
Valley City 32 Ba
Valls 9 Fb
Valmiera 4 Fd
Valognes 8 Cc
Valona 11 Cc
Valparaíso [Chile] 39 Ac
Valparaíso [Mex.] 34 Bb
Valujki 12 Ec
Valverde del Camino 9 Bd
Vammala 4 Ec
Van 21 Cb
Van, Lake– 21 Cb
Vanavara 14 Dc
Vancouver [Can.] 33 Ab
Vancouver [U.S.] 33 Ab

Vancouver Island 31 BCd
Van Diemen Gulf 29 Ea
Vanegas 34 Bb
Vänern (i.) 4 Cd
Vänersborg (l.) 4 BCd
Vanikolo Islands 27 Dc
Vanino 14 GHe
Vanna (i.) 4 Da
Vännäs 4 Dbc
Vannes 8 Bd
Vanoua Lava, Île– (i.) 28 map no.4
Vansbro 4 Cc
Vansittart Island 31 Gb
Vanua Levu (i.) 27 DEc
Vanua Mbalavu (i.) 28 map no.6
Vanuatu (Ind. St.) 27 Dc
Vapnjarka 6 Ib
Var (riv.) 8 Gf
Varanasi (Benares) 20 Fcd
Varangerfjorden (b.) 4 GHa
Varangerhalvøya 4 Ga
Varaždin 6 BCc
Varazze 10 Bb
Varberg 4 BCd
Vardar (riv.) 11 Dbc
Varde 5 Ba
Vardø 4 GHa
Varel 5 ABb
Vareš 6 Dd
Varese 10 Bb
Varkaus 4 FGc
Varna 11 GHb
Värnamo 4 Cd
Várpalota 6 Dc
Vartholomión 11 De
Vasçáu 6 Fc
Vasiľkov 12 Dc
Vaslui 6 Hc
Västerås 4 Dd
Västervik 4 Dd
Vasto 10 Ec
Vasvár 6 Cc
Vatican City (Ind. St.) 10 Dcd
Vatnajökull (gl.) 4 map no.1
Vatneyri 4 map no.1
Vatoa Island 28 map no.6
Vatra Dornei 6 Gc
Vättern (l.) 4 Cd
Vaughn 33 Cc
Vaupés (riv.) 37 Bb
Vava'u Group 28 Ac
Växjö 4 Cd
Veadeiros, Chapada dos– (plat.) 38 Cc
Vedea (riv.) 6 Gd
Vedia 39 Bc
Vegas, Las– [N.M.–U.S.] 33 Cc
Vegas, Las– [Nv.–U.S.] 33 Bc
Vegorritis, Limni– 11 Dc
Veinticinco de Mayo 39 Bc
Vejer de la Frontera 9 Bd
Vejle 4 Be
Velebit (mts.) 6 Bd
Veleta, Pico del– (mt.) 9 Dd
Vélez–Málaga 9 CDd
Vélez Rubio 9 DEd
Velhas, Rio das– (riv.) 39 Da
Velikaja (riv.) 12 Cb
Velikaja Kema 14 Ge
Velika Plana 6 Ed

Velikije Luki 13 BCd
Veliki Ustjug 13 Dc
Veliko Tárnovo 11 Fb
Velingrad 11 Ebc
Velino, Monte– 10 Dc
Veliž 12 Db
Velletri 10 Dd
Vellore 20 Ef
Velsk 12 Fa
Venado Tuerto 39 Bc
Venda 26 BCd
Vendée (phys. reg.) 8 Cd
Vendôme 8 Dd
Veneto (phys. reg.) 10 Cb
Venezuela (Ind. St.) 36 Dc
Venezuela, Golfo de– 37 Ba
Venice 10 Db
Venice, Gulf of– 10 Db
Venice Mestre 10 Db
Vénissieux 8 Fe
Venlo 8 FGb
Venta (riv.) 4 Ed
Ventimiglia 10 Ac
Ventotene (i.) 10 Dd
Ventoux, Mont– (mt.) 8 Fe
Ventspils 13 Bd
Ventuari (riv.) 37 Cb
Vénus, Pointe– (cap.) 28 map no.2
Vera 39 Bb
Veracruz 34 Cc
Veraval 20 CDd
Verbano → Maggiore, Lago– 10 Bab
Vercelli 10 Bb
Verde, Cap– (cap.) 24 Ac
Verde, Rio– (riv.) 39 Cab
Verden an der Aller 5 Bb
Verdon (riv.) 8 Gf
Verdon–sur–Mer, Le– 8 Ce
Verdun 8 Fc
Vereščagino 12 Hb
Verhnedvinsk 4 Fe
Verhneuralsk 12 IJc
Verhni Baskunčak 13 De
Verhni Ufalej 12 Jb
Verhnjaja Amga 14 Fcd
Verhnjaja Salda 12 Jb
Verhnjaja Tojma 12 Ga
Verhojansk 14 Gc
Verhojanski, Hrebet– 14 FGc
Verhoturje 12 Jb
Verhovje 12 Ec
Verin 9 Bb
Vermillion 32 Ba
Vermont (State) 32 Da
Vernal 33 Cb
Vérnon (mt.) 11 Dc
Vernon [Can.] 33 ABab
Vernon [U.S.] 33 CDc
Véroia 11 Ec
Verona 10 Cb
Versailles 8 DEc
Vertiskos Óros (mts.) 11 Ec
Vertou 8 Cd
Vesjegonsk 12 Hb
Vesoul 8 FGd
Vesterålen (is.) 4 Ca
Vestfjorden (b.) 4 Cab
Vestmannaeyjar 4 map no.1
Vestvågøy (i.) 4 Ca
Vesuvius (volc.) 10 Ed
Veszprém 6 Cc

etlanda 4 Cd
etluga (riv.) 12 Gb
etta d'Italia (mt.) 10 CDa
ézère (riv.) 8 De
iacha 39 Ba
iana 38 Cb
iana do Castelo 9 Ab
iareggio 10 Cc
 borg 4 Bd
 bo Valentia 10 Fe
ic 9 Gb
icecomodoro Morambio 42
grid square no.1
icenza 10 Cb
ichada (riv.) 37 BCb
ichy 8 Ed
icksburg 32 BCb
ictor Harbour 29 Ff
ictoria (State) 29 Gf
ictoria [Can.] 33 Ab
ictoria [Chile] 39 Ac
ictoria [H.K.] 15 Dg
ictoria [Mala.] 18 Ecd
ictoria [Malta] 10 Ef
ictoria [U.S.] 32 Bc
ictoria, Lake– 26 Cb
ictoria, Mount– 19 Bd
ictoria de Durango 34 Bb
ictoria de las Tunas 35 Ca
ictoria Falls 26 Bc
ictoria Falls (wf.) 26 Bc
ictoria Island 31 DEa
ictoria Land 42 grid square
no.4
ictoria River 29 Eb
ictoria River Downs 29 DEb
ictoria West 26 Be
ictorica 39 Bc
ičuga 12 Fb
idele 6 Gd
dim 14 Dd
idin 11 Eab
idisha 20 Ed
idzy 4 Fe
iedma 40 Bb
iedma, Lago– 40 Ab
ienna 5 Fd
ienne (riv.) 8 Dd
ienne 8 Fe
ientiane 15 Dh
ieques, Isla de– (i.) 35 Db
ierwaldstätter See 5 Be
ierzon 8 Ed
ieste 10 Fd
ietnam (Ind. St.) 15 Dh
igan 18 EFa
igan, Le– 8 Ef
igia 38 Cb
igía Chico 34 Dc
ignemale, Pic de– (mt.) 8
CDf
igo 9 Aa
ihren (mt.) 11 Ec
iitasaari 4 Fc
ijayawada 15 Ch
ijkitski Strait 14 CDb
ikna (i.) 4 Bb
iktorija, ostrov– 13 CDab
ila Franca de Xira 9 Ac
ilaine (riv.) 8 Cd
ila Murtinho 37 Cd
ilanculos 26 Cd
ila Nova de Gaia 9 Ab

Vilanova i la Geltrú 9 FGb
Vila Real 9 Bb
Vila Real de Santo Antonio 9
ABd
Vila Velha [Braz.] 38 Ba
Vila Velha [Braz.] 38 CDd
Vila Viçosa 9 Bc
Vilejka 12 Cc
Vilhelmina 4 CDb
Vilhena 39 BCa
Viljandi 12 Cb
Viljuj (riv.) 14 Fc
Viljujsk 14 Fc
Villa Angela 39 Bb
Villablino 9 Ba
Villacañas 9 Dc
Villacarrillo 9 Dc
Villacidro 10 Be
Villaco 5 De
Villa Colón 39 Bc
Villa Dolores 39 Bc
Villafranca del Bierzo 9 Ba
Villafranca de los Barros 9
BCc
Villafranca del Panadés 9 Fb
Villagarcía de Arosa 9 ABa
Villaguay 39 Cc
Villa Hayes 39 Cb
Villahermosa 34 Cc
Villajoyosa 9 EFc
Villalba 9 Ba
Villa Maria 39 Bc
Villa Montes 39 Bb
Villanueva de la Serena 9 Cc
Villanueva de los Infantes 9
Dc
Villarreal de los Infantes 9 Ec
Villarrica 39 Cb
Villarrobledo 9 DEc
Villaverde, Madrid– 9 Db
Villavicencio 37 Bb
Villaviciosa 9 Ca
Villazón 39 Bb
Villefranche–de–Rouergue 8
DEe
Villefranche–sur–Saône 8
Fde
Villena 9 Ec
Villeneuve–sur–Lot 8 De
Villeurbanne 8 Fe
Vilnius 4 Fe
Viña del Mar 39 Ac
Vinaroz 9 Fb
Vincennes 32 Cb
Vincennes Bay 42 grid
square no.4
Vinchina 39 Bb
Vindelälven (riv.) 4 Db
Vindhya Range 20 DFd
Vinh 15 Dh
Vinh Loi 19 Eg
Vinita 32 Bb
Vinkovci 6 Dd
Vinnica 13 Be
Vinogradov 5 Id
Vinogradovka 17 Cc
Vinson Massif (mt.) 42 grid
square no.1
Vir 10 Eb
Virac 18 Fb
Virden 33 Cab
Vire 8 Cc
Virgenes, Cabo– 40 Bc

Virginia 32 Ba
Virginia (State) 32 Db
Virgin Islands 36 Db
Virovitica 6 Cd
Virrat 4 Ec
Virtsu 12 Bb
Vis (i.) 11 ABb
Visalia 33 Bc
Visby 4 Dd
Viscount Melville Sound 31
DEa
Višegrad 6 De
Višera (riv.) 12 Ia
Viseu [Braz.] 38 Cb
Viseu [Port.] 9 ABb
Vişeu de Sus 6 Gc
Vishakhapatnam 15 Ch
Viso, Mont– (mt.) 10 Ab
Vistula (riv.) 5 Gb
Vit (riv.) 11 Fb
Vitebsk 13 Cd
Viterbo 10 Dc
Viti Levu (i.) 27 Dc
Vitim (riv.) 14 Ed
Vitória 39 DEb
Vitoria 9 Da
Vitória da Conquista 39 Da
Vitoša (mt.) 11 Eb
Vitré 8 Cc
Vitry–le–François 8 EFc
Vittel 8 FGc
Vittorio Veneto 10 Dab
Vityaz I Depth 27 Cb
Vityaz II Depth 28 Ad
Vityaz III Depth 28 Ad
Vivero 9 Ba
Vize 11 GHc
Vizianagaram 20 FGe
Vižnica 6 Gb
Vjatka (Kirov) 13 Dd
Vjatskije Poljany 12 GHb
Vjazemski 14 Ge
Vjazma 12 Db
Vjazniki 12 Fb
Vjedinenija, ostrov– 13 GHb
Vjosa (riv.) 11 CDc
Vladikavkaz (Ordžonikidze)
13 De
Vladimir 13 CDd
Vladimirski Tupik 12 Db
Vladimir–Volynski 5 Jc
Vladivostok 14 Ge
Vlašić (mt.) 6 Cd
Vlissingen 5 Bc
Vltava → Moldau (riv.) 5 Ed
Vogelsberg (mt.) 5 Bc
Voghera 10 Bb
Voi 26 Db
Voinijama 24 ABd
Vóïon (mts.) 11 Dc
Voiron 8 Fe
Voïviís, Limni– 11 Ed
Vojvodina (phys. reg.) 6 DEd
Volcano Islands 27 Ca
Volčansk 12 IJab
Volda 4 Ac
Volga (riv.) 13 Dd
Volgo–Baltijski vodny put
imeni V.I. Lenina 12 Eab
Volgodonsk 12 Fd
Volgo–Donskoj sudohodny
kanal imeni V.I. Lenin 12 Fd
Volgograd 3 Hc

Volgogradskoje
vodohranilišče 12 Gcd
Volhov (riv.) 12 Db
Volhov 13 Gd
Volinskaja vozvyšennost
(phys. reg.) 6 GHa
Volissós 11 Fd
Völkermarkt 10 Ea
Völklingen 5 Ad
Volkovysk 12 Bc
Volnovaha 12 Ed
Vologda 13 CDd
Vólos 11 Ed
Volsk 13 Dd
Volta, Lake– 24 Bd
Volta Redonda 39 Db
Volterra 10 Cc
Volturino, Monte– 10 Ed
Volturno (riv.) 10 Ed
Vólvi, Limni– 11 Ec
Volžsk 12 Gb
Volžski 13 De
Vopnafjördur 4 map no.1
Vorarlberg (reg.) 5 BCe
Vordingborg 5 Ca
Vórios Evvoïkós, Kólpos– 11
Ed
Vorkuta 13 EFc
Vorogovo 14 BCc
Voronež 13 CDd
Vorošilovgrad → Lugansk 13
CDe
Võrts järv 4 Fd
Võru 4 Fd
Vosges (mts.) 8 Gcd
Voss 4 Ac
Vostok 42 grid square no.4
Vostok Island 28 Bc
Votkinsk 13 Ed
Voúxa, Ákra– 11 Ef
Vouziers 8 Fc
Voznesensk 12 Dd
Vraca 11 Eb
Vranica (mt.) 6 CDde
Vranje 11 Db
Vrbas 6 DEd
Vrbas (riv.) 6 Cd
Vršac 6 Ed
Vryburg 26 Bd
Vsetín 5 FGd
Vukovar 6 Dd
Vulcan 6 Fd
Vulcano (i.) 10 Ee
Vúlture, Monte– 10 Ed
Vung Tau 19 Ef
Vuotso 4 FGa
Vyborg 13 BCc
Vyčegda (riv.) 13 Ec
Vyksa 12 Fb
Vyšni Voloček 13 Cd
Vysokogorny 14 GHde
Vysokoje 5 Ib
Vytegra 13 Ga

W

Wäat Salīmah 25 Db
Wabe Shebele (riv.) 25 Ed
Wabowden 31 Fc
Wąbrzeżno 5 Gb
Wachussett Seamount 28 Bd

Waco **32** Bb
Waddenzee **8** Fa
Waddington, Mount– (mt.) **31** Cb
Wad Madanī **25** Dc
Wafra **21** Dd
Wager Bay **31** FGb
Wagga Wagga **29** Hf
Wagin **29** Be
Wagrowiec **5** Fb
Waha **24** DEb
Wahiawa **28** map no.1
Wahpeton **32** Ba
Waialua **28** map no.1
Waidhofen an der Ybbs **5** Ee
Waigeo, Pulau– (i.) **18** Hde
Waikabubak **18** Ef
Wailuku **28** map no.1
Waimea **28** map no.1
Waingapu **18** Ff
Wajh, Al– **21** Bd
Wajima **17** Ef
Wajir **25** DEd
Wakasa–Wan **17** Dfg
Wakayama **16** Id
Wake Island **27** Db
Wakhan (phys. reg.) **20** Da
Wakkanai **16** Ja
Walachia (phys. reg.) **6** FHd
Wałbrzych **5** Fc
Walcheren **8** Eb
Wałcz **5** Fb
Wales (reg.) **7** DEef
Walgett **29** Hde
Walgreen Coast **42** grid square no.3
Walikale **25** Ce
Walker Mountains **42** grid square no.3
Wallaroo **29** Fe
Walla Walla **33** Bb
Wallis Islands **28** Ac
Walls **7** Fa
Walpole, Île– (i.) **28** map no.4
Walsall **7** Fe
Walsenburg **33** Cc
Walvis Bay **26** Ad
Wamba (riv.) **26** Ab
Wamba **25** Cd
Wanaaring **29** GHd
Wangaratta **29** Hf
Wangiwangi, Pulau– (i.) **18** FGef
Wangpan Yang **16** Fd
Wangqing **16** GHb
Wangxian **15** Df
Wanning **16** Dg
Warangal **20** EFe
Warburton, The– (riv.) **29** Fd
Warburton Mission **29** Dd
Ward, Mount– **42** grid square no.1
Wardha **20** Ed
Wardha (riv.) **20** Ede
Waren [Ger.] **5** Db
Waren [Indon.] **27** Bc
Warmbad **26** Ad
Warnemünde, Rostock– **5** CDab
Warragul **29** Hf
Warrego Range **29** GHcd
Warrego River **29** Hd
Warri **24** Cd

Warrnambool **29** Gf
Warsaw **5** Hb
Warta (riv.) **5** Gc
Warwich **7** Fe
Warwick **29** Id
Wasatch Range **33** Bbc
Wäshim **20** Ed
Washington (i.) **28** ABb
Washington **32** Db
Washington (State) **33** ABb
Washington → Teraina **28** ABb
Washington, Mount– **32** Da
Wasifiya, El– **25** map no.1
Wāsiṭah, Al– **22** Ch
Waspán **35** Bb
Watampone (Bone) **18** EFef
Waterford **7** Ce
Waterloo [Bel.] **8** Fb
Waterloo [U.S.] **32** Ba
Watertown [N.Y.–U.S.] **32** Da
Watertown [S.D.–U.S.] **32** Ba
Waterville **32** Ea
Watford **7** Ff
Watheroo **29** Be
Watrous **31** Ec
Watsa **25** CDd
Watson Lake **31** Cbc
Wauchope **29** Ie
Waukarlycarly, Lake– **29** Cc
Wausau **32** BCa
Wave Hill **29** Eb
Wäw **25** Cd
Wawa **32** Ca
Wāw al Kabīr **24** Db
Waycross **32** Cb
We, Pulau– (i.) **18** Ac
Weda **18** Gde
Weddell Sea **42** grid square no.1
Weed **33** Ab
Weiden in der Oberpfalz **5** CDd
Weifang **16** EFc
Weihai **16** Fc
Wei He (riv.) **16** Cd
Weimar **5** Cc
Weinan **16** CDd
Weipa **29** Ga
Weishan Hu (l.) **16** Ecd
Weisse Elster (riv.) **5** Dc
Weissenfels **5** Cc
Wejherowo **5** Ga
Welkom **26** Bd
Wellesley Islands **29** FGb
Wellington [Austl.] **29** He
Wellington [N.Z.] **27** De
Wellington, Isla– (i.) **40** Ab
Wells **33** Bb
Wells, Lake– **29** Cd
Wels **5** Ed
Welshpool **7** Ee
Wenchang **16** Dg
Wenshan **16** BCf
Wentworth **29** Ge
Wenzhou **16** Fe
Werder **25** Ed
Werra (riv.) **5** Bc
Werribee **29** Gf
Werris Creek **29** HIe
Wesel **5** Ac
Weser (riv.) **5** Bb

Wessel, Cape– **29** Fa
Wessel Islands **29** Fa
West Bengal (State) **20** Gd
West Cape **27** De
Westerland **5** ABa
Western Australia (State) **29** BDcd
Western Carpathians (mts.) **5** FHd
Western Dvina (riv.) **12** BCb
Western Ghats (mts.) **20** DEef
Western Malaysia (State) **18** BCd
Western Sahara (Dep.) **23** Ac
Western Samoa (Ind. St.) **28** Ac
Western Sayans **14** BCd
Westerwald (mt.) **5** ABc
Westfalen **5** ABc
West Falkland (i.) **40** Bc
West Ice Shelf **42** grid square no.2
West Nicholson **23** EFg
Weston **18** Ecd
Weston–super–Mare **7** Ef
West Palm Beach **32** CDc
Westport [Ire.] **7** Be
Westport [N.Z.] **27** De
Westray (i.) **7** Eb
West Siberian Plain **13** FHcd
West Virginia (State) **32** CDb
West Wyalong **29** He
Wetar, Pulau– (i.) **18** Gf
Wewak **27** Cc
Wexford **7** CDe
Weyburn **31** Fd
Weymouth **7** EFf
Whalsay (i.) **7** Fa
Whangarei **27** Dd
Whasington, Mount– **32** Da
Wheeler Peak **33** Bc
Wheeling **32** CDab
Whiehorse **30** EFc
White Bay **31** Jc
Whitehaven **7** Ed
White Nile (riv.) **25** Dc
White River [Ar.–U.S.] **32** Bb
White River [Nb.–U.S.] **33** Cb
White Volta **24** Bcd
Whitney, Mount– **33** Bc
Whyalla **29** Fe
Wichita **32** Bb
Wichita Falls **33** CDc
Wick **7** Eb
Wickham **29** Bc
Wicklow **7** De
Wicklow Mountains **7** Ce
Widgiemooltha **29** Ce
Wieliczka **5** Hcd
Wieluń **5** Gc
Wiener Neustadt **5** EFe
Wienerwald (mts.) **5** EFd
Wieprz (riv.) **5** Ic
Wiesbaden **5** ABc
Wiese, ostrov– (i.) **13** Gb
Wight, Isle of– **7** Ff
Wigtown **7** De
Wilcannia **29** Ge
Wildspitze (mt.) **5** Cc
Wilhelmshaven **5** ABb
Wilkes Land **42** grid square no.4

Willemstad **35** Db
William Creek **29** Fd
Williams Lake **31** Cc
Willis Group **29** Ib
Williston **33** Cb
Williston Lake **31** Cc
Willmar **32** Ba
Willow **30** CDc
Wilmington [De.–U.S.] **32** Dab
Wilmington [N.C.–U.S.] **32** Db
Wilson, Mount– **33** Cc
Wilson's Promontory **29** Hf
Wiluna **29** BCd
Winchester **7** Ff
Windhoek **23** Dh
Windorah **29** Gd
Wind River Range **33** BCb
Windsor [U.K.] **7** Ff
Windsor [U.S.] **31** Gd
Windward Islands **28** Bc
Windward Passage **35** Cab
Winisk **31** Gc
Winneba **24** BCd
Winnemucca **33** Bb
Winnipeg **31** Fcd
Winnipeg, Lake– **31** Fc
Winnipegosis **31** Ec
Winnipegosis, Lake– **31** EFc
Winona **32** Ba
Winslow **33** Bc
Winston–Salem **32** CDb
Winterthur **5** Be
Winton **29** Gc
Wisconsin (State) **32** BCa
Wiślany, Zalew– (lag.) **5** Ga
Wisłok (riv.) **5** Hd
Wismar **5** Cb
Withe Sea **13** Cc
Witputz **26** Ad
Wittemberg **5** Dc
Wittenberge **5** Cb
Wittenoom **29** Bc
Wittlich **5** Ad
W.J.Van Blommestein Meer **37** Db
Wkra (riv.) **5** Hb
Włocławek **5** Gb
Włodawa **5** Ic
Włoszczowa **5** GHc
Woking **7** Ff
Woleai Atoll **27** Cb
Wolf Point **33** Cb
Wolfsberg **5** Ec
Wolfsburg **5** Cb
Wolin (i.) **5** Eb
Wollaston, Islas– **40** ABc
Wollaston Lake **31** Ec
Wollaston Peninsula **31** Dab
Wollongong **29** Ie
Wołomin **5** Hb
Wołów **5** Fc
Wolu **18** Fe
Wolverhampton **7** Ee
Wŏnsan **16** Gc
Wonthaggi **29** GHf
Woodland **33** Ac
Woodroffe, Mount– **29** Ed
Woods, Lake of the– **32** Ba
Woodstock **31** Id
Woodward **33** CDc
Woomera **29** Fe

Wooramel River **29** ABd
Worcester [S. Afr.] **26** ABe
Worcester [U.K.] **7** Ee
Worcester [U.S.] **32** Da
Workington **7** DEd
Worland **33** Cb
Worms **5** ABd
Worthing **7** FGf
Wotje Atoll **27** Db
Wowoni, Pulau– (i.) **18** Fe
Woy Woy **29** Ie
Wrangel Island **41** grid square no.2
Wrangell **31** BCc
Wrangell Mountains **31** Ab
Wrath, Cape– **7** Db
Wreck Reef (i.) **29** Jc
Wrigley **31** Cb
Wrocław → Breslau **5** Fc
Września **5** FGb
Wuchuan **16** Df
Wugang **16** De
Wuhan **15** Df
Wuhu **16** Ed
Wu Jiang (riv.) **16** Ce
Wunstorf **5** Bb
Wuntho **19** Cd
Wuppertal **5** ABc
Wurno **24** Cc
Würzburg **5** BCd
Wurzen **5** Dc
Wushi **16** Bb
Wusuli Jiang → Ussuri **16** Ha
Wuwei [China] **15** Df
Wuwei [China] **16** Ed
Wuxi **16** EFd
Wuxing (Huzhou) **16** EFd
Wuyi Shan (mts.) **16** Ee
Wuyuan **14** De
Wuzhong **16** Cc
Wuzhou **16** Df
Wyandra **29** Hd
Wyndham **29** Db
Wyoming (State) **33** Cb
Wysoke Tatry (mts.) **5** GHd

X

Xainxa **19** Ab
Xai Xai **26** Cd
Xam Nua **19** Dd
Xangongo **26** Ac
Xánthi **11** Fc
Xapuri **37** Cd
Xar Moron He (riv.) **16** Eb
Xiamen **16** Ef
Xi'an **15** Df
Xiangfan **16** Dd
Xiang Jiang (riv.) **16** De
Xiangkhoang, Plateau de– **19** Dde
Xiangtan **16** De
Xiangyin **16** De
Xianyang **16** Cd
Xiaogan **16** DEd
Xichang **16** Be
Xieng Khouang **19** De
Xigazê **15** Cg
Xi Jiang (riv.) **16** Df
Xinghai **16** Ac
Xingren **16** Ce

Xingtai **16** Dc
Xingu (riv.) **38** Bb
Xining **15** Df
Xinkai He (riv.) **16** Fb
Xinmin **16** Fb
Xinpu → Lianyungang **16** EFd
Xinxian **16** Dc
Xinxiang **16** DEc
Xinyang **16** DEd
Xique–Xique **38** Cc
Xixabangma Feng (mt.) **20** FGc
Xuancheng **16** Ed
Xuanhua **16** DEb
Xuanwei **16** Be
Xuchang **16** DEd
Xuguit Qi **14** Fe
Xuwen **16** Df
Xuyong **16** BCe
Xuzhou **15** Df

Y

Ya'an **16** Bde
Yablonovy Range **14** Ed
Yabrin **21** De
Yacuiba **39** Bb
Yafran **24** Da
Yagishiri–Tō (i.) **17** Gb
Yagoua **24** Dcd
Yakima **33** ABb
Yako **24** Bc
Yakumo **17** FGc
Yakupica (mt.) **11** Dc
Yaku–Shima (i.) **16** Hd
Yakutat **31** ABc
Yakutsk (Aut. Rep.) **14** Fc
Yala **19** Dg
Yalata **29** Ee
Yalgoo **29** Bd
Yalıköy **22** Bb
Yalinga **25** Cd
Yalong Jiang (riv.) **16** Be
Yalova **22** Bb
Yalu Jiang (riv.) **16** FGb
Yamagata **16** IJc
Yamaguchi **17** Bg
Yamal, Peninsula– **13** FGb
Yambí, Mesa de– (plat.) **37** Bb
Yambio **25** Cd
Yamdena, Pulau– (i.) **27** Bc
Yamethin **19** Cd
Yamma Yamma, Lake– **29** Gd
Yamoussoukro **24** Bd
Yampi Sound **29** Cb
Yamuna (riv.) **20** Ec
Yamzho Yumco (l.) **19** ABc
Yanbu' **21** Be
Yanchang **16** CDc
Yancheng **16** Fd
Yangchun **16** Df
Yangjiang **16** Df
Yangor **27** map no.2
Yangquan **16** DEc
Yangtze River **16** Ede
Yangzhou **16** Ed
Yanji **16** Gb
Yankton **32** Ba

Yantai **16** Fc
Yanzhou **16** Ec
Yaoundé **24** Dd
Yao Yai, Ko– (i.) **19** Cg
Yapen, Pulau– (i.) **27** Bc
Yap Islands **27** Bb
Yapu **19** Cf
Yaqui (riv.) **34** Bb
Yaraka **29** Gcd
Yarí (riv.) **37** Bb
Yarim **21** Cg
Yarkant He (riv.) **13** GHf
Yarlung Zangbo Jiang → Brahmaputra (riv.) **19** Bc
Yarmouth **31** Id
Yarram **29** Hf
Yarumal **37** Bb
Yasawa (i.) **28** map no.6
Yasawa Group **28** map no.6
Yass **29** Hef
Yata **39** Ba
Yathkyed Lake **31** Fb
Yatsushiro **17** Bh
Yauca **39** Aa
Yavari (riv.) **37** Bc
Yavi **22** Fc
Yaví, Cerro– (mt.) **37** Cb
Yawatahama **17** Ch
Yaxian **16** Cg
Yayapura **27** Cc
Yayladağı **22** EFde
Yazd **21** EFc
Ye **19** Ce
Yecla **9** Ec
Yei **25** Dd
Yell (i.) **7** Fa
Yellowknife **30** GHc
Yellow River **16** Cb
Yellow Sea (Huang Hai) **16** Fc
Yellowstone (riv.) **33** Cb
Yellowstone National Park **33** Bb
Yemen (Ind. St.) **15** Bh
Yen Bai **19** DEd
Yenice **22** Ad
Yenice [Tur.] (riv.) **22** CDb
Yenice [Tur.] (riv.) **22** Ecd
Yenki **16** Gb
Yeo, Lake– **29** CDd
Yeovil **7** Ef
Yeppoon **29** Ic
Yerköy **22** Ec
Yeşilhisar **22** Ec
Yesilırmak (riv.) **22** Fb
Yeste **9** Dc
Ye–u **19** BCd
Yeu, Ile d'– (i.) **8** Bd
Yexian **16** EFc
Yiannitsá **11** Ec
Yíaros (i.) **11** Fe
Yibin **16** BCe
Yichang **16** Dd
Yichun [China] **16** De
Yichun [China] **16** Ga
Yilan **16** Cc
Yıldız dağı (mt.) **22** Fbc
Yildiz dağlari (mts.) **22** Aab
Yiliang **16** Bef
Yinchuan **16** BCc
Yingde **16** Df
Ying He (riv.) **16** DEd

Yingkou **16** Fb
Yining **15** Ce
Yioúra (i.) **11** EFd
Yirga Alem **25** Dd
Yirshi **16** EFa
Yíthion **11** Ee
Yixian **16** Fb
Yiyang **16** De
Ylikitka **4** Gb
Ylivieska **4** EFb
Yogyakarta **18** CDf
Yokadouma **24** Dd
Yokkaichi **16** Icd
Yoko **24** Dd
Yokohama **16** IJc
Yokosuka **16** IJcd
Yokote **16** IJc
Yola **24** Dd
Yom (riv.) **19** Ce
Yona **27** map no.1
Yonago **17** Cg
Yona–Guni–Jima (i.) **16** Ff
Yonezawa **16** Jc
Yŏngan **17** Ad
Yŏngch'on **17** Afg
Yŏngdok **17** ABf
Yongxiu **16** DEe
Yonkers **32** Da
Yonne **8** Ecd
York (riv.) **7** Fe
York, Cape– **29** Ga
Yorke Peninsula **29** Fef
York Factory **31** Fc
Yorkton **31** Bb
Yoron–Jima (i.) **16** GHe
Yoshino–Gawa (riv.) **17** Dg
Yoshiwara **17** Fg
Yŏsu **16** Gcd
Yōtei–Zan (mt.) **17** Gc
Yotvata **22** Eh
Youghal **7** Cf
You Jiang (riv.) **16** Cf
Youngstown **32** CDa
Yozgat **22** Ec
Ypacaraí **39** Cb
Yssingeaux **8** EFe
Ystad **4** Ce
Yu 'Alliq, Jabal– (mt.) **22** Dg
Yuan Jiang (riv.) **16** De
Yuanling **16** CDe
Yuba City **33** Ac
Yübari **16** Jb
Yucatán (pen.) **34** CDbc
Yucatán Channel **34** Db
Yuci **16** Dc
Yuendumu **29** Ec
Yueyang **16** De
Yugoslavia (Ind. St.) **3** EFc
Yukon (riv.) **30** Ec
Yukon Territory **31** Bb
Yulin [China] **16** Cf
Yulin [China] **16** Df
Yulin Jiao **16** Cg
Yuma **33** Bc
Yumen **16** Abc
Yumenzhen **16** Ab
Yunak **22** Cc
Yuncheng **16** Dcd
Yungas (phys. reg.) **39** Ba
Yunnan (prov.) **16** ABe
Yunxian **16** Dd
Yurimaguas **37** Bc
Yushan **16** Ee

Yushan (mt.) **16** Ff
Yutian **20** Fa
Yuyao **16** Fde
Yvetot **8** Dc
Yzeure **8** Ed

Z

Zabajkalsk **14** Ede
Zabib **21** Cg
Zäbol **21** Gc
Zabrze **5** Gc
Zacapa **35** Bb
Zacatecas **34** Bb
Zadar **6** Bd
Zafir, Az– **21** Cef
Zafra **9** Bc
Žagań **5** Ec
Zagora **24** Ba
Zagorsk → Sergiev Posad **13** Cd
Zagreb **6** Bd
Zagros Mountains **21** DEc
Zagyva (riv.) **6** Dc
Zähedän **21** FGd
Zaḩlah **22** EFef
Ẓahrän, Aẓ– **21** DEd
Zaïre (riv.) **26** Ab
Zaire (Ind. St.) **23** DEf
Zaïre → Lualaba (riv.) **26** Bb
Zaječar **6** EFe
Zajsan **13** He
Zajsan, ozero– **13** He
Zakopane **5** Gd
Zalaegerszeg **6** Cc
Zaláu **6** Fc
Zaleščiki **6** GHb
Zalțan **24** DEb
Zambezi (riv.) **26** Cc
Zambezi **26** Bc
Zambia (Ind. St.) **23** EFfg
Zamboanga **18** Fc
Zambrów **5** Ib
Zamora **9** BCb
Zamora de Hidalgo **34** Bbc
Zamosč **5** Ic
Žanatas **13** FGe
Záncara (riv.) **9** Dc
Zanjän **21** Db
Žannetty, ostrov– **14** IJb
Zante (i.) **11** De

Zante **11** De
Zanthus **29** Ce
Zanzibar **23** FGf
Zaoqing **16** Df
Zapadna Morava **6** Ee
Zapala **39** ABc
Zaporožje **13** Ce
Zaqāzīq, Az– **25** Dab
Zara **22** Fc
Zarasai **4** Fe
Zárate **39** Cc
Zaraza **37** Cb
Zard Küh (mt.) **21** DEc
Zarghunshahr **20** Cb
Zaria **24** Cc
Zarkovski **12** Db
Zarqä, Az– **22** Ff
Zarqa, El– **22** CDg
Žary **5** Ec
Zarzaïtine **24** CDb
Zaskar Mountains **20** EFb
Žaškov **6** IJb
Žatec **5** Dc
Zavidoviči **6** Dd
Zavitinsk **14** FGd
Zavolžje **12** Fb
Zavolžsk **12** Fb
Zawi **23** EFg
Zawïlah **24** Db
Zbaraž **6** GHb
Zbąszyń **5** EFb
Zborov **6** Gb
Zbruč (riv.) **6** Hb
Ždanov → Mariupol **12** DEd
Žďar nad Sázavou **5** EFd
Zdolbunov **6** Ha
Zduńska Wola **5** Gc
Zeehan **29** map no.1
Zefat **22** Ef
Zeitz **5** Dc
Zeja **14** Fd
Zeja (riv.) **14** Fd
Zélaf **22** Ff
Želanija, mys– **13** FGb
Zelenoborski **4** GHb
Zelenodolsk **12** GHb
Zelenogorsk **4** Gc
Zelenogorsk–Ilimski **14** Dd
Zelenogradsk **4** Ee
Zelenyi (i.) **17** Jc
Železnogorsk **12** DEc
Želtyje Vody **12** Dd
Zémio **25** Cd

Zemun, Belgrade– **6** Ed
Zenica **6** CDd
Zeravšan (riv.) **13** Ff
Zernograd **12** Fd
Zézere (riv.) **9** Ac
Žezkazgan (Džezkazgan) **13** Fe
Zgierz **5** Gc
Zgorzelec **5** Ec
Zhangguangcai Ling (mts.) **17** IJbc
Zhangjiakou **16** DEb
Zhangye **16** Bc
Zhangzhou **16** Ef
Zhanjiang **15** Dgh
Zhaodong **16** FGa
Zhaotong **16** Be
Zhejiang (prov.) **16** EFe
Zhengzhou **15** Df
Zhenhai **16** Fde
Zhenjiang **16** EFd
Zhenyuan **16** Ce
Zhijiang **16** Ce
Zhob (riv.) **20** Cb
Zhongba **15** Cfg
Zhongwei **16** BCc
Zhongxian **16** Cd
Zhoushan Qundao **16** Fde
Zhucheng **16** EFc
Zhumadian **16** Dd
Zhuolu **16** DEb
Zhuzhou **16** De
Žiar–nad Hronom **5** Gd
Ẓibā' **21** Bd
Zibo **16** Ec
Ziel, Mount– **29** Ec
Zielona Góra **5** Ebc
Ziftá **22** Cg
Žigansk **14** EFc
Zigong **16** Be
Ziguinchor **24** Ac
Žigulevsk **12** Gc
Zihuatanejo **34** Bc
Zile **22** Eb
Zilfi, Az– **21** CDd
Žilina **5** Gd
Zillah **24** Db
Zima **14** Dd
Zimbabwe (r.) **26** Cd
Zimbabwe (Ind. St.) **23** EFgh
Zimnicea **6** Ge
Zinder **24** Cc
Zipaquirá **37** Bb

Žirje (i.) **6** Be
Žirnovsk **12** FGc
Ziro **19** Bc
Žitny Ostrov (phys. reg.) **5** Fde
Žitomir **13** Bd
Zittau **5** Ec
Zlatica **11** EFb
Zlatograd **11** Fc
Zlatoust **13** Ed
Zlatoustovsk **14** Gd
Zlin **5** Fd
Żlobin **12** CDc
Złocieniec **5** Fb
Złotoryja **5** EFc
Złotów **5** Fb
Zmeiny, ostrov– **12** Dd
Žmerinka **6** HIb
Znamenka **12** Dd
Znojmo **5** EFd
Žohova, ostrov– **14** Ib
˙Zoločev **6** Gb
Zolotonoša **12** Dd
Zomba **26** Cc
Zonguldak **22** Cb
Zorritos **37** Ac
Zouar **25** Bbc
Zouïrât **24** Ab
Zrenjanin **6** Ed
Zudañez **39** Ba
Żufār (phys. reg.) **21** EFf
Zug **5** Be
Zugspitze (mt.) **5** Ce
Zújar (riv.) **9** Cc
Zujevka **12** Hb
Žukovka **12** Dc
Zumba **37** Bc
Zumbo **26** Cc
Zunyi **16** Ce
Županja **6** Dd
Zürich **5** Be
Zürichsee **5** Be
Zuwärah **24** Da
Zvishavane **26** BCd
Zvolen **5** Gd
Zvornik **6** Dd
Zwickau **5** Dc
Zwiesel **5** Dd
Zwolle **8** Ga
Žyradów **5** Hbc
Zyrjanka **14** HIc
Zyrjanovsk **13** He
Żywiec **5** Gd